Handbook *of* Process Theology

Handbook *of* Process Theology

JAY MCDANIEL

DONNA BOWMAN

EDITORS

CHALICE PRESS

ST. LOUIS, MISSOURI

Cover and interior design: Elizabeth Wright

Visit Chalice Press on the World Wide Web at
www.chalicepress.com

10 9 8 7 6 5 4 3 2 1   06 07 08 09 10

Library of Congress Cataloging–in–Publication Data

Handbook of process theology / Donna Bowman and Jay McDaniel, editors.
   p. cm.
 Includes bibliographical references and index.
 ISBN-13: 978-0-8272-1449-1 (pbk. : alk. paper)
 ISBN-10: 0-8272-1449-9 (pbk. : alk. paper)
 1. Process theology. I. Bowman, Donna. II. McDaniel, Jay B. (Jay Byrd), 1949-
 BT83.6.H36 2006
 230'.046–dc22
                                    2005025661

Printed in the United States of America

Contents

Acknowledgments

The editors wish to gratefully acknowledge, for their assistance and patience, our editors at Chalice Press: at the origin of the project, Jon Berquist (now at Westminster John Knox); during the last several months, Jane McAvoy, editorial director and vice president, whose sudden death in June 2004 we mourn; and Trent Butler, editorial director who did the final editing of this work. Our authors must also be commended both for their excellence and for their patience, as the project has grown and changed since its inception, necessitating more time between invitation and culmination. Among other notable process thinkers that we contacted, John Quiring and Catherine Keller provided invaluable assistance in suggesting additions to our list of authors.

Thanks to the administration at the Honors College, University of Central Arkansas, Richard Scott and Norbert Schedler, for their support of the time and resources needed to work on this project over a period of years. Blake Vernon at UCA provided manuscript assistance.

Last but foremost, we wish to thank our families for granting us leave from parental and spousal duties for weekends on end to meet, read, write, and discuss this book. Their sacrifice to further the discussion of these ideas and extend the scope of process thought has been notable, and we pray that it will bring forth fruit a hundredfold.

Abbreviations

Works of Alfred North Whitehead frequently cited in this collection are denoted, in the text and in footnotes, by the following abbreviations:

AE   *The Aims of Education and Other Essays.* New York: Free Press, 1929.

AI   *Adventures of Ideas.* New York: Free Press, 1933.

MT   *Modes of Thought.* New York: Free Press, 1938.

PR   *Process and Reality: An Essay in Cosmology.* Corrected Edition. Edited by David Ray Griffin and Donald W. Sherburne. New York: Free Press, 1978 [1929].

RM   *Religion in the Making.* New York: Fordham University Press, 1996 [1926].

SMW *Science and the Modern World.* New York: Free Press, 1925.

Contributors

RONALD J. ALLEN, ordained in the Christian Church (Disciples of Christ), is Nettie Sweeney and Hugh Th. Miller Professor of Preaching and Second Testament at Christian Theological Seminary, Indianapolis. Author or coauthor of almost thirty books on preaching, he recently directed a project, funded by the Lilly Endowment, that studied how people listen to sermons, the results being published by Chalice Press in the four-volume series *Channels of Listening.*

DONNA BOWMAN teaches theology and interdisciplinary studies in the Honors College of the University of Central Arkansas and is the author of *The Divine Decision: A Process Doctrine of Election* (2002). She is also a film critic, wife, mother, and Atlanta Braves fan.

KATHLYN A. BREAZEALE is assistant professor of religion at Pacific Lutheran University, with a focus in feminist and womanist theologies. She is developing a book manuscript entitled *Partners after Patriarchy: A Marriage Theology of Mutual Empowerment.* She is also a peace studies advocate, liturgical dancer, and sailor.

PAUL CUSTODIO BUBE is the W. Lewis McColgan Professor of Religion at Lyon College in Arkansas, where he lives with his wife Joni and two daughters, Melissa and Belinda. He is the author of *Ethics in John Cobb's Process Theology* (1988) and coeditor of *Conversations with Pragmatism* (2002).

JOHN B. COBB JR. is professor emeritus of Claremont School of Theology and founding codirector of the Center for Process Studies. Among his books are *The Process Perspective* (2003), *Christ in a Pluralistic Age* (1975), *Transforming Christianity and the World* (1999), and *Postmodernism and Public Policy* (2002).

MONICA A. COLEMAN is the director of the womanist religious studies program and assistant professor of religion at Bennett College for Women in Greensboro, N.C., with research interests in disability theology and religion and literature, as well as process and womanist theologies. She is the author of *The Dinah Project: A Handbook for Congregational Response to Sexual Violence* (2004), and an ordained elder in the African Methodist Episcopal Church.

JOHN CULP teaches at Azusa Pacific University, where he specializes in philosophy of religion and interdisciplinary courses. He has published essays dealing with Wesleyan theology, process thought, and Wesleyan epistemology. He has also served as a college soccer coach.

BRUCE G. EPPERLY is director of continuing education and associate professor of practical theology at Lancaster Theological Seminary. An ordained minister in the United Church of Christ and in the Christian Church

(Disciples of Christ), he is the author of eleven books, including *God's Touch: Faith, Wholeness, and the Healing Miracles of Jesus* (2001).

DAVID RAY GRIFFIN is professor emeritus of philosophy of religion and theology at Claremont School of Theology. His most recent books are *The New Pearl Harbor: Disturbing Questions about the Bush Administration and 9/11* (2004); *Two Great Truths: A New Synthesis of Scientific Naturalism and Christian Faith* (2004); and *Deep Religious Pluralism* (edited; 2005).

LUCINDA A. HUFFAKER is associate professor of religion at Wabash College and director of the Wabash Center for Teaching and Learning in Theology and Religion (funded by Lilly Endowment, Inc.). The author of *Creative Dwelling: Empathy and Clarity in God and Self* (1998), she is perhaps best known as coeditor of the international journal *Teaching Theology and Religion*.

CAROL JOHNSTON is associate professor of theology and culture at Christian Theological Seminary, and author of *The Wealth or Health of Nations: Transforming Capitalism from Within* (1998). She also works on biblical ecotheology, is a Presbyterian minister, and loves sailing.

JEFFERY D. LONG is an assistant professor of religious studies at Elizabethtown College, in Pennsylvania. He is currently working on his first book, *Universal Hinduism: A Hindu Model of Religious Pluralism.*

SANDRA B. LUBARSKY is professor of religious studies at Northern Arizona University, where she also directs an interdisciplinary master's program on "Sustainable Communities." She is the author of *Tolerance and Transformation: Jewish Approaches to Religious Pluralism* (1990), and coeditor with David Griffin of *Jewish Theology and Process Thought* 1996).

JAY MCDANIEL is professor of religion at Hendrix College in Conway, Arkansas, where he also directs the Steel Center for the Study of Religion and Philosophy. His publications include *Of God and Pelicans: A Theology of Reverence for Life* (1989), and *With Roots and Wings: Christianity in an Age of Ecology and Dialogue* (1995). He is a husband, father, and amateur guitarist.

MARY ELIZABETH MULLINO MOORE, a former director of the Center for Process Studies in Claremont, California, is professor of religion and education and director of women in theology and ministry at the Candler School of Theology, Emory University (Atlanta, Georgia). Her books include *Teaching as a Sacramental Act* (2004), *Ministering with the Earth* (1998), and *Teaching from the Heart* (1998).

LESLIE A. MURAY is professor of philosophy and religion and coordinator of the philosophy and religion area at Curry College, Milton, Massachusetts. He is the author of *An Introduction to the Process Understanding of Science, Society and the Self* (1988).

THOMAS JAY OORD is professor of theology and philosophy at Northwest Nazarene University, Nampa, Idaho, and coeditor (with Bryan Stone) of *Thy Nature and Thy Name Is Love: Wesleyan and Process Theologies in Dialogue* (2001). He is author of *Relational Holiness: Responding to the Call of Love* and *Science of Love: The Wisdom of Well-Being* (2005). Tom is theologian for the

Institute for Research on Unlimited Love, a husband, father of three girls, and ordained elder in the Church of the Nazarene.

RUSSELL PREGEANT is professor of religion and philosophy and chaplain, emeritus, at Curry College in Milton, Massachusetts, and visiting professor in New Testament at Andover Newton Theological School in Newton Centre, Massachusetts. He is the author of the volume on *Matthew* in the "Chalice Commentaries for Today" series (2004), *Christology Beyond Dogma: Matthew's Christ in Process Hermeneutic* (1978), *Engaging the New Testament: An Interdisciplinary Introduction* (Fortress 1995), and *Mystery without Magic* (1988). He is an avid devotee of Cajun cooking.

DAVID E. ROY practices full-time pastoral counseling at the Center for Creative Transformation in Fresno, California, and has written *Toward a Process Psychology: A Model of Integration* (2000).

CLARK WILLIAMSON is Indiana Professor of Christian Thought, emeritus, at Christian Theological Seminary. He is author of *Way of Blessing, Way of Life: A Christian Theology* (1999); *A Guest in the House of Israel: Post-Holocaust Theology* (1993); and *Preaching the Gospels Without Blaming the Jews: A Lectionary Commentary* (2004, with Ronald J. Allen). He is also an avid Chicago Cubs fan.

Introduction

■ DONNA BOWMAN

■ JAY McDANIEL

With a bit more than a half-century of history, process theology is a way of thinking about life, including its ultimate or divine dimension. Based on the thought of Alfred North Whitehead and several followers with similar philosophical commitments, process theology seeks to apply Whitehead's "philosophy of organism" to the study of the divine reality and of everything that is affected by it.

Our Aim: An Overview of the Variety

Several books already exist that attempt to provide more or less comprehensive introductions to process theology. The reader interested in more detail about how process looks at issues in religious studies and philosophy of religion should not hesitate to pick up one of those volumes. The aim of this book, however, is somewhat different.

Process theology has extended its reach in the last several decades into many areas of thought and practice, some of them quite surprising. While the task of providing comprehensive descriptions and analyses of this entire range awaits the encyclopedist, we hope to offer in the meantime an overview, in an accessible form, of process theological thinking in many diverse areas of that vast scope. Process thought has been utilized creatively to think not only about traditional theological topics such as the nature of God, the interpretation of scripture, various tenets of Christian doctrine, and the challenge of religious pluralism, but also about psychology, health, politics, economics, gender, and ecology. In addition, religious traditions other than Christianity utilize process theological thought for reflection on their tenets, practices, scriptures, and enduring questions. We hope to provide a general readership with an indication of process theology's diversity of subject matter and approaches by collecting essays from a variety of American process theologians. The reader will, we hope, gain an appreciation of the variety within process theology and the wide range of topics to which its insights can be applied, while absorbing as well some of the movement's key insights and basic framework.

Permit us to make several further observations before proceeding.

1. Choosing the Topics

No anthology can cover all the topics that are important to process theologians. An example of a topic not explicitly addressed in this volume is the process interpretation of selected fields in the natural sciences, especially quantum theory, relativity theory, and evolutionary biology. To be sure, many of the essays allude to a process interpretation of these fields, but these allusions can be enriched by further explanations. Readers interested in such explanations are encouraged to consider the wide range of materials now available, as illustrated, among other places, in *The Liberation of Life: From Cell to Community* by Charles Birch and John B. Cobb Jr., and *Religion and Scientific Naturalism* by David Ray Griffin. The Center for Process Studies in Claremont, California, can provide bibliographical material on the relation of process thought to science, and on a host of other topics with which this anthology deals.

2. "First person" and "third person" Whiteheadians

The community of process thought has long been divided between what we might call "first-person" and "third-person" Whiteheadians. The difference lies in the thinker's approach to appropriating Whitehead's metaphysical categories for the description of everyday lived experience on the human level. Third-person Whiteheadians tend to feel confident that Whitehead's philosophy accurately and with reasonable completeness describes reality at the level of its smallest individual units (called "actual entities"), but hesitate to apply the same or similar language to the case of more complex experience, such as that of human beings. First-person Whiteheadians, on the other hand, are comfortable using such notions to illuminate subjective, conscious experience as it is lived by higher organisms. The distinction turns on how useful Whiteheadian terminology might be at the level of lived human experience; different thinkers and writers will communicate with different degrees of boldness or qualification, depending on how far they feel the language can be pushed without becoming inaccurate. The reader will notice that both approaches are present in the essays in this book; the former tend to sound more careful and precise, the latter more evocative and suggestive.

3. Use of Technical Jargon

As the above paragraph illustrates with its timid introduction of the term "actual entities," process theology has inherited from Whitehead a vocabulary of technical terminology—a jargon, not to put too fine a point on it. Again, the reader will notice that some essays in this book tend to make freer and less apologetic use of this jargon; others tend to avoid it or translate it into ordinary language.

The need for a technical vocabulary arises because assumptions about reality are built into the structure of ordinary human language. Therefore, if we are using language in an ordinary, commonsense way, certain unspoken and very deep intuitions about reality become concretized in our words. Take, for instance, the subject-object structure of English (and almost all languages). We speak of subjects (easily identified and enduring agents or substances) doing things to objects (easily identified and enduring agents or substances) or having qualities (necessary or contingent, but in any case usually optional, accidental properties). No wonder it was so obvious to Aristotle, whose native Greek shared this structure, that the world is made up of enduring substances that are essentially separate from one another, undergoing changes or having properties that are for the most part external, temporary, and unworthy of sustained remark. Any attempt to challenge this view, so natural to all of us who have grown up talking this way, necessitates a conscious change in the way we use language. To exclude the assumptions that rule our everyday talk, words with a certain ordinary meaning will need to become technical terms, precise and unequivocal.

The danger of using this jargon too frequently in a book aimed at a general readership is that readers will be unable or unwilling to wade through technical language to get at the author's point. Jargon can be severely off-putting to the uninitiated. On the other hand, the danger of using less precise words for the same concepts can lead to serious misunderstandings. Without the advantage of carefully defined language, the author may be unable to prevent those deep-rooted assumptions from misleading readers. We have made efforts to reduce the technical terminology in this book, believing that it is generally possible to be reasonably accurate—or at least not to do serious violence to Whitehead's ideas—without a thicket of jargon. On the other hand, on frequent occasions we asked authors to avoid certain looser terms in favor of more accurate, even jargonistic terms, in order to prevent the reader from drawing implications that would not be in keeping with a process understanding. Later in this introduction we provide a brief glossary of some of the terminology used in this book, and some authors give their own short definitions within their essays for the particular language with which they work.

4. Choice of Authors

While many of the authors' names in this volume will be familiar to readers who have explored process theology, others will be new to most readers. One of our aims for the handbook was to include both senior scholars in the process movement and emerging scholars with interesting specialities. We recognize that important thinkers in both camps exist whom we have not included. The reader familiar with the world of process thought will no doubt be able to think of many names that would be at home on our list of authors. Again, we are unable to be completely comprehensive, but we have attempted to indicate and to represent herein the diversity in this movement–not only of topics, but of scholars.

5. A Christian Vantage Point

Finally (and not unconnected with the preceding point), the dominant vantage point of this book is that of the Christian theological enterprise. This reflects the historical reality that process theology began and initially flourished as a Christian appropriation of Whitehead's thought. Certain sections in this book, notably those on salvation and the Bible, reflect predominately Christian, and perhaps exclusively Abrahamic, perspectives. Other sections, such as those on spirituality, culture, and emerging process traditions, broaden the focus to include non-Christian ways of engaging process thought, and point the way toward new perspectives that may not be as strongly tied to the Christian tradition in the future. We look forward to an anthology, perhaps within the next decade, that will be more deeply informed by a multitude of religious perspectives than this one.

A Brief History of Process Theology

Alfred North Whitehead (1861–1947) is the intellectual father of process thought. The British mathematician and philosopher taught at Harvard, beginning in 1924. He acknowledged a debt to the American tradition of pragmaticism, empiricism, and naturalism, a strain exemplified by William James, John Dewey, and C.S. Peirce. His studies of science convinced him that existing philosophical systems were inadequate to describe the essentially relational character of all reality. Therefore he developed what he called the "philosophy of organism," and insisted that its success be judged by its adequacy to experience and observation, as well as by its logical consistency.

During his time at Harvard, Whitehead was at one point assisted by Charles Hartshorne, a young research fellow also greatly influenced by Peirce. Hartshorne (1897–2000) went on to teach at the University of Chicago in 1928, where he worked on the development of a Whiteheadian metaphysical system, with special attention to its implications for theology. His ideas, along with the Whiteheadian ideas he championed, were taken up by an influential group of students and scholars in Chicago, including Henry Nelson Wieman, Bernard Loomer, Daniel Day Williams, and Bernard Meland. Process theology would percolate in Chicago until the 1960s.

John B. Cobb Jr., the third major developer of process theology, studied with Hartshorne at Chicago. His 1965 book *A Christian Natural Theology Based on the Thought of Alfred North Whitehead* quickly became the preeminent systematic exposition of process theology during its first flowering of widespread influence in the late sixties. After receiving his degree from the University of Chicago Divinity School, Cobb worked briefly at Emory University before finding his eventual home at the School of Theology at Claremont. There, while teaching and writing numerous books and essays, he co-founded the foremost journal of process thought, *Process Studies*, and the Center for Process Studies at Claremont, both of which continue to be the most prominent and influential gathering places for scholars working on Whiteheadian, Hartshornian, or other process ideas. Cobb is still hard at work today, despite his retirement in 1990 from the Claremont Graduate School; we are proud that he has contributed an essay to this volume.

A Short Glossary

The authors of the individual essays have generally attempted to avoid an excess of technical language and often provide their own glosses on terms particularly relevant to their topics. Still, certain words and phrases are so common in process talk, and yet so particular in their definitions, that a short glossary will prove helpful to the reader. The following is by no means an exhaustive list of the process terminology used in this book; rather, it represents a gathering of frequently used terms in one convenient location for ease of reference.

Actual occasion:

A momentary happening or event—a drop of experience—in which many events of the past actual world "become one" through a process of subjective unification. These are the most fundamental units of reality, the ultimately real entities of the universe. Third-person process theologians picture these actual occasions as immensely small (microscopic or submicroscopic) in size and then propose that the larger objects of human sense-perception (rocks and trees) are composed of them. First-person process theologians emphasize that ordinary human experience—as lived from the inside in the immediacy of a present moment—is itself the first and most intimate instance of an actual occasion that we humans know. Both perspectives reflect Whitehead's perspective in *Process and Reality*, and many process theologians shift back and forth from these two points of view.

This process contains its own subjective immediacy or internal aliveness, and its very essence includes an act of decision by which certain possibilities for unification are actualized while others are cut off. Once this unification occurs, the subjective immediacy of the occasion perishes; and the occasion becomes an irreducible fact in subsequent history of the universe; that is, an immortal object to be felt by all events that come afterward. In an actual occasion, then, the many of the universe become one and are then increased by one.

Concrescence:

The process by which an actual occasion unifies the universe in its moment of becoming. This process includes an objective component: namely, the universe itself as it gives itself in the form of the past actual world of the experience. And it also includes a subjective component: namely, the process of feeling the universe and thus gathering it into unity. In its subjective side the occasion begins with a reception of the universe in its sheer givenness. This reception is called the physical pole of the emerging experience, not because it involves a visible body, but because it involves the internal feeling of being affected by something that is given for experience and thus exerts a causal influence upon experience. The occasion then unfolds as a consideration of possible valuations of the data to a final decision, in which the occasion unifies the data in a definite ordering. This consideration occurs in what Whitehead calls "the mental pole of experience." Here the word *mental* does not necessarily presuppose consciousness or abstract forms of thinking, but rather the feeling of possibilities and purposes for responding to what is given by the universe. This feeling or valuation is guided by a subjective aim, which is selected by the occasion itself, but the initial phase of which is given by God. See *initial aim* and *subjective aim* below.

Consequent Nature:

That aspect of God that feels and is affected by the universe. Like all entities, God can be thought of as a process that moves from one pole (in God's case, the mental pole that feels potentialities) to another (in God's case, the physical pole that feels the universe). God's physical pole is termed "consequent" because it is the part of God that results from the decisions of all other entities.

Just as each finite occasion is composed of the universe and its responses to the universe, so the consequent nature is composed of the universe and divine responses to the universe. These divine responses include empathy (a feeling of the feelings of the experiences of all other actual occasions and thus a sharing in their destinies) and judgment (an awareness of what could have been and should have been, given the ideals of truth and goodness and beauty, which either did or did not occur.) It is by virtue of the consequent nature that some process theologians, following Charles Hartshorne, speak of the universe as the body of God. Just as God is in all things, all things are in God; and the consequent nature is the term used to describe God's embrace of all actualities.

Creativity:

The ultimate process or force in the world, expressed by every occasion in its own becoming.

Although God is the ultimate actuality, God is not the only ultimate in the process system of thought, if by "ultimate" we mean something irreducible. In process thought creativity is also ultimate. The nature of reality, in other words, is a drive toward the new and the next; even when no change or difference is discernible to an outside observer, creativity is in operation through each occasion's exercise of freedom in the privacy of its own becoming. Process theologians propose that some religious and philosophical perspectives in the world have awakened to the ultimacy of "Creativity," just as others have awakened to the ultimacy of God, and that there is wisdom in both points of view.

Initial aim:

The way that God is continuously active in the world by providing potentialities for becoming, which add value to the world and enjoyment to the experiencing subject. God's basic function in the process worldview is the infusion of value into the initial stage of an occasion's becoming. This valuation is a seed that allows the occasion's own subjective valuation of the data to proceed, allowing the transmission of order from one occasion to the next, and preventing the dissolution of the universe into chaos or irresolvable competition. In religious terms, we might think of the initial aim as God's choice or God's will for the occasion; it expresses to the occasion God's creative drive toward intensity of feeling, which includes the results of all creaturely processes. Many process theologians speak of two kinds of decision in God: a primordial decision that there is to be an ordered universe at all (there could have been no order), and the moment-by-moment decisions that are given as the initial aims of each concrescing moment. Through these aims, God continually acts in the world, albeit through persuasion not coercion, invitation not force. Initial aims require actualization on the part of concrescing subjects if they are to be realized.

Prehension:

The inclusion of a datum from the occasion's world into its process of becoming.

A prehension is an experiential act of feeling or taking into account something else from a subjective point of view, and it can be either conscious or nonconscious. Every prehension has its object. These objects can include past actual occasions, pure potentialities, or combinations thereof. Through prehensions in the mode of causal efficacy, emerging occasions *prehend* past actual occasions. By means of these prehensions, those occasions are present in the emerging occasion, thus giving the universe its solidarity and unity. Prehensions of potentialities are the means by which valuations occur, including those that select relevant possibilities for rendering the many of the universe into one moment of experience. In process thought, all actualities–including the divine actuality–have a subjective side, whether conscious or unconscious, and this subjectivity consists of prehensions.

Primordial Nature:

That aspect of God, timeless in its own right, that envisions and evaluates all that is possible. This is the mental pole of God's process of becoming, consisting of the primordial divine valuation of all possibilities. From this self-originating act of decision, God's creative drive toward aesthetic value advances in accordance with the state of the world at each new moment. This advance is expressed through the moment-by-moment decisions of God, as expressed in initial aims. Initial aims, then, are the way in which the primordial nature becomes incarnate in the world.

Subjective aim:

The individual entity's own decision about what it is to become. It springs both from the initial aim provided by God and from the standards of value inherited from other occasions in the concrescing entity's past. It is the dimension of freedom and creativity in every occasion, regardless of how slight or seemingly insignificant its decision might seem to an observer.

SECTION I

God and Revelation

Many students and practitioners of process theology find that its most fundamental differences from other theological schools lie in its concepts of God and revelation. We describe our religious convictions fundamentally in terms of the nature of ultimate reality, the need for human relationship with that reality, and the way we come to knowledge of that reality. This section offers essays dealing with process understandings of those core convictions, standing on Christian ground but also looking for ways to engage dialogue with people of other religions.

Notwithstanding the fact that mainstream Protestant and Catholic Christianity each contain several concepts of God, the majority in use derive from the efforts of early Christian thinkers to conceptualize the God spoken about in scripture in terms of the current philosophical thinking of the day. Process theologians find that, because new knowledge (including scientific knowledge) has challenged many aspects of classical and medieval philosophy, parts of the concept of God derived from that philosophy are inadequate to our experience. Donna Bowman's essay argues that process theology's revised concept of God, especially in regard to divine omniscience and omnipotence, is crucial to the relationship between grace, human responsibility, and authentic faith. John Cobb discusses how process theology conceives of the person of Jesus and the function of the Christ as a divine work connecting God's reality with our reality.

Process theology presumes that God is present in the lives of all people and shares in the sufferings and joys of all people. From the vantage point of Christian experience, we cannot help wonder about the relationship of God to people of other religions. Often the question "But are they saved?" represents a sticking point in efforts to establish dialogue between Christians and adherents of other major world faiths. Therefore, it is important to be clear about what we mean by "salvation." The term has a distinguished New Testament pedigree, especially in the writings of Paul. It has been the pivot on which have turned many schisms, denominational splits, and reformations. Christian process theologians typically believe that the exclusionary use of the doctrine of salvation, that is, its use to determine "who's in and who's out," runs counter to the spirit of the gospel. They seek a way to understand salvation that is biblically accurate, experientially credible, and open to the working of God's grace far beyond the boundaries that human legalism often draws.

When process theologians approach the issue of salvation, they usually have in mind the reality of religious pluralism and its unprecedented challenge to Christian concepts in the modern and postmodern ages. John Culp's essay provides an exposition of the doctrine of salvation as process theologians have conceptualized and utilized it during the last half century, with particular attention to the doctrine's connection to the biblical witness. David Ray Griffin then explicates a process theology of pluralism, emphasizing the proposal, common to many process thinkers, that different religious traditions can discover different but complementary truths. Drawing on years of Jewish-Christian dialogue, Clark Williamson first surveys Jewish responses to process philosophy and Christian theology and then identifies tools within process theology for advancing the dialogue.

Christians, along with Jews and Muslims, are "people of the Book"; they look to scripture as an important avenue of access to the revelation of God in history. This means both that they must arrive at philosophies and theologies of interpretation (hermeneutics) and that they must deal with specific texts within the canon that have been particularly influential on their traditions' histories. Although the scope of interpretation and hermeneutical research is vast, Russell Pregeant and Ron Allen aim, in their essays, to develop a distinctive mode of scriptural reading and reflection that arises from process theology. Pregeant situates the process philosophy of interpretation in the larger context of contemporary approaches to scriptural interpretation, showing how it builds on and adds to narrative, deconstructive, textual, and historical criticism. Through this discussion he proposes a way of understanding revelation and authority that draws from process categories of thought. Allen shows how the written word can become a living word in the act of preaching. In a process perspective, he suggests, preaching is a creative and communal act involving listeners and speakers that engages a full range of human responses: imaginative, conceptual, and existential.

CHAPTER 1

God for Us

A Process View of the Divine-Human Relationship

■ DONNA BOWMAN

David Hume, in his classic treatise *The Natural History of Religion,* writes that the gods originated as "invisible, intelligent powers" directing all of the natural processes that seemed so chaotic, irregular, and uncontrollable to ancient people. Once the gods were in place and worship was established, he writes, one particular God would often be elevated above the others:

> ...[H]is votaries will endeavor, by every art, to insinuate themselves into his favor; and supposing him to be pleased, like themselves, with praise and flattery, there is no eulogy or exaggeration, which will be spared in their addresses to him. In proportion as men's fears or distresses become more urgent, they still invent new strains of adulation;...Thus they proceed; till at least they arrive at infinity itself, beyond which there is no further progress.[1]

Hume, with some portion of his tongue resting lightly in his cheek, goes on to say that by a fortunate coincidence, this process arrives at the same perfect being theology to which "reason and true philosophy" lead us. Hume does admit it can easily be pressed too far and result in "inexplicable mystery."[2] Hume astutely notes that we find ourselves in the position of needing to justify our own acts of worship by asserting, repeatedly and in myriad ways, that God is supremely worthy of such.

It seems evident that human beings in more recent times are not immune to this tendency to enlarge and empower their God to the greatest possible extent. John Calvin proclaimed that God's sovereignty is the reason God is to be worshiped and praised, and therefore demonstrations of such sovereignty– even those that violate our human notions of fairness or love–are eminently laudable. Karl Barth, in the same tradition, insisted on the radical transcendence of God, such that no human observation or exercise of rationality can give us any information about the Divine. On a more prosaic note, the brand of evangelical popular piety often on display in Christian media–television, popular music, and packaged revivals–focuses heavily on praise of divine power and majesty. It is hard not to conclude that such displays, however sincere and well intentioned, frequently serve the purpose of congratulating the worshiper on being a subject of the most powerful monarch, or, to put it another way, on backing the winning team.

Process theologians have led the charge in the twentieth century to moderate the practice of paying God "metaphysical compliments," to use Whitehead's phrase. Worshipers' natural tendency is to flatter the one being worshiped to the point of admitting fatal contradictions into the notion of deity itself. In the face of this tendency Whiteheadian process thought seeks to identify God's function in the matrix of reality and to limit its descriptions of God to what is justified by that function. Naturally, such a method of deriving a doctrine of God is vulnerable to the criticism that any God thus described would not be worthy of worship. Stephen Lee Ely wrote the first major scholarly text that makes this critique of process thought (*The Religious Availability of Whitehead's God*, Wisconsin University Press, 1942), but it has been a staple of criticism both in popular and scholarly circles ever since.[3]

In what follows I will offer a defense of the process vision of the divine-human relationship in terms of the faith this vision engenders. It is commonly thought that, to be worthy of worship and to be an object of faith and trust, God must be in direct and primary control of events both natural and human, both present and future. I argue that such a God cannot elicit a response of faith. Only the "limited," immanent, persuasive God that process thought describes produces true faith and true trust from human persons.

Is Process Theology "Natural Theology"?

In much process philosophy indebted to Whitehead, God is considered primarily in respect to God's necessary function in the system of value transmission and the orderly relationship between past, present, and future. In his magnum opus *Process and Reality*, Alfred North Whitehead exhaustively describes the coming-to-be and passing-away of individual events and outlines the types of connections by which disparate events unite and interpenetrate. He then appends a final chapter, somewhat at odds with its predecessors in tone and language, on "God." The placement of the discussion, as well as its function within the book, bespeak its chiefly metaphysical (rather than theological or religious) character. God is the one necessary entity within the system, with a special function and enhanced (although not qualitatively alien) powers, compared to the entities that are the concern of the bulk of the book. God appears in *Process and Reality* as the final factor required to make the system conform to observed experience and provide an explanation for its stability and directionality.

Barth's Denial of Natural Theology

To theologians, especially those touched by the long shadow Karl Barth and neoorthodoxy cast over the twentieth century, such a derivation of God's activity and (to some extent) character from thoroughly mundane systematic considerations is a paradigmatic example of natural theology. Natural theology was a flourishing activity that united scientists, naturalists, humanists, and theologians in the eighteenth and nineteenth centuries, offering hope for the harmonization of all sources of knowledge. But Barth's fervent attacks in the first half of the twentieth century stigmatized natural theology. Barth lambasted all efforts to come to knowledge of God "from below"–that is, by starting from human experience and reason. God's character and activity is revealed to us "from above," preeminently in Jesus Christ. So we must look to revelation for knowledge of who God is and what God does.

Process theologians are certainly used to the charge that they are engaging in natural theology. The foremost among them, John B. Cobb Jr., even celebrated the label by titling his seminal volume of process systematics "A Christian Natural Theology." In general, process thinkers have embraced the epithet in an effort to reclaim it from the post-liberal ghetto. But the substance of Barth's opposition to natural theology has everything to do with the religious adequacy of a given theological formulation, and this side of the criticism is more rarely addressed. Any God who can be *deduced* from observation of and reflection on creation, human nature, the human condition, or metaphysical verities is a cog in the universal machine rather than its master, Barth argues. And this deprives God of the power *over* the system that is needed to save. Natural theology fails because by its own admission, it cannot reach any God that is not already within its grasp. Such a God does not dispense grace. Such a God merely fulfills the metaphysically ordained divine function.

One might argue that the reason natural theology can succeed in finding the transcendent God, creator *ex nihilo*, is that we, as created beings, are already and essentially connected to our source and the source of all things. It's not that God is *in principle* able to be found through reason and observation. It's that the creation bears the traces of the Creator and that human creatures, made in God's image, already have a leg up on the heavenly ladder.

Barth emphatically rejected this argument, based on his understanding of the radical nature of grace. Creation has no claim on the Creator. The special relationship with God that human creatures enjoy in no way reflects some metaphysical constant. It is solely due to the gracious, unmerited, and completely unexpected divine decision to elevate human beings into the divine fellowship. Barth identifies this orientation toward creation with election, but he shifts the focus from God's choosing of individual human beings to God's choosing of God's self in the person of Jesus Christ. Thus the divine orientation toward creation results in the utterly illogical, utterly unsystematic appearance of God in human form, not to rule, but to take on all rejection for human beings so that election can be their lot. Such a paradox can never be discovered through reflection on human beings and their world. It can only be revealed and pondered.

Natural Theology and the "Religiously Available" God

If process thinkers are, in fact, engaging in natural theology, then Barth would argue that the God they find and describe is not worthy of worship. How do process theologians defend their enterprise in the face of such a criticism?

We might try to show that Barth's analysis of worship-worthiness is dependent on a particular view of human beings and the human condition. The reason Barth asserts that we need an utterly transcendent God to save us is that we are completely powerless, not only to save ourselves, but even to affect the conditions in the world that perpetuate sin. The Augustinian-Calvinist doctrine of humanity's "utter depravity" has as its corollary a zero-sum notion of available power. If God is all-powerful, then it follows that human beings are none-powerful. Even if we might be allowed some limited causal efficacy in our immediate environment, we are certainly bereft of true power: the power to determine one's own fate or to effect real good or progress in the world.

Process Theology and Human Power

Process theology disputes this view of human (and, more broadly, creaturely) powerlessness. Taking seriously the message of the biblical creation account that humans are accorded a share of God's creative and ordering tasks for the world, process thinkers further deny that these powers were lost in the fall. Although forces beyond our control determine much about our situation and destination in life, even in the most constricted situation there is always something over which the human being, and the human being alone, has power. As the twentieth-century existentialist writers would assert, we are condemned to freedom. Even when falling off a bridge, when the forces of gravity have converted our bodies into mere objects subject to physical laws, we have the choice of how to respond to this situation, of what meaning to make out of it. In ordinary circumstances, of course, thanks to our flexible brains and technological abilities, we have in fact *far more control* over ourselves and our environment than any other creatures on earth.

Is it possible for us to use that power in the service of any goals other than finite, insignificant, or fatally flawed ones? Do its limitations in time and space make it unworthy of the name "power" at all, especially if we intend to use that word univocally of both God and creatures? Process thinkers assert that the univocal usage is appropriate. Humans exemplify the same basic and irreducible decision-making power exercised by every existing entity–God included. Naturally the scope and extent of that power differs between the creature and God. But the power itself is singular. It is the power to respond to one's unique situation and to become that response. It is the power of self-determination.

God's self-determination uniquely affects all creatures directly. My self-determination, in itself, has a far more limited effectual range. That does not make it any less worthy of being called with the same name and given its due respect.

None of this is to say that human power extends to the ability to "save myself." The pedagogical function of the Calvinist insistence on human powerlessness is to keep us far away from any notion that our salvation is something we could do, or even influence. In the view of process thinkers, the cure has been too radical for the disease—as if a leg has been amputated to treat fallen arches. Under the influence of this extreme doctrine, it's easy to forget that even with an imperfect foot, one can still walk, however haltingly.

If the task set before us is to run a marathon, however, the fallen arches might as well be amputated limbs. To say that human beings can determine themselves, even to the greatest extent possible, is not to say that they can create on their own the divine-human relationship God has envisioned and willed for them. God's power extends to the knowledge and perfect assessment of all possibilities for human beings, their communities, and their surroundings. We cannot act in our own best interests, let alone in the best interests of those we love and those yet unknown, without connecting ourselves to divine power. Yoked to God's perfect knowledge and perfect relationality, human power can begin at last to approach the goals that human beings have long held dear.

Finding God through Human Experience

What does this analysis of human power have to say about the human capacity to come to the knowledge of God? In other words, what are the epistemological commitments of process theology? Whitehead's own God-talk, despite his primary concern with metaphysical system, evinced a mixture of strict adherence to the description of God necessitated by God's place in the system and of the more evocative, poetic, or "religious" language about God's character, love, and "tender care." It seems clear that the philosopher was drawing his data freely from the demands of his systematic commitments and the inspiration of his religious heritage. And I would comment that this, with much more elaboration and methodological hand wringing, is exactly the epistemology that process theologians have practiced henceforth.

Process theology makes a dual effort to bring the "below" of natural theology and the "above" of revelation into communication. For example, the process system sketches a God of infinite relationality ("love") who has a primordial purpose for all of reality, a purpose God is in the midst of creatively bringing about. This vision seems, at first blush, quite conducive to the standard religious descriptions. However, once we begin looking at scripture with an eye to seeing God "in time" rather than outside of it, "in process" rather than archly static, and intrinsically immanent rather than only conditionally (gratuitously) so, revelation appears to bloom with support for the process metaphysic. God is quite naturally and literally pictured as moving through time with the denizens of the Hebrew Bible, observing and reacting to their agency, going to Plan B, even being surprised or dismayed by what God finds. "Perfect being" theists[4] have variously explained much of this narrative picture of God as one of the following:

1. a poor interpretation of God's actual qualities by the human writers (an explanation that has the downside of undermining the perfection of divine inspiration)
2. an accommodation for the weak minds of ancient readers who could not be expected to appreciate metaphysical perfection
3. a set of layers of nonliteral material, of some typological, analogical, or anagogical sort, which give added spiritual meaning to the text while remaining misleading at the literal "plain text" level

Process interpreters are freed from the Ptolemaic epicycles of this kind of avoidance of the text's obvious picture of God. We may, as discerning and educated users of revelation, want to be aware of tendencies in the narrative toward mythological or other genre-specific modes, tendencies that can clothe God in somewhat ill-fitting anthropomorphic terms. Still, within the process paradigm we can return to some of the assumptions about God's nature and character that certainly seem to underlie the text, but which the prevailing theistic interpretations directly contradict.

This dual movement—arcing human knowledge and perception upward toward the heavens and bending revelation down into its original human context—is not the Tower of Babel critics of natural theology condemn as the preeminent case of human overreaching. Nonetheless the dual movement brings to mind a famous disagreement between the liberal theologian Emil Brunner and the fiery neoorthodoxy of Karl Barth. Contemplating the question of how humans come to know God, Brunner posited that human beings must have an inherent built-in capacity for God-knowledge or God-relationship. This "contact point" does not constitute any positive knowledge of God in itself. It is merely revealed as present when we discover that in fact revelation reaches its aim, that humans can come to know and relate to God despite the vast qualitative differences between the finite and the infinite, the human and the divine. Barth famously responded "Nein!" In his book of the same name, subtitled "An Answer to Emil Brunner," he accused Brunner of compromising the radical discontinuity between creation and Creator, of attempting to open a back door to natural theology.

Process Theology and Epistemological Power

Are process theologians claiming as much, or more—that human beings have an innate capacity to know and relate to God? Does that claim collapse the divine-human distinction and, in the name of epistemological explanation, imperil the characteristics that make God worthy of worship?

If process thought marks a radical change in any one particular area from the Augustinian-Reformed view of human power, that area is epistemological power. Process thought holds, first of all, that the power to know is in essence the power to perceive. The power to perceive, moreover, is in essence the power to *feel.* In other words, Hume was half right: all knowledge can be traced to an impression, but sensory impressions—what we ordinarily call "perceptions"—are only a tiny subset of the kinds of feelings that impact creatures. And what we ordinarily call "knowledge," i.e., formed linguistic propositions held consciously in the mind, is only one example of the way the world gets inside us and affects us. To feel God—"prehend" God, in Whiteheadian terminology— is to begin to know God.

Here process thought answers Barth with its own resounding "No!" It is within the power of every human being, every creature of any kind, in fact, to feel God. As we feel our environment at every moment, assembling those feelings into a coherent and meaningful picture on which we can act, God is felt as present in, with, and under that environment. Those who attune themselves to God's presence in their perceived worlds find that they make value judgments about their world influenced and guided by how God values it. Whitehead terms this a "hybrid physical prehension": we prehend an entity in our world; we prehend God's feeling of that entity as part of our prehension of God; and, therefore, God's valuation of that entity is part of our feeling of it. Those astutely attending to this argument, however, will note that we have effected a reversal in the normal conception of power. In ordinary usage, power consists in being able to affect others. Here, power has been redefined as the ability to be affected by others—and by God. In fact, the difference between God and creatures in this quasi-epistemological realm of feeling is that we feel in part and therefore we know in part, while God feels all and therefore knows all.

To those not schooled in the minutiae of Reformed dogmatics, the granting of such a minute power to human beings as the power to receive a perception of God may not seem to threaten the sovereignty of the Divine. After all, scripture claims on more than one occasion that every human being in the world does in fact have the chance to obtain knowledge of God; does that not point to an innate human capacity for God-knowledge? Barth would reply that such statements do not point to what is natural to human beings *qua* human beings; they indicate that God has graciously revealed God's self to all.

The way process thought utilizes a form of natural theology to characterize God and human beings raises a significant question: how can Christians understand grace under this rubric? By his polemic against natural theology, his positing of a vast qualitative gulf between the divine and the creaturely, and his denial of even an epistemological point of contact for God within the natural human being, Barth intends only one thing: to safeguard the radical nature of grace.[5]

Can Grace Be Gratuitous in Process Thought?

The moment of grace's action, in Reformed thought, occurs whenever God deigns to be related to human beings. To posit such a relation as a natural or metaphysical reality apart from God's condescending action, therefore, is to hobble grace, to make it less than grace.

Is there is another moment, equally as vital and equally as primordial, in which grace can be located? If process thought wishes to engage with the mainstream of Christian thought, historical and contemporary, it must affirm that the basic rubric under which God deals with human beings is that of grace. However, it is possible that the "basicness" of this rubric need not be limited to the metaphysical status of creatures relative to the Divine.

Many process thinkers identify grace in God's self-determination to undergo significant and unnecessary risk by fostering the development of complex creatures with very high levels of decision-making power. God's aim, according to Whitehead, is to maximize intensity of feeling in the universe—intensity being defined as an optimal combination of harmony and contrast. It is possible that maximal intensity could be reached by ensuring that little destruction takes place. In that case, God would not encourage the evolution of complex forms of life, preferring the safety of minimal decision-making power (and therefore minimal destructive power), with its steady levels of intensity. But if there is a real possibility for much greater—perhaps even qualitatively greater—levels of intensity of feeling to be achieved through the cooperation of a highly diverse universe, including complex, significantly free, significantly creative creatures, then God might choose this route. The latter option, however, entails a very real risk. Creatures with significant freedom, creativity, and power can destroy as rapidly and as thoroughly as they can create. Such creatures can also suffer in conscious, lasting, and perhaps inescapable ways; their pain detracts from the intensity of feeling God aims to achieve.

God has no way to know with certainty and ahead of time whether the risk God runs in fostering the growth of creatures with the ability to cooperate with and to thwart God's aims in significant ways will pay off. Process theology denies the knowability of the future, for it denies the actuality—the current existence—of the future. The future is "not yet"; it comes to be out of its myriad potentialities, and in the present is revealed as one and only one of those possible outcomes. Then it passes into the past as brute fact, with all those unrealized potentials eternally unfulfilled. What is potential can only be known as potential, not as actual. Certainly God knows with perfect accuracy and comprehensiveness all the possibilities engendered by the risk God runs in encouraging the evolution of complexity. But it is not possible to know what *will* happen, with certainty, even if one knows perfectly all the circumstances and possibilities of present and past moments. Against Laplace and *with* Heisenberg: perfect knowledge of present actuality does not result in certain predictions of the future.

So God's choice to risk setbacks, destruction, and ruin by nurturing complex co-creative creatures is not a mechanically obvious one, made simply by "running the numbers" to see which scenario results in the best (most value-laden, most intensely felt) result. Because the future is open, God can know only possibilities and probabilities ahead of the coming-to-be of the actual events. Whatever choice God makes is not determined by some concept of "best" that exists outside of God. The goal may be set in God's character, but the means to reach it is a matter of free choice among competing alternatives that cannot be mathematically, objectively, or certainly ranked. God's freedom—another key consideration for Calvin and Barth—consists in God's ability to choose to be God, that is, to reach God's goals, in one and only one particular way. That way, it turns out, is to empower co-creators of value, co-feelers of intense feelings—and simultaneously to run the risk that these creatures will spell the doom of the divine goal.

Moreover, grace for Barth and Calvin is most accurately identified with a decision made before time began. Our experience of grace in our temporal lives is simply a playing-out of the predetermined implications of that decision. While it is true that grace stems from God's primordial decision to be for us, that decision, given that the future is radically open, can only be general in its scope and content. Experiences of tragedy mark our lives in time. These tragic experiences are as deeply real as our experiences of grace and redemption. The latter condition the former, but they do not trump them; the reverse is also true. Any view of grace adequate to these existential conditions cannot refer all queries back to a decision made in the solitude of God's primordial being before creation. The book of Job ends not with human submission to the ineffable. Rather it rightly ends with the unresolved conflict between a human being with a legitimate protest against God and a God who refuses to answer, citing executive privilege. Our tragedies refuse to be erased by a smug assurance that it was all part of the plan, that all things work together for good. That may be God for us, in a prospective and autocratic way, but it is not God with us. The circumstances and feelings of creation in their unforeseeable particularity elicit grace and judgment alike. Grace flows not only from God's general decision to be a God for us and with us, but from the specific moment-by-moment decisions God makes in response to our free decisions. Grace encompasses but does not eradicate our real experiences of fragmentation, tragedy, destruction. Grace is present but does not overwhelm the unanswerability that is undeniably a feature of human life. Grace is true to the textures of our experiences, rather than replacing them with its patter, as if our lives were somehow less than real.

Is this not grace, grace in its ultimate form, without hedges placed about it to protect it from itself, without escape hatches into the worship of power by means of which the triumph of good can be guaranteed? If grace is true giving, true risk, true *kenosis*—if grace is God's real character, not just the mask God presents that could change if need be—then I submit that Barth and Calvin, by failing to subscribe to a metaphysical system in which the future is truly open and in which, therefore, the results of God's decision to be God in a particular way are foreknown or predetermined with certainty, have compromised the radical nature of grace. True giving, true risk, true *kenosis*, is not calculated ahead of time. God's decision to be *God for us* is given without the guarantee that this decision will succeed in accomplishing the goal that motivated it. This is grace: true, noble, deep, and worshipful.

Worship-Worthiness and an Open Future

In conclusion, I would like to make a bold claim on process theology's behalf. My contention is that the only God who is worthy of worship is the God who exists in time with creatures, in a time stream in which future actualities are an oxymoron. Such a God, as discussed above, cannot know the future as actual, because the future is merely and solely potential. In addition, the real power of creatures to determine themselves, in degrees ranging from miniscule to significant, means that predictions about what the future holds cannot be made with certainty. The myriad creatures whose decisions affect what will come to pass in the future have some control over what will happen. Their decisions are affected by many factors, but in the final analysis, their self-determining decisions are theirs alone. Creaturely control over what comes to pass, therefore, cannot be gainsaid by any other power.

Divine Inability to Know the Future

Therefore, for these two reasons–the future's lack of actuality, and the responsibility of creatures for what comes to be in every moment–God cannot know the future as an already-existing actuality. In no way do the final days or the end of history exist out there, waiting for us to arrive at them. If such were the case, as believers in prophecy profess, then the final outcome of history is set, fixed, knowable, and communicable. Visions and revelations could transfer some of this knowledge from God to us. We could know, ahead of time, that God will ultimately defeat all forces opposed to the divine will. We could know, ahead of time, that if we align ourselves with God, we are aligning ourselves not only with the forces of good, but also with the side destined to be victorious in the struggle.

Historic Christianity's Understanding of God and the Future

As it turns out, this is in fact the position taken by Christianity historically, under the influence of two factors.

REINTERPRETING APOCALYPTIC

First, as Christianity became quickly distanced from its Jewish roots in the first few centuries of its existence, the genres of prophecy and apocalyptic literature in Judaism just as quickly began to be misunderstood. Prophecy in Judaism was primarily concerned with speaking truth to power, with being an independent voice for God outside the religious and political establishment of society, with calling the people, the rulers, and the priesthood alike to righteousness. The predictive function of prophets always came in conditional phrases: *if* the people do not change their ways, *then* this will happen–but *if,* instead, they do return to the Lord's way, *then* this will be the result. Apocalypticism, on the other hand, arose near the end of the period of development of the Hebrew Scriptures and presented visions of the future in arcane symbolic detail. It expressed a powerless people's longing for power, an oppressed people's longing for political reversal. To give hope, apocalyptic writings were attributed to great Hebrew heroes, and their symbols pointed in no uncertain terms to people, conditions, and events in the present day of the writers and readers. The hope that apocalyptic literature tried to foster was not for a distant redemption, but a present, near-term deliverance. It promised that God would act to restore Israel to its place of dominance and punish her enemies, not in the next generation, but in this one. It sought to give strength for resistance in the here and now, with the assurance that the day of the Lord was at hand, that the visions of ancient heroes were coming to pass before the reader's eyes.

In the Hellenistic and Roman contexts into which Christianity emerged and in which it developed largely divorced of its original Jewish context, prophetic and apocalyptic writings were understood very differently. Gentiles immersed in the empire's pagan culture read them as auguries or oracles, sometimes obscure but always literal descriptions of future realities. In one sense, this continued trends already found in the New Testament literature. Mainstream sects of Judaism (partly due to the influence of pagan empires such as Persia and Greece) had already by the time of Jesus begun to examine the works of the prophets for just such auguries and oracles, especially about the messiah. The synoptic gospels, especially Matthew are full of "prophecies" of this kind lifted from the Hebrew scripture–some from nonprophetic books such as the Psalms–to support Jesus' messianic claim. It made sense for Gentile readers of the New Testament, therefore, to extend that interpretation of prophecy back into the entire genre as found in the Old Testament. In addition, Christianity found itself in a similar position, vis-à-vis the ruling authorities, as Judaism endured during the rise of apocalypticism. The persecution of a majority power that made it difficult, if not impossible, to maintain and exhibit characteristically Christian behavior, belief, and ritual fostered a Christian genre of apocalyptic literature, one example of which survived (not without controversy) in the canon of the New Testament. Jewish apocalypticism cloaked current events in symbolic language to encourage an expectation of imminent rescue. In the same way Christian apocalypticism, including the premier example, the Apocalypse of John, urged believers to stand fast because the return of Jesus Christ in glory was right around the corner; the countdown had already begun, and the events foreordained to come to pass at the end were occurring.

Interpretations of the prophetic and apocalyptic genres already in evidence in the New Testament, then, reinforced the predisposition of Gentile converts to see, in Jewish writing about the future, road maps to an already-existing reality inexorably creeping closer and closer. Such interpretations, and the metaphysic of a fixed, closed future that goes with them, had a natural appeal for communities far outside of the realm of power, waiting for an end to oppression, persecution, and bondage.

PERFECT BEING THEOLOGY

The second factor that influenced the traditional Christian insistence on the actuality of the future and God's perfect knowledge thereof is the emergence of so-called "perfect being" theology, or the classical view of God. The reasoning, originating from Greek notions of perfection, goes something like this: Time, clearly, is the realm of change. Perfection cannot exist naturally in a realm of change, because for anything perfect, change can only be a move away from perfection. Therefore God, being perfect, must exist outside of time. An existence outside of time, coupled with perfect knowledge of all actualities, seems to indicate perfect knowledge of actualities in every temporal moment. To conceptualize this, we must think of time as a line. All of us exist as points on that line, moving forward moment by moment; we do not have perceptual access to any point but those we have been through. The points ahead of us on the line exist, but since we have not passed through them yet, we cannot know them. An observer not existing on the line, however, could have perceptual access to every point on the line. Hence God, not existing in time but outside of it, can perceive any point in time, all of which exist already as parts of a completed whole.

Another method of arriving at the same conclusion is to begin with the concept of perfect knowledge. All of us know imperfectly; we are aware that there are things we do not know. One of the things we know least about is the future. Perhaps some of us have access to some knowledge about the future, through application of natural laws of cause and effect, or even through seers and soothsayers. It appears, then, that knowledge of the future is possible, but for humans it's limited to what is certain because of constant and unchanging physical processes, and to what has been revealed through supernatural means. A being with perfect knowledge, however, would know everything that could be known about the future. The two tastes of future knowledge that we so rarely enjoy–certainty based on the knowledge of present causes or on miraculous revelation–would be available in their fullness to such a being. On the one hand, the perfect knower would know all present causes, and therefore the certainty of all future effects. On the other, the perfect being might well be postulated as a source for the psychic glimpses of the future afforded to imperfect human knowers, since only an actual observer of future actualities would be able to transmit knowledge of them to a human mind stuck in the temporal flow. In any case, the perfect being would be able to know *in toto* what human prophets know only in part, which means that God has perfect knowledge of the future.

Divine Foreknowledge and Foreordination

The twin influences of Jewish prophetic apocalyptic texts—whose proper genre reading was lost in the Gentile context of Christianity's spread—and of Greek philosophical understandings of perfection that seemed to entail divine observation and knowledge of the future, led Christianity to take for granted divine foreknowledge (and even, in many times and places, the more stringent position of divine foreordination) of all events in the universe's future. The first influence is historically conditioned. We now have much more and much better information about how the genres of prophecy and apocalyptic literature in the Jewish tradition were read at the time of their composition. We know that they were not intended to be road maps to a far distant future. The second influence has also been compromised by modern discoveries. Relativity theory, and then quantum physics, confirmed that perfect knowledge of present actualities would not equal perfect predictive power for all future occurrences. The glimpses of the future that some human beings claim have not proven to be verifiable by empirical means, our most solid source of knowledge. In fact, based on the exposure of many similar claims as frauds and cheats, one could solidly infer that no one has the access to future knowledge that such people routinely claim.

Defining Perfection

The one line of reasoning left standing, then, is the one that begins with assumptions about what perfection is. Here we are not on very solid ground, either, although millions of believers still take for granted that the Greek mode of thinking about perfection is still the obvious and only reasonable definition. Philosophers and theologians down through the centuries have enjoyed stumping their students and teasing their own brains with conundrums and paradoxes intrinsic to perfection so understood—most of them centering on omnipotence. Could God create a rock so heavy God couldn't lift it? Could God create a round square? Less playfully, such difficulties extended to the reconciliation of perfect divine knowledge of all future actualities (necessitated by the definition of perfection) and the free will of creatures (necessitated by the perfect justice of God in holding us accountable for our sins). How can we truly be said to be free—that is, to have real options to do either this or that—when what we will do already exists as an actuality in a future moment and is eternally known by God?

The answer, of course, is that omnipotence and omniscience, those divine perfections of power and knowledge, have never meant simply, bluntly, or naively the power to do everything and know everything. Instead, they identify perfect power as the power to do everything logically possible to do (no round squares). Perfect knowledge, similarly, is the *knowledge of everything knowable.* And as stated above, it is by no means a simple matter to declare the future actual and therefore knowable as actual. There seem to be very good scientific and philosophical reasons for believing that the future is not actual and is therefore not knowable as actual, even by a perfect knower. The perfect knower knows the future as potential, which is all that it is. God knows those potentialities perfectly, of course. But perfect knowledge of a potentiality is not equivalent to knowledge of an actuality. Twentieth-century revolutions in physics and cosmology reveal that the condensation of actuality from potentiality is not a simple transformative process. Rather it is a process deeply and thoroughly shot through with uncertainty. This process abounds with the real (sometimes miniscule, sometimes significant, but always real) possibility for something unexpected to occur–something not merely unexpected to common sense or to crude probabilistic judgments, but truly unable to be confidently expected even by the perfect Expecter.

Uncertainty and Faith

This climate of uncertainty is the best and most honest understanding we have reached of reality at the dawn of the twenty-first century. What, therefore, can we make of those who cling to belief in a fixed future, an end of time that we are rapidly approaching like a train approaching a station? I can only conclude that for such believers, the benefits of security outweigh the benefits of assuming faith's risk. For these believers, to assure themselves that they will be vindicated in the end is of paramount importance. They are unwilling to take on the risk of faith without a guaranteed reward.

Of course, this approach to faith negates faith's very nature. It is not a risk if a payoff is assured. Faith is not enough for this kind of believer; they must supplement their faith, or rather replace it, by adopting a doctrine of an actual, already-existing future in which their choice is vindicated by their side's eventual victory.

In this age of pluralism, we have at last begun to realize that Christian triumphalism is antithetical to Christian faith. The God who is for us and who asks us to be for God is truly Emmanuel, God *with* us in the stream of time. This God-with-us is supporting us in our free choices for the good, the true, and the beautiful. This God is redeeming the sins that set those causes back by working through them creatively to advance God's will. Yet many still worship a god whose most crucial attribute isn't goodness or grace or love or beauty, but power. This god becomes worthy of devotion primarily for winning in the end. Only the God who, as process theology describes, shares the risk of faith in a set of values and a vision of the future intrinsically worth enacting, is truly worthy of worship. This God demonstrates solidarity with creatures by graciously fostering the development of significant free will and decision-making power that they exercise alone, without coercion. In this God-for-us, we can place legitimate, human, valuable, and fruitful faith.

CHAPTER 2

Jesus and Christ in Process Perspective

■ JOHN B. COBB JR.

Jesus

Who was Jesus? Since this man has played a greater role in shaping the history of the West, and possibly the world, than anyone else, the question is of general importance and interest. For those of us who are personally committed to follow him, the question has heightened urgency.

For two centuries now, the question of Jesus' identity has prompted critical historical research. The historical reconstructions of Jesus and his times have varied widely. A few scholars have concluded that a religious community made up the stories about Jesus with no historical basis at all. On the whole, however, the consensus is that "Jesus" names a real person and that some of the New Testament accounts are reasonably accurate indications of what he did. Few doubt that he lived in Galilee, was baptized by John, gathered disciples around him, and was crucified by the Roman government. But just which of the other stories about him have a factual basis remains a subject of dispute.

Even more important are uncertainties about his message. A generation ago, cutting edge scholars depicted Jesus as an apocalyptic. That is, they thought that the reported sayings about the imminent coming of God's reign were authentic. They interpreted Jesus' message in light of this expectation. Of course, the scholars did not believe that his predictions were accurate. But many thought that the understanding of human existence associated with the erroneous, mythological belief was relevant for us as well. The greatest New Testament scholar of the twentieth century, Rudolph Bultmann, called for "demytholo-gizing" Jesus' message, by which he meant interpreting it existentially. Bultmann taught that, moment by moment, we are called to take responsibility for our lives with a decision that expresses love rather than to allow ourselves simply to reflect the culture of our time.

Today many cutting edge scholars are convinced that a later generation of believers added the apocalyptic sayings attributed to Jesus. Jesus himself, they think, was a wisdom teacher who challenged the dominant structures and authorities of his time in the name of compassion for the poor and devotion to God. One expression of this scholarship is the Jesus Seminar and its determination of the degree of likelihood that the putative sayings of Jesus were really his.

Fortunately, not everything changes according to these important judgments! We can say with some confidence that Jesus emphasized God's love for us and the importance of our loving our neighbors. Jesus challenged the religious and political authorities of his day in terms of his vision of God's purposes for the world. That vision turned upside down values that were common to that society and ours. Central to his teaching was the coming of God's *basileia* (God's reign or commonwealth). Jesus called people to live toward that world in which God's purposes will be fulfilled on earth as they are already fulfilled in heaven. Much in this message continues to inspire and direct us.

Regardless of the outcome of continuing debates, the resulting picture of the historical Jesus will be very different from traditional christology. For many centuries Jesus was not viewed as a humanly understandable Galilean teacher but as a divine being, different in kind from all other human beings. The great drama was that of descent from heaven and return to heaven. The primary work was either the defeat of Satan or the appeasement of the just wrath of God the Father. In short, the church's teachings about Jesus focused on incarnation, crucifixion, atonement, resurrection, ascension, and anticipated return.

Some theologians have replaced the Christ of the creeds with the Jesus of the historians. Others have refused to do so. They draw a contrast between the Jesus of the historians and the Christ of faith. The Christ of faith is Jesus as the believing church has understood and experienced him. The Christ of the creeds was developed to account for the faith of the church, not to explain the historians' reconstruction of Jesus.

These alternatives have been posed sharply in the twentieth century. The work of historians has become increasingly influential in shaping the understanding of Jesus in more liberal churches, as well as in the wider culture. But the most important theological movement of the twentieth century, associated with Karl Barth, denied the relevance of the work of historians to Christian faith.

This has not been a matter of naïve opposition to critical scholarship. For Barth, scholarship has its place, and the church has no business opposing it or trying to restrict its freedom. Nor does Barth's rejection of the historians' Jesus for theological purposes express indifference to the "real" Jesus. Instead, Barth's rejection was based on a fundamental fact about what modernity considers good scholarship. Such scholarship is nontheistic. For Barth, reconstructions of Jesus that leave God out of the picture do not tell us who Jesus was.

Barth appeals instead to the witness of believers as found in the Bible. For us to be believers is to share in their faith and vision. We do not become believers by examining the evidence provided by historians. Faith is a gift of the Holy Spirit.[1]

Process theology responds to this situation by opposing the dualism of the Jesus of history and the Christ of faith, while agreeing with Barth that the worldview presupposed by modern historians is unacceptable for faith. This worldview is inadequate for anyone who has an appreciation of the New Testament text. For example, the New Testament account of Jesus is full of miracle stories. Most historians simply assume that these are untrue. They do not, therefore, examine the evidence in favor of their authenticity. In other words, those who know in advance that miracles do not occur have no need to sift evidence as they would with stories that do not describe miracles.

The situation today is a bit less rigid than it has been in the past. We know so much about the role of mental states in healing that the flat dismissal of "faith-healing" is no longer universal. But the healing miracles are still treated peripherally and skeptically for the most part, despite their central role in the gospel accounts. The *a priori* dismissal of other miracle stories continues. In the background is the Enlightenment assumption of fixed laws of nature that admit of no exceptions, along with the understanding of miracles as violations of such laws. In contrast, process thought argues that most of these laws are statistical generalizations about the habits of nature when primarily physical events are not influenced by primarily mental ones. How mental states affect the behavior of physical objects (beginning with human bodies) requires separate investigation. Stories of extraordinary influence deserve respectful consideration.

Process theologians can celebrate the softening of the exclusion of the effects of faith on human health. We hope for more movement in this direction. Just as historians seek to decide other matters of history with real openness to evidence, we hope for the day when miracle stories will be treated on the same basis. If, as process thinkers believe, the mental and the physical are intimately interconnected, we cannot place an *a priori* limit on what people of extraordinary spiritual power may do. We need to examine the evidence in particular cases. When historians bring their skills and their methods to bear, without negative presuppositions, we will be in a much better position to reconstruct the ministry of Jesus.

The critical "miracle" for theological reflection is the resurrection of Jesus. Historians generally assume that what the New Testament reports about this cannot have taken place. They do not deny that Paul had a vision, and they allow that others may have had similar visions earlier. But the implication of their presuppositions is that these visions were hallucinatory. They assume that the crucified Jesus cannot have actually appeared to his followers.

One major theologian, Wolfhart Pannenberg, has challenged the historians with historical arguments.[2] Of course, he must oppose their tendency to reject events that are too unusual. He calls for openness to uniqueness. If the prejudices of historians are set aside, he believes, they will find strong historical evidence for the resurrection appearances of Jesus as objective events rather than hallucinations. As a process theologian I am inclined to agree.

Although process thought is open to dramatic novelty, process theologians find factual claims more plausible if the events that are asserted to have happened have analogies that can be studied. Pannenberg notes the frequent reports of appearances to loved ones by those who have recently died. Students of these appearances find considerable evidence that at least some of them are not mere hallucinations. Sometimes the recipient has no prior knowledge of the death. Sometimes information is imparted that is hard to explain in any other way. That Jesus also appeared to some of his followers does not seem incredible in this context.

Pannenberg also makes a case for the empty tomb. As a process theologian I do not absolutely exclude the possibility that a physical body can be transformed into a spiritual one, but I am skeptical that this occurred. The evidence seems too weak. In other cases of appearances of the dead, their bodies were not affected.

I have pursued this discussion primarily to indicate how I believe process thought can and should affect historical reconstruction. I do not mean to say that all process thinkers would come to the same conclusions. Although process thought is open to paranormal (or miraculous) phenomena in a way that Enlightenment metaphysics was not, nothing requires process thinkers to take an interest in such matters.

This openness to a variety of judgments is based on a second characteristic of process theology, which further differentiates it from Pannenberg. For Pannenberg, the affirmation of the factual resurrection of Jesus is *the* cornerstone of theology.[3] For process theology, the issue is important but not decisive. The resurrection of Jesus does not prove that his teachings are correct or that everyone should become a Christian. A Jew can believe that Jesus appeared to his disciples without becoming a Christian. A Christian can believe that the resurrection signifies only changes in the attitudes and beliefs of the disciples without ceasing to be a Christian.

Nevertheless, that Jesus truly appeared to his disciples after death is not an unimportant belief. It supports the conviction that life does not end with the grave. It affords deep joy that his religious and political enemies did not defeat this remarkable man. It helps us understand the passion and conviction with which discouraged disciples gave themselves to the spread of the faith.

For process theology, no one belief is absolutely necessary for Christians to hold. Christianity is a process, a sociohistorical movement. Such a movement certainly requires beliefs about its origins, about its nature and mission, and about the world. These beliefs change and develop from generation to generation. The task of theologians is to help shape them in faithfulness to the movement's history and its new situation, so that they will be as honest and truthful as possible, and as helpful in guiding responses to changing challenges.

Our current task is to come to terms with the evidence that lies before us about who and what Jesus was. So far, I have suggested that, when approached from a process perspective, this evidence encourages reaffirmation as historical probability of parts of the New Testament picture of Jesus that recent historians have rejected. But I have said nothing about Jesus as the incarnation of God. Process thought allows us to move to that topic as well without sharp discontinuity with an enriched historical thinking.

The Word Became Flesh

For process theology, God's being present or immanent in Jesus is a matter of historical fact. We believe that God is immanent in every event whatsoever. The exclusion of talk of God from factual discourse is, from our point of view, an error. This means that talk of how Jesus was related to God can and should be discussed in continuity with what we learn about Jesus through historical research. The "Christ of faith" is continuous with the "Jesus of history." To reflect intelligently on these matters, we need to consider, first, how God is in all things and especially in all people, and, second, how God was present in Jesus.

God in All Things

According to Whitehead, each unitary event or actual occasion comes into being out of all the occasions that lie in its past. "The many become one and are increased by one" (PR 21). The new occasion is different from all the others precisely because its past is not identical with that of any other event. In the moment of coming to be, it has its own unique subjectivity.

However, this is only a partial account. In itself it explains how the past shapes the present. If this were the whole story, then the present would be nothing but the predetermined outcome of the past. Whitehead and his followers share with many others the conviction that we are not automatons. That means that just how we constitute ourselves, moment by moment, is not strictly determined by the past. In part we decide what we become.

The question is how we can have real alternatives among which to decide. Whitehead shows that we can have such alternatives only if, in addition to taking account of, or "prehending" past actual occasions, we also "prehend" possibilities not derived from the past. Whitehead calls these "pure possibilities" or "eternal objects." We face an infinite number of such possibilities, but we prehend those that are relevant to the particular past out of which we arise each moment. Each actual occasion of human experience constitutes itself through the integration of such possibilities with the actuality of the past.

We do not experience the alternatives among which we choose neutrally. Some appear to us better than others. "Better" does not mean only more pleasant and enjoyable, although these are important positive considerations. A better possibility is one that enriches our experience in the immediate present more and also contributes more to the relevant future, our own and that of others.

This possibility often invites us to take a risk or to break with long-established habits. There is no certainty, in any moment, that we will choose the best.

If the totality of things were exhausted by the facticity of the world, that is, by all that has happened in the past, no prehensions of pure possibility would call us to creative self-actualization. Indeed, we would face no decision at all, since everything would be pre-decided. How, then, can we explain the real effectiveness of previously unrealized possibilities in our experience? Whitehead believes pure possibilities cannot influence us if they are only abstractions. They must inhere in actuality. That actuality he calls God. God's inclusion and ordering of the whole realm of pure possibility is God's "Primordial Nature." God's Primordial Nature participates in the coming to be of every creaturely event.

The Primordial Nature of God plays a necessary, although rather limited, role in the constitution of elementary occasions. These are predominantly physical. That means that they overwhelmingly conform to their past. Life brings a breakthrough. We distinguish the living from the inanimate by the role that novelty plays. Then, some living things develop the capacity for the more complex integrations of novelty into their physical existence. These integrations introduce thought and intelligence. In these primarily mental occasions, the role of God's presence greatly expands.

Process theologians have noted a remarkable affinity between a plausible account of how the Primordial Nature of God functions in the world and what is said in the prologue to the gospel of John about the "Logos" or "Word" of God. "In the beginning was the Word, and the Word was with God, and the Word was God. He was in the beginning with God. All things came into being through him, and without him not one thing came into being. What has come into being through him was life, and the life was the light of all people" (Jn. 1:1–4).

Given this similarity, process theologians often identify the Primordial Nature of God with what John calls the Word. This leads to similarities between process theology and the Logos theologies of the early church. They are alike in seeing that the Divine that was present in Jesus is also present in all of us and in the whole of creation.

God Present in Jesus

But a christology must deal not only with how Jesus was like all other human beings, but also with what is distinctive about him. Why do we single him out for special attention and reverence? Was there anything different or unusual about the way God was present in him?

John describes the difference as follows: "The true light, which enlightens everyone, was coming into the world" (1:9); and "the Word became flesh and lived among us" (1:14a). The latter formulation has been immensely important in the formulation of Christian teaching, since becoming flesh means being "incarnated." What becomes flesh is that which already enlightens everyone. It is hardly a total break. Yet it is clear that for John the difference is important, and it has been important for the church since then.

The questions for process theologians are two. First, is there historical evidence that Jesus' relation to God was unusual? Second, if so, how can we best understand that in process terms?

Historical Evidence for Jesus' Unusual Relation to God

Much historical evidence shows that Jesus had remarkable powers. This is especially so when we read the New Testament as process thinkers. We need not suppose that all the miracles occurred just as they are reported. We know that followers embellish and invent. But the likelihood remains that Jesus performed startling healings and other miracles. He attributed these to the power of God working through him. Few of us claim comparable power.

Further, he spoke with extraordinary authority. He seems to have associated himself with God in astoundingly intimate terms, addressing God as "*Abba*," or "Daddy," and identifying the authority of what he said with God's. He did not base his authority on his scholarly expertise in the interpretation of scripture, but even set it over against traditional teaching. What he taught comes to us, even today, with something of that authority. We are unlikely to follow his teaching straightforwardly, but we cannot dismiss it.

Understanding Jesus' Relation to God in Process Terms

Can process theology throw light on these remarkable characteristics of Jesus? If God is in all of us, what could differentiate God's presence in Jesus from that in others? The easiest answer is based on differences in the extent to which we embody the Primordial Nature of God moment by moment. If in one moment we resist the possibilities that come to us, the possibilities in the next moment will be more limited. We can harden our hearts toward God. That will never end God's role in our lives, but it will greatly reduce our freedom, making us more and more determined by our past and by our context. If, on the other hand, moment by moment we respond to the fullest possibility God offers, new possibilities open to us. We become more and more free. Our positive response to God's call becomes increasingly spontaneous.

Most of us fall somewhere between these extremes. The differences among us are a matter of degree. But differences of degree can be very dramatic. We speak of conversions and becoming a new person. If Jesus from his youth was unusually responsive to God's call, we can have some clue as to how in his maturity he had a spiritual power and authority that was very distinctive indeed.

We also are called to play different roles. Our calling depends on the circumstances in which we live and our genetic constitution. It depends also on the needs of our society and world. People equally responsive to God may lead very different lives. One may be a mother bringing up her children and managing her family. Another may be a social reformer seeking to overthrow unjust institutions. A third may be a scholar, patiently advancing historical knowledge. Jesus' calling differed from all of these, and it turned out to be of enormous importance for the future of the world. About most people, however faithful, we know nothing. So we never raise the question of their distinctive relation to God. In Jesus' case, because beliefs about him still shape our world, it is natural and appropriate to ask the question.

Most process theologians will agree that Jesus was called to a unique mission and that he responded with extraordinary faithfulness. Our question now is whether the uniqueness of Jesus goes still further. Was Jesus so related to God, at least part of the time, that God's incarnation in him is distinct from God's mode of presence in us? Most of the tradition has thought so. Faith does not depend on a positive answer, but if the evidence encourages us to move closer to the tradition, we should do so.

I personally have engaged in speculations about the multiple ways in which an occasion of human experience can be structured. Since the prehension of God is a factor in all human experience, this variety of structures involves a variety of roles for God. I propose that in Jesus, part of the time, the self or "I" was co-constituted by the prehension of Jesus' personal past and the prehension of God. If so, this would provide a process equivalent to what is said of Jesus in the Chalcedonian creed. That speaks of one person coming into being through the union of the Divine and the human. The creed was composed by persons who thought in terms of a divine substance and a human substance, and of a person as a substance. Given those metaphysics, they had a difficult task indeed to maintain both the deity and the humanity of Jesus as a person. For process thought, the one person of Jesus can be understood as co-constituted by the presence within him, moment by moment, of both God and his personal past. If God was in Jesus in this unusual way, it is easier to understand his extraordinary spiritual authority. It might also justify our speaking of a unique incarnation of God in Jesus.

It may help to contrast this structure with the one more familiar to us. For most of us most of the time, the "I" is constituted by prehensions of the personal past. We prehend God also, but we experience God as one who is other to ourselves. At best, we experience God as gracious to us. Sometimes, instead, we experience God as calling us to something we don't want to do. When we refuse, we sometimes experience God as judging us. We do not experience God's presence as co-constituting our selfhood.

Such speculations illustrate the ability of process theology to contribute to ideas about the form that incarnation took in Jesus. They are certainly not binding on process theologians or anyone else. Some prefer to stay closer to the findings of contemporary scholars. Some prefer to be guided by the kerygma, the earliest proclamation of the church. Adoption of the process conceptuality does not necessitate any particular speculation about him.

Christ

We have spoken of Jesus and of the Word that was incarnate in him. But what do we mean by "Christ"? We can use "Christ" as one of the titles of Jesus—"the anointed one." This is its literal meaning. The first Christians claimed that Jesus was the long-awaited messiah and would return soon to fulfill the messianic role. But for the Greeks, the specific relation to Israel bound up with messianic expectations was of less interest than the conviction that in Jesus God had come to the world to effect salvation for all. Incarnation came to be more central to what was understood by "Christ." This remains true in the church to our day. To call Jesus "Christ" usually implies that God was in Jesus working for our salvation.

In the language of the church, "Christ" often refers to the divine reality as incarnate. This frees the word from too close an identity with a single historical figure, although its use is always bound to the knowledge of God we gain from Jesus. We can speak of Christ as present throughout the cosmos and especially in the poor and oppressed. We see Christ in our needy neighbor. Luther said that we should be Christs to one another. The church is the body of Christ.

Process theology offers its distinctive account of what characterizes those persons or groups in which we see Christ. They are especially clear instances of "creative transformation." This requires explanation.

As noted above, God's presence in each occasion of human experience provides possibilities for being something other than the sheer, predetermined outcome of the past. This does not reduce the role of the past in the present. Indeed, the incorporation of novel possibilities often enables the present to include more of the past. An occasion can transform elements that would otherwise be mutually exclusive into what Whitehead called "contrasts."

This can be understood more easily with examples that take more than a single occasion of experience to transpire. Consider the case in which one who believes that Jesus is the only savior encounters those who look to Gautama Buddha for their spiritual guidance and inspiration. The exclusivist belief about Jesus seems to be incompatible with the spiritual preeminence of Gautama. It seems that one must reject one affirmation to embrace the other. Many have done so.

But novel ideas and fresh thinking can come into play and lead to a much more creative response. One may consider much more carefully in what way Jesus saves us. One may see that this is quite different from the enlightenment attained by Gautama and sought by his followers. In the contrast, the distinctive work of both becomes clearer. The believer in Jesus as savior may recognize the reality and great value of the enlightenment Gautama realized. This recognition need not weaken faith in Jesus. It can transform such faith. Faith in Jesus is now seen as opening us to appreciate and even to appropriate the great spiritual attainments of other religious leaders and communities. These can be understood as needed for the coming of God's *basileia*, which Christians believe to be the fullness of salvation. The move in this direction is a creative transformation of individual believers and, through them, of the Christian movement. In such a development, process theologians see Christ—that is, God—at work in the world.

Obviously, most instances of creative transformation, occurring moment by moment, are not so dramatic and history shaping. They are, however, always instances of enlargement, in which one retains the richness of one's personal history but incorporates also the new opportunities of the moment. In the process, the meaning of what one inherits from one's personal past changes and develops. The process of growing from childhood to adulthood, if it is healthy, contains numerous instances of creative transformation. The way mature Christians think of God is different from the way they thought of God as children, but, ideally, it is not discontinuous. It has been transformed by taking account of many things that were outside of the child's experience.

Paul wrote: "Do not be conformed to this world, but be transformed by the renewing of your minds" (Rom. 12:2a). The idea of creative transformation can be understood as an elaboration of that text. It is also closely related to a term much more common in the New Testament: *metanoia*. This is usually translated "repentance" and too often understood simply as regret. But the central meaning is "change of mind." When *metanoia* occurs, we see things differently and follow a different course of action. We may not be ashamed of how we have acted in the past, but now that we understand reality differently, we would be ashamed to continue to think and act in that way. We can understand this as creative transformation. Where it occurs, we see Christ.

Wisdom

Recently, process theologians have been influenced by somewhat parallel reflections about the earliest christologies and about the implications of Whitehead. Feminists have shown that in the New Testament the Divine that is present in Jesus is spoken of more often as "Wisdom" or "*Sophia*" than as "Word" or "Logos." Even the prologue to John, quoted above, may have originally spoken of *Sophia*, who is imaged as feminine. One speculation is that the church moved from a Wisdom christology to a Word christology partly to avoid including the feminine in God. Today we are trying to reverse that process and depict God as equally feminine and masculine in character. This leads many to renew a Wisdom christology; and process theologians, who have long critiqued stereotypically masculine images of God, are fully supportive.

This could be done, of course, simply terminologically. We could replace Word with Wisdom in writing about Christ while making no other changes. But further reflection on Whitehead's own writings suggests another, congenial, change. When Whitehead wrote about God, he usually had reference only to the Primordial Nature. But when he entered the sphere of religion, he emphasized the "Consequent Nature," God's inclusion of the world. Whitehead saw particular religious importance in the conviction that not only is God in us but also we are in God. God takes us up into the divine life as we perish moment by moment. What is ephemeral in the world lives on in God. We find meaning in the belief that all that we do we contribute to the divine life forever.

At the very end of *Process and Reality* Whitehead makes clear that he believes that, as is true of all other things, God's Consequent Nature is felt, or prehended, in the world. He calls this "the particular providence for particular occasions"

(351). In other words, the way God is present in a human occasion is affected by how previous occasions have affected God. Our experience of God can be of the fullness of the divine actuality instead of only the possibilities God orders for us in the Primordial Nature.

The concluding passage of *Process and Reality* raises many questions, and even process theologians may be more comfortable to limit themselves to the major themes of the book. But whereas the Primordial Nature is appropriately thought of as Word or *Logos*, when we consider the Consequent Nature, which includes the world along with the Primordial Nature, Wisdom or *Sophia* suggests itself. It seems appropriate to imagine that God's Wisdom is incarnate in Jesus.

This needs unpacking. In Greek thought, the Logos was the principle of reason embodied both in the human mind and in the order of the cosmos. The Primordial Nature of God, in Whitehead, plays that role. In the prologue to John's gospel, the concept is enriched by its association with life, which suggests that it is the source of vitality and novelty as well as order. The Primordial Nature of God plays that role also. It is quite natural to consider that, in a general way, what Whitehead names as the Primordial Nature of God is what the prologue to John calls the Logos.

But this identification leaves out much that is important about God. God not only orders the world and gives it novelty; God also saves the world in God's own life. God integrates the eternal Logos with the ever-expanding world of creatures. By incorporating that world in the divine life, God suffers with those who suffer and rejoices with those who rejoice. All of this seems to be revealed by and incarnate in Jesus.

Further, the way God is present in believers involves the integration of this internalization of the world with the more abstract Primordial Nature. The knowledge that results from this integration is more naturally thought of as Wisdom or *Sophia* than as Word or reason or Logos. To understand that God is present to and in us as Wisdom enriches and personalizes our relationship to God. To understand that God's Wisdom was incarnate in Jesus enriches our christology.

This also makes better contact with the teaching of Paul, who thought of incarnation in terms of God's Wisdom rather than God's Word. Paul's most extended discussion of Wisdom is in 1 Corinthians 1:17 through 2:13. Here Paul makes clear that Christ is the Wisdom of God. This Wisdom is in marked contrast to what the world in general understands to be wisdom. God's Wisdom appears to most people as foolishness, and God's power appears to them as weakness. But those who believe find God just where the world does not seek the Divine.

Whitehead himself pointed out the difference between what is revealed about God in and through Jesus and the dominant ways in which God had been, and indeed, has continued to be, understood. His analysis is congenial to Paul's reflections. Sadly, the church as a whole preferred largely to ignore this revelation in its official teaching and to hold on to the views of God that expressed worldly wisdom. One way of understanding process theology is as the effort to bring the church back to that understanding of God that Paul saw as uniquely manifest in Christ as the Wisdom of God. Whitehead wrote:

> In the great formative period of theistic philosophy, which ended with the rise of Mahometanism, after a continuance coeval with civilization, three strains of thought emerge which, amid many variations in detail, respectively fashion God in the image of an imperial ruler, God in the image of a personification of moral energy, God in the image of an ultimate philosophical principle...

> There is, however, in the Galilean origin of Christianity yet another suggestion which does not fit very well with any of the three main strands of thought. It does not emphasize the ruling Caesar, or the ruthless moralist, or the unmoved mover. It dwells upon the tender elements in the world, which slowly and in quietness operate by love; and it finds purpose in the present immediacy of a kingdom not of this world. Love neither rules, nor is it unmoved; also it is a little oblivious as to morals. (PR 342–343)

In light of Whitehead's comments, we realize that process theology can indeed be seen, not as an exception to, but rather an extension of, the Galilean origins of Christianity. Process theology proposes, not only that Jesus is an incarnation of God in many important ways, but also that God is like Jesus in equally important ways. God is the great companion: a fellow sufferer who understands, absorbing the world's sins and sufferings, and who guides the world, not by violence or blind decree, but rather by love.

CHAPTER 3

Coming to Salvation
A Process Understanding

■ JOHN CULP

Many people today reject traditional Christianity but seek spirituality and salvation in a variety of ways. For some people, salvation involves an intensely personal experience of God's love. For others, salvation means deliverance from a terrorist bombing or a debilitating illness. Some long for meaning in the daily routines of life. Contemporary ideas about salvation range from personal beliefs about life after death to highly developed theological concepts derived from interreligious dialogue. Amid these diverse approaches exist the common themes of a need for change and the actual occurrence of a change. Meaningful expressions of these themes typically involve attention to the need for salvation and the source of salvation. The crop-destroying drought brings cries for deliverance from hot dry days; and yet, when reflected upon, the cry reveals a longing for a more permanent state of satisfaction, sometimes called eternal life. The question then emerges: Is there a reality that can bring this about? For many people, that reality is God. My aim in this essay is to present a process approach to salvation that responds to these dynamics.

Process theologians describe salvation at three different levels. Historically, process thought began with a metaphysical description of reality that showed how salvation was possible, and what it involved, by talking about God and the preservation of value.[1] In a time when it was difficult to understand the structure of reality in a way that allowed for divine action to bring about salvation, process thought offered the possibility of creative change due to God's actions. Later, process thinkers developed explicitly theological statements about salvation based on these ideas.[2] In more recent times, process theology has sought to explain the experiential aspect of salvation.[3] I will begin with the experiential and then consider the theological and metaphysical aspects of salvation.

The Experiential Aspect of Salvation

People frequently seek for salvation prior to reflecting on the idea of salvation. Spirituality, as living theology, longs for more than the ordinary. Whitehead also affirmed the centrality of experience for understanding human life.[4] Process theology, drawing on Whitehead, continues to be concerned with experience. Examining individual accounts of salvation reveals frequent references to the feelings that were experienced. These feelings cannot be described only in terms of physical sensations. These feelings may be physical or mental, conscious or nonconscious. Feelings of a need for deliverance and feelings that deliverance has happened commonly occur in accounts of the experience of salvation.

Feelings of a need for deliverance arise in a variety of situations. When a young person dies, others begin to deal with the possibility of their own deaths. Is deliverance from death possible? Experiencing oppression has resulted in responses such as rage, singing, and action. In these responses, people seek for some deliverance from the meaninglessness of their lives. At times, experiences of death or oppression include the feeling of personal responsibility for the situation. Frequently when confronted with suffering, oppression, disaster, or death, a person will respond with feelings of guilt and responsibility for the loss and destruction that has occurred. Religiously, this sense of responsibility often includes the feeling that God's expectations have been violated. In these situations, the need for deliverance is often felt as a need for forgiveness from God.

Experiencing deliverance in salvation results in a variety of feelings. There may be feelings of spiritual, emotional, or physical well-being. A person may feel accepted by God. There may be a discovery, or recovery, of the meaning of a person's life. A person's ordinary accomplishments become significant. The experience of salvation includes, at times, a feeling of freedom from what limited earlier activities. The person who could not forgive, now forgives. Often the experience of salvation is accompanied by a strong sense of being loved and cared for. This feeling grows out of an awareness of God's love and concern. The feeling of being loved may also be based on the feelings of being cared for and loved by other people. Many times, feeling forgiven by God and others provides the core of the experience of salvation. At its heart, feeling forgiven includes feeling acceptance from those who have every right to refuse acceptance. However, true acceptance does not ignore or trivialize the actions that brought about rejection. If the offense is trivialized, acceptance avoids the problem rather than dealing with it. That finally is not acceptance because when the problem can no longer be avoided the acceptance is withdrawn. Feeling truly loved and forgiven by God may result in feelings of personal communion with God.[5]

The variety of feelings in the experience of salvation carry implications for how salvation is understood. The need, nature, and means of salvation implicitly structure the understanding of the experience of salvation. The need for salvation arises out of feelings that in some way involve a feeling of loss. The loss may be the loss of meaning, relationships with others, personal value, or relationship with God. Ultimately what has happened in such feelings of loss is a reduction of value. The need for salvation does not arise out of every occurrence of loss. Instead, the failure to bring about some increase in value, or the intensity of existence, gives rise to the need for salvation. Choices that fail to increase the possibilities for future choices cause a loss of value. Value is not a static accomplishment but is the creative advance that is possible in each situation. Value is creative within the order established by the past and leads to a more complex order in the future. At the most foundational level, rejecting God's purposes in the world causes the loss of all types of value affecting one's self, other people, the world, and God.

Salvation, in its nature, then brings about an increase in possibilities in response to the loss of value. Feelings of salvation express that more than ordinary existence is possible even in the middle of ordinary life. The feeling that salvation by nature goes beyond the ordinary points toward the dependence of value on God's preservation of value that has been accomplished. The preservation of value depends on God's restoring a creative relationship with God. Without this restoration, forgiveness for wrongs can never be complete. Restoration does not ignore or deny the loss that decisions have caused for God and God's purposes. God accepts loss as part of God's activity in restoring the relationship between an individual and God. The message of God dying in Christ, Christ's self-emptying, and references to God's weakness[6] demonstrate God's overcoming opposition and separation without destroying the source of opposition or denying the reality of the opposition. In accepting loss, God trusts future relationships to be meaningful and accepting. Thus God's action creates without destroying. If God defeated evil only by destroying rather than redeeming evil, salvation would not be possible for those who were destroyed; and God could not save all.[7] God's action making salvation possible must be universal. If salvation is not available for all, salvation becomes limited and loses significance. God's action must be continuous and continuing if a favoritism for the few is not to take the place of an experience of salvation that is extraordinary because it can be experienced by all individuals.

Finally, experiences of salvation include a feeling that the source of salvation is God both in creating and in completion of creation through the preservation of value.[8] Feelings of God as the source of salvation do not specify a detailed analysis of how God provides salvation or the nature of the work of Christ. What is felt is that this deliverance or restoration occurs because of God's action. By implication, if God is understood as the source of life, value, and meaning, then God as Creator of this universe must offer some means of avoiding death and other destructive changes in the world. Furthermore, the need for salvation is such that only God can bring deliverance or restoration.[9] God provides salvation by making both change and continuation possible. Human choice against change or continuation limits God's use of both change and continuation. Thus the need for salvation is intensified by the denial of the source of salvation.

Process theology offers two correctives to popular misconceptions of the experience of salvation. Recognizing the relatedness of all experience rules out understanding salvation as a strictly solitary experience. The contemporary interest in spirituality runs the risk of centering on the individual's spirituality and experience of salvation. This loses sight of the Old Testament's description of salvation as experienced by the family of Abraham, the Hebrew people as they leave Egypt, and the nation of Israel during David's reign. Paul's concept of the church as the body of Christ continues the communal understanding of salvation. Basically, the feeling of forgiveness establishes relationships among those who have been forgiven and those who have forgiven them.

Process theology also understands the experience of salvation realistically. At times people think that salvation means immediate deliverance from all difficulty. Any sickness should end now; a job will come today; shattered relations will be resolved in a moment of time. However, process theology notices that salvation often involves feeling the presence of One who suffers with a person. God's love and care lead God to enter into horrifying circumstances to enable a person to retain a sense of personal value through feeling God's care even in the struggle. At times, this sense of presence includes the assurance that no matter what the outcome is, God preserves the value of that person's struggle.

Theological Explanations of the Experience of Salvation

The theological level of salvation builds upon the feelings present at the experiential level of salvation. Christian theology makes explicit the implicit assumptions involved in the experience of salvation. The discipline of theology at its best does not impose foreign concepts on the experience of salvation but instead provides a more complete and conscious understanding of the experience of salvation. However, a dynamic relationship exists between theological understanding and experiential feelings. Although theological reflection begins with the feelings experienced in salvation, subsequent experiences of salvation are influenced by theological concepts. The usual theological analysis of the experience of salvation speaks of the need for salvation, the process of salvation, and the fulfillment or conclusion of salvation.[10] This conceptual structure describing salvation helps in organizing the chaotic experiences of salvation and thus facilitates communicating salvation to others. Paul's address to the Athenians illustrates the usefulness of clear thought. Paul proclaims the gospel of salvation as the fulfillment of concepts with which his Greek audience was familiar.[11]

The Need for Salvation

Theological reflection about salvation begins by explicitly identifying what in the nature of reality makes salvation important. Salvation is important because of experiences of destruction. Destruction of any aspect of reality threatens all of reality and makes salvation from that destruction important for the reality of what is being destroyed as well as for all of reality. The destruction or threat of destruction may involve only an external threat. The person infected with a cold virus seeks deliverance from the effects of that virus. However, a more important type of destruction grows out of the response to the destruction or threatened destruction. A person can be consumed by anxiety over the danger of infection through an airborne cold virus. The anxiety about the possibility of infection may become more destructive than the infection itself.

In the contemporary world, destruction takes the basic nature of the loss of freedom because of the centrality of freedom to the identity and value of the person.[12] Loss of freedom means the loss of self-control and places a person under the domination of another person. The dominated person becomes an expression of the dominator no matter what distinctions exist. The parent who seeks to live through the child destroys any independent value for the child. Threats to the freedom of a group occur as well as threats to the freedom of the person. To destroy the freedom of the group is also to cause a loss of identity and value. Thus, the loss of freedom destroys the individual, the group, and threatens all of reality. Again, this loss of freedom may be due to external events or to the fear of external events resulting in a more problematic loss of freedom due to fear.

To understand the destruction caused by the loss of freedom and how that destruction contributes to the desire for salvation, freedom itself must be carefully explained. Today the concept of freedom depends on a concept of a self as will or intention. The freedom of a self then involves two elements, creativity and context. The notion of creativity involves spontaneity, intentionality, and novelty to some degree. Creativity makes it possible to avoid limiting the understanding of freedom to the absence of restraints. Freedom involves individual creative action. The basis for affirming creativity in every actuality is that each actuality involves a response to prior events. The response to prior events becomes creative because each event decides on a new utilization of the past events through the selection of a response to the past that differs from the past event.

Context is also part of freedom because each decision occurs in a context, in relationship with past events. Without the prior events, there would be no options to choose among. The recognition of context in freedom avoids unrealistic understandings of freedom that fail to recognize the impossibility of absolute freedom. Absolute freedom as the absence of limits is impossible because without a context there can be no selection of possibilities and without selection there is no freedom.

Sin results from individuals seeking to avoid decisions by trying to control a situation completely or to surrender all control. Freedom includes deciding whether to respond to the structures of freedom in a manner that affirms a realistic freedom or in a manner that denies realistic freedom composed of creativity and context. The conditions of freedom elicit anxiety about freedom from humans. This anxiety leads to the denial of freedom and sin because the denial of freedom seeks to find security by limiting freedom. In that denial of freedom, the person denies God's purpose in presenting possible responses to the past.

Rather than affirm their freedom, individuals deny their freedom through pride or sensuality.[13] Pride denies the limitations of context in human freedom. One manifestation of pride ignores dependence on any one or any reality. Another, more insidious, expression of pride refuses to recognize that one of the limits of freedom is equity in that no one merits more of the resources for self-creativity than anyone else. Sin as sensuality denies human capabilities, usually by reducing human agency to the forces that act on humans and thus denying responsibility. Sin in both forms may be subjective and objective. Subjectively, sin becomes self-deceptive and thus hides itself within the self. In this way the sinful person denies responsibility for sin by suppressing the knowledge of individual sin. In its objective expression, sin manifests itself beyond the individual self and takes on its own power. This power is expressed in structures that are personal, social, and natural.

Although the Christian tradition has often focused on death as the outcome of sin, the most significant result of sin is the destruction of the fulfillment of possibilities that God has offered and thus the loss of participation in God's purposes. In its basic nature, sin opposes salvation by limiting the possibilities that are present in a situation. Rejecting the possibilities for the future restricts what God and the person can accomplish in a situation. Sin, then, denies freedom. Death is the outgrowth of the loss of future possibilities rather than an unrelated or specific punishment imposed for sin. Death, as the wages of sin, limits the possibility of life and the possibilities in living. The spiritual nature of separation from God has more important implications than just physical death. Sin as the self's denial of freedom results in spiritual death, which is the loss of confidence in the ultimate value of freedom. The significance of physical death is that it finalizes the degree of death that the soul has experienced.

The Process of Salvation

The theological description of salvation requires concepts of judgment by God, Jesus Christ as God's response to judgment, and development in the experience of salvation. In a theology of salvation, the concept of God's judgment makes clear that the loss of freedom, or sin, is not merely a part of the structure of reality. If the nature of reality requires the loss of freedom, judgment of individuals as responsible beings appears impossible or unjust. But the human attempt to avoid freedom by not making a choice establishes individual responsibility. God's judgment confirms that individuals are responsible for their response to freedom. However, God's ability to create novel possibilities relevant to each situation might be understood to make judgment unnecessary because God could act as though there had been no rejection of God's purposes. Such an understanding would make individual decisions insignificant. Choices to reject possibilities are meaningful because real loss occurs. God's judgment then retains the integrity of God's purposes by distinguishing the actualization of God's purposes from the rejection of God's purposes.

The biblical account of God's judgment of Israel by means of exile points out the contrast between carrying out God's purposes, expressed as commandments, and rejecting those purposes. If God had ignored Israel's transgressions, then we today would have little sense of God's purposes in the world. In other words, God's love opposes the rejection of God's love and the destructive nature of that rejection. God's love teaches through judgment without destroying freedom. God preserves even what was actualized in rejecting God's purpose by contrasting that to what could have been actualized.

God's judgment makes clear the need for affirmative responses to God's purposes in order to demonstrate the fulfillment of freedom. These affirmative responses to God's purposes initiate the process of salvation. Biblically, the concept of the kingdom of God describes the experience of salvation as the fulfillment of choices to put God's purposes into action.[14] The New Testament indicates that Jesus Christ makes possible the coming of the kingdom of God by demonstrating God's purposes in the world. Not only does God identify creative advance by contrasting it to destruction, God enables humans to see, experience, and understand the presence of freedom in creative advance. The crucifixion of Jesus appeared to end this demonstration of the fulfillment of God's purposes in actuality, but Jesus' resurrection shows the possibility of salvation. The resurrection made it clear that the kingdom of God involves transformation. Jesus' resurrection resulted in transformation of ordinary existence rather than in a separate type of existence that differed because it was spiritual. Jesus empowers persons to actualize the freedom they possess through his resurrection by affirming God's freedom from human rejection of God's purposes. Finally, Jesus' actualization of God's defeat of destruction becomes an influence on all subsequent events.

Self-transcendence through transformation characterizes salvation as present existence. Self-transcendence becomes possible through a positive response to God's activity. Self-transcendence becomes clearest in situations in which a person is enabled to love others than himself. God's activity does not impose change on a person from outside of the person but enables her to love the other. God's acceptance frees a person to love without being made to love. Christian existence involves a presentation of the possibilities for the Christian through the memory of Jesus, transmitted by tradition and by the presence of the resurrected Christ. This experience provides the basis for all other experiences of God even though it is nonconscious. The awareness of God may also take the form of the experience of peace. Peace arises out of the apprehension of one's relatedness to the Divine in the universe and is experienced as the harmony between the soul's activities and God's purposes that transcend personal satisfaction. Peace is the spiritual completion of life in the here and now.[15]

In a Christian understanding of salvation, the feeling of God or peace is not a static state of existence. Salvation is not accomplished at one moment and then retained as a specific, unending condition or type of existence. Salvation, as an ongoing process, begins with a person's initial response to God's purposes. In the context of Christian culture, God's purpose is most clearly experienced initially in Jesus Christ. Succeeding responses to God's purposes lead to a pervasive pattern of the acceptance of God's purposes and more significant contributions to God's influence in the world. The initial acceptance becomes an ongoing commitment rather than an occasional response. This ongoing commitment to God's purposes brings about the experience of salvation as a way of living. Salvation as a way of living requires concepts of both God's creative and saving activity.[16] God's creative activity provides salvation as freedom from the restrictions of the past. Without God's creative action, the world would exist only as chaos or endless repetition. In God's saving activity, God retains the value accomplished by each occasion. Because of God's relation to each occasion, God feels the value that each occasion accomplishes and makes that a part of God's continuing response to the world. In this retention, God values the intensity of feeling that each occasion achieves regardless of the loss that may have occurred in that event. Salvation thus involves both God's agency and human agency.

The kingdom of God represents the fulfillment of both divine and human freedom because human activity assists in constituting reality. But, as the fulfillment of divine and human freedom, salvation is never completed at one point in time either in the past or future. Salvation is a dynamic reality calling each moment to a richer fulfillment of its possibilities. Thus salvation, the kingdom of God, is the conjunction of every experience of freedom with its redemptive promise rather than a specific culmination of all events. No final description of fulfilled freedom is possible because freedom itself is dynamic, self-surpassing, and spontaneous.

The conscious experience of God's love and acceptance may play an important role in a person's religious development. The conscious sense of God's presence develops out of the nonconscious feeling of God. God may present the possibility of a conscious awareness of God's presence to the individual. This conscious awareness of God is not essential to Christian experience, nor is it given to all Christians. At the same time, the conscious awareness of God has intrinsic value and is beneficial. As a gift from the Holy Spirit, conscious awareness of God provides assurance.

The Fulfillment of Salvation

In a Christian understanding of salvation, discussion of the need for salvation and the process of salvation usually concludes with a discussion of the fulfillment of salvation. Often this fulfillment is described as eternal life or life after death. Christian process theology affirms that salvation may include life after death. The possibility of human immortality depends on a nondualistic understanding of the body and soul of an individual.[17] Both the physical and psychic aspects of human existence are experiences. Thus experience includes physical and mental components in differing degrees rather than being two discrete substances. The human soul then consists of a succession of human experiences inheriting from past experiences with a special fullness related to that specific individual. Conscious memory may be part of what is inherited, but it is not the entirety of the soul. In this understanding of the soul, continued existence after death involves the occurrence of later experiences that belong to the series constituting that particular soul.

Life after the death of the brain is possible because brain events do not exclusively constitute human occasions. Based on the understanding that a "person" is a unity of a chain of events, or experiences, eternal life could take place if God calls into being new events that have a strong continuity with the chain of events that identified the person prior to death. Because these are new events, they may be experienced by other events, or by living people. These new events are not bodily events although they have a strong connection to prior physical events. This existence after death would not be radically different from existence prior to death since both types of existence are characterized by God's grace in calling life into existence and by God's judgment of the response to that grace.

Existence after death need not be everlasting because resurrection is most crucially a quality of existence rather than length of existence. A new kind of existence does not require that existence be everlasting or unending. Thus the resurrection of the soul could be a temporary existence rather than being either immortality of the soul or resurrection of the body as forms of unending existence. Understanding resurrection of the soul as involving both physical and mental events is similar to Paul's concept of a spiritual body. Ultimately eschatology in the theological concept of salvation rejects limiting salvation to continued existence. The biblical image of God being "all in all" conveys a more radical goal for history and physical existence and does more justice to both the significance of God for salvation and the importance of individual existence than a concept of salvation as continued existence.

The end of things is their relation to God rather than their unique existence. This relation to God does not deny unique existence because we do live in the wholeness of our psychosomatic existence forever in God.[18] The goal of the continuation of the best of existence in response to God must recognize that human decisions in rejecting evil often bring new problems. A new type of existence is necessary. This new existence goes beyond what can be expected in this existence and is crucial for human hope.[19] But this suprahistorical hope requires some continuity between historical and suprahistorical existence to avoid introducing a destructive arbitrariness into human existence. Where no connection exists between historical and suprahistorical existence, historical existence becomes devalued; and suprahistorical existence functions as a distraction to historical existence. The retention of value in God provides the fulfillment of what has been achieved. Furthermore, this retention of value retains the significance of individual decision by building on those decisions in God's presentation of possibilities to future occasions.

The Metaphysical Basis for Salvation

Whitehead's concern to draw on experience in his philosophy makes the experiential level of salvation important to any attempt to state a doctrine of salvation. The theological understanding of salvation adds a reflective aspect to the experiential level of salvation (RM 15, PR 15). Considering the metaphysical level of reality broadens the experiential and theological understandings of salvation. Whitehead's concern for cosmology, and thus metaphysics, provides the broadest understanding of reality and a basis for critiquing specific religious doctrine. Metaphysical statements provide universalization that might be lost due to the intensity of religious feelings.[20] Whitehead's explicitly religious statements about "Galilean Christianity," the "tender elements in the world," and "love" (PR 342–43) connect the religious aspects of experience to the nature of reality. These statements describe the way in which God functions to preserve the world rather than calling for a change of life through commitment to the vision of God as Savior. A comprehensive process doctrine of salvation requires explicit recognition of the metaphysical basis for the doctrine of salvation in Whitehead's affirmation that the ultimate nature of the universe recognizes the importance of value for both God and every actual entity (RM 59, 100).

God plays a crucial role in making value actual and in preserving value. In terms of the general nature of reality, God makes it possible for specific realities as valuable to exist. God makes possible new events by presenting possibilities to each situation. Instead of an endless repetition of the past, God's presentation of possibilities calls new events into actuality, into existence. Whitehead described the past as the "dead level of ineffectiveness, with all balance and intensity progressively excluded by the crosscurrents of incompatibility" (PR 247). In presenting new possibilities, God seeks the value of intensity in feelings (PR 244, RM 100). God's presentation of novel possibilities saves the world from the destructive nature of repetition. This is evil for Whitehead because its triviality precludes experiences of greater value.

The structure of reality that results both in the loss of the past in order for the present to be actualized and in responsibility arising out of the possibility of choosing challenges the continuation of salvation in Whitehead's metaphysics. God must do more than simply present possibilities to a world if salvation is going to be anything more than the actualization of possibilities. The preservation of value is also important. The value achieved by any actual event gains a certain level of preservation in the evaluation that future events will make of it. By means of this evaluation, past events continue to influence the future, and their value is transmitted. A person's memory of a parent continues the value achieved by that parent.

However, this type of preservation involves some loss for the actual occasion in that the preservation does not include all of the occasion. Preservation by succeeding events does not avoid the "perpetual perishing" Whitehead discovered throughout reality (PR xiii–xiv, 29). Although this perpetual perishing makes possible the attainment of new actualities and thus new values (AI 204), loss still occurs. Preservation by later events is haunted by the possibility of a complete retention of value (PR 340). The complete preservation of value without loss occurs through God's harmonization of events in God's Consequent Nature. This harmonization by God retains even the value of evil events. Evil, as loss in its basic nature (PR 340, 346), destroys value by replacing the positive advance of value that could have taken place with its own triviality. This triviality destroys evil itself by making it insignificant for the future (RM 95–96). God overcomes even this self-destructiveness by means of contrasts between creation and destruction. God saves evil events by relating them to the completed whole.

Identifying salvation at the metaphysical level makes the contrasts between a process understanding of salvation and many other views of salvation apparent. Salvation from nonexistence does not begin with an isolated action by God. Instead, God enables actuality to occur. Furthermore, salvation of what has become is not accomplished by God's unilateral action defeating whatever threat to value arises. God does not utilize coercive force to overcome other forces at work. Whitehead described salvation as God's patience, where God conceptually harmonizes the actual events that have occurred. Whitehead also differed from many concepts of salvation because he was not certain that preservation of value required life after death.[21] While he did not rule out the possibility of immortality, or life after death, he did not take a position on the metaphysical reality of such life. Instead, he held that the reality of such life should be settled according to special evidence, religious or nonreligious, as long as it was reliable (RM 110).

Themes in a Process Doctrine of Salvation

Process notions of salvation have appeared at the experiential, theological, and metaphysical levels of understanding. In a variety of ways, four themes can be found at each of these levels of understanding. The most obvious theme is that God provides salvation by preserving the value achieved by each person and actuality. That abstract statement contains important implications for a theology of salvation. God plays the crucial role in salvation. Without God, there is no preservation of value, no salvation. As vital as the response to God is, salvation occurs through God's action to preserve the value that has been actualized. The nature of God's preservation of value also implies important considerations for a theology of salvation. God preserves all the value that has been achieved because God preserves each actual realization of value. Thus salvation includes the full importance of each individual. No one is excluded, and no accomplishment is lost.

A second theme in process concepts of salvation is that God's salvation is experienced in the origin of each event. Salvation occurs in the present moment as God's presentation of possibilities enabling each occasion to accomplish more than the repetition of the past and more than its own specific interests. This salvation is described variously as God's provision of novelty, empowering to love, manifestation of freedom, reassurance of justice, and transformation of the past. God's action has significance for present existence. All that comes to be results from God's call to actualize possibilities that are unique to the present moment. Salvation is not only the culmination of a long process; salvation begins the process.

Third, process doctrines of salvation emphasize the mutuality of the relation between God and the world. All doctrines of salvation describe a relationship between God and the world. Process thought about salvation makes very clear that this relation is a mutual relation. God acts to make salvation possible and to preserve value. God does not act by causing events to happen. The mutuality of this relationship can be seen in the importance for God of the response to God's possibilities. In this mutuality, the value of each moment finds confirmation in the very structures of reality. God's relationship to each person acknowledges the significance of that person's decision.

The final theme is the identification of sin as the rejection of God's purpose in the actualization of the possibilities that God presents to each becoming occasion. The rejection of God's purpose of increasing value requires redemption or salvation. The need for salvation arises from the decision of each occasion, which points to the responsibility of each actuality for its decisions. Sin does not arise out of the structures of existence. Although the loss that occurs when a person chooses one option over another limits the person's opportunity in the future, that loss does not determine the choice that each person makes. Each person chooses which course of action to take. If that choice rejects the freedom to transform the past that God presents, real loss occurs. Deliverance from the control of the past that destroys freedom comes through God's new action to present the best possibility in response to the destructive choices from the past.

CHAPTER 4

Religious Pluralism

■ DAVID RAY GRIFFIN

Religious pluralism, besides being one of the central issues in contemporary religious thought, is also an issue to which process theology has made an especially important contribution. Although religious pluralism may arise as an issue in any of the religious traditions, most of the discussion of religious pluralism has occurred within the Christian tradition. Accordingly, I will, partly for this reason and partly for the sake of simplicity, deal with religious pluralism as it has been discussed by Christian theologians and by process Christian theologians in particular.[1] I explain first what religious pluralism is and why it has arisen. I then discuss widespread criticisms of religious pluralism, pointing out that most of them are based on a version of religious pluralism that is very different from process theology's version. In the final section, I discuss this process version as pioneered by John B. Cobb Jr., showing how it avoids the problems associated with the other version.

What Religious Pluralism Is

"Religious pluralism" is not simply the sociological fact that there are many different religions. That fact is usually called "religious diversity." To be a religious pluralist is to make two assertions. First, religious pluralists reject any *a priori* claim that their own religion is the only valid one. For example, John Hick says that pluralism rejects the view that "there can be at most one true religion, in the sense of a religion teaching saving truth."[2] Pluralists are open in principle, in other words, to the possibility that other religions may be valid. The second assertion goes beyond this mere statement of possibility to affirm that other religions are indeed valid, as when Christians, in Hick's words, assume that their "Jewish or Muslim or Hindu or Sikh or Buddhist friends and acquaintances are as fully entitled in the sight of God to live by their own religious traditions as we are to live by ours."[3]

To be a religious pluralist, therefore, is to reject absolutism, according to which one's own religion is considered the "One True Way." The most severe form of Christian absolutism is *exclusivism*, according to which no one can be saved except through Christian faith. A less severe form of absolutism is *inclusivism*, which says that, although people in other religious traditions may be saved, they are saved only by virtue of God's saving act in Jesus Christ. The inclusivist, like the exclusivist, denies that other religions can be authentic paths to salvation. The pluralist says that other religions can be this and that at least some of them are.[4]

Why Religious Pluralism Has Emerged

Religious pluralism has become an increasingly important factor since it began to emerge in the seventeenth and eighteenth centuries. It has developed for at least five reasons: theological, ethical, sociological, scientific-philosophical, and dialogical.

The major *theological* motive has been the doctrine of divine love. John Hick said that he became a pluralist because he could not reconcile the idea that God is "infinite love" with the idea that "only by responding in faith to God in Christ can we be saved." This would mean that "infinite love has ordained that human beings can be saved only in a way that in fact excludes the large majority of them."[5] Catholic theologian Paul Knitter felt a tension "between two fundamental beliefs: God's universal love and desire to save, and the necessity of the church for salvation." He decided that the doctrine of God's universal salvific will implies that the revelation given to others must be a potentially *saving* revelation, so that "Christians not only can but must look on other religions as possible *ways of salvation*."[6]

The *ethical* motivation behind religious pluralism begins, Mark Heim observes, "with revulsion at the crimes of religious pride."[7] To illustrate this point, Hick devotes several pages to the "destructive effects of the assumption of Christian superiority." He points out, for example, that "there is a clear connection between fifteen or so centuries of the 'absoluteness' of Christianity, with its corollary of the radical inferiority and perverseness of the Judaism it 'superseded,' and the consequent endemic anti-Semitism of Christian civilization," which led to the Holocaust.[8] If each religion could overcome its absoluteness "by the realization that one's own religion is one among several valid human responses to the Divine," Hick argues, "religion could become a healing instead of a divisive force in the world."[9]

These theological and ethical motivations for pluralism have been supported by a *sociological* fact about the modern world—that many Christians, through increased familiarity, are overcoming old stereotypes about other religions. Besides learning about these religions from books and mass media, Christians increasingly have neighbors belonging to other religious traditions. When they compare the lives of these people with that of fellow Christians, it becomes increasingly difficult to maintain the old view that the spiritual and moral fruits produced by Christianity prove it to be in a class by itself.[10]

Another external push toward pluralism has come from a *philosophical* result of the encounter with *modern science*. More important than any particular discovery or teaching of modern science is what can be called the scientific community's *presumption of naturalism*. Although sometimes the term "naturalism" is used to mean a materialistic, atheistic worldview, the basic meaning of naturalism–and the only meaning that science necessarily presupposes–is the denial of supernatural interruptions of the world's normal causal processes.[11] Much modern theology–that broad movement often called "liberal theology"– has accepted scientific naturalism in this sense. Hick, for example, says that the form of Christianity that "believed in miracles which arbitrarily disrupt the order of nature" is "incompatible with the scientific project."[12] This rejection of supernaturalism does not necessarily mean a rejection of theism. Many liberal theologians (including process theologians) have developed doctrines that can be called "theistic naturalism," or "naturalistic theism."

This denial of supernatural interventions does not even entail that these theologians reject ongoing divine activity in the world (as process theologians especially show). But it does mean that they no longer assume that the founding events of Christian history involved a divine incursion into the world that was different in kind from the way that God works always and everywhere. For example, Ernst Troeltsch, the first major pluralist of the twentieth century, rejected, in Knitter's words, "concepts of revelation that had God swooping down from heaven and intervening into history at particular spots."[13] Another major Christian pluralist, Wilfred Cantwell Smith, rejects the idea "that God has constructed Christianity" in favor of the idea that God "has inspired us to construct it, as He/She/It has inspired Muslims to construct what the world knows as Islam."[14]

The doctrinal revisions undertaken by pluralistic theologians have especially focused on traditional Christian theology's supernaturalistic christology. According to that christology, points out Hick, Jesus "was God–more precisely, God the Son, the second person of the Holy Trinity–incarnate." Such christology implied "that Christianity, alone among the religions, was founded by God in person." Christianity was, therefore, "God's own religion in a sense in which no other can be."[15] Process theologian John Cobb's first statement of his pluralistic position was entitled, significantly, *Christ in a Pluralistic Age.* Cobb rejected the traditional "supernaturalist and exclusivist" interpretation of the incarnation of the divine Logos in Jesus, according to which Jesus was "a supernatural being," namely, "the transcendent, omnipotent, omniscient ruler of the world…walking about on earth in human form."[16]

The rejection of supernaturalism applies also to the traditional idea of salvation, according to which salvation involves a divine decision, based on arbitrary standards, that saves some people from eternal damnation. Hick recognized that Christian exclusivism and inclusivism both depend on some such definition of salvation, such as "being forgiven and accepted by God because of the atoning death of Jesus." He responds by suggesting that "we define salvation…as an actual change in human beings," which involves "a long process," not a sudden, supernaturally effected transformation.[17] Cobb, likewise, speaks of "salvation as something we participate in here and now rather than, or in addition to, life beyond."[18]

A fifth motivation behind the development of pluralistic forms of Christian theology has been what some have called the *dialogical* imperative.[19] This imperative has both ethical and theological motivations. The major *ethical* motivation is the recognition that many problems of our planet are so great that they can be overcome, if at all, only through the cooperation of the world's various religions. Knitter, for example, argues that all the religions today are facing the human demand for "some form of this-worldly, earthly (as opposed to purely spiritual) *liberation*," so that "*liberation*–what it is and how to achieve it–constitutes a new arena for the encounter of religions."[20] The major *theological* motive for dialogue is that, once we see that our own religion is not the one and only true religion, we realize that other traditions may have truths and values that are not provided, at least as clearly, in our own religion. The conclusion that Christianity, like every other religion, is limited, says Knitter, leads to the dialogical imperative, because through dialogue with members of other religious traditions "we can expand or correct the truth that we have," thereby overcoming the "limitations of our own viewpoint."[21] This motive, as we will see, is central to Cobb's pluralistic theology.

Criticisms of Religious Pluralism

Although, for many theologians, the need for Christianity to embrace pluralism is now beyond question, not all theologians agree. From the perspective of many Christian thinkers, "Christian pluralism" is a self-contradiction. One cannot hold Christian faith in an authentic form, they believe, and be a pluralist. Much of this rejection of Christian pluralism arises from an absolutist, supernaturalist notion of Christian faith, which simply presupposes that the only authentic form of Christian faith is one that assumes, *a priori*, that it is the only religion sanctioned by God. This kind of criticism can be largely ignored by pluralists, because the controversy is not about pluralism as such but about the proper Christian response to modern thought–whether the liberal rejection of the supernaturalist framework is a necessary adjustment by Christian faith or a betrayal of that faith.

Another criticism, however, must be taken more seriously. According to this criticism, pluralism inevitably leads to a kind of relativism that is antithetical to Christian faith. In a landmark book, Alan Race pointed out the centrality of this issue. He wrote: "The pertinent question mark which hovers over all theories of pluralism is how far they succeed in overcoming the sense of 'debilitating relativism' which is their apparent danger." By "debilitating relativism," Race meant the view that all religions are equally true in a way that makes them equally false.[22] At least one pluralist theologian, Langdon Gilkey, believes that this danger cannot be avoided. Seeing "no consistent theological way to relativize and yet to assert our own symbols," Gilkey concludes that giving up our absolute starting point leads to an "unavoidable relativism."[23]

The reason this concern looms so large is not only the fact that the way to affirm pluralism without relativism is not immediately obvious, but also the fact that some of the most prominent pluralists have been led to relativism. For example, Ernst Troeltsch has been called not only the first great Christian pluralist but also "the first great Christian relativist."[24] And the position of John Hick has been widely criticized as leading to a complete relativism. This fact is of great significance because Hick's version of pluralism, besides being the version that has been discussed far more than any other,[25] is widely taken as representative of pluralism as such. For example, Kevin Meeker and Philip Quinn say that they reserve the term *religious pluralism* "to refer to the position John Hick adopts in response to the fact of religious diversity."[26] Mark Heim, seeing Hick as having made "the philosophical case for a pluralistic outlook," treats Hick's position as the paradigmatic pluralistic theology.[27] Any weaknesses in Hick's position, therefore, have widely been taken to be weaknesses of pluralism as such. It is, accordingly, important to see that the weaknesses in Hick's position, which have led to such widespread criticism, follow from his particular version of pluralism, rather than from pluralism as such.

Hick's move to pluralism began, as we saw, with his conviction about what the divine love would not do. The particular way Hick worked out his pluralistic position then led him to the conclusion that personalistic words such as *love* could not be applied to the Divine Reality in itself. A fact combined with an assumption led Hick to this conclusion. The fact was that the reports of profound religious (mystical) experience can be divided into at least two major types:

1. those that describe communion with a good, loving, personal deity, distinct from the experiencer
2. those that describe a realization of identity with ultimate reality experienced as formless, impersonal, ineffable, and "beyond good and evil"

The existence of these two types of religious experience creates a problem in part because they are both reported, as Caroline Franks Davis points out, as apprehensions of "the nature of *ultimate* reality."[28]

But this fact would not have created a problem except for a crucial assumption on Hick's part. This assumption was that, as Cobb puts it critically, "what is approached as 'ultimate reality' must be one and the same."[29] As Hick himself puts it, "there cannot be a plurality of ultimates."[30] Given that assumption, Hick faces a serious question, which is, in Davis's words:

> How can "ultimate reality" be both a personal being and an impersonal principle, identical to our inmost self and forever "other," loving and utterly indifferent, good and amoral, knowable and unknowable, a plenitude and "emptiness"?[31]

In seeking to answer this question, Hick decided that as a pluralist he could not play favorites. He could not say that the one kind of religious experience was more authentic–more revelatory of ultimate reality–than the other. He decided, accordingly, that ultimate reality in itself–which he often calls simply the "Real in itself"–must be considered completely unknowable (like Immanuel Kant's "noumenal reality") and must, therefore, be distinguished from all human ideas about ultimate reality. These human ideas are then divided into two types: divine *personae*, such as the biblical God and Advaita Vedanta's Saguna Brahman (Brahman with qualities), and the *impersonae*, such as Advaita Vedanta's Nirguna Brahman (Brahman without qualities) and Buddhism's "Sunyata" (usually translated "emptiness"). None of these human ideas about ultimate reality correspond to the ultimate reality in itself, says Hick, because the Real in itself "cannot be said to be one or many, person or thing, substance or process, good or evil, purposive or non-purposive."[32] Therefore, Hick says, we cannot apply to ultimate reality in itself any substantive predicates, such as "being good," "being powerful," and "having knowledge."[33]

Hick's position thereby does lead to the "debilitating relativism" of which Alan Race spoke. In his eagerness to show all religions to be equally true, Hick has in effect declared them all to be equally false, thereby undercutting their support for moral and spiritual attitudes. Hick does, to be sure, claim that "the major world religions constitute varying human responses to the transcendent Reality, and are thus at least to some extent *in alignment with that Reality*," so that they can to that extent provide criteria for valuing various human attitudes.[34] For example, pointing out that saints in all religious traditions manifest "compassion/love towards other human beings or towards all life,"[35] Hick implies that this attitude is in alignment with "transcendent Reality." However, given Hick's assertion that this "transcendent Reality" is entirely devoid of purpose, goodness, compassion, and love, he cannot legitimately say that the saint's "compassion/love" is any more in alignment with it than Hitler's hate and indifference. Hick's version of religious pluralism is widely rejected because of this complete undermining of Christian faith and ethics.[36]

Another widespread criticism is that Hick's so-called pluralistic position is not really pluralistic. This criticism is based on the fact that Hick says not only that all religions are oriented toward the same ultimate reality but also that they all aim at essentially the same "salvation," which Hick describes as a "transformation of human existence from self-centredness to Reality-centredness."[37] One problem created by this lack of genuine pluralism, Heim points out, is that by implying that "the specific and special aspects of another faith tell us [nothing] that is of significant importance," it provides no motivation for dialogue.[38]

Heim's equation of pluralism with Hick's specific version of it is shown by his comment that "the pluralistic hypothesis" rests on two dubious assumptions: "a metaphysical dogma that there can be but one religious object, and a soteriological dogma that there can be but one religious end."[39] By virtue of thereby equating pluralism with Hick's position, Heim ends up with a paradoxical position. On the one hand, saying that, "Despite their appropriation of the title, ['pluralistic'] theologies are not religiously pluralistic at all," Heim argues that we need a "truly pluralistic hypothesis."[40] On the other hand, repeatedly referring negatively to "pluralism" and "pluralistic theology,"[41] he calls for a "post-pluralistic" theology.[42] This second conclusion—which comes through as the book's dominant message[43]—reinforces the view of others who have used the problems inherent in Hick's version of pluralistic theology to call for leaving pluralistic theology as such behind.[44]

Process Theology's Complementary Religious Pluralism

Whitehead's process philosophy provides the basis for a different version of religious pluralism. Two features of Whitehead's philosophy are especially relevant. One of these is his concern, in dealing with different systems of thought, to show how assertions that at first sight appear to be *contradictory* may actually express *complementary* truths. Whitehead suggested this approach with regard to science and religion, saying that a clash between their teachings is "a sign that there are wider truths...within which a reconciliation of a deeper religion and a more subtle science will be found" (SMW 185). He also suggested it with regard to Buddhism and Christianity, saying that instead of sheltering themselves from each other, they should "[look] to each other for deeper meanings." In each case, the task is to overcome formulations that, while expressing a measure of truth, have done so in "over-assertive" ways, "thereby implying an exclusion of complementary truths" (RM 146, 145, 149).

The other feature of Whitehead's philosophy that is especially germane to pluralism is his view of the relation between *God and creativity*. "Creativity," which involves a generalization of the physicist's "energy," refers to the power embodied in all actual things—both God and finite actualities. According to Whitehead's view of actual entities, they are momentary "actual occasions," which come into existence out of the causal influence of the past, exercise a degree of self-determination, and then come to completion, after which they exert causal influence on future actual occasions. Your experience during a few seconds, for example, is composed of a number of actual occasions—also called "occasions of experience." Whitehead's term "creativity" points to the twofold power of each occasion of experience to exert a degree of self-determination in forming itself and then to exert causal influence on the future. Whitehead's term "creativity" thus provides a new understanding of what previous philosophers have simply called "being" or "being itself," and which theologian Paul Tillich called "the power of being." But for Whitehead, unlike Tillich, God is not simply being itself, understood as the power of being, but the ultimate *embodiment* of this power.

The distinctive feature of Whitehead's position is that God and creativity are equally primordial. Although traditional theologians regarded the power to create as eternal, this power belonged to God alone—the fact that a world with its own power exists was due to a voluntary divine decision. This idea was enshrined in the doctrine of *creatio ex nihilo*, according to which our world was created out of a complete absence of finite actual entities. Whitehead rejected this doctrine, suggesting instead that our world was created–as the Bible itself suggests[45]–out of a primeval chaos. Although our particular world is a contingent divine creation, there has always been *a* world, in the sense of a multiplicity of finite actualities embodying creativity, and therefore the twofold power of exerting self-determination and exerting causal influence on other things. To say that God has always coexisted with creativity, therefore, means that creativity has always been embodied in a world as well as in God–that there has always been worldly creativity as well as divine creativity.

This doctrine is doubly important for the issue of religious pluralism. In the first place, this doctrine explains the impossibility of supernatural interruptions. Traditional theism's supernaturalism was undergirded by its doctrine of *creatio ex nihilo*. By saying that the very fact that a finite world exists at all is because of God's free decision, traditional theists implied that all the principles embodied in our world–not only what we call the "laws of nature" but also the most fundamental causal principles–were freely created. And what was freely created could be freely interrupted. This doctrine, besides giving traditional theists an insoluble problem of evil,[46] also lay behind their absolutist view that Christianity is the only divinely ordained religion. Thanks to supernatural intervention, the fallibility that is involved in all human thinking could have been divinely overcome in the case of the authors of the New Testament, resulting in an infallibly inspired book.

Process theologian Marjorie Suchocki has developed the implications of this Whiteheadian view of the God-world relation in her highly readable book, *Divinity and Diversity*, which is subtitled *A Christian Affirmation of Religious Pluralism*. Because all creatures have their own creativity, hence their own freedom of response–as the creation narrative in Genesis itself suggests–God's activity in the world must take the form of "call and response." Because the various creatures will often use their freedom to respond in different ways, diversity arises. God's call at any time will be relevant to the responses previously made by a particular species, or a particular religious tradition. Accordingly, Suchocki concludes:

> If God works through call and response, and if human freedom introduces variety into the response, then shouldn't we expect to find different stories, rituals, orders of social structure, and senses of the sacred, but all tending toward creating the good within human forms of community?[47]

In developing the implications of this view for the Christian understanding of the "reign of God," she says that we are today called "to live a reign of God that reaches not toward an imperialism of one religion–our own!–sweeping the planet, but that reaches toward a new form of community: a community made up of diverse religious communities, existing together in friendship."[48]

Equally important for religious pluralism is the fact that the distinction between God and creativity provides a basis for speaking of *two* ultimates. John Cobb has most fully worked out this idea. Cobb's position, in contrast with Hick's identist pluralism, can be called "complementary pluralism."[49] Different religions, Cobb holds, have seen different truths and have offered different paths to salvation.

In developing the idea that there are two ultimates, Cobb suggests that one of these, corresponding with Whitehead's "creativity," has been called "Emptiness" ("Sunyata") or "Dharmakaya" by Buddhists, "Nirguna Brahman" by Advaita Vedantists, "the Godhead" by Meister Eckhart, and "Being Itself" by Heidegger and Tillich. It is the *formless* ultimate. The other ultimate, corresponding with what Whitehead calls "God," is not Being Itself but the *Supreme* Being. Far from being formless, it is the world's source of all forms, such as truth, beauty, and justice. It has been called "Amida Buddha" or "Sambhogakaya," "Saguna Brahman," "Ishvara," "Yahweh," "Christ," and "Allah."[50]

Cobb believes that there are good reasons to prefer this hypothesis to Hick's. One reason is that Cobb simply does not find it illuminating to say that God, who is *worshiped*, and Emptiness, which is *realized*, are "two names for the same noumenal reality."[51] Cobb's hypothesis allows us to recognize them as the different realities they seem to be. A second advantage of this alternative hypothesis, Cobb says, is that it allows Christian theologians to avoid the "relativization and even negation of basic Christian commitments" implicit in Hick's hypothesis.[52] "[T]hose who assume that all traditions must be focusing on the same aspects of reality," Cobb says, are led to believe that what Zen Buddhists call Emptying "must be the same as God," which can in turn lead the Christian thinker to "employ the negative theology on the Christian heritage so radically as to dissolve God into Emptying. In that process everything distinctive of the biblical heritage is lost."[53] Whiteheadian pluralists, by contrast, can affirm the existence of a Divine Actuality with many characteristics in common with the biblical God, including those that support the concern for a just social order, without disagreeing with the description, provided by nontheistic Hindus and Buddhists, of ultimate reality as formless. Finally, Cobb says, "When we understand global religious experience and thought in this way, it is easier to view the contributions of diverse traditions as complementary."[54]

This last point is crucial, given Cobb's view that the challenge of interreligious dialogue is "to transform contradictory statements into different but not contradictory ones," thereby moving "toward a more comprehensive vision in which the deepest insights of both sides are reconciled."[55] One basis for such reconciliation is to recognize that claims that may at first glance seem contradictory are really answers to different questions. "[T]here is no contradiction in the claim of one that problem A is solved by X and the claim of the other that problem B is solved by Y...The claims are complementary rather than contradictory."[56] For example:

> Consider the Buddhist claim that Gautama is the Buddha. That is a very different statement from the assertion that God was incarnate in Jesus. The Buddha is the one who is enlightened. To be enlightened is to realize the fundamental nature of reality, its insubstantiality, its relativity, its emptiness...That Jesus was the incarnation of God does not deny that Gautama was the Enlightened One.[57]

Another example involves the tension between the Christian assertion "that Jesus is the Christ" and the Jewish insistence "that the Messiah has not come." Jews and Christians, Cobb suggests, should "work together repeatedly to clarify the difference between what Jews mean by 'Messiah' and what Christians legitimately mean by 'Christ.'"[58]

Alan Race, after warning of the danger of "debilitating relativism," pointed to Cobb's version as an exception. "The virtue of Cobb's contribution," said Race, "is that he combines fidelity to Christ with unqualified openness to other faiths."[59] Cobb illustrates this assessment by saying that, to enter into interreligious dialogue, "we do not need to relativize our beliefs...We can affirm our insights as universally valid! What we cannot do, without lapsing back into unjustified arrogance, is to deny that the insights of other traditions are also universally valid."[60]

CHAPTER 5

The Dialogue between Jews and Christians

■ CLARK WILLIAMSON

The conversation of Jews and Christians with each other has been going on intensely since the 1960s. The conversation intensified after the Second Vatican Council's issue of *Nostra Aetate* (*In Our Times*), expressing new attitudes toward Jews and Judaism after the Nazi Holocaust in which so many Christians and churches were complicit. At the same time, and parallel to this development, intra-Jewish and intra-Christian dialogues about Jewish and Christian understandings of each other, have also taken place, resulting in a number of significant publications.[1] Several Christian theologians have taken a hard and critical look at Christian teachings and practices toward Jews and Judaism and have made constructive proposals in the effort both to restate Christian teachings and reshape Christian practices.[2]

Jewish and Christian Process Theologies: A Narrative

This essay is a narrative account of the development of Jewish process theologies parallel to the development of Christian process theologies. There have been Jewish process theologians for as long as (or almost as long as) there have been Christian process theologians. Here we describe that history, briefly. Then we will look at Jewish criticisms of Christian process theology. Finally we will pay attention to the contributions process thought can make both to the dialogue between Jews and Christians and to the reconstruction of Christian theology in the light of that same dialogue.

Jewish Process Theologies: History and Development

Process thought was a philosophy (or group of philosophies sharing family resemblances) before theologians began engaging it in conversation and finding in it resources for rethinking matters of faith. That process thought is a philosophy means that theologians of various faith traditions can engage it in conversation. Jewish process theologians have worked with process thought for as long as Christian process theologians. Mordecai Kaplan, the founder of the Reconstructionist Movement in Judaism, read and responded to Whitehead's books as they were published.

On November 18, 1929, Kaplan reports that Whitehead's *The Function of Reason* "was an eye opener to me."[3] He writes that "Whitehead's philosophy fills the void created by Dewey's Pragmatism." Kaplan is widely and rightly regarded as having played down metaphysics. Even so, he claims here: "If then faith and salvation are to be proved tenable as matters of individual conviction it is essential that we have resort to philosophy and metaphysics for a conception of God compatible with our present knowledge of the universe and of human nature."[4] On January 19, 1930, Kaplan mentions (in passing) that "in the afternoon I read Whitehead's new book *Process and Reality.*"[5] In a lecture on "The Changing Functions of Religion," outlined on November 19, 1931, Kaplan asserts that "the term God comes now to connote the totality of existence (interpreted pragmatically by Hocking and metaphysically by Whitehead)."[6] Like many others, however, Kaplan took Whitehead's remark that "religion is what the individual does with his own solitariness" out of context. He argued, to the contrary, that "the time to experience the reality of God is when we are in the midst of those who are kindred to us in soul by reason of common hopes and difficulties."[7] Whitehead, however, also comments that "religion is world-loyalty"(RM 59). As a thinker for whom relations are essential to individuals, Whitehead placed great value on community: "There is no such thing as absolute solitariness. Each entity requires its environment. Thus man cannot seclude himself from society" (RM 132).

Kaplan's work has inspired most of the numerous Jewish process theologians. Robert M. Seltzer suggests that "the most generative aspect of Kaplan's theology" may have been "his pointing the way to a modern Jewish natural philosophy akin to the process theology developed by Charles Hartshorne, John B. Cobb, and Schubert Ogden."[8] An incomplete list of Jewish process theologians would have to include the following: Max Kadushin,[9] Milton Steinberg,[10] William Kaufman,[11] and Emanuel S. Goldsmith.[12] More recently, some Jewish women theologians have, happily, also engaged process thought in their rethinking of Judaism. These include Lori Krafte-Jacobs[13] and Sandra B. Lubarsky, coeditor of and contributor to *Jewish Theology and Process Thought.* Perhaps not surprisingly, Jewish process theologians are drawn to the same elements in process thought that attract Christian process theologians. Like Whitehead, Steinberg thought that religion needed grounding in metaphysics: "an indispensable function of churches is to furnish their communicants with a philosophy of the universe. Without such a theological base a religion is 'jelly.'"[14] According to Simon Noveck, Steinberg "credited Hartshorne's social conception of theism for emancipating him 'from servitude to the classical metaphysicians and their God who in his rigid eternal sameness is not God at all, certainly not the God of whom Scripture maketh proclamation nor whom the human heart requires.'"[15] Lubarsky looks at the neoclassical understanding of divine perfection of God as becoming (the self-surpassing surpasser of all) and genuinely affected by relationships. She points out that this view accords with the "the God with whom the biblical authors were convinced we interact, the God who is not an unmoved mover, but who is (in Fritz Rothschild's words, describing Heschel's God) 'the most moved mover,' the God who is perfectly *related to each of us*."[16]

Equally important to Jewish process theologians, however, is another emphasis of process theology, that on God as the One apart from whom "there could be no relevant novelty" (PR 164). The understanding of God's Primordial Nature as the creative or transformative Logos plays a large role in the theology of John B. Cobb Jr.[17] In Henry Nelson Wieman's version of process theology, God is identified with the process of creative transformation (Wieman termed it "creative good" or "creative interchange") as it works itself out primarily in relationships among human beings.[18] Wieman was concerned with God not, in the manner of John Dewey, as "our ideals," but as the creative, transformative source of the continuing renewal and transformation of our ideals. For Wieman, overcommitment to specific moral ideals was worship of the creature instead of the Creator who is ever leading us on to even better ideals. Greatly committed to the down-to-earth, practical transformation of the arrangements by which human life is shaped and governed, Wieman was convinced that they needed radical transformation. All this accorded quite well with the strongly practical-ethical emphasis of Judaism and particularly with Kaplan's attempt to "reconstruct" Judaism in a contemporary context. Kaplan had his students read Wieman's books and shared with Wieman a commitment to transform faith in the service of human well-being. For Kaplan, God "is identical with the totality of creative processes in man and nature that make for self-transcendence and self-perfection." God is the "functioning in nature of the eternally creative process, which, by bringing order out of chaos and good out of evil, actuates man to self-fulfillment."[19]

Long ago, for both Kaplan and Wieman, this understanding of creative transformation was applied to interfaith relations and to the dialogue between Jews and Christians. Their shared approach to diversity was "to relate to other faiths in the spirit of creative intercommunication and mutual learning in depth."[20] Wieman and Kaplan not only came to know each other's works but, as Emanuel Goldsmith points out, "to publicly acknowledge their mutual understanding and respect."[21] This remains an entirely appropriate and healthful way to engage in interfaith conversations.

On a related point, Nahum Ward points out that, for Judaism, "the Torah is about transformation." The Torah speaks of God calling human beings to transform their lives. "The God of the Torah is forever breaking into the human scene to shatter old forms and to offer a new form, a higher covenant. This God opens avenues of liberation, which move people past prior limitations."[22]

Agreeing with William Beardslee that the contrast between the biblical vision and our own worldview can result in creative transformation of our worldview, Ward suggests that a classic rabbinic method of interpretation was to use some issue, question, or problem in a text as a "springboard for a new teaching."[23]

For Judaism, halakhah (law, way, path), is not so much "law" as it is an ongoing process of interpreting and reinterpreting law, explicitly recognizing that the God who gives the law also transcends it and that no law is ever final.[24] The recurrent themes of Israelite and Jewish law are the protection of families; the treatment of the stranger; the plight of orphans and widows and "the least of these"; the oppression of the poor by the rich; and the cruel and unjust behavior of kings and rulers. Law in Judaism is, indeed, as Edward Farley points out, "the voice of the vulnerable other."[25] That this is so is perhaps reflected in the fact that the most frequently repeated biblical mitzvah, commandment, is "you shall not oppress a [stranger]" (Ex. 23:9), "you shall love the [stranger] as yourself" (Lev. 19:34). Repeated thirty-six times in the scriptures of Israel, this is arguably the most important commandment. Its frequency supports Farley's claim that in torah, halakhah is the voice of the vulnerable other.

Equal to Kaplan in importance among seminal Jewish thinkers, however, is Abraham Joshua Heschel. Heschel, unlike Kaplan, developed an understanding of God as a being who interacts with the world, who is affected by and "sympathizes"–feels with–the world. For all his adult life, Heschel stressed what he called a divine "anthropotropism," God's turning toward the person. He distinguished this from what he regarded as the "modern" reduction of God to an aspect of human experience, of our "theotropism" or turning toward God, a turning that modernity could always explain away. As Heschel put it in his Ph.D. dissertation at the University of Berlin: "Whatever occurs in history, [God] feels it inwardly. Events and actions provoke in [God] joy or suffering, acceptance or discontent."[26] Relying on sources from Kabbalah and Hasidic literature, Heschel claimed that "every event within the world brings with it an event within God."[27] Heschel stood for what he called a "Religion of Sympathy," arguing that biblical faith "is an emotional religion of sympathy [with God's pathos]" and that the prophets could therefore "devote to God their inmost depths, their enthusiasm and their fervor."[28]

Heschel does not seem to have expressed his understanding of God's power as directly as process theologians do. He understood that, as Kaplan and Dresner express it, "human indifference can inhibit the Divine."[29] Heschel spoke while the Nazis persecuted the Jewish people and drove them into a new exile in concentration camps. He recalled the rabbinic and Hasidic view that "the Shekhinah [the All-present One] lies in the dust," that God is in exile and that human beings, even in exile, have to help God.[30] Jewish theologians such as Sol Tanenzapf and William E. Kaufman have brought Heschel into conversation with Whitehead and Hartshorne. Heschel strongly attacked Parmenidean[31] views of God as utterly static and unchangeable and as denying that God can be affected. He put up an equally strong defense of a "dynamic" view of God as given voice by the prophets of Israel. Pathos is, for Heschel, God's way of interacting with the world, although Heschel refused to attribute pathos to God's essence. In this respect, both Whitehead and Hartshorne allow for respects in which God does not interact with the world. That God is and who God is are, for Hartshorne, absolute and abstract aspects of God. It is God's actuality, God's experience, that is affected by the world.[32]

Jewish Criticisms of Jewish Process Theology

All this is not to say, however, that no issues divided Jewish and process theology. Several Jewish commentators note that Whitehead's "all-encompassing aesthetic viewpoint...seems to run roughshod over Judaic ethical sensitivity."[33] That Whitehead made a slipshod reference to the God of the prophets (or perhaps of Judaism?) as "a ruthless moralist" (PR 343) does not help matters in this discussion, particularly as Whitehead went on to say that love is "a little oblivious as to morals."

Among Jewish theologians, Harold M. Schulweis makes the strongest arguments against process theology on this point. He contends that the mark of God's ultimate goodness, according to process thought, "is in the adequate taking into account of all possible and actual interests, each being given its due."[34] "Therefore," he contends, "[God] cannot wish the sick child well without caring about the woes of the bacteria." Schulweis finds inadequate to Jewish moral concerns the understanding of God's providence as setting limits to the free interplay of finite agents lest there be sheer chaos. And he claims that to call into question "the priority of human over simian or amoebic values...is a far cry from the affirmations of man's [humanity's] centrality which inform the ethic of the Judaeo-Christian tradition."[35] All this follows, for Schulweis, from a dependence on aesthetic metaphysics, as evidenced in Whitehead's remark that "the real world is good when it is beautiful."[36] He concludes that Jewish process theological defenders of Heschel deal inadequately with Heschel's "perception of the Bible and of prophecy [which] makes moral demands upon God and His providential care which neither supranatural or naturalistic metaphysics is able to satisfy."[37]

Schulweis's argument, in essence, is that the aesthetic approach to metaphysics engenders an egalitarian view of divine sympathy that makes it difficult to make moral distinctions, such as that between the well-being of a child versus the well-being of the bacteria making the child ill. This is an issue with which Christian process theologians have also been concerned, leading them to discuss "gradations of intrinsic value," which clearly affirm that the child possesses more intrinsic value than do the bacteria and is more important to God than are the bacteria.[38]

Process Tools for Dialogue

That this argument can be answered is a task to be taken up by process theologians, whether Jewish or Christian. Without going into more detail than is possible in this chapter, we shall outline two points that could be made in response.

First, it is a merit of the scriptures of Israel and of rabbinic Judaism that they have developed a covenantal ecology or "Jewish land ethic," something that has, on the whole, been absent from Christianity, which is, if anything, more anthropocentric than Judaism.[39] The covenant of the rainbow with Noah and all his descendants (all humanity) was also with "every living creature" (Gen. 9:10). The prophets reiterated this ecological covenant: "I will make for you a covenant on that day with the wild animals, the birds of the air, and the creeping things of the ground; and I will abolish the bow, the sword, and war from the land…" (Hosea 2:18). Rabbi Johanan ben Zakkai said: "If you have a sapling in your hand, and it is said to you, Behold, there is the Messiah–go on with your planting, and afterward go out and receive him."[40] Concern for the well-being of all God's creatures is not an alternative to concern for the well-being of humans; it is essential to the well-being of humans.

Second, Whitehead does state that God's aim is at the "evocation of intensities" or at strength of beauty in finite occasions. This is misconstrued, however, if it is understood to be at the expense of moral concerns (PR 105). The genius of process thought on this issue is that, as in other matters, it overcomes traditional dichotomies, such as those between grace and freedom or spirit and matter or the holy and the common. Simply put, morality, which introduces width of outlook into the perspective of a person, is itself always part of God's aim at strength of beauty. God is ever calling us out of the narrowness, limitations, and contradictions of the past. The Jewish-Christian dialogue itself can be best understood as a consequence of God's calling us, particularly us Christians, out of our narrowmindedness and stupidity with regard to Jews and Judaism. Autobiographical testimony from Christians engaged in this dialogue provides ample testimony to the fact that greater understanding of Jews and Judaism has led them to a more intense and, hence, beautiful appropriation of their own faith.[41]

Criticism of Traditional Christian Theology

Last, the Jewish-Christian dialogue generates criticism of traditional Christian theology. This is particularly the case for Christian process theologians since it raises a host of issues that need to be addressed. With some exceptions, Christian process theologians have largely ignored these issues. Christians have traditionally claimed to supersede, that is, displace Jews in the covenant with God.

Supersessionism takes several forms in the history of the church. First, it can argue that Jewish history is a "trail of crimes," culminating in deicide (killing God in the crucifixion of Jesus), and resulting in God's abandonment of the people Israel and, instead, electing a new people–the church–to covenant with God.

Second, it can argue that Christianity is that new, universal, spiritual, Gentile religion that is everything new, spiritual, and universal that old, carnal, and ethnocentric Judaism can never be; ours is in every respect the better religion.

Third, it can read the Bible on the model of the classic creeds—creation, fall, and redemption in Jesus. God creates the world (Genesis 1 and 2); Adam and Eve fall (Genesis 3); God redeems the world through Jesus (the New Testament). In this structural supersessionism, the scriptures of Israel and the history of the people Israel with the God of Israel are qualitatively unimportant after Genesis 3 in helping Christians understand God.[42]

Fourth, Christian theology can give Jews and Judaism the silent treatment, rendering Jews and Judaism invisible by rendering them unworthy of mention.

In any or all of its forms, this Christian "teaching of contempt" for Jews and Judaism raises innumerable theological problems.[43] It is not merely a bias occasionally expressed in anti-Jewish tracts (so called because that is what they often call themselves: e.g., *Tractatus Adversus Judaeos*). Consider, rather, that in Christian anti-Judaism the following are the case:

1. God is the kind of God who would abandon a people because of its failures.
2. The scriptures are properly read and interpreted as supporting such a theology.
3. Jesus was the kind of mediator who would cut a supersessionist deal with God.
4. In his ministry Jesus was constantly in conflict with Jews and Judaism, taught against Jews and Judaism, died at the hands of Jews and Judaism and was raised by God in victory over Jews and Judaism.
5. The Holy Spirit is the spirit of the church, the Christian community, and is at work in the new, "spiritual" Israel, not in the old Israel according to the flesh.
6. The church is the replacement people of God, us, the ones for whose benefit all this anti-Judaism pays off.

Process Resources for Overcoming Supersessionism

Because supersessionism is the church's oldest ideology (distortion of truth in the interest of power), it is often the way Christians think without being aware of it. Process theologians can, without meaning to, fall into its clutches. When process theologians announce that Jesus taught with a kind of authority not shared by scribes and Pharisees, not only do they uncritically assume that Mark 1:22 is accurate but reflect an unfamiliarity with the Mishnah. In the Mishnah Pharisees do nothing but teach with authority. (The later Talmud is at pains to show that what they taught can be derived from the written Torah).

Nonetheless, the process philosophies of Charles Hartshorne and Alfred North Whitehead give no support to the traditional Christian ideology of supersessionism. On the contrary, their understanding of divine creativity argues that God generates diversity of all kinds and regards diversity as enriching, rather than impoverishing, our lives. Learning to appreciate diversity, to affirm the other as other, intensifies the beauty of our own life. Also, the process christology of Schubert M. Ogden, which unabashedly declares that "no other word is spoken in Jesus that is everywhere spoken in the actual events of nature and history and specifically witnessed to with more or less adequacy by 'the law and the prophets.'"[44]

A few Christian process theologians have undertaken to rethink Christian teachings as radically, in light of their new understandings of Jews and Judaism, as process theologians long have attempted to do so in light of process philosophy. Bernard J. Lee, S.M., has done so with the figure of Jesus of Nazareth;[45] Michael E. Lodahl has done so with the doctrine of the Holy Spirit;[46] Pamela Payne has done so with feminist christology;[47] and I have taken up the task of rethinking Christian systematic theology.[48] This task, however, is no doubt still in its beginning stages among Christian theologians in general and among Christian process theologians in particular.

The story of the relation of process theology to Jewish theology has a considerable past to it. If nothing else, this essay has shown that fertile ground abounds for conversation between Jewish and process theologians and that such a conversation has long been underway. But this relationship also has an incredibly bright possible future ahead of it, if Christian process theologians take up this challenge as daringly as they have long taken up many others.

CHAPTER 6

Scripture and Revelation

■ RUSSELL PREGEANT

Most process theologians identify with the progressive end of the theological spectrum; they are sensitive to the problematic character of both scripture and revelation for many persons in our contemporary world. However, they still accord an important place to scripture, viewing its authority as dialogical and persuasive rather than unilateral and coercive. That is, while rejecting the notion that the Bible speaks directly and simplistically for God, they affirm its role in fostering a genuine encounter with God and a meaningful struggle to discern God's will.

Biblical scholars informed by this perspective have developed a critical hermeneutic, or approach to biblical interpretation, that reflects such an understanding. This approach positions itself between those who look to the historical-critical method for the delineation of stable and normative meanings and those who tend to dissolve the meaning of texts into the subjectivity of individual readers or interpretive communities. It understands biblical interpretation rather as a process in which meaning emerges through a dynamic interaction of text and reader.

A majority of process theologians also embrace a doctrine of revelation. They understand it, however, in a way that does not involve God's literal intervention in the world. This is because process thought rejects a dualism that divides the world into "natural" and "supernatural" realms, as if the former somehow operated on its own and God could act within it only by entering it from "outside." Process theology therefore understands God's communication in nonsupernaturalistic terms. This communication, in other words, does not involve the violation of the order of the natural world. And a process approach to revelation also calls into question the sharp distinction some theologians make between "universal" revelation (knowledge of God communicated to human beings generally through ordinary experience) and "special" revelation (knowledge of God communicated through the events in the history of Israel and the life, death, and resurrection of Jesus).

The rejection of revelation as God's supernatural communication with the world, however, is bracketed by a clear endorsement of the notion of divine action. Process theologians understand revelation as God's self-disclosure, not the purely human process of discovery. Also, in keeping with a theological trend since the mid-twentieth century, this divine self-disclosure is to be distinguished from the communication of propositional truth or a body of doctrines, although it does entail cognitive content.

Revelation and the Action of God

Process thought opposes the notion of a closed universe of sheer cause and effect, finding degrees of indeterminacy at all levels of complexity in the universe. Whitehead's cosmology not only makes room for the activity of God but also considers it as a necessary component of change. This is one reason it views God's contribution to the world process in nonsupernaturalistic terms. Far from an interruption of that process, divine action makes available the possibilities out of which the future arises. Understanding God's action as persuasive rather than coercive, moreover, process thought excludes the notion of unilateral means of making the divine will known. Not only must revelation involve the actual reception of potential disclosures, but it also takes place within the confines of God's ordinary way of relating to the world.

Although working primarily from a different philosophical perspective, H. Richard Niebuhr makes use of Whitehead to frame a classic nonsupernaturalistic account of revelation. Likening revelation to the experience of coming "across a luminous sentence" in a difficult book, "from which we can go forward and backward and so attain some understanding of the whole," he goes on to quote Whitehead: "Rational religion appeals to the direct intuition of special occasions, and to the elucidatory power of its concepts for all occasions." For Niebuhr, Christians look to Jesus Christ as the special occasion from which they "derive the concepts which make possible the elucidation of all the events in our history"; and revelation "means this intelligible event which makes all other events intelligible."[1]

As helpful as it is, Niebuhr's statement lacks a full account of how the elucidation constitutes an act of God. Process theologians, however, find further resources in both Whitehead and Hartshorne that serve this end.

Marjorie Suchocki employs Whitehead's view of the process through which events occur in her explanation of general revelation. Each emerging event receives from God an initial aim, or possibility for realization, "that has been particularly fitted to it in light of its particular past." The occasion then adapts God's initial aim, so that "the completed occasion is the result of what it has done with the aim from God." Thus every event has potential elucidatory power, enabling the discernment in nature of a divine order and the workings of a God of persuasive love.[2]

Revelation is indirect and ambiguous, however. For it "is two stages removed from the divine harmony in which it originates," requiring interpretation, and it is possible to read nature as malevolent as well as beneficent. Thus what one makes of the revelation given in general experience is deeply affected by one's situation. But this does not mean that the order discerned in nature "is only in the eye of the beholder, for the beholders themselves are part of the world perceived. Order within the observer is therefore order in the world as well; further, order apparently gives rise to its very perception."[3] The revelatory process is thus highly fallible, but it does not consist in sheer subjective interpretation; in it genuine knowledge of God is possible.

From a process perspective, revelation has an event-character, as it does in so much recent theology, commensurate with its nature as divine self-disclosure rather than the communication of propositional truth. It takes place precisely in the occasions of experience, and the apprehension of God's aims is, in fact, the experience of God's immanence in the world. However, Suchocki is clear also that human consciousness provides a platform for the disclosure of ideational content. "If God is truly persuading the world toward depths of harmony that are reflective and therefore revelatory of God, then surely as the world attains consciousness God will utilize consciousness to achieve a fullness of revelation...The aims of God pull the world toward the image of God."[4] Through revelation, human beings thus can come to *understand* something of God.

Schubert Ogden treads on similar ground as he draws on Hartshorne in approaching the problem of God's action in history. He first notes a sense in which all creaturely acts are acts of God, since God includes all beings. Even though all beings possess a measure of freedom, "each creature is what it is only by partly reflecting or expressing in its being God's free decisions."[5] But then Ogden identifies a stronger meaning of "act of God," rooted in the human "capacity of consciousness or self-consciousness." Because human beings are able to understand human existence "and express its meaning symbolically through word and deed and can...also re-present or speak for the divine," they are able to receive any event as an act of God. They have, however, no guarantee that any given reception of an event will accurately reflect God's intention.[6]

This second meaning lays the groundwork for an understanding of the notion of a special or a decisive act of God. Just as some human actions are more expressive of a person's character than others, some can become more revelatory of God than others. "[T]o say of any historical event that it is the "decisive" act of God can only mean that, in it...the ultimate truth about our existence before God is normatively re-presented or revealed."[7]

Process theologians in general relativize the difference between universal and special revelation, but David Griffin thinks Ogden compromises the force of God's decisive action in Christ. Objecting specifically to Ogden's contention that God's action in Christ is no different "from the way in which [God] acts primordially in every other event," Griffin insists that "[u]nless there is something about God's action in Jesus that differs from [God's] action elsewhere, it is misleading to speak of Jesus as God's special or decisive act."[8]

What Griffin finds "[m]issing in Ogden's analysis of the meaning of a 'special act' is any mention of the intention of the agent whose special act it is supposed to be."[9] He argues that Ogden neglects aspects of Whitehead's thought that could provide a more adequate account of a "special" act. The key point is that for Whitehead, "God acts differently in different events," since "the content of [God's] aims for them differs greatly." And on this basis Griffin argues that God provided special aims for Jesus, associated with his becoming "*God's supreme act of self-expression.*"[10] Ogden, however, has his own way of affirming that something about Jesus made his reception of the Christ-event appropriate and not mere subjective prejudice: it is the content of "his outward words and deeds."[11]

Process thought is a natural ally of the notion of progressive revelation, although various theologians embrace it in different ways. Ogden accepts the need for tradition to be made intelligible in ever-new contexts but also seeks a stable norm to determine adequacy to that tradition and thus tends toward the definition of an essence of the Christian faith.[12] John Cobb, however, denies such an essence and envisions the continuing transformation of the faith through encounter with other traditions, while Benjamin Reist writes of "processive" revelation and locates the Christian essence precisely in "a historically productive power." Along similar lines, Delwin Brown finds the search for a stable norm futile.[13]

In summary, despite some important differences among theologians employing process thought, they evidence substantial agreement on some fundamental points regarding revelation:

- that revelation takes place in concrete events and involves divine activity as well as human reception
- that revelation occurs in a nonsupernaturalistic mode
- that revelation involves God's self-disclosure in both concrete events and ideational content, but is not the direct communication of propositional truth
- that it is necessary both to make a distinction between special revelation and general, natural, or universal revelation and to recognize that they are not fundamentally different in nature
- that revelation is in some sense progressive or processive

Scripture, Revelation, and Authority

Two aspects of Suchocki's account of revelation are particularly pertinent to the relationship of revelation to scripture: her affirmation that revelation conveys actual knowledge of God and her acknowledgement of the interpretive element involved and hence of the indirectness and ambiguity of the knowledge gained. To the extent that scripture witnesses faithfully to revelatory events, it is possible to receive it as holding revelatory potential itself and hence to foster both encounter with and conceptual knowledge of God. The ambiguity of revelation, however, makes impossible any equation of scripture with truth.

To say that scripture is capable of fostering knowledge of God is also to say that it is referential—a point that sets the process perspective off against all theories of language and interpretation that understand texts as making meaning solely within a self-enclosed linguistic world. More proximately, however, the texts of scripture are referential in two other senses. They refer, first, to worlds behind the texts—the life-worlds of the original authors and recipients—and thus reflect the historical milieus in which they were generated. So a process understanding of scriptural interpretation will not take a purely textual or nonhistorical approach but will affirm the historical-critical method as one important tool in seeking meaning.

Texts are also capable of referring outside the text in another direction, however: to the life-worlds of readers. And this means that historical-critical investigation alone by no means exhausts the significance of a text. Nor can we make an absolute distinction between what a text meant in its original context and what it can legitimately come to mean in a later interpreter's situation, for both reading and historical investigation are necessarily shaped in part by our own interests and collective life-worlds.

The assertion that scripture is capable of fostering actual knowledge of God has sometimes led to the criticism that process interpreters view it as conveying straightforward metaphysical information. As we have seen, however, the ambiguity of revelation forecloses the equation of a scriptural claim with truth.[14] And this becomes clearer as we examine Whitehead's epistemology and theory of language.

According to Whitehead, perception as we normally think of it is actually the synthesis of two more basic modes of perception. One, termed "presentational immediacy," is based on sense data. More basic, however, is a nonsensory type of perception he names "causal efficacy." One example of this is the memory of an immediately past emotion. Another is the vague awareness we have of the organs of our bodies as the channels of sense data—the feeling we have of ourselves as we "feel" the outside world.[15]

What Whitehead calls "symbolic reference" is a combination of these two modes. Apart from causal efficacy, sense data would have no context. And the synthesis of the two modes necessarily involves valuation, since it takes place precisely by giving meaning and significance to the sense data. Thus all knowledge is at base participatory: "It must be distinctly understood that no prehension, even of bare sensa, can be divested of its affective tone, that is to say of its character of 'concern' in its Quaker sense" (AI 182).

More immediately relevant to the nature of scripture are the implications that this general epistemology has regarding language. If perception is participatory and valuational, the language that emerges from it will necessarily be "incomplete and fragmentary" (AI 227). And Whitehead's sense of universal relatedness also means that language is necessarily abstract. To signify meaningfully, we focus on some aspects of reality for emphasis, lifting them out of their web of relationships. Thus, as Lyman Lundeen comments, our linguistic forms ignore the connections of objects with any "concrete perspective, purpose, or process" and treat them "as though they were independent of the contextual relationships."[16]

The abstract, fragmentary, value-laden character of language is unavoidable, but a problem arises when we ignore it. We commit the "fallacy of misplaced concreteness," deceiving ourselves by assuming that language signifies in a more precise and exhaustive way than it actually does.

Attention to the limitations of language thus underscores the ambiguity of revelation. If language is inexact in even mundane signification, how much more so must it be as it gropes toward God and the ultimate structure of the universe? Thus if process thought accepts the notion that God is in some sense revealed through scripture, it also insists on critical interpretation. And in this way it makes a partial alliance with those contemporary schools of literary interpretation that give individual readers and interpretive communities considerable freedom in the shaping of meaning.

Process theologians also tend to acknowledge the variety of perspectives found in scripture, and they sometimes look behind the canon for a norm or at least focal point. Griffin thus accords a central place to the pre-conceptual "vision of reality" expressed by the historical Jesus as God's decisive revelation.[17] And Ogden looks to the apostolic witness or pre-Easter Jesus-kerygma, the earliest testimony to Jesus that takes the form of a presentation of his words and deeds, as the norm by which to evaluate the various scriptural witnesses.[18] Some process thinkers, however, reject any effort to identify absolute, stable norms as too suggestive of the notion of an essence—either of a text or of the Christian faith—which they consider incompatible with Whitehead's insight that reality is fundamentally processive in nature.

In any case, reference to the historical Jesus or the apostolic tradition is only one way that a critical element can be brought to bear on the question of the authority of scripture. Ogden, for example, radicalizes Bultmann's demythologizing program by loosening it from the vestiges of an exclusivist christology and also proposes his own program of "deidologizing" to speak to the concerns of liberationist and feminist theologians.[19] Here again, other process thinkers argue for a hermeneutical model that draws more fully on process categories. But virtually all who employ a process conceptuality recognize the necessity of a critical hermeneutic and therefore understand biblical authority as dialogical and persuasive in character. Scripture has a normative standing but must be subject to an interpretive and evaluative process that gives weight to the life-world of the contemporary interpreters and communities of faith.

The Use and Interpretation of Scripture

The normativity of scripture is qualified in process theology not only by the necessity of critical reading or hermeneutics but also by a parallel function of scripture. Whitehead placed great emphasis on feeling and intuition and was critical of religion that treated its dogmas too rigidly. "Feeling" in his vocabulary means more than mere emotion, but his use of the term reveals a conviction that our relationship to our environment involves a mode of apprehension entailing something other than formulation of concepts on the one hand, or mechanistic causation on the other. If experience is always value-laden, a believer's relationship to a religious tradition is most fundamentally intuitive rather than conceptual.

Whitehead's classic statement on the limitations of dogma has important implications for how process theology should approach scripture:

> Religions commit suicide when they find their inspirations in their dogmas. The inspiration of religion lies in the history of religion. By this I mean that it is to be found in the primary expressions of the intuitions of the finest types of religious lives. The sources of religious belief are always growing, though some supreme expressions may lie in the past. Records of these sources are not formulae. They elicit in us an intuitive response which pierces beyond dogma. (RM 144)

Although the exclusive emphasis on religious lives in this statement scarcely does justice to the richness of scripture, the reference to the elicitation of intuitive response transcending dogma resonates with one aspect of how the Bible has functioned for many people of faith throughout the centuries. While theologians and scholars have habitually mined the texts for their doctrinal content, many "ordinary" folk and mystics have treated them rather as platforms for meditation and sources of inspiration. Thus process thinkers reflecting on spirituality may find something quite different in the texts than theologians concerned primarily with ideas.

Similarly, biblical scholars influenced by the recent emphasis on the narrative aspects of scripture may also be able to employ process insights to good advantage in probing the significance of these materials. Also, process interpreters have a natural affinity not only with explicitly ideological interpreters but also with those who stress the vitality of the "nonprofessional" readings of scripture–through sermon, story, song, and other forms of imaginative response–including those that arise in non-Eurocentric communities. Broadly speaking, then, a grounding in the process world view should sensitize any reader to the inspirational, imaginative, and liberating potential of the texts.

To some extent, bridging the gap between ideational and affective approaches are some concrete exercises in biblical interpretation that have emerged under the rubric of "process hermeneutic." These endeavors have taken two different forms, although they are often found working in tandem.[20] The first is the use of process categories as keys to illumining the texts, which often enables the identification of elements that run counter to the tenets of traditional theology informed by the Greek philosophical tradition. The second is the use of a process theory of interpretation, often done to make sense of the confluence of discordant elements within a text.

The first approach has the double effect of unveiling aspects of the text often obscured by traditional readings, and showing the affinities between process thought and the biblical thought worlds. Process interpreters and others have laid great emphasis on those aspects of scripture that image God's action in the world as persuasive rather than coercive, but they often ignore many other points of contact, which Robert Gnuse has pursued systematically in a recent work.[21] One example is the presence of a preexisting chaos in Genesis 1, which resonates with the process rejection of *creatio ex nihilo* in conjunction with an understanding of the universe as God's body. Another is the frequent reference to God's change of mind, which is suggestive of the process insistence that God is affected by interaction with the world. In a variation on this latter theme, Gerald Janzen finds the suggestion of divine mutability in Hosea 11 as God engages in agonizing self-questioning, contemplating the destruction of Israel, and is transformed through the absorption and transmutation of the wrath resulting from Israel's unfaithfulness.[22]

The examples could be easily multiplied. Closely related to the theme of divine mutability is that of the suffering of God, to which Terence Fretheim has devoted an important volume,[23] while Gnuse has found that process categories are helpful in understanding the concept of covenant.[24]

The second way in which biblical scholars have made use of process thought–as a basis for a theory of interpretation–may in a narrower sense be understood as "process hermeneutic." If Lundeen's *Risk and Rhetoric in Religion* constitutes a hermeneutic of religious language in general, others have mapped out an explicit theory of biblical interpretation. The most comprehensive work along these lines to date is Ronald Farmer's *Beyond the Impasse: The Promise of a Process Hermeneutic.*[25]

Fundamental to process hermeneutic in this sense is Whitehead's epistemology, involving the distinction noted above between presentational immediacy and causal efficacy. Whitehead affirms the possibility of knowledge "about the world as it is" while at the same time acknowledging the "contributions of our minds in shaping our perceptions."[26] Of more immediate relevance to the interpretive process is the way in which Whitehead, moving beyond the question of perception, takes account of the creative imagination. At this level, he introduces the notion of propositions, which are concrete possibilities that emerge in the self-creation of any event. These propositions are "prelinguistic, and, for the most part, preconscious,"[27] but they can be evoked–albeit imperfectly–by linguistic formulations. Interpreters must therefore be prepared to treat the text as open-ended and evocative, pointing beyond itself not only to an extra-linguistic world, but more proximately to propositions–suggestions for meaning–that engage the imagination. Whitehead's famous statement on propositions and truth makes room for both investigation behind the text into external reality and appreciation of its ability to generate creative response: "[I]t is more important that a proposition be interesting than that it be true. The importance of truth is that it adds to interest" (PR 395f).

One element in a process hermeneutic is therefore a recognition of the fragmentary and open-ended character of signification, which is the root of ongoing reinterpretation. But such a hermeneutic also takes account of Whitehead's dictum that "every proposition refers to a universe exhibiting some general systematic metaphysical character," so that it is necessary also to trace out the metaphysical implications of the various strains of meaning that can be identified.[28] The groundwork is thus laid for a way of dealing with disparate aspects of scripture without necessarily negating any. Some interpreters have, for example, sought to correlate competing significations by identifying those strands that can best withstand metaphysical scrutiny, making them the base of a theological reading, and valuing the competing strands more for their imaginative force.

This move, however, is only one form of a broader strategy: the use of Whitehead's notion of "contrast"–the synthesis of contradictory elements into a higher unity. Whitehead used the term to describe a component in the emergence of new realities generally, but it can be fruitfully applied to the interpretive process. The interpreter seeks to bring disparities within a text, or among various texts, or between the life-worlds of text and interpreter, into conjunction through their creative transformation.

To illustrate this hermeneutic at work, we may begin with Farmer's discovery in the book of Revelation of subtle suggestions of God's persuasive action and the contingency of the future. These elements comprise an "undercurrent" that competes with a more dominant strand of deterministic thought portraying God's action as coercive. But Farmer finds that the "deterministic language can evoke nondeterministic" possibilities for meaning and so offers a novel synthesis in which the dominant strain is valued as a nonliteral, imaginative expression of the view that "creative-responsive love…is the most powerful force in the universe."[29] In a parallel way, I have argued that the undercurrent of extra-christological salvation that appears at several points in Matthew can be synthesized with the dominant strain of exclusivism. We effect this synthesis by valuing the exclusivism strain as imaginative reinforcement of "a universalistic soteriological principle," based on the love command, "that transcends the entire confessional dimension of Matthew's christology and which actually contradicts a univocal understanding of it."[30]

These two studies value one strain of meaning for its imaginative force, while another is allowed a more univocal meaning and logical force. Others have employed Whitehead's notion of contrast in maintaining a more tensive union of elements. David Lull, for example, holds together two sets of opposites in Paul's understanding of the Spirit in Galatians. Paul's first set presents the Spirit as working coercively on the one hand, and "as a power in relation to which human effort has some efficacy" on the other. The second set gives his negative view of nature as over against an implicit affirmation of redemptive action within nature.[31] Similarly, in a feminist evaluation of Revelation, Catherine Keller maintains a creative tension between the positive and negative aspects of the text itself and the long history of its effects.[32]

To the extent that process interpreters seek to embrace diverse strands of signification in texts and accept the open-endedness of meaning, they show affinity with a contemporary school of interpretation known as deconstructionism. Interpreters working from this latter perspective stress the inability of any text to present a fully self-consistent point of view, since it will inevitably draw on modes of thought that run counter to other significant strains of meaning. Thus a deconstructive reading will often show how a text, on close reading, ultimately collapses in on itself, undercutting its own apparent meaning. They also deny the ability of a text to convey reliable knowledge of the world outside the text or of the ultimate nature of things. Since all terms used in a text gain their meaning from other terms, which are themselves dependent on yet other terms, the interpreter is caught in an endless chain of deferred meaning. Therefore, we can never pin down the exact meaning of a text.

Despite important points of agreement with deconstructionists, however, process interpreters assume that language can convey a real but relative knowledge of reality. And their use of Whitehead's contrast model, while containing a deconstructive moment, provides a constructive alternative to simply watching a text collapse. Although texts do in fact contain competing strains of meaning, it is a valid move on the interpreter's part to seek precisely the kind of synthesis described in the preceding discussion.

This does not mean, however, that process interpreters find all texts or strains of meaning worthy of positive valuation. Although it is theoretically possible to create a positive pattern of meaning out of any set of complexes, the dialogical and persuasive character of biblical authority mitigates against any hermeneutic of unqualified consent. For process hermeneutic as well as for deconstruction, a moment of evaluative decision remains.

The Evolution of Tradition

Beyond the actual interpretation of texts, process-oriented scholars and theologians have also applied the notion of process to the changing understandings that that have emerged throughout biblical (and later) history. Gnuse, for example, employs Whitehead's notion of concrescence to illumine the evolutionary character of biblical thought as well as to reflect on the concept of salvation history–which understands God's action in the world in terms of a progression of divine self-disclosures in the history of Israel.[33] In a similar way, Lewis Ford states that "[t]he biblical drama is the biography of God," acknowledging the remarkable evolution in the human understanding of God that took place in ancient Israel.[34] And John Cobb draws on Whitehead's concept of "living historic routes" to describe the history of tradition.[35] These and similar reflections suggest that process thought can provide a way of understanding the biblical tradition as reflective of God's ongoing involvement in history.

Process interpreters, however, can hardly give unqualified endorsement to typical theologies of salvation history. Thus Gnuse finds it necessary to broaden this notion of God's self-disclosure to include nature as well as history and to avoid the implication of interventionism.[36] Any designation of the biblical story as the biography of God must be nuanced by a recognition of the ambiguity of revelation. Whitehead's emphasis on freedom, moreover, forecloses any notion of inevitable progress or guaranteed historical outcome. If process sensitivities caution against a simplistic rejection of later New Testament writings, such as the pastoral letters, as sheer degeneration, they also alert the interpreter to the negative fallout from the resurgence of patriarchy and hierarchy as well as the developing doctrinalism that Whitehead found so problematic.

Attention to the evolutionary character of biblical thought does not generally figure explicitly into "process hermeneutic," at least in the narrower sense; but it does carry important hermeneutical implications. Certainly, the tensions that appear within a given writing, among various writings, or between biblical and contemporary perspectives are sometimes the products of evolutionary change. And recognition of this fact will have impact on the questions of authority and normativity. However, the evolutionary explanation of a given set of tensions by no means exhausts their significance, for from a purely textual perspective these tensions, no less than any others, are suitable material for treatment under the category of a Whiteheadian contrast.

In any case, the textual and historical approaches are not incompatible from a process perspective. And the need for a critical hermeneutic remains central for all who approach the text from this point of view.

Concluding Comments

This essay began by noting that process theologians generally identify with the progressive end of the theological spectrum. Thus their commitment to scripture and their acceptance of revelation as a valid theological category are subject to the terms that I have tried to elucidate. But their intention to honor tradition is real and not at all surprising in light of Whitehead's understanding of the world process as involving the creative transformation of disparate elements. If their doctrines of scripture and revelation are "revisionary," one must also understand that continual transformation is a necessary aspect of tradition. And if process theologians are progressive, they do not pursue their agenda in dichotomizing fashion but in an effort to make creative use of the past in forging new futures.[37]

CHAPTER 7

Preaching as Conversation among Proposals

■ RONALD J. ALLEN

Each theological family births an understanding of the nature and purposes of preaching that flow from that theology's convictions concerning God, the world, the church and the listener.[1] This article develops a process-relational notion of preaching as a conversation with proposals on ways to consider God and the world.[2] The chapter meditates on what happens when the sermon comes to life and ponders how God is involved in all phases of the message from preparation through afterglow.[3]

Proposal as Lure for Feeling

This process-relational approach to preaching is based on the notion of preaching as a lure for feeling. When making a proposal, a person or community offers a perspective of an aspect of God or the world to self or others (PR 224, 184ff). In essence, a proposal asks people to believe that God or the world is the way described in the proposal. Because the self is a gestalt, a proposal affects thoughts, emotions, and behaviors simultaneously. People can respond to a proposal in multiple ways: they can accept or reject it; they can suspend making a decision as they envision what might happen if they accept or reject it; they can ignore it. People can be affected unconsciously but powerfully by propositions.[4]

Whitehead describes a proposition as a lure for feeling (PR 186). "Feeling" bespeaks the full functioning of human awareness and knowledge. Susanne K. Langer offers one of the most elegant definitions of feeling in the corpus of writings influenced by process perspective. "The word 'feeling' must be taken here in its broadest sense, meaning everything that can be felt, from physical sensation, pain and comfort, excitement and response, to the more complex emotions, intellectual tensions, of the steady feeling-tones of a conscious human life."[5] Feeling includes "the whole gamut of our sensibility—the sense of straining thought, all mental attitude and motor set. These are the deeper reaches that underlie the surface waves of emotion and make human life a feeling instead of an unconscious metabolic existence interrupted by feelings."[6] Feeling is a realm of understanding. Indeed, Whitehead says, "We think with our bodies,"[7] and Bernard Meland reminds us, "We live more deeply than we can think."[8]

Proposals sometimes take the form of informational verbal language. However, propositions can also be expressed in other media—e.g., poetry, fiction, music, dance, the visual arts, social circumstances or movements, and through the world of nature. A proposition lures feeling.

Human beings are affected by proposals at two simultaneous levels.[9]

1. A proposal appeals to the conscious mind.
2. It kindles the unconscious depths of the self.

William Beardslee and colleagues point out that ideas are never pure intellectual abstractions. An idea "is always clothed with emotion" that touches the inchoate depths of the self and stirs deep processes of feeling that may overflow into insight and action.[10]

For instance, a proposal in the mode of dance may prompt the audience to feel the world from the perspective of the dance. By watching the dance, the viewer feels something of the meaning of the dance even if that knowledge cannot be fully articulated in informational language, or even in metaphorical speech.

Whitehead says, in a famous remark, "It is more important that a proposition be interesting than that it be true" (PR 259), for proposals alert us to fresh possibilities for life. Proposals play an important role in community in that they "pave the way along which the world advances into novelty."[11] By encouraging a community to become aware of the multiple possibilities available for life, proposals enhance the sense of freedom in a person or community.[12] Even when people decide that they cannot embrace a particular proposition, the process of considering the proposition is enriching for it helps the audience clarify why they find some propositions promising and others less so. Whitehead insists we must critique proposals and judge which ones are more and less promising.[13]

Preaching as Conversation among Propositions

The preacher voices proposals concerning God, how God is luring the world, and how responding to the divine lure might be enriching. The sermon itself is a lure that arises out of conversation among propositions.[14] A preacher intends to help the congregation name, critically assess, and respond to ways of perceiving God and the world that are aligned with God's purposes.[15]

Preaching involves conversation in two arenas:

1. In sermon preparation, the preacher considers different proposals that come from voices in the past and the present. The preacher seeks to honor

the otherness of each voice; the preacher wants to hear the distinct propositions of others, and not to impose the preacher's predilections (no matter how worthy) on them.[16]

2. The sermon itself typically has the quality of conversation.[17]

David Tracy frames this approach to preaching. "Conversation in its primary form is an *exploration of possibilities* in the search for truth."[18] Conversation is the movement of question and response, give and take, as the partners in the dialogue clarify issues and seek resolution.[19] "In conversation, we find ourselves by losing ourselves in the questioning provoked by the text [or other source of a proposition]. We find ourselves by allowing claims upon our attention, by exploring possibilities suggested by others, including those we call texts."[20] In conversation, "we notice that to attend to the other as other, the different as different, is also to understand the different *as* possible."[21] We must speak clearly, respect others, and be open to changing our own opinions when other viewpoints prove convincing.[22] Participants in a conversation "try on" how they might experience the world from the standpoint of the other. The conversation may cause those involved to reinforce or enlarge the viewpoints, reframe them, imagine fresh alternatives, or reject them.

Voices in the Preaching Conversation

The voices in the preaching conversation include the Bible, Christian tradition, voices from beyond the Christian community, the congregation, the preacher's deepest theological convictions concerning the divine presence and purposes, and the Holy Spirit.[23] The preacher asks of each conversation partner, "What does this voice ask us to believe concerning the subject of the sermon?" Pastor and people want to know how each voice can help them identify points at which the proposal is promising and points at which it is not, so that the community will not respond to the proposition by default but on the basis of a clear and critical assessment of the proposition.[24]

Many voices put forward points of view that make positive contributions to the message. Some voices likely offer ideas that preacher and congregation cannot follow. However, a community often finds it valuable to consider proposals that the group cannot endorse because doing so helps the community clarify their evaluation of a proposition.[25]

Recent biblical scholarship views the Bible less as a single book and more as a library of different theological perspectives. From process perspective the Bible is a collection of proposals of possibilities for understanding God and the world. We can identify distinct theological interpretations with proposals from Elohists, Yahwists, deuteronomists, priests, sages, apocalyptists, Hellenistic Jewish writers, and early Christians. Within each theological trajectory individual voices speak in their own accents. The preacher wants to know, "What does a text ask to us to believe to be true of God and the world?" A sermon is often a conversation beginning with this question.[26] If the community can affirm the proposal of the text, preacher and congregation think through implications. If not, the community ponders alternatives.[27]

In many times and places, scripture has helped communities discern the purposes of God. A preacher in the process tradition should recognize, however, that communities sometimes drift into myopic relationships with the Bible. While the Bible is an important guide, it is not imperious. Other voices also lure the community toward divine aims.

The notions *Christian history* and *tradition* refer to the many Christian witnesses, events, and practices–from the Bible to the present–that interpret Christian faith. It is commonplace to lament the biblical illiteracy of today's church, but the church is even more illiterate concerning post-biblical witnesses and practices, especially among non-Western Christian traditions. Yet, as Delwin Brown points out, a tradition can have long-lasting effects even when a community no longer remembers the tradition per se.[28] By bringing such voices into the sermon, the preacher helps people reflect critically on how the voices contribute to the community's current thinking, feeling, and acting.[29] Such voices also often offer perspectives that the current community has overlooked.

A preacher may seem overwhelmed when turning to "the tradition." However, a preacher can usually identify a few persons, events, or practices pertinent to a given sermon. For example, many pastors have trusted friends in Augustine, Calvin, Wesley, Campbell, and the affirmations of faith, not to mention practices such as fasting and reconciliation.[30] Preachers need to remember that tradition is not a fixed, unchangeable deposit, but is perpetually in the process of critically reevaluating itself.[31]

The *voices beyond the Christian community* are too numerous to catalog, e.g., philosophy, social sciences, natural sciences, arts, and social events. Other religions often posit striking proposals.

The *congregation* is a primary voice to whom the preacher attends. The recent literature of preaching emphasizes that each congregation is a distinct culture. The preacher needs to engage pastoral listening to discover the unique character of the community and frame the discussion of proposals so the congregation will have a good opportunity to consider them seriously.[32] Although the congregation is a community in which all people are inherently interrelated, it is also diverse.[33] Different people have different attitudes. Each congregation contains multiple subcultures and world views.[34] Hence, the preacher needs to ask how the different subcommunities might react to a particular proposal.[35]

Preachers also attend to their own *life experiences* and to their *deepest theological convictions.*[36] Preachers do not come to sermons as blank slates, but enter the preaching conversation already loaded with preassociations with the text: life experiences, ideas, feelings, and predispositions toward the text and toward the other voices in the conversation. A sensitive preacher needs to name these qualities and to deal with them critically.

A minister seldom simply "preaches the Bible." Ministers tend to preach their own deepest theological convictions in dialogue with scripture and other sources. Preachers need to be conscious of the distinctiveness of their convictions and of how such beliefs relate to those of other theologies and world views.

As developed in the last section of this article, God is always at work in all phases of the conversation.[37] According to process theologians, the Spirit is inherently present.

The preacher needs to help the congregation take account of *those affected by the proposition.* Who might be touched by the proposition and how? These may include the congregation as well as persons and communities (including nature) beyond. Would the quality of their lives be increased or diminished by the attitudes and behaviors encouraged by this proposal?

Bernard Meland reminds the preacher not to be reductionistic when listening to the various voices in the conversation. Meland eloquently says, "...perceptual experience is a richer event than conception can possibly be, providing every occurrence of awareness with a 'fringe,' implying a 'More,' much of which persistently evades conceptualization."[38] Preachers need to become sensitive to insights and intuitions that come to them via this route. Such awareness is more than passing emotion. It is a fabric of feeling. Though neither preacher nor congregation may be able to explain it fully, they are often aware of it. In each moment and circumstance, there is More than meets the eye.

For the process-relational preacher, culture can be a source of theological insight.[39] Human beings are always immersed in culture. God is omnipresent in the midst of a particular culture and the interactions of different cultures. Consequently, all inhabitants of the earth already have some acquaintance with God through being alive. Many of these awarenesses never rise above the level of intuition. One of the preacher's callings is to help folk name theologically their experience so that they can respond as fully as possible to the divine presence. A minister may not need to provide people with what they do not have, or tell them about what they have not experienced, but may need instead to help them recognize how God is present and graciously active in their behalf. At the same time, a pastor is also called to theologically critique culture and its relativities. Just as culture can mediate the holy, so culture can distort it.

Despite the fact that a pastor cannot completely describe a proposal and its depth implications, the preacher needs to help the congregation name as many aspects as possible since the congregation is then usually able to respond to them more fully than when they are unnamed.[40] The conscious awareness of the More can become a resource to which the congregation can turn. Or, the preacher may name aspects of experience that work against the efforts of the Holy. Such forces can be especially pernicious because they erode community without anyone noticing the damage.

The preacher develops proposals to put before the congregation by bringing the perspectives of the various conversation partners into dialogue and critically reflecting on them. Through critical reflection, the preacher identifies the strengths and limitations of the contributions of the partners and formulates a proposal that has a good possibility of helping the community respond optimally to God's purposes.[41] Meland clarifies:

> The constructive use of reason in theology is not that of bringing life and faith into a domesticated situation of reasonableness; but to provide us with vistas of the mind by which we can best apprehend and be responsive to what really constitutes the circumstances of reality as lived; to provide an orientation, as it were, within which we can respond to these immediacies with a sense of their depth and ultimate import, as being constituent of the Creative Passage, which in religious language, is to speak of our life in God.[42]

Reason is not an arbitrary anvil on which the preacher hammers the content of the sermon. Reason is a companion to help preacher and congregation perceive lures in their depths, complexities, implications, and interrelatedness. Reason helps preacher and community articulate proposals that are consistent with their real theological convictions.

Sermon Itself as Conversation about Propositions

Thinking of the sermon itself as a conversation does not require that the preacher engage the congregation in give-and-take in the worship space.[43] Reuel Howe distinguishes between form and function with regard to monologue and dialogue. The form of a sermon may be monologue, but its function or quality may be conversation. As Howe points out, in a dialogical situation one person "feels responsible for and responds to the patterns of experience and understanding" of the other person(s) involved so that they are "encouraged to grapple with" their own preexisting meanings "in relation to the speaker's meaning."[44] A sermon is conversational when the congregation recognizes itself in the sermon—its questions about life, its experiences, its affirmations—and is moved to reflect on them.[45] Such conversation uses language that is evocative for the congregation and that brings the experience of the congregation into the sermon.[46] Although listening to one voice, the congregation feels involved in the questions raised in the sermon and in the journey to explore them.

The preacher hopes the sermon will persuade the congregation that the proposition the sermon puts before them is sufficiently promising for them to adopt it. Persuasion in the world of process thought is not manipulation. Manipulation is the attempt to get people to believe that their options are more limited than they really are. From process perspective, a sermon is persuasive not by attempting to close off the congregation's awareness of options, but by holding up the beauty and promise of the proposition, especially in comparison and contrast with other possibilities. When the full range of interpretive possibilities is known to a listening community, they can reflect critically on the various options in relationship to the proposition of the sermon. The preacher hopes the congregation will see possibilities for life-enhancement in the sermon. However, because people enjoy a significant measure of self-creation by accepting (or turning away) particular life choices, the listeners make their own judgments on whether or not to understand themselves in the terms of the sermon.[47]

The Form of the Sermon

Process-relational thought has its greatest impact in regard to the content of the sermon. Yet, this conceptuality is also suggestive for the form and movement of the sermon. Process-relational thinking about the movement of sermons makes use of the key insight that each event comes to life in its own way depending upon the persons, proposals, and forces involved. A sermon, of course, is an event. Consequently, the possibilities for sermon form and movement are limited only by the capacity of the preacher and the congregation to imagine them.

From the vantage points of form and movement, the preacher needs to ask, "What needs to go into this sermon so that the congregation can adequately perceive the lure of the sermon and have an opportunity to respond to it? How can the sermon be arranged so that the congregation is likely to be receptive to the movement of the sermon?" The form of the sermon serves the aim of the sermon.

Fred Craddock, whose initial work on preaching shows some influence from Whitehead, speaks for many in the preaching community today. "*How* one communicates comes across to the hearers as *what* one communicates… There is no avoiding the fact that the medium is a message, if not the message."[48] A preacher speaking out of the process-relational world seeks consistency between the experience of life (especially the experiences of discovery and insight) and the experience of hearing the sermon. In the optimum turn of events, the sermon is an occasion when the congregation not only conceptually understands the proposal but feels it.

Imagination is the ability to envision aspects of life that are other than our immediate, actual experience. An act of imagination enables us to picture how others experience and how the world could be different for us. "The significance of the imaginative mode, as employed by the poet, the artist, or by anyone concerned with sensitive inquiry attentive to the penumbra of the experience-able meaning of events, is that it both enlarges the range of awareness and discerns its subtle qualitative depths."[49]

We have already noticed that imagination helps the preacher prepare the sermon by making it possible for the preacher to envision how the world feels to the conversation partners in the developing sermon. Imagination is especially important as the preacher ponders how the congregation may feel about the proposal(s) in the sermon. The sermon can include materials, and unfold in such a way, as to encourage the community to imagine the world from the viewpoint of the proposition.

Without intending to do so, Whitehead himself, in his philosophy of education, poses a sequence of three moments that serves some sermons (AE 17–20).

1. *Romance* (fascination). People are naively fascinated by bits and pieces of the subject. A preacher might call attention to questions raised by the text or the topic, or to incongruities between aspects of the text or topic and our experience. What does this naïve encounter with the text or topic seem to invite the congregation to believe, feel, or do?

2. *Precision.* A preacher would help people seek a more precise apprehension of the subject through research and reflection. What does this mature understanding of the text or topic invite the congregation to believe?

3 *Generalization.* The preacher helps the people generalize on the relationship between the discoveries gained from the moment of precision and other moments or other data. The learner seeks to generalize from the particular precision associated with the previous moment to other situations.

Sermons can be structured in many other ways that are congenial to process conceptuality:

- unfold in the sequence of the moves and questions of a conversation[50]
- be like a jigsaw puzzle as people and congregation put together questions and pieces of insight into a gradually enlarging picture of meaning
- resemble Whitehead's radial pattern of thought in which the preacher looks at the subject again and again, each time from a different elevation and angle[51]
- follow the form and function of the biblical text[52]
- recreate the preacher's encounter with the text, that is, the structure of the sermon is the same series of steps in which the preacher initially worked with the text or topic and developed the proposal[53]
- take a trip in which congregation and community make a journey toward understanding[54]
- tell a story that creates a narrative world into which the congregation enters and has an imaginative experience of what their experience in the everyday world could be like if they accept the proposal of the sermon[55]

Some weeks a congregation may be similar to a car owner standing before an automobile that does not function and simply needs a repair manual. A pastor might just directly relate the proposal to the community.[56]

The Sermon Comes to Life

A sermon is not fully a sermon until it is spoken in the presence of the congregation.[57] Whitehead notices that when someone speaks,

Hands and arms constitute the more unnecessary parts of the body. We can do without them. They do not excite the intimacies of bodily existence. Whereas in the production of sound, the lungs and throat are brought into play. So that in speech, while a superficial, manageable expression is diffused, yet the sense of the vague intimacies of organic existence is also excited. Thus, voice produced sound is natural symbol for the deep experiences of organic existence.[58]

Generating and receiving sound waves touches a person at a primal level.

The oral-aural dimension is important. Preaching, like other forms of speaking, "evokes in the speaker feelings of causal efficacy—feelings of that power whereby our reality emerges and which gives us our identity. In short, the spoken word reinforces the speaker's sense of being an efficacious agent in a world of such agents."[59] A similar experience pertains for those who hear sermons (and other oral communications). The act of speaking produces sound waves that pass through the air and physically touch the eardrums of the listeners. The eardrums and the air in the ear canals actually move. The body becomes directly involved in processing the words that strike the ear. The words that come to the listener through preaching stir the self at the level of feeling.

Hence, if a person seeks to preach from a process-relational stance, the sermon must be oral-aural in character. It needs to have the quality of living speech. The preacher should be as fully as possible present to the community. This feeling of presence has less to do with whether the preacher uses notes, an outline, or a complete manuscript, and more to do with the character of the moment of preaching.

Process-relational preachers should be sensitive to another, often overlooked aspect of preaching: the value of silence. Meland explains:

> It does not follow, however, that the realities of these lived experiences lay dormant or unexpressed, except as they can break forth verbally in language. Nor is living with integrity, with style and beauty, always, or necessarily, the fruition of language employed instructively, testimonially, or with moral direction or insistence. *Presence*, sheer presence in and of itself is a mode of communicating.[60]

Indeed, "there is language in silences."[61] In silence we become aware of the depths of reality in ways that we cannot fully express in words or even in the arts. The preacher who honors silence by being silent, from time to time, may help the congregation become aware of God as sheer presence. When preacher and congregation are silent, if only for a moment, they may become aware of God touching them at the level of feeling.[62]

God Is Omnipresent in All Phases of the Sermon

God is present and purposive in all phases of the preparation, embodiment, and afterglow of the sermon.[63] Moment by moment, God offers the preacher the most relevant available intuition, thought, sensitivity, discovery, feeling, or other awareness. God shares the joy of the preacher's moments of discovery;

God struggles with the complexities, ambiguities, questions, and doubts that come to the preacher while developing the proposal. God is with the preacher as the preacher ruminates on what to say and how to say it. The preacher who is in tune with the divine intention for a particular sermon may even feel inspired. Preachers do not always respond favorably to the divine lure, of course, and at such times, God persists in offering possibilities that can be as renewing as possible for pastor and people given the other choices that they have made.

God is similarly present and purposeful when the preacher is actually speaking the sermon. God seeks to help the pastor and the congregation live into the optimum possibilities for the message. God is at work to increase the receptivity of the listening community to the lure of the sermon. God feels the congregation feeling the sermon. God is present in the internal relationships among preacher and congregation, attempting to help all members of the community be appropriately responsive to one another. God seeks to intensify the experience of all involved in the world of the sermon.

God continues to work in the afterglow of the sermon by nurturing the feelings generated by the sermon that contribute positively to the congregation and the larger world. Because sermons are spoken and heard by finite people, God aims to limit the distortion and damage from the sermon. As implied earlier, God takes the effects of the sermon and feeds them into depths of experience out of which the community will continue to live. Indeed, Marjorie Suchocki points out that because all entities in the universe are internally related and affect one another, the effect of the sermon extends beyond the immediate congregation to the farthest atoms of the universe.[64]

Even though the preacher stops speaking, the sermon is truly not over. The contributions of the sermon are effective as long as life process continues. One might even say that God continues preaching the sermon long after pastor and listener have consciously moved to other topics.

A homily is seldom spoken *to* God. Nevertheless, the process-relational point of view reminds us that a sermon (like all other things) does affect God. When a message is consistent with the divine will for all entities to experience blessing, a message intensifies God's joy. When a message diminishes or distorts God's aims for the world, it grieves the divine spirit. Ministers, then, preach not just to express themselves, nor simply to affect their congregations. In the deepest sense, the preacher speaks with God. That awareness should enhance the preacher's sense of calling.

SECTION II

Spirituality and Daily Life

Along with many other schools of Christian thought, process theology realizes that the religious life is more than the holding of praiseworthy convictions, although it includes such convictions. The religious life also involves the full range of human experience: inner and outer, sensory and imaginative, bodily and psychological, pleasant and painful. In a modern context, this aspect of the religious life often falls under the rubric of spirituality. Process theologians will usually emphasize that spirituality, properly understood, is not equivalent to narcissistic escapism nor reducible to forms of mysticism that have indeed played an important role in Christian life. They emphasize that spirituality cannot be separated from, and in fact arises from, the joys and struggles of ordinary life.

Bruce Epperly describes how process theology offers a decidedly integrative approach to healing and health, which can include the best of scientifically informed medicine while remaining open to alternative forms of healing. In addition, he emphasizes that healing itself is an ongoing process, coincident with (rather than external to) the course of a life. David Roy builds upon years of pastoral counseling to show how process theology proposes a distinctive psychology of religion, which weaves together attention to interior movements of the soul and heart with recognition of the social conditions and family traditions that shape human life. Kathlyn Breazeale then takes these insights into the realm of sexual partnerships, proposing that process theology yields new insights into power structures, religious attitudes, and models for healthy intimacy in a changing public climate. Donna Bowman then uses process categories to describe how the medium of film evokes the two major dimensions of spirituality, sacramental awareness and discernment, and proposes that both the nature and the utilization of film offer its audience an experience of the sacred depth of each moment.

CHAPTER 8

Process Theology and the Healing Adventure

Reflections on Spirituality and Medicine

■ BRUCE G. EPPERLY

New Frontiers for Spirituality and Medicine

In the centuries before the first Europeans sailed across the Atlantic, cartographers labeled the western extremities of their maps with the words, *ne plus ultra*, "there is no more." Following the voyages of Columbus and other European adventurers, mapmakers revised western edges of their maps with the words, *plus ultra*, "there is more," even though they could barely imagine the wonders and wealth of the mysterious land and its first inhabitants.

Today, physicians, nurses, complementary healers, and spiritual leaders are revising the maps of Western medicine with the recognition that "there is more" to healing and medicine than contemporary Western medicine had previously imagined. In light of newly emerging images of reality and human existence, traditional Western medicine is embarking on a healing adventure that embraces modalities as diverse as acupuncture and antibiotics, computerized tomography (CT) scans and compassionate touch, medication and meditation, and prayer and Prozac™. A broader vision of human life is emerging; and with this new vision comes a new understanding of the interplay of medicine, healing, and spirituality. The dualism and materialism that undergirded modern medicine is being eclipsed by a relational and spiritual vision of reality. Individualistic notions of health and illness are giving way to planetary and communal images of wholeness. This new vision of healing and medicine is expressed in the surprising and dramatic transformation of medical practice and research.

First, science is studying the sacred. While religious beliefs and spiritual practices were once considered irrelevant, if not detrimental, to physical and mental health, today medical scientists are discovering that religious commit-ment promotes emotional, physical, and relational well-being. As researcher Jeff Levin suggests, we can now articulate an epidemiology of spirituality, based on hundreds of scientific studies that associate religious behaviors with both the prevention and recovery from illness.[1] Committed religious behavior is associated with[2] longer life, fewer incidents of heart disease, stroke, and cancer, and decreased substance abuse. Elders who are religiously active respond more creatively to chronic illness, surgery, and bereavement.[3] While medical research cannot fully explain why religion is beneficial to health, the results suggest that religion promotes greater self-respect, a healthier lifestyle, a sense of meaning and competence in dealing with illness and tragedy, social support, optimism and hope, and a greater ability to respond to stress.

Yet, beyond the association of certain religious behaviors with positive health outcomes, certain studies point to a metaphysical foundation for health and healing. Intercessory prayer and distant healing techniques have been associated with fewer side effects following heart bypass surgery, reduction of depression, enhanced healing of wounds in mice, and increased growth of certain grasses and fungi.[4] In reflecting on these studies, some commentators have suggested that the effectiveness of distant prayer is grounded in nonlocal causation and the intricately woven ecology of life.

Further, the interplay of psyche and soma has been irrefutably demonstrated by numerous studies, indicating that spiritual practices such as meditation and centering prayer as well as the secular relaxation response significantly contribute to the reduction of blood pressure, metabolism, and stress.[5]

Second, the emerging medicine of the future integrates technology and touch in its embrace of complementary forms of medical care. Fifteen years ago, when I began teaching courses on spirituality and health at Georgetown University School of Medicine, my first year medical school students scoffed at Bill Moyers's video on traditional Chinese medicinal practices such as Qi Gong and acupuncture. Today, my medical students recognize that acupuncture and ayurvedic medicine may complement treatments routinely prescribed by Western medical practitioners. Many physicians and nurses recommend once-ridiculed practices such as acupuncture, homeopathic and herbal medicine, energy work, massage, and meditation as adjuncts to their own therapies.

Third, a wholistic and relational vision of reality is replacing the individ-ualistic worldview upon which modern Western medicine has been based. Led by medical pioneers such as Herbert Benson, Deepak Chopra, Larry Dossey, and Dale Matthews, physicians are discovering the enchanted universe of quantum physics in which relationship, nonlocal causation, universal creativity, and the role of the spirit are at the heart of reality. According to this innovative vision of reality, our lives weave together mind and body in such a way that health and illness are never purely somatic, but always reflect and shape our emotional, spiritual, and relational lives.

Finally, a new partnership is emerging among physicians, nurses, comple-mentary health care practitioners, and spiritual leaders. Physicians and other health care givers are recognizing the essential role of spiritual beliefs and practices in preventing illness, responding to chronic and life-threatening physical conditions, facing death, and finding guidance in facing difficult ethical issues surrounding birth, death, and medical experimentation. In this context, religious institutions are reclaiming their historic role as channels of healing for mind, body, spirit, and relationships. Among Christians, the healings of Jesus have been reclaimed as means of responding to illness in a scientific age. Jesus has been rediscovered as a spiritual healer whose healing ministry joined somatic medicine, healing touch, energy healing, prayer, psychotherapy, the placebo effect, and social and economic justice.[6]

A Healing Vision of Reality and Human Life

In a highly influential essay, written in 1977, George Engel expressed the need for a new model of medicine. According to Engel, the growing crisis in modern medicine originated from "an adherence to a model of disease no longer adequate for the scientific tasks or social responsibilities of either medicine or psychiatry."[7] The biomedical model of health and illness, Engel believes, "embraces both reductionism, the philosophic view that complex phenomena are ultimately derived from a single primary principle, and mind-body dualism, the doctrine that separates the mental from the somatic."[8]

While the biomedical model successfully addresses significant somatic issues, its failure to address the spiritual and emotional lives of patients renders it ineffective in dealing with chronic and terminal illness, patient responsibility for self-care, and bioethical decision-making. Its technological orientation has saved countless lives and will continue to do so, but, on its own, the purely somatic approach is unable to address the deeper issues of meaning and values that are raised by critical illness and mortality. In its isolation of the patient from significant spiritual, relational, and environmental resources, biomedicine has added to the suffering of many patients. Further, its adherence to a linear cause and effect understanding of reality has blinded it to the impact of economics, emotions, spirituality, and the environment on issues of health and illness. Such adherence has also prevented it from recognizing the potentially hazardous side effects of certain medical interventions and pharmaceutical interactions.

Fortunately, Western medicine is in a time of transformation as physicians, nurses, and medical institutions are beginning to utilize the resources of complementary medicine, spiritual formation, and psychological counseling. At Georgetown University School of Medicine and Medical Center where I once taught, courses in complementary medicine, spirituality and health, and death and dying are now routinely offered along with the hard sciences. Sigmund Freud would be astounded if he were to drop in on my workshops in meditation and lectures on modern spiritual movements to psychiatric residents. This same spirit is evident in the everyday realities of medical care. When a friend was going through a difficult time, her physician suggested that she practice centering prayer and walk daily along with taking the Prozac™ he had prescribed.

Despite these changes, the dualistic and somatic vision of reality still shapes the thinking of most physicians, insurance companies, government policy-makers, hospitals, and patients. To enhance the well-being of patients, the insights of the Newtonian-Cartesian world view that undergirded Western medicine for four centuries must be supplemented and embraced by a more adequate and comprehensive vision of reality.

We need flexible and expansive maps of reality and human existence to help us navigate the new frontiers of spirituality and medicine. While not providing specific medical answers, the maps provided by process-relational theology proclaim that "there is more" to our personal health than somatic well-being. These maps give us directions toward the exciting frontiers that lie ahead for medicine and spirituality.

Process-relational theology expands our maps of reality, human life, and medicine by inviting us to reflect on the following themes:

1. the relatedness of all things and the ecology of health
2. the interweaving of mind and body
3. the role of the environment and economics in health and illness
4. the symbiotic relationship of technology and values
5. the importance of spirituality in health and illness
6. the impact of our visions of God on our health

In the paragraphs that follow, I will briefly describe the resources of process-relational theology for the transformation of medicine in light of the growing partnership of spirituality and medicine.[9]

Relationships and the ecology of health. Process theology affirms the essential interconnectedness of life. Each moment of experience arises out of the universe and contributes, by its own process of self-creation, to the universe beyond itself. While each moment of experience is a locus of creative transformation and a unique center of experience, the materials of self-creation arise from its immediate and distant environment. This environment both limits and inspires the process of self-creation.

In contrast to this vision of universal interrelatedness, the Newtonian-Cartesian vision of reality holds that substances, especially mind and body, are essentially independent and isolated from one another. Their interactions are ultimately accidental, rather than essential to their nature. In a world of isolated substances, the body can be treated in a piecemeal fashion, without consideration of the rest of the organism or its immediate environment. In a universe of independent substances, the physician has little need to consider the impact of medical interventions on other organ systems or to keep in mind the role of family life, sense of meaning, or hope for the future in health and illness. Further, in the Newtonian-Cartesian model, the ideal venue for understanding the patient's health is the "clinic," the closed-system, antiseptic environment that isolates the patient from the complications, and also the concreteness, of her or his family, occupation, religion, or neighborhood.

In contrast, process-relational thinking asserts that all medicine and spirituality is interactive and communal in nature. The body and mind are woven together seamlessly, and this same fabric of relationships characterizes the person and her or his environment. In a dynamic and relational universe, the sources of health and illness are complex and multifaceted. Process-relational thought asserts that the medicine of the future must address issues of economics and global warming, and asbestos and job satisfaction, as well as stress, family life, self-care issues, and accessibility to health care. From this perspective, an adequate "medical history" must include questions about religious background and personal values as well as family health history and personal lifestyle.

The interweaving of mind and body. Process-relational theology and metaphysics proclaims that we live in a psychosomatic, or panexperiential, universe. The ecology of our personal lives reflects the interconnectedness of the universe. Mind and body interpenetrate one another. Each occasion of experience is both physical and mental in nature: it is grounded in the causal impact of the past, but it also aims toward creative transformation in the present and the future. While what we typically describe as "mind" and "body" differ quantitatively in terms of richness, complexity, and novelty of experience, they are similar in kind. The basic units of reality, "drops of experience" or "actual occasions," that make up both minds and bodies are lively and experiential in nature. From this perspective, the notion of unfeeling matter is an abstraction, the result of the apparent stability of physical objects. Yet, beneath the apparent stability of the body is a dynamic microcosm of relationships in which inheritance, subjectivity, and novelty join in the ever-evolving dance of creativity. In contrast to the modern image of a disenchanted universe, populated by isolated and insentient objects, process-relational thought affirms the vision of the psalmist, who proclaimed that the heavens declare the glory of God. But, more than that, process-relational thought equally proclaims that our lymphatic, cardiovascular, nervous, digestive, and reproductive systems also declare God's lively handiwork and glory. In their essential unity, body is "inspired" and mind is "embodied" as reflections of divine artistry and care.

Dynamically interconnected, mind constantly shapes the body even as the body continuously conditions the mind. Meditation lowers blood pressure and enhances the immune system. Hope and optimism enable us to cope emotionally and physically with the challenges of personal setbacks, illness, and bereavement. Visualization exercises, affirmations, and counseling marshal our resources for dealing with the diagnosis and treatment of cancer as well as shifts in our relationships with children and spouses. On the other hand, hopelessness depresses the immune system. For example, in the year following the death of a spouse, widows and widowers are more susceptible to depression, illness, and mortality.

The body also affects the mind. Persons treated medically for chemical depression need spiritual and psychological counseling as well as appropriate medication to restore their spirits and enable them to see themselves as whole persons despite their illness. Treatment for a broken bone is not fully complete until the patient recovers a sense of overall well-being and confidence in her or his ability to walk or run. Accordingly, from a process-relational perspective, every somatic intervention has emotional and spiritual consequences. Conversely, every spiritual, emotional, or mental change is registered throughout the body.

The role of the environment and economics in health and illness. All health is environmental health. This insight was recognized by the Hebraic prophets who proclaimed the vision of *shalom,* God's reign of wholeness and justice that embraced personal well-being, economic structures, social justice, and governmental policy. Jesus' healing ministry joined the cure of the body and spirit with the transformation of social relationships in light of the reign of God. Similarly, Hippocrates asserted that "the well-being of a person is influenced by environmental factors…the quality of air, water, and food; the winds and topography and general living habits."[10] In the modern era, the World Health Organization affirmed the essential unity of personal and environmental health with its definition of health in wholistic terms as "the state of complete physical, mental, and social well-being and not the absence of disease and infirmity."[11] The ecological nature of health is noted by Gary Gunderson, who asserts that the primary indicator of a child's long-term health is her or his educational level, grounded in her or his parents' economic condition.[12]

We are connected to the universe. The places we work, the quality of the food we eat, the air we breathe, and the water we drink profoundly effect our health and well-being. We live in a world characterized by incidents such as Chernobyl, Three Mile Island, Love Canal, and the terrorist attacks of September 11, as well as toxic physical and emotional environments. In such a world Whitehead's affirmation of the intricate relationship of humans and their environment challenges medicine to expand the scope of its interest to include the workplace, natural environment, nuclear wastes, economic justice, and accessibility to health care. As Whitehead notes,

> In fact the world beyond is so intimately entwined in our natures that unconsciously we identify our more vivid perspectives of it with ourselves. For example, our bodies lie beyond our own individual existence. And yet they are part of it. We think of ourselves as so intimately entwined in bodily life that man is a complex unity–body and mind. But the body is part of the external world, continuous with

it. In fact, it is just as much a part of nature as anything else–a river, a mountain, a cloud. Also, if we are fussily exact, we cannot define where the body begins and nature ends. (MT 21)

Health and healing are both local and global in nature. In bringing healing to families, workplaces, and social structures, we promote well-being at every level of life. Much to the surprise of traditional physicians, medical studies indicate that patients have shorter hospital stays, on average, if their rooms have pleasant and open vistas. Healthy and just environments contribute to physical as well as spiritual well-being.

The interplay of technology and value. In its primary focus on bodily survival and health, modern Western medicine has often neglected its spiritual roots in the teachings of Hippocrates and the compassion of Jesus. Health care has been defined in terms of objective test results and technological interventions. While we cannot underestimate the significance of today's technological marvels, we must also recognize that nonquantifiable issues such as values, belief systems, and ethical principles have often been forgotten or given purely cursory, and mandated legal, attention in the desire to sustain physical existence at any cost. In so doing, somatic treatments solely aimed at extending the patient's life often result in diminishing her or his overall physical, emotional, relational, and spiritual well-being. The growing interest in physician-assisted suicide and euthanasia is a direct result of persons' fears that aggressive medical treatments will rob them of dignity, integrity, and choice in the final months of their lives.

Process-relational metaphysics maintains that value and existence are coextensive. To exist, even in the most rudimentary manner, is to be locus of value and meaning. Existence implies the dynamic interplay of experience and response, aversion and adversion, and physical health and mental decision-making. From this perspective, all medicine, by definition, embraces value and meaning. There is no purely objective technology, medical care, or data. Accordingly, issues of ethics, personal decision-making, and spiritual formation are essential to medical care. At certain times, issues of faith, family life, and personal perspective may become more compelling than application of technological care or the preservation of physical life. This is especially true at the descending edges of life where medical interventions must be congruent with the quality of life of the patient and her or his personal values and faith. Though physicians must always treat somatic diseases, process-relational thinking reminds them that the patient as a whole is the ultimate locus of concern, and not merely her or his physical ailment or the preservation of somatic existence.

The importance of spirituality and decision-making in health. One of the side effects of somatic-oriented medicine has been the disempowering of patients. Western technological medicine assumed that physical functions were automatic and entirely somatic in nature. Though they recognized the ephemeral "will to live" as having some bearing on a patient's survival, most physicians assumed that the various organs and bodily systems functioned in strict isolation from a person's emotional and spiritual life. Over the past thirty years, however, medical research has indicated the fallacy of this position. On the one hand, studies clearly indicate the negative physiological side effects of prolonged feelings of stress, hopelessness, loneliness, and competition. On the other hand, practices such as meditation and deep prayer have been identified with positive changes in blood pressure, metabolism, and stress. In light of these findings, many health caregivers and spiritual guides now explicitly encourage patients to deepen their spiritual lives and reflect on their deepest values as adjuncts in the prevention and response to illness.

Process-relational thought affirms that in each moment the quality of our lives is determined by our openness to intensity and depth of experience. Even the simplest drop of experience makes decisions that shape its integration of the world in its process of self-creation. The experience of value, meaning, choice, creativity, and freedom are coextensive with reality. Accordingly, even when death is imminent, we can always do "something more" to bring greater wholeness to our lives and the lives of others. In the spirit of Viktor Frankl's reflections on life in the concentration camp, while we cannot fully determine the events that externally dominate our lives, we always have the freedom of choice in responding to these events. While our freedom is always contextual, and thus limited by our current physical condition, environment, accessibility to treatment, and communal values, our moment-by-moment choices can mean the difference between health and illness and life and death. Even as we are faced with chronic illness and death, our faith can make us whole and bring us peace of mind.

The significance of our image of God and the nature of God's presence in our lives. Our images of God can be factors in health and illness. This is evident in religious groups that create a chasm between faith and medicine by asserting that any recourse to medical care is a sign of faithlessness. It is also evident in the toxic images many persons have of God. These images constellate around the following assertions:

1. illness results from sin, while health reflects personal righteousness.
2. illness is caused by divine punishment for our behavior or thoughts.
3. illness is God's will.
4. illness exists to teach us a lesson or enable us to inspire others spiritually.
5. we create our own realities and, thus, our health and illness is entirely the result of our faith and attitudes.

Further, many persons envisage God as a parent who absents herself or himself from our ordinary lives, but shows up with signs and wonders at the divine whim or at the pleading of her or his children. These images of the relationship between spirituality and illness are ultimately linear and unilateral in nature: either everything comes from God, or everything is the result of our own behaviors and thoughts. In either case, the victim is banished to isolation, guilt, and impotence.

In contrast, process-relational thought proclaims a dynamic, relational, and multifactorial understanding of health and illness. Our health condition is the result of many factors: physical condition, environment, our attitudes and beliefs, health care accessibility, genetics, spiritual life, prayers of others, and the presence of God. In the interplay of health and illness, process-relational thought affirms that God aims at intensity, depth, and beauty of experience. As creative-responsive love, God's presence is characterized by intimate companionship, gentle and persistent persuasion, and constant personal guidance, rather than arbitrary and coercive interventions. God is present as the lure toward wholeness within each moment of experience. In the interplay of personal openness to divine activity and environmental influence, God aims at the "best for the impasse" (PR 224). As Whitehead asserts, "every act leaves the world with a deeper or fainter impress of God. [God] then passes into [the] next relation to the world with enlarged, or diminished, presentation of values" (RM 122). The intensity of divine presence varies from occasion to occasion. God's presence may, in the interplay of events, bring dramatic changes of body, mind, spirit, and relationships, often identified as "miracles." In contrast to the modern vision of miracles that sees these intensifications of divine presence as violations of the law of nature, process-relational theology sees God as an essential component of every occasion, working within all things to bring forth the best possibility, be it incremental or dramatic in nature. While our personal or social decisions may limit God's actions in a particular situation, God is always and everywhere on our side. God wants us to experience the wholeness and well-being congruent with the wholeness of all things.

Process-relational theology sees God's healing presence in terms of responsiveness as well as creativity. We find wholeness through the awareness of God's embrace of the totality of life—our own and the lives of others. As the fellow sufferer who understands, God embraces each moment of experience and affirmatively receives all things into becoming. At every stage of life and state of health, we are known and loved fully by God. With the author of Psalm 139, we find reassurance in God's eternal openness to the totality of our lives. Our lives make a difference to God. God cherishes our lives and receives our pain and struggle, as well as our joy, into God's own experience. At the descending edges of life or in moments of despair, we can cry out to God, knowing that God hears us, knows us, and loves us.

The process-relational God is the ultimate image of hope. God is unambiguously on our side, working within our lives to bring forth experiences of beauty and wholeness. God supports medical care but equally supports human decisions that place meaning and quality of life above mere survival. As the source of hope and optimism, God's presence promises a spiritual healing even if there is no physical cure. This faithful and loving God inspires our creativity, intellect, relationships, and even our immune system in the divine-human quest for abundant life.

Healing Practices

Process-relational thought is profoundly concrete. Rising out of reflection on ordinary as well as uncommon mystical experiences, process thought articulates a vision of reality as a whole and then tests it within the concreteness of everyday experience. Process-relational theology not only illuminates the relationship of spirituality and medicine, its metaphysical and theological insights also provide practical guidance for health care givers, spiritual leaders, and laypersons.

First, process-relational thought challenges medical education to embrace images of wholeness at every level of the curriculum, including the well-being of physicians. In the course of medical school and residency programs today, virtually no attention is given to the health and well-being of future physicians and other health care givers. Process theology inspires a curriculum that encourages students to see their lives as laboratories of health and healing. From reflection on their own experience, medical students and residents become more mindful of their own health, including their experience of stress and illness, attitudes toward their bodies, and self-care strategies. Mindful medicine enables young physicians to become more empathetic toward the experiences of their patients. Further, this process invites students and residents to become "healthy healers" through their participation in, and eventual teaching of, courses in meditation and stress reduction, healthy lifestyle, and relationship between professional, personal, and family life. In addition, the curriculum would include courses on religious traditions in medicine, mind-body medicine, and global medicine.

Today, due to the generosity and insight of the John Templeton Foundation, over seventy medical schools now have courses in spirituality and health. However, more attention to the relationship of spirituality and health is needed both at the educational and institutional level. The global spirit of process-relational theology affirms the virtues of Western technological medicine as it places them in the context of the many streams of healing (for example, traditional Chinese, ayurvedic, Native American, and touch healing) that reflect today's global culture. Students and practitioners alike would be invited to embody new models of partnership with clergy, nurses, and complementary caregivers to enhance the healing potential of their patients.

Second, process-relational theology invites clergy to explore their own wholeness. Mirroring the curricular emphases of current medical education, seminary education currently gives little curricular attention to matters of pastoral wellness and spiritual formation. Issues of family life, sexuality, self-care, and stress management are at the periphery of seminary education even though neglect of these issues may be a factor in professional misconduct and ineffectiveness among many religious leaders today. Sadly, at many seminaries courses in spiritual formation and psychological wholeness are optional in the training of future religious leaders. In contrast, a process-relational seminary curriculum and continuing education program for clergy joins spiritual formation with professional training. Students and clergy would learn to integrate prayer and preaching, lifestyle and liturgy, wellness and worship. Focus on healthy spiritual strategies for responding creatively to conflict as well as balancing family life and ministry would complement and enrich traditional courses in theology, pastoral care, homiletics, scripture, and church administration. Clergy would discover the essential unity of spiritual and professional growth in the ecology of pastoral well-being. In so doing, clergy would reclaim their essential role as healing partners with physicians, nurses, psychotherapists, and complementary health care givers.

Third, the social nature of reality places social responsibility at the heart of medical care. All health is public health. As medical education and practice is transformed in light of the process-relational vision of reality and human existence, the hospital and health care system will also be transformed. Process-relational thought affirms the importance of structures of relationships that nurture beauty and intensity of experience. The ever-present aim at beauty and intensity of experience is multidimensional and can be articulated in terms of *preventative, positive*, and *responsive* medical care.

As *preventative*, the aim at beauty undergirding the medicine of the future seeks to eliminate any factor that minimizes or denies wholeness of experience. Today, a holistic medical-spiritual vision advocates the creative transformation of health care, economics, education, ecology, and family life. In America, this means, first of all, universal health care, advocacy for the marginalized, accessibility of necessary treatments, architectural accessibility for persons with disabilities, and healthy workplaces. It also means a profound commitment to joining issues of homeland security with economic justice, quality education, and training in parenting and family life. In the profound interconnectedness of life, process-relational theology inspires us to mend the world and not just our own land. Our own well-being is ultimately connected with careful stewardship of the rain forests in South America, economic and social justice in the developing world, peace in the Middle East, an end to global hunger, and creative responses to HIV/AIDS in Africa and North America.

As a *positive* factor in the aim at beauty, process-relational thought encourages training in nonsectarian as well as sectarian spiritual formation and healthy living habits by schools, churches, and community organizations. In the spirit of Whitehead's comment that the art of life is not only life itself, but living well, and living better, we need to incarnate the divine dream of growth and beauty by encouraging lifelong learning and creativity as well as generosity and service.

As *responsive* to tragedy and sickness, process-relational thought nurtures healthy environments and treatment practices for persons recovering from illness as well as for those who are dying. At the beginning and end of life, process-relational thought challenges us to aim at beauty and companionship by supporting young parents and embracing persons with life-threatening illnesses. We live well when we are born into loving arms and die surrounded by loving arms. Medical practices are not merely about bodies. They also embrace values, emotions, and spirituality. At every season of life, we can find spiritual and relational wholeness as members of healing communities nurtured by healthy environments.

As we revise our maps of reality to include the partnership of spirituality and medicine, uncharted frontiers lie ahead of us. Beyond the isolation and individualism that characterized Western medicine for four centuries, we must aim at a social and planetary order that promotes beauty, health, and community. In the adventure of personal and global healing, process-relational theology will be a leader in inspiring the whole person interplay of spirituality and medicine toward which God lures us.

CHAPTER 9

The Creative Adventure of Pastoral Counseling

Process Illuminations and Assurances

■ DAVID E. ROY

Even after nearly thirty years, I continue to experience pastoral counseling[1] as a creative adventure. I delight in the unknown of each new session or conversation. What subtle yet amazing developments will emerge in this scheduled hour? I never know for certain. Instead, many sessions amount to a brief "theater of the improv," a brief work of art. Even when I think I know in advance how things will go, my ideas often do not predict the ultimate of the hour. This does not mean the sessions are without any sense of purpose or direction. In retrospect, most appear to have been highly purposeful. This is particularly true when there is more than a bit of mystery about process and outcome.

These are some of the core reasons I am glad I have the comfort, guidance, and challenge of the process metaphysics and the theology that is given such rich voice through this metaphysics. Process thought encourages tendencies to be inquisitive, playful, and innovative. It provides a powerful rationale to practice the art of healing souls at a deep level. It makes available the means to integrate mind-body-spirit, a feature of particular importance to pastoral counseling as well as to any psychotherapist who intuits the worth and beauty of this union of these essential dynamics of the universe. In that same context, it clarifies the centrality of the role of the sacred in the healing process without being narrowly sectarian. It offers clarity about how we perceive, including why there are so many problems in this area. It affirms the power and role of consciousness in human growth and healing. It even outlines a model of human development. And there is more.

The balance of this article is a brief elucidation of fourteen areas in which process thought provides what I am calling illuminations and assurances for pastoral counseling. This list is incomplete and not rigorously systematic. It is not, however, arbitrary. Each topic will be handled briefly; far more could be said at each point.

1. The Ultimate Value of Creativity

The process metaphysics assures us that God is the Creative Adventurer who seeks real and novel solutions to human dilemmas. This can serve as a model for our professional work. That is, the process understanding that creativity is the ultimate principle of reality and that even God is characterized by this principle[2] supplies what may be the ultimate ethic for pastoral counseling.

This affirmation can play a very important role in shaping the moment-by-moment flow of therapy.[3] When novel ideals bubble up, when mysterious hunches and vague impressions emerge, process principles tell us to be consciously aware that these are good things that we should attend to. This is important because often these hunches are fragile and tentative: Is this really important; could this really be the case? Often these intuitions lack corroborating evidence. Yet, time and time again, I discover that these hunches are at the heart of what is going on with the client. At times they are off the mark, of course, and need to be tossed aside. Insisting on the rightness of these intuitive flashes and imposing them on the client is unhelpful and quite possibly destructive.

To be creative in this manner requires listening carefully and with fresh interest and delight to the *details* of the person's story. If a person is vague, overly general, it is more difficult to reach into that deeper place where the novel insights emerge. We have to listen until we can feel the *subjective form*[4] of the client's experience. Once this is reached, we usually can feel some of what is going on, we can experience some of what it is like to be this person. It often is at this point that the creative impulses tend to emerge. These impulses may lead to interpretations, to guiding questions, or to suggestions for action.

2. Sacred Love and Wisdom as Intimately Immanent

The process metaphysics assures us that God's creative, loving, compassionate, fitting, and hopeful inspiration is bubbling within each person we meet, and bubbling within us as we join them. This inspiration invariably points the way toward the healing that is needed. Part of our job is to shine an affirming light on this inspiration as it emerges.

For example, I worked with a woman who felt "one down" to her husband and sons. She said repeatedly, "I'm not very smart" compared to them. Simply telling her that was not true did not change her mind. One day I felt a strong flash of energy directing me toward her performance at work. When I asked her if her boss (a demanding consultant) would keep someone on his staff for years who was "not very smart," she said, "No, he would not. He has very high standards." The door to a change in her self-perception had been opened, and an initial step had been taken. Many more steps would be needed before this change in perception would be solidly integrated, but the first step was crucial.

According to Whitehead, this sacred inspiration is the result of the interweaving of God's two primary natures, the Primordial (wherein God holds and orders all pure possibilities) and the Consequent (wherein God receives the actual world with unconditional tenderness). This sacred inspiration, rooted in these two natures, comes to the core of every person as two sacred gifts. One is a potent germ of intrinsic and complete validation (the love) and the other is the dispassionate and noncritical knowledge of how things can be improved for the future (the wisdom). The development of a healthy psyche depends in part upon the successful balancing of these two dynamics.

Both dynamics are essential and, when out of balance, can create intense disharmony. A major cause of the imbalance is the result of the introduction of the world's valuation, in contrast to that offered by God. While God's wisdom is dispassionate and noncritical—God's unconditional love will be offered again and again no matter what the person does or does not do with the lure for change—the world's valuation is often in sharp contrast and makes love conditional upon change. The intensity of the world's negative valuation can be massive and therefore can, functionally, vastly overshadow the sacred, unconditional love and validation.

Yet, this sacred love cannot be eliminated no matter how far into the background of the soul it may recede. In fact, even in the worst situations it will be known by its absence. That is, when a person feels unloved and unaccepted by the world, that person will feel variously ashamed, depressed, and angry. These emotions are the result of the contrast between the unconditional love, held out of awareness, and the highly conditioned acceptance of which the person is aware. In other words, something deep within each of us says over and over and over, "I am a precious person. I am worthy of love. It makes me embarrassed, hurt, sad, and angry to be treated as though I am not." One main therapeutic task is to lift this contrast to consciousness and to help the person become aware of this deeply buried inner experience of grace (love and acceptance) that resides within the person's own soul, within the person's own deepest experience of self. This experience of grace has to be balanced with the world's view of the person, even when there may be merit in at least some of the critique the world offers: "I may not be perfect, but I am precious and beloved nonetheless."

The paradox is that the more a person is able to embody the sacred love, the more creatively responsive to the lure for growth and change the person becomes. The sacred wisdom, which after all is a form of divine judgment, is experienced not as condemning criticism, but as opportunities for a more abundant, freer, healthier life. Pointing to this inner wisdom and encouraging the person's grounding in his or her own source of novel solutions is a second and equally important therapeutic task.

3. Mind-Body-Spirit: Different Facets of the Same Universe

The process metaphysics rigorously supports the understanding that we live in but one universe with different facets. The Cartesian framework, out of which virtually all experimental psychology has emerged, can be collapsed and discarded. This in turn will permit the collapse of the barrier between intuitive approaches to psychotherapy and those developed with the guidance of the scientific methodology. The black box—what Skinner and others called the mind or psyche—*does* matter. This is not a call to abandon the scientific approaches; they are of high value to the field. Instead, this is a call to allow other dynamics, including those that cannot be as easily reduced to objective measurement, to be seen as having an equal value to the healing practices of good psychotherapy. This includes the dimension most often vehemently excluded, namely the spiritual. If the spiritual dimension is indeed a fact of reality and a factor in all healing, it would be foolish, even unethical, to exclude this aspect from both theory and practice. Here pastoral counseling can and should take the lead. The process metaphysics gives our field a clear voice and a clear area of leadership in helping other, secular practitioners integrate spirituality into their work.

The core of this integrated world view comes from how Whitehead defines the basic unit of reality, what he called an *actual occasion*. What is being described here pertains to every such occasion or event, ranging from those events that constitute the natural world to the inner world of our minds. Every actual occasion has both a physical pole and a mental pole. This dual nature is essential to all of reality; however, it is not a duality that splits nature into the physical and mental, for they are two facets of the same indivisible entity.

The physical pole is where the past is experienced as definite, concrete fact; the mental pole is where the becoming subject creates itself out of what it has included from the physical pole.[5] The physical pole receives and conforms to that which is given to it; in that sense, it is the foundation of what we normally think of when we consider the so-called physical world. This is a world of causal events. Yet it is only one dynamic in each and every event. The other is the mental pole, within which the event is given the opportunity to introduce new possibilities as elements of change. And the source of these new possibilities? Whitehead calls this the *initial aim* of the becoming subject and the initial aim is given to each event by God. This is a spiritual process that is an intimate and inseparable part of each physical-mental event. Hence, the unity of what traditionally is called mind-body-spirit.

This integrated world view supports the sensibility of most clients whom I have seen over the years, and not simply those who are religious in more traditional ways (such as participating in faith communities on a regular basis). My impression is that many people have a need to know that their spirituality is respected and its role in their healing is valued even if it is not discussed in any formal fashion.

Even when the spiritual is excluded from consideration, other features of this integration are helpful, in particular knowing how the mind and body are intimately related. For example, this helps resolve the dilemma that many feel at having to choose a physical or a mental cause to their issues. With the process perspective, such an either/or choice is not required. The mentality that characterizes the psyche is understood to be just as real in an ontological sense as the physicality that characterizes the body. Within the process framework, these are simply two different dimensions of the same unit of reality, not two different kinds of reality. This paves the way to understanding that the psyche and the soma have a great deal of mutual influence, even if they have different roles in the constitution of the whole person. The psyche receives massive and potent influence from the body, the brain in particular. In turn, the body receives strong and definite influence from the psyche, particularly where the brain is concerned. Without the brain, there would be no psyche; without the activity of the psyche, there would be no central organization to the person.

This perspective also argues that there can be multiple places to intervene to promote mental health. With depression, to take but one (albeit important) issue, one can intervene chemically at the synapse level. Or, one can intervene with the mentally driven issues of meaning, mourning, motivation, and so forth. Or, one can intervene with both (a finding supported as the best of the three choices through a variety of clinical studies). Clients cannot simply dismiss their depression as a chemical imbalance of unknown origin, a perspective of personal helplessness that is upheld by some pharmaceutical and managed care companies. Instead, they have to take responsibility for at least some of the cause as well as the healing. Paradoxically, adopting this position of personal responsibility also is empowering–I can do something about this–which in turn is an offset to the helplessness of depression.

4. Human Beings as the Proud Possessor of a Self

Any deep and penetrating psychological consideration of the human condition inevitably will encounter such themes as the self, self-esteem, narcissism, and shame. Process metaphysics clarifies these topics and their mutual relationship, and also suggests a rationale for both their existence and the direction for maturation.

Human beings both are a self (the *self as agent*) and have a self (the *self as object*).[6] The reigning mental event at any given instance is the self for the person. However, human beings also come to form a sense of themselves that they can experience in a variety of ways. Because of the technical requirements of Whitehead's philosophy, anything that is *experienced* has to be an object, something that is not a becoming event. This means that when we experience ourselves, we are experiencing something that is a construct of some sort; and that which is doing or being the experiencing is the becoming event–the central organizing event of the psyche or the self.[7] Why is this important? Because it means that people are more than the self they believe themselves to be. The totality of their psyche invariably includes aspects and dynamics that they are used to ignoring, denying, or even despising. These dynamics may be ones that cause problems for them and whose recognition can yield healing and integration. These dynamics also can provide missing elements that these people need to face current challenges. A passive person sometimes needs to find his or her aggression. A reactive person sometimes needs to be able to wait to respond constructively.

This distinction also is a part of another aspect intimately involved with the origin and development of the self as object. This can be understood as self-esteem or self-love. While the connotations of these two are quite different, they are pointing to different aspects of the same struggle. Psychologically, positive healthy self-esteem is an essential element of good mental health. It is associated with success and even positive care for others. Poor self-esteem is associated with depression, failure, and a host of other difficulties. Self-love, on the other hand, usually is viewed in a negative light, as virtually synonymous with self-absorption, selfishness, callousness toward others, and so on. However, the active self at any given instance (self as agent) cannot esteem or love itself; it can only esteem or love (or detest) the self as object, the self that has come to stand for the person. This argues that self-esteem and self-love are really the same and, in turn, sheds light on the real problem. This is the healthy resolution, or lack of it, of the tension between the unconditional divine love and the inevitable failures and associated shame of being a finite, fallible, incomplete human being. This tension requires attention throughout life. This will enable a person to arrive at a point of clarity about being unconditionally unique and precious *and* being imperfect in virtually all areas of living. Such clarity will prevent the recognition of imperfection from overwhelming the feeling of having unique value. The need for feeling unique value then does not blind the person to the realities of imperfection.

5. The Realities of Perception

Whitehead's theory of perception, initially put forth in *Symbolism, Its Meaning and Effect*,[8] became joined with his theory of concrescence (the process of becoming) in *Process and Reality*. His theory of perception brings to the fore several critical ideas that help us understand the vagaries of human perception, particularly as this pertains to the process of psychotherapy.

In sum, Whitehead proposed the existence of two direct, pure modes of perception and a third mode produced by the combination of the two. The two direct modes are *causal efficacy* and *presentational immediacy*. The combined mode is *symbolic reference*. *Causal efficacy* is the experience of the world being thrust upon us; it is the force of the past pressing itself upon the present; it is our sense of being connected. This is akin to that feeling we get in our gut. It is vague, massive, and hard to localize. This mode is most often the source of meaning. *Presentational immediacy* is the experience of world as it is being presented to us in the present. It is precise, detached, and easily localized. This is akin to our visual experience. This mode is most often the source of symbols. *Symbolic reference* is the mode produced by combining the two pure modes, by combining meaning and symbol. Most human perception falls into this category. It is the mode of perception that produces consciousness.

One of Whitehead's most important contributions is the recognition of the foundational reality and importance of causal efficacy. This mode underlies our sense of connection to others, our experience of feeling "caused," and plays an important role in the formation of intuitions. This mode often is ignored, denied, minimized, and even disparaged. However, it is the ground of all perception. Radically, it is a means of direct, nonmediated perception at a distance. It is the world in us, that feeling in our guts, that intuition that arises from the background. It accounts for knowledge that comes to us from others about their condition that is not the result of visual or auditory perceptions. My experience is that this most often has to do with sensing mood and emotion. This includes subtle shifts that are not always visible on the surface.

Whitehead also helps us see that human beings virtually never perceive the fullness of reality, never perceive sheer actuality. This paves the way for error. One of my favorite cartoons in this context is a "Frank and Ernest"™ strip with a sign announcing a speech: "Tonight's Topic: What is Reality?" Frank says to Ernest, "I think reality is just a good guess." Human beings perceive actuality primarily by means of what Whitehead called *transmutation.* In this a huge number of occasions are seen as a unity based upon one or more common qualities. This is how we come to see a wall or a door or a window, for example. This also is how we come to see other human beings. We do not perceive individually the trillions upon trillions of occasions that make up another person at any given moment. Instead, we abstract certain qualities from those trillions of occasions that constitute that person. Thus we create what is for us a finished picture. Invariably, the picture is incomplete, potentially inaccurate, and therefore subject to error.[9]

Whitehead recognized other forms of error in human perception. In fact, his complex analysis can account for the logical possibility of what have been termed false memories. In these cases, a possibility comes to be perceived as an actuality. By the same token, Whitehead's theory supports the logical possibility of repressed memories; or, better, memories that are diminished to the point they are not recognized as memories.

These understandings are helpful to the work of pastoral counseling in a number of ways. They provide a solid conceptual basis for telling clients they cannot assume they ever fully know what another human being—or even themselves—is like. This is a critical element of virtually all relationship counseling. Another implication of these ideas is the realization that both camps in the false memory vs. repressed memory debate have the potential to be accurate *and* in error. This supports the larger understanding that Whitehead most often supports the creation of understandings that bridge opposing positions (he calls these *contrasts*). For Whitehead, *and* is most often the operative conjunction, instead of *or.*

6. The Power and Importance of Consciousness

Whitehead, like many of the pioneers of psychotherapy, understood consciousness to be a small but highly potent aspect of human psychic experience. According to process thought, one of the central functions of consciousness is to contrast with clarity and great intensity what actually exists with what might be but is not. This is the foundation of all change. Clearly, consciousness is the peak of human experience and essential for psychotherapy. Lifting unresolved issues to consciousness is a powerful way for people to change, to bring into reality what might be, but has not yet been, actualized. This argues for approaches that emphasize the importance of this in distinction from those approaches that attempt to effect change in clients without client awareness.

There is more. When the two pure modes of causal efficacy and presentational immediacy are fully included and fully balanced in the mode of symbolic reference, I believe the stage is set for the experience of detached yet lively interest characteristic of what Buddhists call *mindfulness.*

The original theory underlying Gestalt therapy developed the idea of what it called the three modes of the self. The two pure modes were the *id mode* and the *ego mode.* These are relatively easily correlated with causal efficacy and presentational immediacy.[10] The combination of these two modes is referred to as the *middle mode,* correlated with symbolic reference. Middle mode experience is characterized by *spontaneity* and is the source of creative problem solving, where need and possible solutions seem to grow together until the resolution is actualized. All of this is accompanied by full and intense awareness, in the Gestalt therapy model. Thus Gestalt therapists work form the belief that awareness is curative.

7. A Model of Human Development

As developed elsewhere,[11] the process modes of perception also form a basis for a model of human development. The development of a genuinely robust, mature self takes several years and fairly optimal conditions. Three phases can be identified in the development of the mature self. Each phase is dominated in turn by one of three different modal experiences of the self (self-modes for short). The three phases are dominated, in succession, by the *confluent mode* of the self, the *discernment mode* of the self and the self-transcending or *spiritual mode*[12] of the self. These three modes are derived from Whitehead's three modes of perception (causal efficacy, presentational immediacy, and symbolic reference). The argument is that these modes, while all present at each stage of personal development, dominate the subjectivity and therefore the person in successive phases. That is, the progression of confluent, discernment, and spiritual phases reflects the general contours of psychological development. The developmental differences have to do with the degree to which the self is characterized by the qualities associated with each of the modes.

The confluent mode is the mode of experience early in life. This mode includes the experience of the past flowing into the present. Whitehead uses the word *conformal* to describe the dominant experience in this phase. This mode is the experience of "gut" feelings (which can be intense) characterized by vagueness, heaviness, primitiveness, and meaning. The person experiences a lack of engagement, a sense of extreme relaxation, passivity, a receptive attentiveness. The sense of the body looms large. So, potentially, do emotions. When this mode is pervasively dominant, as in early childhood, we may feel we have no boundaries. This mode underlies the experience of being other-determined or other-caused so prevalent in childhood and in many pathological conditions in adulthood. In addition, however, it is through this mode that we can experience mystical union with another or with God. It is the foundation for intimacy.

The second phase of development is dominated by the discernment mode of the self.[13] In this mode the seeds of novelty find some fertile soil. In the discernment mode, the self is dominated by the experiences of detachment, separateness, discrimination. Experience is organized. Perceptions are vivid and distinct. Discernment corresponds with Whitehead's perception in the mode of presentational immediacy and symbolic reference. The self takes the vague, chaotic welter of data and weaves a unique, unified and harmonized creation. Perceptions in this mode are much more manageable than in the first mode; they are "to a large extent controllable at will."[14] This understanding underlies the power of conceptual reframing, a major component of cognitive psychotherapy.

This mode accounts for our usual sense of being a separate human being, separate from the elements around us. This mode, highly correlated with and dominated by vision, tends to be normative for subjective human experience. When we shift from this mode in adulthood, we tend to feel we are having an altered state of consciousness. These shifts can result from meditation, trauma, drugs, sleep- and sensory-deprivation, and so forth.

This mode is also the source of all projection, both accurate and inaccurate. That is, what comes into the psyche in the confluent mode is projected back onto reality in the discernment mode, enabling us, among many other things, to maneuver physically in the world. However, it is entirely possible to receive data that arise from a different time and place and project them onto the here and now. This happens frequently in therapy. It is the foundation of transference, for example.

This mode brings with it a sense of self-determination; the sense of being self-caused belongs to this mode. This mode allows us to accomplish great things, but if our experience is continuously dominated by this mode, we also run a very real risk of creating the very problems that plague our culture and inflict at least some of the damage on the people we see in therapy. For example, when this mode dominates, we tend to emphasize our separateness and our detachment. In the extreme, this yields a cold, uncaring heart, unconcerned about our fellow humans, let alone our world. The dominance of this mode also accounts for our loss of the sense of the sacred in ourselves and in the ordinary world around us.

The spiritual mode of the self, the third phase, comes into being long before the self enters the spiritual phase of development. As previously stated, all three modes are present to some degree all along the developmental continuum.

One of the characteristics of this third mode is that it is the experience of the relationship between the two previous modes. In some fashion, symbol (discernment) is joined with meaning (confluent).[15] For Whitehead, the interrelationship between the two modes can also result in consciousness.

Connecting the symbol with the meaning can be a very intense, rich, powerful experience. For example, a man had had recurring images of a face contorted with rage. The image was detached, both visually and emotionally. He had sometimes wondered if it were his mother, but dismissed this idea, for his memories of her did not include this kind of rage. One day in a session, the image of the face began to look more like his mother; then it was followed by an image of a breast. He also became aware that he was salivating profusely. Despite wanting to dismiss the experience as meaningless, he continued to hold all of this in awareness. Suddenly he burst into tears, saying that his mother was screaming at him because he wanted to be fed. Though his mother was dead, he was able to learn from his father that his mother found breastfeeding extremely difficult and painful. As he reflected on the paradigm of this memory, several significant and confusing pieces of his life finally made sense (why, for example, he would be in relationships where he would be attacked when he tried to meet a natural need).

On the one hand, the spiritual mode allows us to perceive the world as it is; and on the other, as it might be. Therapy often involves helping people be clear about both perceptions. As suggested by the perception of what might be, but is not yet, the introduction of novelty is an important function of this mode. It is the interplay between what is vs. what might be—with a full, deep experience, knowledge, and perception of each—that is perhaps the core characteristic of the spiritual phase, yielding eventually the soulful self.

According to Whitehead, one of God's chief aims is the evocation of intensities. This is accomplished through the introduction of novelty. The psyche and the self are caught up in this drama—indeed, they are primary instruments for this drama. The psyche is the presiding or dominant occasion in each instant, presiding over and inheriting from the brain and the body. However, the psyche does not simply repeat its predecessor. It is a new creation each moment, with far less allegiance to the past when compared with, say, occasions that make up the body. The role of the initial aim (which introduces novelty) potentially can be quite significant for the psyche. Thus, each moment can be quite different from the previous moments. In the extreme, this is chaos. In moderation, this can be an experience of creative ecstasy.

As the mature self develops, it gradually increases in its ability to integrate change. It does this by gradually learning to transcend itself. (This process includes such concepts as the observing ego, the self-reflexive self, and the self-transcending self.) The self at the moment of subjectivity does not really look at itself (this is an ontological impossibility in Whitehead's system). However, it does observe its predecessors from a different point of view. To achieve this, it must stand outside of or diminish the influence of its predecessors. The causal force of the past is weakened; the new instance of the self is not fully conformal to its predecessors. This has the effect of increasing the role of the initial aim in making changes for the future.

Clients are frequently dominated by old self-objects or parts of themselves, yet remain unaware of these parts as parts. They so identify with the part that they take it as "themselves." When they finally become aware that this is a part, they begin for the first time to have some real measure of relationship and therefore influence over the feelings and behaviors associated with this part. For example, a woman had been subjected to severe torture at approximately the age of four. As a result of this trauma, she developed a number of traits, including a very quiet, intensely watchful manner. For reasons that are peculiar to the details of the trauma, she also developed an extremely high need for precise accuracy. When she was dominated by this part, mistakes were absolutely not allowed! When she was not dominated by this part, she could be relaxed, spontaneous, playful. After considerable work with this part, she finally developed the capacity to see it and relate to it without either being taken over by it or banishing it. One day she spontaneously realized she was caught up with the mood of this part, and laughed, saying, "You've seen a lot of her over the years, haven't you."

As this kind of experience becomes more and more important for how the self comes to constitute itself, it becomes both increasingly spiritual and soulful. It is increasingly spiritual because the role of God's Spirit (via the initial aim) becomes increasingly the dominant influence in the self. It is increasingly soulful because it also gains in its capacity to include all that is present in the psyche (or soul). As the past is re-presented in the present, this means that the soulful self is increasing in its capacity to integrate the full measure of the past in a new and healing way in the present.

8. The Real Impact of Our History

The process model helps us understand how our history can be efficaciously present in the now of our lives. From the process perspective, past events induce a conformal response at the first phase of becoming[16] (a process Whitehead called *concrescence*) of new events. This accounts for the continuity of reality, including the general continuity of each human person. This is why, for example, each new moment of experience is basically identical to the preceding moment.

However, there is no ontological reason that the influential past events have to be limited to those that immediately precede the newly becoming event. In fact, from the process perspective, it is the entire (!) past universe of events that impinges upon each newly becoming event. Obviously, the vast majority of these events are rendered trivial in terms of influence. However, those events in our personal history that include "unfinished business" can certainly be re-presented in the new moment.

Our unfinished business typically is characterized by unresolved tensions, tensions that are clamoring for a resolution–to "be harmonized" in Whitehead's language. A frightened child needs protection and reassurance. If the child receives this at the time the fear was triggered, most likely this issue becomes adequately resolved at the time. If this does not happen, and if the fear is exceedingly intense or repeated often enough, then a yearning for resolution develops, a yearning made intense by the original intensity or by the repetition of the dilemma. This yearning, then, can reach across years of time and is triggered any time a similar fear is encountered in the present.

The search for a resolution to the pain and trauma involves the creation of what Whitehead calls *contrasts*. A contrast for Whitehead is when previously unharmonized dynamics, dynamics that war with each other, are brought together into a new, intense, and harmonized unity. The frightened child aspect of the adult is finally understood and validated in therapy, for example. This is the basis for a great deal of what happens in pastoral counseling, for the healing that occurs in therapy and the rest of life. The guidance for the creation of these healing contrasts comes via the initial aim; in other words, this is a sacred, spiritual process.

9. The Importance of Going Deep

Deep is where we find the initial aim, where we encounter the Divine in our souls. Enlarging its influence has to be one of the primary goals of all pastoral counseling (though we have to be ultra-careful not to impose or attempt to promote our ideas of what the Divine in another may be like). To accomplish this, we cannot always stay on the surface, either with our client or ourselves. We must permit and nudge the encounter to deeper and deeper levels through any of a variety of means: guided imagery, dream work, meditation, conversations that break through the surface gloss by pursuing the somatic-mental yanks that come along in most sessions and encounters. These often are those moments when we feel a charge of excitement and sense we are stepping out into the risky unknown.

Again, it is crucial that we as caregivers have done or are doing our own work, for if the motivation for this risk comes from one of our own immature, unintegrated aspects and not the sacred wisdom at our core, we can do a great deal of damage. Care also needs to be taken to monitor the process so that the individual does not become too unsettled; this requires familiarity with the other person's ability to dis-integrate and re-integrate.

10. Human Beings as Internally Related to the World– and Vice Versa

One of the most glorious and far-reaching insights of Whitehead is his clear understanding of how all of reality is essentially and internally related. Yes, that is an intellectual mouthful. What this means is that who we are at any given moment is literally constituted out of what is, for all practical purposes, the people and world around us, in addition to our own body and history. *How* this is put together is defined entirely by us at each moment. This self-definition is what we impose on what we have taken into our core. What is taken in, *per se*–our past, our body, and the world that impresses itself upon us–is not under our control. This means, for example, that the people we love *and* the people we hate are all a part of who we are. This means that God's shining love and wisdom is part of who we are. This means that the sweet flowers from the natural world are a part of who we are. Likewise, the destruction of this world, the human-to-human and human-to-world violence and other nastiness are a part of who we are.

This understanding becomes the basis for supporting clients in their efforts to create a beautiful place within which to live, a place of *shalom*. It becomes a rationale for encouraging clients and others to care for themselves, for those near to them, for their physical environment, and even their social-political environment. None of these is irrelevant for "mental health."

As caregivers, this understanding helps us know that we are a part of those with whom we work–and *visa versa*–for better and for worse. This should not be taken as a premise to strive for inner perfection or as a premise to avoid taking great pains to keep our caregiving relationships as safe and other-focused as possible. It is a premise that argues strongly for ongoing inner work, particularly if we seek to enter into the deepest portions of another's inner world.

It also helps us realize that we are definitely influenced and potentially shaped and changed by those with whom we work, particularly when this work is at a deep level. We are not the unmoved mover in these relationships. When and particularly how we are moved actually can become a critical part of the counseling. Freud called this *projective identification,* a term that refers to how a client sets up in the therapist (counselor, caregiver, pastor, employer) the feelings, moods, and even somatic dynamics that pertain to the issue with which he or she is struggling. This information can be a critically important clue. Over the years, I have been adored, idealized, despised, and detested by clients. I have been invited to be overly caring and invited to be a sadistic tormentor. In addition, I have had clients induce in me anxiety, sadness, manic energy, dissociation, as well as stomachaches, choking sensations, and other somatic events. All of these are potential clues as to the issues of the client. In all cases, I have to make sure these feelings and sensations are not originating from my own issues. Once that is settled, then they can become a powerful guide for my work.

The idea of internal relations also helps us see that if we are really disturbed by someone we encounter, disturbed to the point we too intensely dislike or too intensely like that person, it will distort not only the relationship but the other person as well. Even if these feelings are masked and never spoken of openly, they can have a powerful and potentially destructive influence. In these cases, if we cannot resolve the feelings in our own therapy or consultation, we must terminate and refer these people to others.

11. Decision Making as an Essence of Being Human: Leverage for Change and a Source of Hope and Pleasure

One of the less obvious but primary essences of being human is making decisions. From a process perspective, every moment is a new opportunity for a unique and potentially critical decision. This grows out of the fact that, according to the process metaphysics, each *actual occasion* makes a final determination (decision) as to how it will be for all eternity. While decisions at this micro level are not what we normally refer to when we use the phrase "making a decision," nonetheless any macro decision we make is constituted out of numerous micro decisions.

Why is that important? Because it is with decisions at the micro level that we as change facilitators have the most potential to make an impact. By burrowing down the minute details of a given decision, we have the power to illuminate what is really happening on a moment-by-moment basis. I have found that it is at this level that we can tease out the subtle differences to help a person gain control over his or her inner world. For example, if we say to people, "You need to get your act together," most likely they will not have a clue as to what to do or where to look. On the other hand, if we can help them discern the subtle nuances that go into their staying stuck, they will begin to get a handle on the tiny decisions in which they really have the power to make changes.

For example, a person in recovery from an addiction has to learn that the idea of stopping has to be reaffirmed on a moment-by-moment basis. This is the wisdom underlying the dictum, "One day at a time." Each impulse to drink or smoke or use gets countered with a solid "no" on an instance-by-instance basis. This is where the person has real power, instead of at the more general level of, "I must quit drinking, smoking, using; I must stay clean and sober." Persons attempting to make difficult changes, in which there are powerful and countervailing forces, have to learn to look below the generalized surface and get down to the details of their inner flow and see the situation afresh.

A second reason for the power of this perspective is that it makes clear that, despite the force of inertia (called *physical purpose* in the process scheme), we have the potential of small but radically new changes every single moment of existence. We never run out of opportunities to change until the moment we die. These new possibilities are offered afresh at every new moment. This is a powerful reason for hope.

Moreover, decision making can be a deep source of pleasure, particularly those decisions that we can recognize as our own, unique, individual decisions. This reflects the ontological essence of each actual occasion lifted to the full intensity of conscious awareness.

12. Goals for Therapy (and Life)

The process scheme holds out certain general values as ultimate, affirming that these values are the aim of both creation and the Creator. If these values are indeed ultimate, then it would be reasonable to make them the goals of all pastoral counseling, all psychotherapy, and of life itself. These values include intensity of experience as well as beauty, harmony, complexity, enjoyment, creativity, growth, diversity, inclusiveness, openness to others coupled with self-definition (autonomy), and pursuit of the common good.

This approach does not specify the specific plans, but provides instead a measure of the general worth of those plans. Hence it maximizes freedom and creativity, yet it is simultaneously capable of supporting a process of discernment. For example, while intensity of experience is perhaps the highest value,[17] nonetheless, it is important that this intensity be harmonized and produced by complexity with an aim at maximizing the common good. A cannon shot by itself could be judged as intense, but it would be downrated in comparison with a passage from the *1812 Overture* that includes such sounds. In a number of psychological conditions people exhibit great intensity of experience: relationship conflicts, a manic condition, certain facets of the borderline personality disorder experience, certain aspects of the schizophrenic experience, among others. In different ways, however, they would fail to embody some of the other central values.

In general, pastoral counselors (and all psychotherapists) should consider helping clients align themselves with these central values so that they can be in harmony with the direction of the universe, with the divine intention. It is crucial that the caregivers attend to these values in their own lives as well!

13. Clarifying Other Issues of Theory and Practice

Process thought can relate to a number of other issues in the theory and practice of pastoral counseling in a helpful and clarifying fashion. Elsewhere,[18] Whitehead's categories have been used to show why boundaries (a perpetually hot topic for therapists and the general public) are possible, necessary, yet difficult to maintain. The issue turns on the fact that at the physical pole of an actual occasion, the event has no boundaries; it is entirely open to the impact of the impinging world, entirely other-caused. At the mental pole, by contrast, the event has impermeable boundaries; it is entirely self-caused in this phase. When people are having struggles maintaining boundaries, they are allowing the physical pole of their experience to be overly influential. By contrast, when people are having struggles being open to others, they are allowing the mental pole of their experience to be overly influential.

Process thought has also proved valuable in illuminating dissociation,[19] projection,[20] and metaphors[21] (among other topics). While this brief essay is not the place for more expansion of these and other ideas, it is my experience that when process metaphysics is brought to bear upon a given topic, greater clarity inevitably results. This will need to await further development in other writing.

14. The Basis for a Metatheory of the Psyche (and Psychology)

Whitehead's metaphysics aims at universal applicability. As such, to the degree that it succeeds, it provides the broad and diverse fields of psychology and psychotherapy with the potential to guide the development of a metatheory. No theory or approach to theory or treatment has to be excluded due to arbitrary reasons or reasons of personal preference. This is not to imply that the process perspective will be equally supportive or validating, for it will not be.

What might be the value of a metatheory? While the full value of a metatheory ultimately will be known only after it has been created, some of the value can be predicted:

1. A good metatheory should lead to new and more productive lines of research and beneficial applications. If a comprehensive theory better matches the actual world (the goal and test of a good theory), then it is reasonable to assume it will result in improved research and results. On the other side of this coin, a strong metatheory could diminish the pursuit of conceptual and empirical dead-ends.
2. A strong metatheory can function as a *lingua franca*, a common language for communication across all of psychology. This would permit those in far-flung areas of psychology more easily to exchange ideas. Today, by contrast, these disparate areas tend either to ignore or deride what lies outside their particular boundaries.
3. By the same token, a viable metatheory could eliminate at least some of the time, energy, and money wasted in countless professional and personal exchanges in which colleagues are talking at cross purposes with each other.

Whitehead's metaphysics is a promising basis for this proposed metatheory because increasingly it is being taken seriously by key physicists, as well as biologists, educators, feminists, mathematicians, philosophers, political scientists, psychologists, and theologians, among other professionals.[22]

Concluding Thoughts

This essay has attempted to provide a reasonable array of topics important to the professional of pastoral counseling to which process thought speaks. No doubt, another author would highlight other issues. Nonetheless, the hope is that this article covers enough ground to trigger in the reader some new and tantalizing insights, sufficient to motivate you to pursue all of this more fully. And that has been my personal, ongoing relationship with these ideas. They continue relentlessly to function as lures for my own conceptual and personal growth. I hope that this essay will do the same for others.

CHAPTER 10

Process Perspectives on Sexuality, Love, and Marriage

■ KATHLYN A. BREAZEALE

Love…is a little oblivious as to morals.
It does not look to the future;
For it finds its own reward in the immediate present.

ALFRED NORTH WHITEHEAD (PR 343)

In spite of Whitehead's view that love "is a little oblivious as to morals" and not concerned for the future, process thinkers throughout the decades since Whitehead wrote these words have proposed theologies of love, sexuality, marriage, and sexual ethics. Following the theories of Whitehead's contemporary Sigmund Freud, process thinkers have argued passionately for the centrality and power of sexuality in human life. However, they have used the biblical doctrine of the goodness of creation to argue for the inherent goodness of sexuality. Many have discussed relevant biblical passages to demonstrate that their position is not opposed to biblical teachings regarding particular sexual practices. They have utilized Whitehead's philosophy to explain the relationship between God and human sexual love, to overcome the Western dualism of body and soul, and to propose sexual ethics. Thus, process thinkers have much to offer to our contemporary debates about heterosexuality, homosexuality, love, and marriage.

The first part of this essay presents a historical overview of the theologies and ethics developed by four first and second generation process theologians: Henry Nelson Wieman, Daniel Day Williams, W. Norman Pittenger, and John B. Cobb Jr.[1] I discuss how each theologian's view of sexuality, love, and/or marriage emerges from the theologian's key theological point and how the theology then leads to a particular ethical imperative. In the second part of this essay, I draw on this rich heritage and subsequent process thinkers to construct a process theology of intimate partner relationships as one response to the current debates about marriage. This essay concludes with a summary of the primary themes in process understandings of sexuality.

A History of Process Perspectives: Wieman, Williams, Pittenger, and Cobb

We must conceive the Divine Eros as the active entertainment of all ideals, with the urge to their finite realization, each in its due season. Thus a process must be inherent in God's nature, whereby his infinity is acquiring realization. (AI 277)

Whitehead's vision of God as Divine Eros captured the imagination of these four process theologians who addressed issues of sexuality, love, marriage, and sexual ethics. A common theme in much of their work is that human sexuality is one means for humans to participate in and manifest divine love,[2] and thus sexual activity should be guided by God's purposes.

In *The Source of Human Good*, Henry Nelson Wieman asserts that the source of human good is the "creative process" that always transforms the human mind toward the intrinsic good or "qualitative meaning."[3] Sexuality has an important role to play because "more than anything else, [it] is what renders [humans][4] capable of undergoing great creative transformations in the direction of an indefinite increase of qualitative meaning."[5] For Wieman, sexuality has this transformative power because he believes that "the major transformations leading to richness of meaning" are occasions associated with sexuality: birth, adolescence, finding a life partner to love, marriage, and the birth of children.[6] However, human expressions of sexuality are not limited to a fixed pattern or only for the purpose of reproduction; rather, "there is no known limit to [sexuality's] transformability and the richness and variety of qualitative meaning that it may yield."[7] Thus, human sexuality provides "enormous potentialities for good and for evil."[8]

Wieman also has high regard for sexual love because the "coercive outreaches of sexuality" break down the "protective resistances to human responsiveness" necessary for the development of other kinds of love, and sexual love is perhaps most "effective in opening the way for the work of creative transformation."[9] Wieman utilizes the construction of the two traditional categories of human sexuality, male and female, to argue that the primary social unit is the "intimate group," not the "biological individual."[10] This fact of relatedness is fundamental to Wieman's definition of humanity and provides an example of how sexuality is related to Whitehead's theory of internal relations: "The human being is simply not human except in relation to the intimate group."[11] For Wieman, the work of creative transformation in the intimate group is idealized as "the undreamed of transfiguration of a world [that] hovers over every union of man and woman where love breaks the constraints of self-protective concern, opening the way to deepest appreciative interchange."[12]

Wieman's view of sexual ethics follows from the centrality of sexuality in the work of creative transformation:

> Moral standards are effective not primarily by establishing prohibitions but by directing interest, impulse, and behavior into channels which open the way for creative transformation in the direction of richer meaning. One of the dangers which moral standards should be set up to prevent is the narrow obsessive interest which sex may come to possess.[13]

Precisely because sexuality is such a central and powerful force for the work of creative transformation, sexual ethics should serve to direct this force for the good. The proposition that ethics should submit sexuality to the greater good will be articulated by subsequent process theologians as well.

While there has been debate about whether or not Wieman can be considered a Christian theologian,[14] the next group of process theologians who addressed issues of sexuality explicitly claimed their positions were informed by their Christian faith. Writing in the context of the mid-twentieth-century sexual revolution that advocated freedom of sexual expression with the goal of personal fulfillment, John B. Cobb Jr., W. Norman Pittenger, and Daniel Day Williams often admonished and challenged the church as they developed their theologies of sexuality, love, and sexual ethics.

For example, in 1960 Cobb proposed "The Christian Understanding of Sexuality" in an unpublished paper. In this paper, Cobb advocates that the church encourage a return to the New Testament view of sexuality in which there is "no suppression or repression of sexual interests, no prudery, but there is a spontaneous transference of the center of concern which relegates questions of sex to a secondary importance."[15] Cobb works out a process philosophical basis for his position that sexuality should be subordinated to larger concerns in his discussion of love and ethics in *A Christian Natural Theology*. Here Cobb acknowledges Whitehead's statement that love is somewhat oblivious to morals (see the quotation at the beginning of this chapter). However, Cobb asserts that although a "real tension" exists between love and ethics, the two are not contradictory because "only as there is love of one's own future self and love also for other persons, and finally, for humanity as a whole, can there be any meaning to the ethical imperatives."[16] While love is "unjust" in that we love some people more than others, human freedom enables us to resolve the tension between love and ethics. Following Whitehead's philosophy, freedom exists in the individual's ability to modify its "subjective aim" or purpose. Thus we can choose to balance desires for immediate fulfillment with future possibilities, and we can commit ourselves to codes of conduct that will enable the fullest future possibilities for all.[17]

In contrast to Cobb's discussion of the tension between love and ethics, Daniel Day Williams in *The Spirit and the Forms of Love* posits the *agape* of God as the locus for sexual ethics. Williams is concerned to explore the relationship between agape and human eros. One clue to understanding this relationship is the fact that all loves, including sexual love and God's love for humans, "work within the history of the self's becoming. No love...is a 'thing,' a static pattern or form. It is a spirit at work in life and taking form in the process of becoming."[18] Therefore, Williams holds that in establishing a Christian sexual ethic, the first principle is that sexuality "should be so ordered, disciplined, and released that sexual love becomes a creative aspect of the life of agape, the giving of each person in service to God and...neighbour [sic]."[19] Furthermore, Williams attributes great value to sexuality when he asserts that sexuality is "a human analogue of the creativity of God, and a primary source of human creativity."[20] However, human creativity includes "pain, discipline, frustrations, and ambiguities" as well as "delight and joy."[21]

This acknowledgment of the ambiguous power of creativity leads Williams to his second principle for a Christian sexual ethic: Sexuality is both essentially good and distorted by sin. Thus, sexual ethics should not be focused on judging particular acts as inherently good or bad. Rather, "the ethical test of any action [is] its consequences not only for one individual, but for the whole community."[22] The new sexual freedom of his time had aroused public debate about the issues of premarital intercourse, marriage fidelity, and divorce. In response Williams asserts that the basis for "Christian judgment about sexual practice" is "what does the practice do to the creation of loving mutually supporting persons who can grow in love to God and the neighbour [sic], who also have tendencies to exploit one another, and who must find disciplines of self-protection and self-restraint for the sake of love?"[23]

Williams advocates the Christian ideal of monogamous marriage as the best possibility for the development of such loving persons:

> But the Christian conception of the life commitment of one person to another in a sexual union is justified fundamentally as a recognition of the highest possibilities of human love, not as a concession to human weakness or a search for a convenient way to preserve social order.[24]

Williams believes that the revolt against Christian standards was occurring because the church had tended "to treat sex as incidental to the fulfillment of marriage," and left the area of sexual experience before marriage "in a limbo of silence or prohibition."[25] Thus, while affirming the Christian ideal of marriage, Williams is offering his Christian sexual ethic to break the silence of the church's teachings and provide guidance for both unmarried and married persons.

Another process theologian who sought to provide such guidance was W. Norman Pittenger. One of the most prolific process thinkers in addressing issues of sexuality, he published seven books dealing with this topic between 1969 and 1982. Similar to Williams, Pittenger uses his understanding of God's love as the foundation for his Christian theology of sexuality and ethics. However, whereas Williams starts with the New Testament concept of the agape of God,

Pittenger begins with human experience. In *The Only Meaning* Pittenger writes that God "is known to us chiefly in our own human loving."[26] Love is "the only meaning" to which the title of this book refers. Pittenger claims that love is the core of God's identity and mode of operation as known through Jesus of Nazareth. Here Pittenger adopts Whitehead's claim that "the Galilean origin of Christianity" presents an image of God as "dwell[ing] upon the tender elements in the world, which slowly and in quietness operate by love;...Love [that] neither rules, nor is it unmoved" (PR 343). With this concept of God as the "chief exemplification" of the "highest and best" of human love, Pittenger asserts that sexual expression brings fulfillment of God's purposes "only in the context of commitment, mutuality, fidelity, tenderness, and hope."[27] Pittenger holds this context as the ideal love for both heterosexual and homosexual persons: "To ask them [homosexuals] to deny that love would be to demand that they cease being human;...for God's sake,...remembering...that God *is* love...let us not seek to kill love."[28]

In *Making Sexuality Human,* Pittenger continues to develop his position regarding the relationship between sexuality and humanity. He asserts that "to 'make sexuality human,' in the most profound sense, is to open up for it the opportunity to be an instrument in the hands of God himself, so that God may express his own creative nature and delight in what it brings about."[29] Pittenger offers his definitions of God as "the cosmic Love or Lover" and of a human as "lover-in-the-making."[30] He holds that these definitions are consistent with Christian faith and with process thought:

> Thus there is no contradiction, in this [process] conceptuality as a context for Christian faith and commitment, between God's purpose for [humans] and their own decision, taken with the freedom that is appropriate to them, to move in this or that direction towards the fulfillment of their potentialities in community with other [humans]– and in relationship to the natural order as well as to the divine Love.[31]

Pittenger's position sets out these key points:

1. sexuality is human when it is open to God the cosmic Lover's purposes.
2. human becoming or lover-in-the-making is social as well as personal.

Based on these, Pittenger offers a sexual ethic founded on three words: *permissiveness, affection,* and *responsibility.* By *permissiveness,* Pittenger means that human beings must live in a society in which they are free to make their own decisions. Otherwise, moral agency disappears. In the sexual realm, Pittenger defines *affection* as genuine love or total commitment to the other's well-being and fulfillment of potentiality, free of coercion or pressure. *Responsibility* is understood as considering the consequences of one's actions for oneself, one's partner, and society.[32]

Pittenger states that "most people, most of the time" will fulfill this ethic through marriage. He affirms the traditional Christian views of marriage as "a sign of God's action in the world" and as a symbol of "the fellowship that [humans are] intended to enjoy with [their] Creator."[33] Pittenger also advocates his sexual ethic for homosexuals whose "aim should be at establishing a relationship with another that will be as permanent as possible," marked by the qualities of genuine love as described above.[34]

In *Love and Control in Sexuality,* Pittenger elaborates on his ethic of sexuality. Because humans have a degree of freedom to make decisions, "self-imposed controls" are needed to move us "toward our fullest possible selfhood as lovers."[35] Controls are also needed to reduce the proliferation of sin, which Pittenger defines as breaking the "relationships given in and intended for growth in love" among humans and between God and humans.[36] Pittenger is adamant that these controls are not externally imposed; rather, these controls "are intimately present in human nature itself, since *love* is what [humans are] becoming and [love] is therefore integral to [them] in that becoming."[37] In the "permissive society" of the 1970s, Pittenger implores Christians to use this ability given by God to formulate controls of love for sexual expression.[38]

Pittenger thus defines "human" as a process of becoming more loving in relationship with other humans and with God who is the cosmic Lover. He views creating a union of mutual fulfillment as the primary purpose of human sexuality. On this basis Pittenger, as a Christian theologian, affirms homosexual love. In *Time for Consent: A Christian's Approach to Homosexuality* and *Gay Lifestyles: A Christian Interpretation of Homosexuality and the Homosexual,* Pittenger presents his case for why the church should welcome homosexual persons and bless their desire for long-term committed relationships. Pittenger asserts that homosexual persons have "the need to give oneself to another who gives in return [that] is so deep in our common humanity." He argues: "When homosexual men and women try to live 'in love,' in the sense here defined, they are fulfilling themselves and acting in accordance with God's purpose."[39]

Pittenger believes that "holy union," not "marriage," should be used to designate committed homosexual relationships because of the accumulated historical, sociological, ecclesiastical, and legal aspects of the institution of marriage, which designates a particular heterosexual relationship that usually includes the expectation of procreation.[40] And, in contrast to his earlier affirmation of the Christian marriage ideal, Pittenger is critical of the "closed character" of conventional marriage. He advocates the "open marriage" approach as more realistic and growth-producing for both homosexual and heterosexual couples.[41]

Pittenger wrote two more books that include chapters addressing issues of sexuality: *The Lure of Divine Love: Christian Experience and Christian Faith in a Process Perspective* and *The Meaning of Being Human.* Pittenger reiterates his belief in the centrality of sexuality for humans as "lovers-in-the-making" by designating human sexuality as "a symbol for the ambiguity of all human life in its genuine potentiality and in its tragic failure."[42] He makes a plea that young people be assisted in making responsible decisions about sexual activity before marriage, that divorce be accepted as the best decision in some situations, and that because marriage is an opportunity for "the development of selfhood," marriage partners should respect each other's "distinctive personalities" so that a "real union of two" is possible.[43] Pittenger affirms homosexual love because this type of love reminds us that procreation is not the primary purpose of human sexuality; rather, "the real purpose of sexual relationships is union and sharing...mutuality and giving-and-receiving at the deepest level of the two selves."[44]

In 1984, John Cobb wrote what became the first in a long series of publications challenging the church to thoughtfully address issues of sexuality. In "Is the Church Ready to Legislate on Sex?" Cobb answers this question in the negative. However, he affirms that the church is ready to *think* about "the whole range of issues related to sexuality before reverting to blind moralism" regarding the issue of the ordination of homosexuals.[45] Cobb identifies these issues as heterosexual activity outside of marriage, divorce, successive marriages, and all homosexual activity. In his discussion of homosexuality, he questions why the church "appears to make no distinction between long-term faithful relationships and utter promiscuity."[46]

Why did Cobb choose to begin writing again on issues of sexuality after his previous work on this topic some twenty years earlier? Cobb explains:

> I have never been condemnatory of gay people. But for much of my career, I thought this negative virtue was sufficient. There were, I supposed, more important issues to deal with...In the mid-seventies I was aroused from this complacency by a Mexican-American friend, Ignacio Castuera. Castuera had introduced me to Latin American liberation theology, and I admired his leadership in that field. But I was startled when he began speaking publicly against the moral condemnation of homosexual acts. Would it not be better, I asked him, to concentrate on the important issues raised by liberation theology?...Castuera replied that if he were to be true to liberation theology, he must be especially concerned for those who are *most* oppressed in our society. He had come to the conclusion that these are gay people...Since then I have not been able to be silent.[47]

I have quoted this candid statement at length because it enables the reader to sense the person behind the theological and ethical writing. Cobb as a Christian theologian is driven by his own ethical commitments to take a stand on controversial issues.

Cobb's next major treatment of sexual issues was a chapter in *Matters of Life and Death* in which he proposes a Christian ideal: "The ideal is of sexual activity only within committed relations, serving the deepening and personalizing of these relations, and subordinating even these relations to larger purposes."[48] Cobb explains these "larger purposes" in two principles that undergird this ideal. First, sexuality is good, yet if sexual fulfillment becomes an end in itself, it becomes "idolatrous and, therefore, demonic." Second, because life is lived in community, the best decisions "will express the mutual responsibility that sustains the community."[49] Cobb believes that this consideration of "larger purposes" is "essential to a Christian approach to sexuality" and is the central point "lacking in the sexual revolution."[50] Cobb urges the church to adopt this ideal as the criteria for "open affirmation and sanctioning of both heterosexual and homosexual bondings other than heterosexual marriage."[51]

Cobb explicitly articulates how process thought informs his views on sexuality in "The Mission of the Church, Part II."[52] By transforming dualisms (the more of A, the less of B) into polarities (the more of A, the more of B), process thought offers an alternative to either/or thinking. Thus, for example, "we become wiser not by denying our bodies but by becoming more sensitive to them."[53] Cobb urges the church to apply this process perspective to the debates about homosexuality as a third option between simply adopting biblical teachings abstracted from their historical context or trying to identify a few basic Christian principles that are unaffected by time.[54] "The process approach is to find in the scriptures themselves changing teachings adapting the Jewish and early Christian movements to their circumstances and mission."[55] With this understanding of the past teachings as continually changing to meet the challenges of the time, the process approach "seeks to discern the patterns of sexual practice today that are most faithful to the living God here and now."[56]

Cobb continued his explanation of a process view of homosexuality in "What Shall the Church Say about Homosexuality?" co-authored with Mary Ellen Kilsby and William A. Beardslee. After discussing points made in Cobb's previous publications, the authors explain how a process perspective disputes essentialist and legalistic thinking.

The notion that homosexuality is against nature is based on the natural law theory that procreation is the essential purpose of sexual intercourse. This "essentialism" is unacceptable because the purpose of sexuality can be found in the purposes of those who engage in sexual acts, not in a single essence that defines its universal purpose. Nothing is "unnatural" about heterosexuals engaging in sexual acts only for mutual enjoyment; thus there is no reason to deny homosexual acts for mutual pleasure.[57] Legalism occurs when a particular act is judged apart from the intentions and consequences in the particular context. Whereas "both Jesus and Paul encouraged freedom from the law," therefore Christians are "to become sufficiently mature to discern what is called for in diverse situations" and thus order sexual activity to the "larger purposes" of the "service of God and other people."[58]

Thus a process perspective does not simply judge homosexual acts as inherently wrong, nor does it endorse the view that "sex is for enjoyment."[59] Rather, the process perspective challenges the church to be concerned about the "wider framework" in which both homosexual and heterosexual relations take place. Although Paul believed marriage often interfered with Christian service, he taught it was better to marry than "to be aflame with passion"

(1 Cor. 7:9b). This same truth applies to homosexuals, yet the church is more ready to tolerate secret casual acts than public long-term faithful relationships between two women or men who ask to be treated as a couple.[60] A process perspective calls the church to repentance:

> It is a severe criticism of the church that its negative teaching and practice…have frequently made it more difficult for gay men and lesbians to find stable and committed relationships, for it is in such a setting that sexual intercourse can express full personal affection and trust.[61]

By establishing the norm of faithful, committed relationships as the best context for heterosexual and homosexual intercourse, the church can use this as the criteria for evaluating both heterosexual and homosexual candidates for ministry. "From the point of view of process theology, this would be justice."[62]

Cobb continued to advocate justice for homosexuals in "Being Christian about Homosexuality."[63] After establishing his case that homosexual acts are not inherently immoral (as detailed above), he reiterates his plea that the church recommend a lifestyle for Christian homosexuals with consideration for both the individuals and society. He asserts that the Christian goal is "human flourishing, holistic personal fulfillment for all." Most Christians believe that this "occurs best in the context of committed relationships that include sexual love."[64] Thus, the church should "teach this ideal without apology" for both heterosexuals and homosexuals.[65]

Supplementary to his writing to the church, Cobb addresses society as a whole in *Postmodernism and Public Policy: Reframing Religion, Culture, Education, Sexuality, Class, Race, Politics, and the Economy.*[66] Here he is concerned in bringing a process perspective to bear on the formation of public policy. Following his vision for church polity, he advocates that society should offer the ideal for sexual expression as "long-term equal bonding" in which "mutual responsibility and love are secured" as the best option for individuals and for society.[67] Yet, behavior that "falls short of these ideals should not be condemned as immoral or made illegal, except when it endangers or damages others."[68] Reiterating his advocacy for homosexual unions, Cobb asserts that the legal and ecclesiastical sanctioning of these unions is "the most urgently needed step in the process of ending discrimination against gays and lesbians." He holds that patriarchal society's "demand for universal heterosexuality is one of the most obvious" forms of patriarchal oppression.[69]

Toward a Process Theology of Partnership: Redemption through Intimacy and Mutual Empowerment[70]

The same-sex marriage controversy has demanded public debate about the institution of marriage. Yet amidst this controversy about homosexual unions, the fact is that heterosexual marriage is in trouble in the United States: 65 percent of marriages end in divorce, and wives initiate 60–75 percent of these divorces.[71] One implication of these statistics is the breakdown of traditional religious beliefs regarding heterosexual marriage roles. Thus as we enter the twenty-first century, we have the opportunity to reconsider our theological understanding of one of the most intimate aspects of our lives. So, we ask: How could a feminist process perspective contribute to creating a post-patriarchal theology of union and marriage?

Whitehead's theory of relationality holds that we are continually being constituted by our relationships. Our personal and corporate identity is dynamic; just as we are shaped by external influences, so we impact that which is other than ourselves: "There is no entity which enjoys an isolated self-sufficiency of existence."[72] Marjorie Hewitt Suchocki poetically describes this ontological relatedness of all creation when she writes: "The world as described by process thought may indeed be beautiful, but it is also dangerous."[73] The danger arises from the fact that relationality is an inescapable fact of existence, making us peculiarly vulnerable to each other. Thus, our intimate partner relationships are one of our greatest opportunities both for sin and for redemption.

I define sin as a violation of our interrelatedness that causes harm to oneself or to another. I understand redemption as creative transformation toward the good (following Wieman as described above), and I agree with other process thinkers (for example, Suchocki) who have argued that redemption can occur only in community.[74] In proposing how a process theology of partner relationships can enhance our opportunity for redemption through intimacy, I discuss three issues: power, the concept of God, and the relationality between body and soul.

Power

Marriage has been an unequal power relationship throughout most of Western history, with the husband having legal and religious power over his wife. During the Roman period, only upper-class men and women were allowed to marry, and these men had the power of life and death over their wives through the law of *pater familias*.[75] In England, medieval and Reformation period husbands could exercise their power through the common law "rule of thumb," which gave a husband permission to beat his wife with a stick as long as the stick was no thicker than his thumb.[76] The battered wife had virtually no power to seek redress from either religious or legal authorities.

For example, most Christian leaders held that wives should submit to their husbands based on biblical texts such as Ephesians 5:22: "Wives, be subject to your husbands as you are to the Lord."[77] Legally, wives had virtually no identity separate from their husbands until the early decades of this century when women won the right to vote.[78] One ramification of these centuries of power imbalance is the current statistic regarding violence against women: three out of four offenders committing domestic violence are spouses, ex-spouses, boyfriends, or ex-boyfriends.[79]

Process theologians have argued that the concept of power as dominance over others creates a barrier to love and intimacy. For example, Bernard Loomer writes:

> If power always means the exercising of influence and control, and if
> receiving always means weakness and a lack of power, then a creative
> and strong love that comprises a mutual giving and receiving is not
> possible.[80]

Rita Nakashima Brock builds on Loomer's work as she describes how the
traditional dominant male/subordinate female arrangement exploits both
women and men:

> While the male seeks to dominate those with less power, he is expected
> to sacrifice himself to God, country, or company. Hence, while self-
> sacrifice and martyrdom seem more feminine, being exploited is
> expected of men for the sake of higher authority...In addition, both
> male domination and female dependency require the suppression of
> the self's own feelings.[81]

Thus as we are socialized to behave according to gender role stereotypes,
we must suppress our own feelings. This suppression creates effective barriers
to the genuine intimacy we could experience with each other.

In contrast to the concept of power as dominance and control, or unilateral
power, Loomer identifies an alternative concept of power as relational.
Relational power "is the ability both to produce and to undergo an effect...[it]
involves both a giving and a receiving."[82] Similarly, Brock describes relational
power as the power that exists in the interactions of the relating:

> We must move away from seeing power as a commodity possessed
> by a self toward seeing it as the bonds which create and sustain, and
> are recreated and sustained by relational selves.[83]

In a process theology of intimate partner relationships, both partners are
empowered through the practice of relational power. This practice releases
each partner from preconceived power roles of dominance or submission.
Through both giving and receiving, partners are free to express their authentic
feelings, thus creating bonds of mutual empowerment and possibilities for
genuine, redemptive intimacy.

In suggesting the concept of redemptive intimacy, I am building on
Loomer's notion of the "true good." He asserts that the "true good is an emergent
from deeply mutual relationships."[84] Loomer argues that even when love for
the other motivates one to seek to control the other for the other's good, the
exercise of unilateral power has the limitation of a preconceived good. The
preconceived good is a limitation because it "often exemplifies the conscious
or unconscious desire to transform the other in one's own image."

For example, if I seek to transform you in my own image, I pressure you
to suppress your authentic feelings. Then intimacy is blocked. I have sinned
against you by seeking to limit the possibilities for the self you are becoming
and the possibilities for the selves we can become together. Loomer describes

how the possibilities for each partner emerge from the particularities of the partner relationship itself:

> A wife is not the occasion whereby a man actualizes husbandly possibilities that reside or subsist wholly within the confines of his enclosed selfhood. The husbandly and wifely possibilities of the respective partners are peculiar to and are created out of that particular marital relationship in which each helps to create the other. The more deeply mutual and creative the relationship, the wider the range of emergent possibilities for those participating in the relationship.[85]

God

In seeking to conceive how partners can experience redemption through practicing relational power, one must also address the traditional concept of God. This is necessary because the association of the husband's authority with divine authority has been one of the primary justifications for the traditional power imbalance between husbands and wives. In 1998, the Southern Baptist Convention affirmed this power imbalance with their resolution that: "A wife is to submit graciously to the servant leadership of her husband even as the church willingly submits to the headship of Christ."[86] Proposing an alternative to the traditional concept of power in partner relationships thus necessitates proposing an alternative to the traditional concept of God.

In contrast to the omnipotent, impassible, "unmoved mover" of traditional Christian theology, Whitehead proposes that God's "Consequent Nature" is determined largely by the actions of the world (PR 345). Embracing Whitehead's notion of the Consequent Nature of God enhances our capacity for intimacy in relationship because this notion of God's relationship to humans is intimate: We participate in God's becoming complete.[87] History has demonstrated that our human relationships mirror our image of our relationship to God. For example, the image of God ruling over creation is mirrored in the image of the husband ruling over his wife. Following the Whiteheadian notion of God, this hierarchical image of God's rule is turned on its side; power flows from God to creatures *and* from creatures to God. We become co-creators with God, and we experience our relationship with God as a creative process. This experience can encourage us to risk a relationship of creative process with a human partner. This creative process includes the practice of relational power, the giving and receiving necessary for honest communication and empathy. Whitehead's description of God's love as both giving and receiving becomes the ultimate model for how we can love each other and create genuine intimacy.

> What is done in the world is transformed into a reality in heaven, and the reality in heaven passes back into the world. By reason of this reciprocal relation, the love in the world passes into the love in heaven, and floods back again into the world. In this sense, God is the great companion–the fellow-sufferer who understands. (PR 351)

Body and Soul [88]

Similar to the traditional correlation of God's authority with the husband's authority to legitimize the husband's rule over his wife, the association of male with the superior soul and female with the inferior body has been another primary justification for the rule of the husband. These associations from classical Greek philosophy were incorporated into Christian theology and have functioned to devalue both the body and women. This devaluation has been further exacerbated by the Christian association of sin with women, the body, and sexuality.[89]

An alternative to this traditional Greek and Christian hierarchy of male/soul over female/body is found in Whitehead's ontology of relationality between body and soul. Foundational to Whitehead's conception of how body and soul are related is his principle that reality is composed of occasions of experience. As each occasion of experience is coming into being, it has a "physical pole" through which it receives the influence of the past or actuality, and a "mental pole" through which it entertains the possibility of novelty. Both body and soul are composed of occasions that have physical and mental poles, so a simple association of physical with body and mental with soul is not accurate in Whitehead's philosophy.

Although the mental pole of every occasion, cellular or psychic, is the occasion's entertainment of new possibilities, the body is organized as to allow one type of occasion, that which constitutes the soul, to be especially affected by novelty and then to transmit that novelty to successive occasions so that the novelty is cumulative. This accumulation constitutes the soul as a "living person." As a result, the soul is the locus of the entertainment of ideas for the whole body (AI 275). Because the body is organized so that bodily sensations or feelings are "poured" into the ongoing moments of the soul (MT 211), the occasions of experience that constitute the soul can include more elements of bodily experiences than any other individual part of the body. Thus the body depends on the soul as a center of organization for the perceptions of the human being. Yet simultaneously, the soul depends on the body. The body provides the most immediate and most influential environment for the soul as the body mediates the contemporary world to the soul through experiences of space and time. Whitehead explains this bodily mediation as the "withness of the body":

> For we feel *with the body*. There may be some further specialization into a particular organ of sensation; but in any case the '*withness' of the body* is an ever present, though elusive, element in our perceptions… (PR 311–12, emphasis in original)

Although the soul is not limited to the influence of the bodily environment–for example, the soul can directly prehend the past through memory–the body is primary because the soul is constituted by the actual world of experience mediated through the body. The soul also depends on the body to provide for the ongoing existence of the soul: "The continuity of the soul–so far as concerns consciousness–has to leap gaps in time. We sleep or we are stunned. Yet it is the same person who recovers consciousness…Thus…the body in particular provide[s] the stuff for the personal endurance of the soul" (MT 162). Thus Whitehead understands that the soul depends on the body and the body depends on the soul in a relationship of mutuality.

This process of mutuality through which body and soul develop is also evidenced as body and soul guide each other through shared experiences. Through the body's perceptions of its surroundings, the body guides the soul; the soul receives both the influence of the past and God's best possibility for the person at that moment in the given situation. The soul is free within the context of its present to appropriate the past without being bound to the past. In this way the soul guides the body. The traditional hierarchy of superior soul over inferior body is overcome through Whitehead's metaphysics of reciprocity between body and soul.

Extending his theories beyond the individual human being, Whitehead also describes the relationship between the soul and the world:

> the experienced world is one complex factor in the composition of many factors constituting the essences of the soul…in one sense the world is in the soul. But antithetical[ly]…our experience of the world involves the exhibition of the soul itself as one of the components within the world. (MT 163)

Thus Whitehead's metaphysics provide an explanation of the relationality of all creation: the world is a factor in the constitution of the soul, and the soul is one more factor that constitutes the world.

Whitehead's metaphysics of body-soul relationality overturns the traditional hierarchy of superior soul over inferior body, providing clues for developing a theology of intimate partner relationships. First, the body is not inferior to the soul because both body and soul are constituted by shared experiences in a relationship of reciprocity as body and soul alternately guide each other. The body is a source of wisdom for the soul as the body mediates experiences of the actual world to the soul. Thus, the bodies of both partners should be reverenced as the body has a primary role in physical and spiritual development.

Second, Whitehead's position undercuts the traditional association of soul with male and body with female because gender is not assigned to either body or soul. Therefore, the primacy of the body in daily experience is acknowledged for both partners as human beings. Whereas the body is not inferior, and woman is not associated with the body, therefore the wife is not considered to be inferior to her husband. The theological justification for her subordination to him on the basis of her inferiority is repudiated.

In summary, based on the Whiteheadian principle that our personal identity is constituted by our relationships, I have suggested that our intimate partner relationships are one of our greatest opportunities both for sin and for redemption. I have proposed how partners might experience redemptive intimacy by practicing relational power, thus creating the "true good" that can emerge only in mutual relationships. Furthermore, I have described how our capacity for intimacy is enhanced by embracing the Whiteheadian notion of the Consequent Nature of God. As we experience the intimacy of co-creating with God by participating in forming the divine nature, we can be encouraged to risk the intimacy of co-creating mutuality with a human partner. Finally, I have shown how intimacy is also enhanced through Whitehead's conception of reciprocity in the relationship between body and soul. Freed from the traditional associations of male/superior soul ruling over female/inferior body, partners are enabled to practice relational power.

A Response

How can this process theology of intimate partner relationships be helpful in the current marriage debates? One answer to this question is found in the fact that in the process world of relationality, my partner and I not only influence the becoming of each other for good or evil, we also influence the becoming of our community. Suchocki describes this dynamic influence:

> The value of communities as well as the value of individuals is to be judged finally not simply in terms of self-significance, but in terms of significance for others in the increasingly wider communities of the world and universe.[90]

Therefore, I hold that one criterion for determining sanctioned partnerships in our society is not the gender of the two persons, but rather, what quality of partner relationships will enable the greatest development of good for the partners and in the community? In agreement with Loomer, I have argued that the "true good" can only emerge through the practice of relational power in deeply mutual relationships. With relational power as our criterion, we could simultaneously strive toward mutual empowerment in our intimate partnerships and work to change social structures that perpetuate violence and oppression through unilateral power.

Clearly, the continued practice of unilateral power will facilitate the destruction of all of us in our ecologically fragile nuclear age, ravaged by war and threats of war. However, as Loomer writes:

> the practice of relational power is an incredibly difficult art to master. This type of power requires the most disciplined kind of mutual encouragement and criticism. The creative openness to this type of relationship involves possibilities of the greatest advance and the greatest risk.[91]

My hope is that we will develop the "mutual encouragement and criticism" to risk mutual empowerment both in our intimate partnerships and in our communities.

Conclusion: God, Sexual Love, and Ethics in Community

The contributions of process theology to understandings of human sexuality can be summarized in three areas: as defining God's nature and the relationship between God and human sexual love; overcoming the views of the self as a discrete individual and the dualism of body and soul developed in traditional Western philosophy and theology; and proposing sexual ethics for both heterosexual and homosexual persons.

Process understandings of God challenge the image of an apathetic, impassible Being. God is named as Divine Eros, Creative Transformation, Agape, and Cosmic Lover. Part of God's nature develops as God relates to creation, a creation in the process of being constituted by interdependent relationships. Thus human possibilities for intimacy are enhanced as humans relate to God and to creation. Whitehead's philosophy postulates that both body and soul are composed of shared experiences as the human is continually coming-into-being in community with God and creation. Body and soul develop in a mutually dependent relationship as each alternately guides the other. Dualism is transformed into polarity so that the wisdom of the body and the wisdom of the soul develop in proportion to each other.

With these foundational understandings of God, body, and soul, process theology suggests that human sexuality is both an opportunity for God to express God's own creative nature and a primary, powerful source for human creativity. As humans have the freedom to express creativity through sexual intimacy, our sexuality has enormous potential for good and evil, for sin and redemption. Precisely because sexuality is such a central element in the developing of human life and God's life, process theology argues that sexual expression should be ordered toward the good of the fullest possibilities for all in the community. Process theologians have argued that humans can best fulfill our possibilities for participating in Divine Love and for loving ourselves and others when our sexual love is expressed in committed, mutually empowering partnerships that sustain the community. Thus process theology offers a sexual ethical ideal for gay men and lesbians, as well as for heterosexual couples before and during marriage. This ideal offers a vision of God, intimate partnerships, and community in which the richest possibilities for both love and justice can be fulfilled.

CHAPTER 11

Reflections on Cinema, Spirituality, and Process

■ DONNA BOWMAN

The power of artistic productions to mediate or even elicit spirituality has been well known, if infrequently theorized, throughout human history, and perhaps prehistory as well. In fact, the function of art tended to be primarily spiritual and religious, at least in the West, until the birth of secularity in the Renaissance and Enlightenment. We have since been influenced, however, by several centuries' worth of artistry in which the secular and religious functions are clearly separated, both in the work itself and in the culture that produced it. In that context, it becomes difficult to talk about the connection of art in general to spirituality in general. Nevertheless, the power of artistic works to inspire spiritual reflection is evident in a wide variety of settings. At the same time as the natural connection between art and spirituality has been erased in much popular conversation, explicit theorizing about that connection has exploded in academic circles.

By "spirituality" or "spiritual reflection," I mean two things: First, what Christians have long termed *discernment*, a way of thinking deeply through matters of value and of finding meaning in the truth. This side of spirituality links with the age-old wisdom traditions of Judaism, as well as with other religions and philosophies from around the globe. The aim is to change one's own practice, one's own life, by the creative experience of applying deep spiritual knowledge. The result is a movement toward the future, an action that arises out of the spiritual insight.

Second, spirituality also includes a kind of *sacramental awareness*. This side of spiritual reflection also has roots in the Christian tradition, especially in its monastic history; but it is more closely and thoroughly associated for contemporary practitioners with Eastern meditative styles, especially various forms of Buddhism. Here the spiritual consciousness seeks to attend to what presents itself in the moment, on its own terms and for its own sake, trusting that something valuable or sacred is therein revealed. This moment can include the past and the future within its own horizons, even as it is not entirely reducible to them. The aim is to discover the depth in the particulars of each instant in a changing present, to avoid precipitously moving toward abstraction, generalization, and universalization. Rather than reflecting on being, the aim is simply to be. The result is an appreciation for the value and meaning of the evanescent and an experiential awareness of one's own consciousness beyond the objects of which one is conscious.

To demonstrate how art might exhibit, comment on, and provide a setting for a type of spirituality related to process thought, we focus here on one very contemporary art form: cinema, a moving-picture technology with just a little more than a century of history. More than other art forms such as literature, visual art (painting and sculpture), the theater, ballet, or opera, film reaches huge audiences in the United States and around the world. Simultaneously, film has demonstrated a capacity for depth of theme, variety of style, nuance of the medium's employment, and presentation of human character. Such a capacity may be one hallmark of a true art form, rather than simply an escapist entertainment medium. It has also spawned a number of other moving-picture media that have taken film (in all its variety of uses) as a model; television is the most pervasive example. Although since the mid-sixties the recording medium of TV and other moving-picture formats has diverged completely from cinema, the vocabulary, grammar, and syntax of those formats remain almost wholly derivative from it.

Parallels between Art and Process

One immediate and striking parallel between the world-description (and resulting spiritual awareness) provided by process theology and the particular characteristics of film is the indispensability of the element of time. Film shares with music, dance, and drama the characteristic of unfolding over time, in a series of causally connected moments that collectively form the work in question. Similarly, process thought asserts that all living beings and enduring realities unfold in this way: moment by moment. Substance ontologies—such as that of Aristotle, who spoke in terms of enduring (or even permanent) substances with accidental (changing) properties—align more naturally with static arts such as photography, painting, and sculpture. Temporal art forms, however, exhibit an attention to the intersections between moments and to the flow of time itself in ways that cannot be summarized or captured in any static note or image.

Another aspect of cinema that resonates with a process perspective is the near-universality of collaboration as a means to producing artistic works in the medium. While some offshoots of cinema, such as video, can be and sometimes are the work of single individuals, nearly all cinematic productions require many people to complete. Major productions require hundreds of collaborators, including technicians, writers, directors, and actors. Some influential film theories (notably the "auteurism" emanating from postwar France) hold that among these many contributors, often one dominant vision discernibly shapes the end product. Nevertheless, no one claims that the contributions of the many are simply mechanically effective in producing the artwork. The creativity of the many, perhaps (but not necessarily) filtered through the presiding creativity of one or few, produces the unitary film, subsequently reproduced and experienced by many.

Once again, this is not unique to film, although the number of collaborators and their intensive specialization may be extraordinary. Drama, music, ballet, and opera all rely on performers and interpreters of written notation to produce actual instances of the work in question. And again, this seems similar to the understanding of cause and effect in the production of every subsequent moment found in process thought, and dissimilar to ostensibly more solitary artistic pursuits such as are found in the visual arts. In the latter, the elevation of one artistic idea and one executing hand into a sole author of the work tends to obscure the collaborative, weblike nature of even those art forms, in which influences–from other humans, the environment, and the artist's personal history–the producers of physical or technological materials, and even the constraints of the medium necessarily act as co-creators. Process thinking sees the emergence of every new moment as a collaborative process involving the individual's immediate past world (including all individuals within that world), God's contribution of valuation and order, and the individual's own final decision about the whole to be made out of all those parts. Every moment is self-creating, but no moment can "go it alone"–it is dependent upon a great cloud of witnesses, a host of those who have come before, in its climb toward becoming itself.

Particular Affinities between Film and Process Thought

So far film evinces the same compatibilities with process thought as several other art forms–perhaps most or all other art forms–when they are stripped of the individualist mythology of Western modernism. Is there any particular or peculiar way in which film can be an example of spiritual life and spiritual perception for twenty-first–century media consumers? I would like to suggest that the very concreteness and particularity of the film experience can serve as a way into spiritual reflection on the deep reality of our particularity. Let me give several examples.

Intentionality

First, most narrative, live-action films are *intended* far more thoroughly, actively, and comprehensively than viewers realize. By intended, I mean that they are the product of innumerable conscious decisions made by multiple decision-makers. Because realistic narrative films aim to create believable, organic worlds, viewers often consider them "given," simply present and available to the filmmakers as places and situations in which to set stories. We accept an on-screen living room, for example, as a real living room in a real house in which the cast and crew happened to find certain furniture or certain décor, even though some of us know, if we were to think for a moment, that movies are usually shot on sets rather than in real houses. In reality, accidents are few and far between on a film set, developing lab, or editing room. A human agent actively decides upon every detail of the finished film, from props to clothing to sound effects to lighting to color quality. Even in documentary films, where the camera catches "accidental" details not set up by the filmmakers, the editing process involves the addition of the filmmakers' intention to whatever footage winds up in the finished product. The artists must decide, for every frame, whether this is what they will show and say. In animated, computer-generated, and other types of non-live action film, the level of intention is often far greater. The filmmakers must physically add every detail to the cel painting, computer graphic, or even directly to the celluloid emulsion. For these films, nothing "already exists" in the real world to be filmed. A new world must be consciously constructed from the ground up, and active decisions must be made about its persistence from frame to frame.

Especially in the case of mass-distributed narrative movies, the intentionality of film has been disguised by its realism. In the same way, the universality of decision-making power in the real world—of creativity, prehension, and concrescence (as process terminology puts it)—has been obscured by our human-scale, macro perspective. From this point of view, many phenomena, especially events that follow so-called "natural laws," look like products of a mechanistic chain of cause and effect. When the operation of innumerable decisions is invisible because the perceptible effect doesn't look to us like consciousness or life, we easily infer or conclude that no analog to consciousness or life exists at any level in the effect. Similarly, we fail to notice with conscious awareness the innumerable intended details in a realistic film or the role of human intention in shaping documentary film. The smoothness of a movie's exploitation of audience psychology, expectations, and persistence of vision can even lull us from our knowledge that an animated or constructed film is as completely devoid of unintended detail as it is possible for a human creative product to be. In both cases, the *appearance* of accident or randomness doesn't count in any way against the truth of universal, repeated, and inescapable intentionality exercised by countless agents at every step in the process of production.

Particularity

Second, film (especially in its narrative mode, but also often in experimental or avant-garde modes as well) demonstrates the *particularity of value* that process thought also describes. To put it another way, the meaning or value that film mediates arrives almost exclusively through the contemplation of particulars, rather than universals. Process theology notes the priority of the concrete, specific, and particular over the abstract, generalized, and universal in the bedrock function of all reality: the creation of value. Far from merely providing instances of the truly real, the Platonic Idea or the essence, these concrete, temporal, and passing particulars of our experience are the ultimately real things of which the world is composed.

In cinema, conscious and immediate abstraction of the sort that is uniquely possible in pure language, where words for universals have the same linguistic status as words for particularities, is almost impossible. Not only is the mainstream history of the film medium narrative and representational, but cinema by nature arrests the viewer at the level of the image itself and its connection to a real-world original. While contemplating abstraction or universalization in a static visual art form, the viewer is free to move her consciousness at will toward and away from the image itself, advancing at her own pace into the larger meaning or significance that abstraction facilitates. In film, by contrast, any connections to a nontemporal universal or abstraction emerge upon reflection about the film experience; while immersed in the experience, the viewer must attend to the details of the actuality on the screen, including any changes over time.

Narrative film is closely tied to the particular and resistant to the premature or illegitimate move toward abstraction. In narrative film storytelling, even at the less realistic end of the continuum, all universals that are being illustrated remain intrinsically tied to the characters or objects that appear onscreen. Filmmakers have no way to evoke a universal without the use of a concrete particular. Even when critical, thematic reflection is underway, the particular image or person stubbornly refuses to disappear or become merely an instance. Instead, the particular becomes an indispensable medium through which the abstract can be communicated or talked about. This is as close to the process view of the priority and ultimacy of concrete actualities[1] as I can perceive in any art form. It's possible that theatrical art shares this quality with film, but because thoroughgoing realism, at least since the early decades of the twentieth century, is not a central aim in the theater, theatrical artists often attempt to evoke abstraction directly and create pure symbolism.

Such irreducible particularity, especially when added to the temporality that is the essence of the cinematic medium, evokes the dimension of sacramental awareness mentioned above. Our attention is drawn first and foremost to the specific contingencies of character, event, emotion, decision, and consequence. And at every moment, those contingencies shift, requiring the viewer to maintain a flowing awareness of the present. Unlike literature or visual art, the medium of film involves artistic control over the temporal element of the viewer's experience. We see and hear what the filmmakers have decided we will see and hear, for exactly as long as they have decided we will see and hear it. As viewers, we are not able to dwell on a passage or a particular image at our leisure, nor are we able to rush past them to what comes next. Film forces us into the present moment, then into the next and the next. What we are attending to in those fleeting moments is not theme or abstraction, but incident and particularity. To the extent that those incidents and particularities in the flowing present of the film evoke the depth, the meaning and value of moments, agents, patients, events, emotions, decision, and consequence, the awareness thus achieved can become sacramental. It can reveal and mediate the depth of things, the significance of "thusness."

Of course, when we watch most films, most of us don't feel like we enter a meditative state of the sort associated with sacramental awareness in a religious context. Some special sorts of films, often described as "hypnotic" or "dreamlike," approximate the state that most people associate with meditation. Many viewers say they "turn off their brains" when watching movies, letting the images and sounds wash over them without critically evaluating them. By this they do not seem to mean that they are fully in the present in a meditative way, or that they are more awake to the present moment than they are ordinarily. Instead, they mean that they do not think *about* a movie while watching it. By contrast, the films that are most strongly associated with a meditative state are those that make the viewer more aware of his thoughts while watching—those with long takes, slowly flowing imagery, surreal or incongruous incidents, or stylized design in visuals and sound. Avant-garde films are often of this type: Michael Snow's classic *Wavelength*, the painted abstractions of Stan Brakhage, and especially the computer-generated mandalas of James Whitney's *Lapis*. Recent narrative films that are associated with a meditative state are Terrence Malick's *The Thin Red Line*, David Lynch's *Mulholland Drive*, and films featuring the slowly moving camera of Russia's Andrei Tarkovsky, the ultra-long-take cinema of Hungary's Bela Tarr, and the "master shot" cinema of Taiwan's Tsai Ming-liang.[2]

Yet not only do these directors' works evoke sacramental awareness in the viewer but their style facilitates a special kind of film experience that makes one aware of the awareness! In fact, I would argue that the value of this style of film, which is growing increasingly popular in many countries, lies in its ability to expose what all film has the potential to accomplish. Just as meditation is a special practice that aims to help us achieve sacramental awareness in everyday experiences, "meditative" films, which highlight the viewer's conscious interaction with onscreen events through unfamiliar pacing and other stylistic innovations, help us perceive the activity of the film medium itself, placing us in a flowing present and focusing our attention on its particularities. With practice, we can become consciously aware of film's spiritual dimension, its uncovering of depth in the particulars of each moment, its function (through artificial means of control) to preclude our tendency to move too quickly away from real, concrete things toward abstractions and universals, its ability to hold our attention where value is truly to be found.

Relationality

If I may be permitted a spatial metaphor: So far we have explored two dimensions or axes of the film experience, considered from the point of view of spirituality. First are the images and sounds depicting incidents onscreen—the surface of the film. Let's think of that as a flat rectangle like a movie screen. I have just tried to highlight a second dimension of depth revealed underneath those incidents whenever artist and viewer cooperatively achieve sacramental awareness, attending to the value in those particulars in the present moment. It's as if we rotated the flat screen and discovered layers upon layers underneath or behind it, extending back into a depth dimension not readily apparent when we are facing the screen.

This picture has a third dimension as well. If we tilt our stack of screen-shaped layers obliquely and catch the light just right, we may see a latticework pattern come into view—a grid or matrix that extends outward in all directions from the stack. This is the network of relationships between the particularities and meanings of the moment and other moments, events, and entities. Here we are leaving that sacramental awareness of the present, having plumbed its depths and appreciated its singular reality, and we begin once again to notice how each instance (or instant) of existence extends itself into others.

As we have seen, process thought identifies concrete contingencies as ultimately real, the foundational *existanda* of the universe. But their reality as building blocks of larger structures arises from their co-construction, their dependence on each other for their very existence. Process philosophy terms this fact "internal relations," signifying that each instance of reality interpenetrates with others in a causal web. It's not as if billiard balls bounce off each other and go their way internally or essentially unchanged, save for accidental properties such as velocity and direction. Instead, each individual constructs itself out of the myriad other individuals in its immediate past, and then becomes the raw material for yet another act of construction by the next individual. To say that every moment is part of a causal web of relationships, then, is to say that every moment is constituted, essentially and thoroughly, by its relationships.

For our purposes in this essay, this third dimension raises two questions. First, how does cinema embody or illustrate it? Second, how does this dimension contribute to spirituality or spiritual reflection?

The relational dimension is inescapable in the film medium. Every element of film—frame, shot, scene, sequence—has meaning only in the relation to the other elements with which the filmmakers have juxtaposed it. For example, consider an individual frame on the celluloid strip. A frame of film, in itself, is a still photograph or image. But this is precisely why a frame of film is not a film. Film consists of frames joined in a particular sequence and displayed to a viewer at a particular rate, such that the disjunction between frames disappears and the illusion of continuous images in motion is achieved. For that to happen, what is crucial is not the frame, but the relationship between frames. Animation provides a handy reference point. We know that the illusion of motion in stop-motion animation[3] is produced by snapping a still picture, moving the models slightly, snapping another picture, and so on, through thousands of iterations. Watch a cel animator at work, and you will see her flipping back and forth repeatedly between one drawing and the next. Only in their relationship can the cinematic effect emerge. This is true even in cases in which the filmmaker is not trying to achieve the illusion of realistic motion. Avant-garde films such as Paul Sharit's *T,O,U,C,H,I,N,G* juxtapose frames or very short multiframe sequences with images that aren't causally related, creating a strobe or stutter effect. Yet here, just as with realism, the film itself is created by the relationships that emerge between the still images thus juxtaposed; and one cannot say one has experienced the film until it has been viewed at the correct rate of projection, causing the desired effect.

Another example, moving away from the fundamental technology of film into its evolution as an artistic medium, is the editing of shots. Each shot of a live-action film is a continuous exposure of film frames, at a predetermined rate, creating an image of the objects, people, and action within range of the camera. But a film, as we know it and as we use the term, is created by the editing decisions made by the filmmakers. What shots will be edited together—juxtaposed, put in relationship? What "take" will be used for each shot? How long will each shot be allowed to continue before an edit? When will the juxtaposition create a change in camera angle, resulting in a "movement" of the viewer in relation to the scene? The answers to all these questions depend not on the qualities of the shots, but on their effect when put into relationship. Indeed, for experienced filmmakers, the eventual relationships they envision will determine what shots they choose to record!

The "internal relations" created between shots in a film were most famously illustrated by Lev Kuleshov, a Russian filmmaker in the early twentieth century, in an experiment he created to demonstrate the power of montage. Kuleshov shot an actor whom he instructed to assume an impassive expression. He then juxtaposed the actor's face with images–a bowl of soup, a girl, a toy, a child-sized coffin–and showed the resulting film to viewers. They "read into" the actor's expressionless face emotions commensurate with the images presented immediately before, swearing that he was hungry, satisfied, lustful, tender, happy, or sad, according to their own emotional reaction to the objects. The shot itself is neutral. Yet the shot is not the film. In the film, the shot has a meaning created by its relationship to the other elements present–and the film would not be the particular film that it is without the exact juxtapositions and resulting meanings, emotions, information, *et cetera*, that put these elements in relation to one another.

Cinematic Relationships and Spirituality

Film, then, is an art form that is essentially relational, a characteristic it shares to some extent with other art forms (literature in the arrangement of words, sentences, chapters; drama in the arrangement of dialogue, scenes, characters; visual art in the composition of shapes, colors, and other imagistic components). The relationality of film is a heavier accent than these other creative endeavors. This is true, on the one hand, because of film's unique ability to juxtapose images from completely disparate times, spaces, and styles with the stroke of an editing knife, and on the other because of the temporal control film exerts over the viewer. The latter point is the final focus of this essay, and the answer to the second question I asked above: How do the relations exhibited by film contribute to spirituality or spiritual reflection?

Like literature and drama, narrative film requires that the viewer actively construct the complete effect through the exercise of memory and anticipation. In other words, the relationships constructed in a temporal medium complete their connection, ultimately, in the mind of the viewer. A complete story–beginning, middle, end–can only be understood if the one to whom the story is told participates in the construction of the whole. It is also the case that the *meanings* of a story–its connections to deeply resonant themes and values– cannot emerge without the participation of the audience. The listener or viewer recognizes symbols, pointers, and hints of larger, more general meanings in the particularities of the story's incidents and characters. The listener or viewer brings both her knowledge of other expressions of that theme and her experience with the situation and its attendant emotions to the way the theme plays out in the story.

Seen from the other side, however, the story offers more than just an illustration of the theme or meaning–more than just an instance of the universal. By evoking the theme in the midst of concrete particulars, the story has multiple possibilities. The story can show a new facet of the theme. The story can bring the film's meaning or significance home with new force. The story can connect the theme to new situations. The story can confront the audience with the power of novelty and specificity intertwined with the depths of antiquity and universality. One's experience of meaning, value, and theme in a narrative may become a paradigm, a touchstone, able to spill over and influence past and future instances of similar meanings. Because of the powerful exploration of postmodern masculinity in David Fincher's *Fight Club*, for example, many young men will experience their own gendered nature with a different conscious awareness and will encounter other stories about manhood differently. In short, a story can enrich its themes, just as themes can enrich a story.

What film adds to this narrative power is its intrinsic, thoroughgoing focus on the particular and the present combined with its complete control over the temporal flow of the story. These factors produce an art form that can aid discernment, one of the components of spirituality mentioned early in this essay, by revealing connections without losing sight of the particularities that first prompted reflection. Discernment might be described as the way one goes about answering the question, "How shall I then live?" It connects the good, the true, and the beautiful in their transpersonal, abstract, deficiently actual forms, with the particular and real situations, characters, and incidents of a life, lived as it is in contingencies and uncertainties.

Too many narratives we absorb, from birth to death, seem intended to disappear even as they are told, leaving only a lesson or a moral–some timeless absolute that is the "real message." Stories can then seem to be mere ladders we climb to new realizations; once the ladder has been ascended, it can be discarded. Indeed, it can seem that if there were some way to get the message without going to the time and trouble of absorbing the story—some "Cliff's Notes" or condensed version—we should profitably make use of it. This attitude toward narrative is a symptom, I believe, of a larger attitude toward contingency and particularity and concreteness: that these passing shades of this world are less important—that they *matter* less—than the absolutes and abstractions and timeless verities out there somewhere. Discernment is not served by this desire to jump right to the meanings and skip their source in lived human experience, because discernment involves linking meanings that arise out of our experience to the decisions that now face us. Both the experiences and the decisions are concrete, specific, contingent. So discernment begins and ends with particularity, passing through its depths and extending outward into its myriad relationships on the way.

Some will assert that the task of discernment becomes necessary because we are merely finite beings in the face of a God or universe that contains all the answers, if only we could grasp them. Like children whose parents tell them stories to teach lessons, we are often told that our task is simply to find what part of the already existing, already complete, and always absolute truth to apply to our lives to pass over our problems with ease. But for process thinkers, neither the universe nor God nor any other existing reality contains all the answers. Just as we are incomplete but in the process of becoming, God, the universe, and all that has been, is, and will be are growing and becoming as well. Wholly new situations and new truths come to be every day and will continue to arise; novelty is real. Everything is unfinished, and everything has the possibility of becoming more. So it is impossible for all the answers to be already available, in principle or in reality. Discerning an answer is a creative, synthesizing process, one in which my particular perceptions, feelings, past experiences, and future anticipations truly matter. Particularity is not to be put aside in the search of a timeless truth, of which I seek to become a mere instance. The truth I make of my life will be singular, unique, particular, and (in the memory and creative power of God) everlasting.

Conclusion

As we have seen, film resists fading into abstraction, even in its nonnarrative forms. Its images and its flow are deliberate, intended, and thoroughly specific. Yet film mediates dimensions of depth and extent that lend meaning, value, and worth to the particularities portrayed. Film shows us how contingencies *matter*—how everything changes because of what they turn out to be. Recently, more and more filmmakers around the world have resorted to manipulating film's temporal dimension to make this point: fracturing the timestream of the narrative[4] or reordering it in reverse[5] to demonstrate the nodes of contingent decision making that send consequences spiraling in one direction or another. But we experience all narrative film, and indeed all narrative, as a sequence of contingencies, even if the film purports to be about fate; we *wait to see* what will happen, and we are interested in what will happen because it *matters* in some way.

The unique power of film to reveal and aid the spiritual practice of discernment lies in its own nature as a process, and one in which the two basic attributes of a process—particularity and time—are inescapably present and deliberately controlled. We attend to exactly the particularities given in the film, exactly for the amount of time the film lasts. While connections to more general meanings, themes, and values emerge during the film's running time, they do not compete with the particularities on the screen; rather, they deepen those concrete actualities and reveal connections between them. At the same time, we exercise discernment as we attend to the relationships between past, present, and future onscreen, anticipate responses and actions from the characters, and make judgments about the advisability of those decisions. Forming a relationship with the narrative as it unfolds, we may include ourselves—our own experiences, emotions, and hopes—in our response to the story. The events onscreen may cause us to question or even change our values in the real world as we use these particularities, in all three dimensions, to inform our response to the question, "How shall I then live?"

Sacramental awareness and discernment are the fruits of a spiritual way of being in the world. But not every way of conceiving the world, its creatures, and its divine component is able to engender and sustain these fruits. Process theology offers conceptual and empirical resources for understanding the depth, value, and momentousness of the flow of contingencies in which we live and for understanding the intimate connections—the internal relations, cooperation, or co-creativity—among those contingencies. Cinema offers a vivid, controlled, and rich experience of those contingencies—appearing, changing, and perishing moment by moment, redolent with the dimensions of particularity, transcendent meaning, and thoroughgoing relationality. In many ways, film provides an especially apt illustration of the process outlook. But it also can become, especially for the attentive, educated, and open viewer, an avenue for spiritual reflection. As the film unreels, framing our world for a time, yet with the frame boundaries invisible to us, we practice attention to the present moment and revel in its concreteness. As its story unfolds, reaching beyond that cinematic world yet remaining an "epiphenomenon" of it, we sense the connections between actualities, meanings, and the future, pregnant with possibilities. Our spiritual lives are enriched by the touch of transcendence, even as they remain wholly immersed in the deep contingencies of art as well as life.

Culture and Social Change

Religious commitments have traditionally been understood to play out in two different realms: *theoria* (theory, or intellectual assent) and *praxis* (practice, or action in the world). Although individual process theologians may emphasize one or the other, the two realms are intimately intertwined in nearly all process thought. Whitehead insisted that *theoria* should be consistent with lived experience, and that *praxis* should cohere with the concepts used to reflect upon it. Following his lead, and affirming the twentieth-century tradition of engaged theology (theology of culture, as Tillich put it), process theologians frequently extend their reach into their social settings, reflecting on realities and advocating change in their times, places, and communities.

The selection of essays in this section demonstrates a few of these cultural and social concerns, out of the wide range of possible disciplines and topics in which process thought has been found to be useful. Paul Bube begins by considering the ethical dimension that flows out of the emphasis on relationship found in process thought, contributing a christological emphasis as well as illustrating some possibilities for application in the realm of environmental action. Monica Coleman's essay, from a Womanist perspective, proposes connections between process views and the resources available in literature by black women that reveal their visions of possible futures. Lucinda Huffaker shows that feminist theologians and process theologians stand together in their efforts to affirm relational thinking and to revise patriarchal and power-based images of the Divine. Carol Johnston's essay examines and critiques existing economic systems, such as capitalism and Marxism, and offers alternatives based on the process view of individuals as intrinsically communal and capable of more than just pleasure-seeking behavior. Mary Elizabeth Moore focuses on current world conflicts, and proposes that a new approach to education informed by process thinking and emphasizing the role of imagination can help to bring about lasting peace. Then Les Muray argues that ecologically sound policies and democratic political institutions can be pursued together, developing a concept of relational power to undergird the goal of fostering flourishing "individuals-in-community." Finally, Jay McDaniel connects process themes to the quest for sustainable ways of organizing human life and community on the planet, with the principles of the Earth Charter as a guide to the values necessary for ecological thinking and acting.

CHAPTER 12

Process Theological Ethics

■ PAUL CUSTODIO BUBE

Process theology is, in a fundamental way, a world view. It is a way of understanding ourselves, the world, God, and the interrelationships these have. From that perspective, process theology provides a way of illuminating, guiding, and shaping ethics. Since process theology might better be characterized as "process theologies," any attempt to outline a process theological ethic must necessarily be selective. We can choose from a number of excellent starting points for explicating a process theological ethics: Henry Nelson Wieman (e.g., *The Source of Human Good*[1]), Schubert Ogden (e.g., *Faith and Freedom*[2]), Franklin Gamwell (e.g., *The Divine Good*[3]), Marjorie Suchocki (e.g., *God, Christ, Church*[4]), Catherine Keller (e.g., *From a Broken Web: Separation, Sexism and Self*[5]), not to mention Alfred North Whitehead and Charles Hartshorne. Since it is not possible to do justice to the full range of these thinkers, the following discussion will draw primarily upon John Cobb's vision of process theology. Since Cobb's theology has grown (and continues to grow) through interaction with these and other thinkers, his theology is a particularly apt starting point.

General Ethical Theory

For process thought, the fundamental aspect of reality, the actual occasion of experience, is a dynamic integration of past influences and novel possibilities into a unity of experience. This integrative process, or "concrescence," is guided by the occasion's "subjective aim" at "satisfaction," that is, an aim at the realization of value for that actual occasion, which in turn becomes an influence upon all future occasions. Four points about this understanding of reality are relevant for theological ethics.

1. The satisfaction of the occasion is an achievement of value that is fundamentally an aesthetic experience. Whitehead and Hartshorne refer to it as an experience of "beauty."[6]
2. The subjective aim is the occasion's autonomous appropriation of the aims of the past it has inherited and of the aim of God, the initial ideal aim, for realization of novel value relevant to the inherited past.

3. The actual occasion's achievement of value contributes to the actualization, and thus value, of all future occasions and of God; i.e., all that comes to be is interrelated with all that has come before and will come after.

4. Every actual occasion of experience has some level of subjectivity–from the virtually trivial to the most profound and complex–and thus, has value for itself.

These points, taken together, suggest several key elements in process theological ethics.

Aesthetic Nature of Value and Moral Obligation

Hartshorne and Whitehead understand aesthetic value or beauty as harmonization of diversity in intensity of experience.[7] Cobb has used the terms "strength of beauty"[8] and "richness of experience."[9] The aesthetic nature of value is basic to all forms of value. Hartshorne writes that "values may be considered under three heads: acting rightly, thinking correctly, and experiencing well or satisfyingly. In other words, goodness, truth, and (in a generalized sense) beauty."[10] He continues, "If we know what experience is, at its best or most beautiful, then and only then can we know how it is right to act; for the value of action is in what it contributes to experiences."[11] Whitehead makes a similar claim when he says that "it is more important that a proposition be interesting than it be true. The importance of truth is, that it adds to interest" (PR 259).

The strength of beauty attained by each actual occasion is both intrinsically valuable in the satisfaction attained in the occasion's subjective immediacy, and instrumentally valuable in the contribution that the actual occasion's aesthetic achievement may provide for other occasions in the future. For example, Hartshorne's ornithological studies show that birds often sing simply for the enjoyment of their song. Their experience is intrinsically valuable. Moreover, the beauty of the song that is intrinsically valuable for the bird may also have instrumental value to the enjoyment of the bird watcher.[12] Note that in spite of process terms like "enjoyment," beauty is not simply pleasure. Pleasure has value if it contributes to beauty, but beauty may allow for pain, as a form of contrast or discord, that is taken up into a wider harmony–a point that John Stuart Mill intuited when he said it is better to be a dissatisfied human than a satisfied pig.

If beauty depends upon harmonization of diversity and intensity of experience, then evil is one of two extremes: discord, the extreme diversity that threatens harmonization; or triviality, what Whitehead has called "anaesthesia,"[13] the diminishment of diversity and repetition of the past. In other words, both extreme violence and extreme apathy are evil. (Consider T. S. Eliot's lines from "The Hollow Men": "This is the way the world ends / Not with a bang but a whimper."[14]) Hartshorne remarks that this view of good and evil corresponds to Aristotle's principle of the golden mean, since beauty is a mean between too much and too little complexity and diversity relative to the actual circumstance of the experience.[15] For example, the ideal achievement of beauty in a simple bird's song will be considerably different from the ideal achievement of beauty in an opera singer's song where the complexity and diversity of sound inherited by the opera singer is far greater.

What are harmonized in the concrescing occasion are the aims of the occasions preceding it as well as God's aim for it. Put differently, the value achieved by an actual occasion results from its unique harmonization of the diverse aims it inherits from the past with the initial aim provided by God. The more fully the actual occasion's subjective aim corresponds to God's initial ideal aim for it, the greater the value it achieves. Of course, the process view of internal relatedness means that the value an actual occasion achieves is not merely for itself, but contributes to the value for others in the future, and for God. Acting rightly, as Hartshorne implies, has to do with conforming to God's initial ideal aim, which is the possibility of achieving what is "most beautiful" in that situation. God's initial ideal aim is thus experienced by the actual occasion as a feeling of *obligation*. Hence, the foundation of morality is the obligation to promote the increase of value in the universe. In other words, in the most general sense one's moral obligation is to maximize beauty as inclusively as possible.[16] "Inclusively as possible" is implied by the very definition of good as harmonization of diversity in intensity of experience and follows from the process view of interrelatedness to all reality.

Although it may appear that process theological ethics succumbs to the naturalistic fallacy, it should be emphasized that process theology is not saying that one ought to maximize beauty for oneself and others because that is the way the universe generally tends. From a process perspective the distinction between fact and value is arbitrary and misleading, since all facts, i.e., all actual occasions, are achievements of value. Where there is no value, there is no experience.[17] Moreover, where there is experience, there are feelings of obligation, namely the feelings aiming at actualization accompanying the inherited past and the feeling aiming at actualization that accompanies God's initial ideal aim for the occasion.

Process theology understands the feeling of obligation that accompanies God's ideal aim as specifically *moral* obligation. In a general sense, every experience has a moral dimension. However, the human experience of moral obligation is capable of coming into self-conscious awareness, a highly complex integration (thus, a beautiful form) of experience. That is, human beings experience moral consciousness. The human potential for achievement of value is thus extraordinarily great; consequently, so is the human potential for destruction of value. Therefore, the moral significance of human decisions has a vastly wider and more profound impact on the world than that of any other creature we know, which is precisely why moral responsibility is so central to what it means to be human.

Because God experiences all that is experienced, all that we do has everlasting implication for God and all entities, who in turn affect all that comes to be. In God's Primordial Nature, God aims at the achievement of maximal beauty of every actual occasion. Since creatures (especially human beings), in their freedom, do not always conform to God's primordial aim at maximal beauty, the becoming universe falls short of the ideal. However, in God's Consequent Nature, all that is achieved is taken into God's divine satisfaction and brought into a greater harmony. Put differently, God loves the world by willing what is best for it, and God loves the world by accepting it with its imperfections into the divine life. In traditional language the love of God is beneficence and empathetic relationship, *agape* and compassion; it is both law and grace, judgment and forgiveness. For Whitehead, this is the final attainment of value, the Harmony of Harmonies, that he calls "Peace."[18]

Freedom and Autonomy

Freedom is found in an individual's ability to choose from the possibilities that God provides for realization. In its achievement of value or satisfaction, each actual occasion exhibits some degree of autonomy or self-determination in the way it constitutes its subjective aim—ranging from the virtually negligible to the highly spontaneous. Freedom is real, yet limited. Significant in this understanding is that God's interaction with creation is not only noncoercive, i.e., does not interfere with the freedom of each actual occasion (a point that is important to process theology's theodicy), but that God's luring interaction with each actual occasion is a necessary condition for freedom. The initial ideal aim God provides to each occasion is a "lure for feeling" that is the basis of the occasion's freedom insofar as it provides graded possibilities of realization that transcend repetition of the influences of the past.[19] Put differently, God provides each actual occasion with an initial aim that includes the ideal aim along with other possibilities for realization that are relative to the actual occasion's immediate past, i.e., its context or situation. The actual occasion freely decides among those possibilities. If there were but one possibility, there would be no freedom because there would be no alternatives from which to choose. If there were infinite possibilities with no attached feeling of obligation that some were better than others, then only randomness would be possible.

Moreover, since freedom enhances diversity and intensity of experience— key elements of beauty—God aims at the enhancement of freedom, particularly in human beings where free decision is capable of coming into conscious awareness. As the human capacity for freedom is promoted, so is the human capacity to attain greater achievements of beauty, but also to achieve greater evil. When we choose less than the ideal in the initial aim, we choose lesser value over higher value. From a process perspective, sheer freedom is not freedom at all. If there were only novelty, we would not have harmonization and unity of experience, only pure discord. Rather, true freedom is always, in the root sense, *responsible* freedom, i.e., freedom in responsibility.

Indeed, much in a process view of value and obligation is in line with H. R. Niebuhr's "responsible self." Process ethics may be interpreted primarily in teleological form where right action and rules are defined in terms of the attainment of beauty (Niebuhr's "man-as-maker"), or interpreted primarily in deontological form as obedience to God's initial ideal aim (Niebuhr's "man-as-citizen"). A fuller appreciation of the process model lends itself to being interpreted dialogically, finding a "fitting response" to one's situation (the inherited past), to God's lure to the future, and to the ideal of beauty (Niebuhr's "man-the-answerer").[20]

Interrelatedness

Whitehead characterized the process of becoming as "the many become one, and are increased by one" (PR 21). That is, each actual occasion prehends those that have become prior to it and adds its own satisfaction to those that come after it, and to God. This idea of internal relatedness, that entities are constituted in large part by their relationships, highlights the fact that the freedom of an entity is expressed in responsible relationships. From an ethical standpoint, all decisions have some moral significance in their effects upon others. Moreover, all decisions have everlasting significance in the life of God.

At the level of living organisms, for example, all things exist within what Birch and Cobb have called a "web of life," an interdependent web of mutually sustaining relationships constituted by a diverse but continuous range of species, from single-cell organisms to human beings. However, the web includes what we typically call the inorganic as well as the organic. Living creatures are constituted by their relationships to air, water, and soil, as well as their relationships to one another. Birch and Cobb characterize this as an "ecological model" of reality that has important implications for environmental ethics, as will be discussed below.[21]

Intrinsic Value and Rights

Whitehead gave the earliest process formulation of the nature of rights in *Modes of Thought:*

> The basis of democracy is the common fact of value experience, as constituting the essential nature of each pulsation of actuality. Everything has some value for itself, for others, and for the whole. This characterizes the meaning of actuality. By reason of this character, constituting reality, the conception of morals arises. We have no right to deface the value experience which is the essence of the universe. (MT 111)

Christian ethics has been sharply criticized in the last forty years for promoting human domination and exploitation of the nonhuman world, resulting in a worldwide ecological crisis that includes escalating extinction of species; worldwide pollution of waterways, air, and soil; depletion of the ozone layer; and global warming. The heart of this criticism points to the biblical tradition that only humankind is made in the image of God, and thus of all that is valued, humankind is valued supremely. To the extent that other values conflict with human values, they are almost always trumped by human values. Deep Ecologists have been particularly critical of this Christian anthropocentrism, and many have argued for alternative spiritualities that promote a view that every living thing has sacred value and ought to be revered.[22]

Process theology agrees with the criticism of anthropocentrism and affirms with Deep Ecology that all beings have intrinsic value and therefore ought not to be viewed in purely instrumental terms. That is, process theology eschews anthropocentrism as inconsistent with the way the world really is and even with the meaning of the biblical tradition.[23] Moreover, the ecological model advanced by Birch and Cobb highlights the way that entire species and ecosystems are achievements of value and warrant respect. Birch and Cobb develop this vision into a biocentric ethics, an ethics centered upon Life. Life is not an abstract concept or the mere sum of living creatures, but rather a way of talking about God's activity in the universe as that which lures the universe toward greater achievements of value. Operative in this image of Life is the process view of God as Primordial and Consequent, as directing all things and as experiencing all things. Thus a biocentric ethics for process theology is also a theocentric ethics.

Process thought departs from Deep Ecology in the process view that intrinsic value varies according to what Cobb calls "capacity for richness of experience." This view addresses the main criticism leveled at Deep Ecology's bio-egalitarianism, viz., its lack of a way to adjudicate competing claims among various centers of value, e.g., the value of mosquitoes versus that of chimpanzees. While process theology affirms that all not all entities have equal capacity for richness of experiencing, by viewing variations among rights in terms of the capacity for achieving richness of experience (which includes potential for suffering) for the individual and those most directly affected by the individual, Birch and Cobb attempt to provide a rough scale for adjudicating competing rights among various entities.[24] For example, to borrow an example from Gustafson,[25] the right of a wasp not to be exterminated does not outweigh the right of a human child not to suffer injury from a wasp sting since the capacity for rich experience for the wasp is dramatically less than that of the child. However, Birch and Cobb's approach is problematic since the experience of being swatted *for the wasp* may involve profound suffering, while the experience of being stung is for the child usually less intense. As Hartshorne said of birdsong, "a bird song that seems trivial to us need not be trivial to a bird."[26] To strengthen Birch and Cobb's criteria, it is helpful to recall that to respect entities' ability to attain strength of beauty is also to respect their freedom. The capacity for freedom, hence the capacity for attaining strength of beauty, observably varies among entities. Unlike the subjective experience of value, freedom is an objectively observable correlate to the achievement of value, and in ethical theory has traditionally been tied to the idea of rights. Thus, a process view of rights would benefit by taking into account the capacity for freedom and self-determination of creatures.

Rights also need to be appreciated within the context of the ecological model that holds that all beings are constituted, in large part, by their relationships to others. Process thought does not limit rights to individuals only. Rights of groups and thus of species come into play because the autonomy of individuals is socially constituted. This is important for creatures with limited freedom. The rights of an individual chicken to survive may be relatively small, but the right of a species of chicken to survive is considerably greater.[27] Even with regard to the rights of animals with considerable capacity for freedom, such as chimpanzees, if the emphasis is only upon the rights of individual animals, those rights might be adequately protected simply by assuring those animals' places in zoos rather than in assuring their ability to sustain themselves in their natural environment as a species. Moreover, respect for and promotion of freedom within the context of the ecological model ties the idea of environmental responsibility to liberation. Indeed, what is needed for many threatened species is not human management aimed at preserving or even promoting their right to exist, but rather liberating them and their ecosystem from human interference, allowing them to return to free wilderness.

The rights of individual animals do become important in ethical consideration, especially when the well-being of highly evolved animals, i.e., animals with significant capacity for freedom and self-determination, is threatened. For example, if we only respect the rights of species, the right of a species of whale to survive may be respected so long as they are hunted in limited numbers. But the capacity of whales for freedom and achievement of richness of experience is so great that the individual whale has a right not to be harmed in addition to the right of its species to survive. The rights of individual animals become particularly relevant in areas such as animal experimentation. Here, a species is not threatened, but individual animals' welfare is at stake. A process view of rights that takes into account the animal's capacity for intense experience and freedom helps to illuminate our common intuition that medical experimentation with rats is morally more acceptable than experimentation with primates. While hard cases abound (e.g., experimentation upon dogs) and exceptions arise, a process view at least provides a framework within which rational judgments can be worked out in context.

Christ in Process Theological Ethics

It would be misleading to construe from the previous analysis that process theology is merely theistic and does not draw upon themes that are central to the *Christian* faith. At least for process thinkers like John Cobb and Schubert Ogden,[28] christology plays a central role in their theology and ethics.

Central to Cobb's christology is his interpretation of Christ as Logos/Sophia. Logos and Sophia are the traditional theological terms used to describe God as present in and guiding the world. From a process perspective, Logos is understood as the way in which God offers God's ideal aim to the world, namely, as creative transformation. Sophia is understood as God's wisdom or full experiencing of the world offered back to the world.[29] In other words, Cobb understands Logos/Sophia as the way the dipolar nature of God is present and effective in the world. The Logos/Sophia precedes the historical person, Jesus, who is Christ because the incarnation of the Logos/Sophia in him was powerfully and perhaps uniquely immediate in his structure of existence. Christ, then, is the creative transforming power and wisdom of God incarnate in the world, which is uniquely witnessed to in the gospel portrait of Jesus, yet discernable in artistic creations, scientific advances, the evolutionary process, and wherever there are advances toward more intense, inclusive, and diverse syntheses of experience. For the Christian, Jesus is a central part of the past that continues to influence the present, particularly in how Jesus directs the Christian toward the way the Logos/Sophia continues to be effective in the world. "Putting on Christ" has ethical significance, pointing to a style of life (and thus to a theory of virtue) constituted by conformity to the creative transformative work of the Logos/Sophia.

Creative transformation, however, fulfills the general aims of justice. As a normative principle, creative transformation calls us to take into account competing claims or perspectives to arrive at a fuller, more inclusive view—a view that might properly be called "impartial" insofar as impartiality connotes giving consideration to all relevant perspectives. Birch and Cobb refer to this inclusion of perspectives as "sharing one another's fate."[30] The impartiality of creative transformation does not assume that it is a standpoint untouched by any perspective. Rather this impartiality begins with the assumption of diverse, valuable perspectives that need to be taken into account—a conclusion that seems in keeping with feminist and liberation theologians who reject so-called "disinterested" views of justice in favor of passion or perspectival analysis.[31] Inclusion of valid perspectives rather than the absolutization of an ideal perspective is the heart of creative transformation and the goal of justice.

Douglas Sturm takes a similar position when he argues that justice is best grounded in the "principle of intersubjectivity." This is a "dialogic" model of social relationships. It respects "divergence of perspective" and finds its social embodiment in an "energetic democracy." In this democracy political and social life is understood as "an encounter among people with differing interests, perspectives, and opinions…[in which conflict] is handled in democratic ways, with openness and persuasion."[32] Sturm concludes that the purpose of justice "is to construct the conditions whereby the genius of each individual and each culture…might enrich the lives of all others; it is to encourage new forms of creative intercommunication."[33]

The view of justice as creative transformative change bears some resemblance to Reinhold Niebuhr's view of justice as a balancing of competing interests. However, there are significant differences. For Niebuhr, justice, which is primarily a rational ideal, is necessarily in tension with love, a religious ideal.[34] Justice is always only approximated; it is always a compromise. For process theology, although creative transformation is an ongoing process that does not achieve a static ideal, its aim is not compromise, but inclusion of the most diverse interests possible. Moreover, creative transformation does not stand in opposition to love, as Niebuhr would hold. Rather, love is the perfection of creative transformative change. That is, creative transformation requires love, as compassion or empathy, as the way that the aims of others are taken into account. Indeed, when we consider that Christ is creative transformation incarnate in the world, justice is as much a religious ideal as is love—a view that seems ultimately more biblical. In short, unlike Niebuhr who sees love as an external measure of justice, process theology understands love to be internally related to justice.

Illustration of Praxis–Social Justice

Drawing upon the foregoing analysis, we can characterize the application of a process view of justice to social issues. Such application is the attempt to arrive at a creative synthesis of competing values that promotes participation of the affected parties in a way that enriches interrelationships and achieves greater value for all. Sturm provides one helpful way to conceive this effort. He calls for a "new social covenant" embodied in "social democracy" that incorporates "public determination into the functions of allocating investment, organizing production, and distributing wealth with the governing intention of enhancing the quality of relationships throughout the community of life."[35] Sturm's terms–social, democratic, covenant–are apt: "social" highlights the process vision of interrelatedness; "democratic" highlights the process vision of intrinsic value and self-determination; and "covenant" recalls the theological basis of the process vision. While Sturm tends to give most of his attention to areas of political and economic life, he recognizes these are intimately bound up with the well-being of the environment.[36]

From the standpoint of justice as creative transformation, social justice is wedded to environmental justice rather than an alternative to environmental welfare. This is probably best illustrated in the approach that John Cobb and Herman Daly take in their analysis of economics and environmental sustainability.[37] Where many environmentalists tend to see market economics as antithetical to environmental sustainability, Cobb and Daly are more interested in avoiding an either/or analysis and ask how the market values and environmental values can be creatively transformed. Thus rather than simply rejecting free market economics in favor of socialist or other alternatives, they explore ways that free market mechanisms can be incorporated into regional market systems so that human freedom and well-being are promoted alongside greater environmental sustainability.[38] Similarly, rather than get caught up in a trade-off between urbanization and re-ruralization, they ask how both can be promoted in a way that is environmentally sustainable. Thus, they affirm the work of Paolo Soleri's arcologies, or architectural ecologies, on the one side, and Wes Jackson's call for movement toward smaller, self-sufficient rural communities, on the other.

In short, application of a creative transformative view of justice to problems analyzes problems in their interconnectedness rather than in isolation. Problems of poverty and hunger, sexism, agricultural sustainability, meaningful work, species extinction, disparity of wealth between first and third world nations, racism, overpopulation, energy consumption, political participation, global warming, etc., are fundamentally interrelated. True justice must promote the values that address all of these issues. Process thinkers such as Sturm, Daly, Cobb, (as well as Charles Birch and Ian Barbour), apply a creative transformative model of justice to these issues that seeks, in simple terms, "both/and rather than either/or" solutions, which serve the attainment of value that is most inclusive of all entities involved.

Final Thoughts: Role of Intercessory Prayer in Process Christian Ethics?

The process view of God is that God is supremely affected by all that occurs in the world and is perpetually active in the world as a persuasive, directive agency who aims at ever-increasing richness of experience for all actualities. This view lends itself to affirming that intercessory prayer affects God's actions and events in the external world. Intercessory prayer is a type of self-constitution by an individual. This self-constitution becomes a direct influence upon God's self-constitution, on the one hand, and both a direct influence in the self-constitution of all other individuals in the future, and an indirect influence upon those same individuals through their experience of God whose self-constitution includes the original influence. Moreover, the influence of the same prayer is also felt indirectly in the self-constitution of each occasion through one another.

Like any event or series of events that contribute to God's self-constitution, prayer does not change God's basic aim at increasing richness of experience in all creatures, but it can hinder or aid in God's effectiveness as a persuasive agent. To the extent that a prayer is in line with God's specific aim for, say, peace in the Middle East, the effectiveness of God's lure for that event is reinforced and compounded. Needless to say, the effect of prayer is further compounded when many individuals share in it and when its aim is specific. To the extent that one's prayer deviates from God's specific aim, God's effectiveness is impoverished—though never eliminated. Hence, in this view, self-examination and alignment with God's aims affects the efficacy of one's prayer—to the extent that one's prayer conforms to God's aims, one is a coworker with God.

Process theology affirms that intercessory prayer influences God's activities, but it hardly advocates moral quietism over social action. The recognition that prayer influences God follows from the recognition that all we do influences the self-constitution of all future events, including God. To recognize that all one's actions, whether they be prayers, attitudes, lobbying, picketing, etc., have important consequences for the future establishment of justice would seem to do more to encourage active involvement than discourage it. Indeed, the apparent logic that sincere belief in intercessory prayer tends to lead to moral quietism generally presupposes a false understanding of God's activities in the world. Such a view sees God's activities as akin to those of a superman who forces his will upon the world rather than as one who persistently and patiently persuades the course of events.

The concern that belief in the efficacy of intercessory prayer encourages a view of God as a mere means to one's end is a more important objection for a process theological interpretation of intercessory prayer. Superficially, it may seem that process theology's view of God as supremely affected by the world lends itself to viewing God as susceptible to manipulation. However, to say God takes into account one's desires and prayers is not the same as saying that God is determined by them. Process theology affirms that God is supremely self-determining. Besides, one's prayers are a small, though significant, influence among the multitude of influences contributing to God's self-constitution. Moreover, a process theology of prayer still affirms a basic tenet of all Christian prayer, namely, that the ideal petition is that God's will be done. The purpose of intercessory prayer, as of all Christian social action, is ultimately to contribute to the realization of God's will.

CHAPTER 13

An Exchange of Gifts

Process and Womanist Theologies

■ MONICA A. COLEMAN

Police and firefighters charge fines and rob citizens more than protecting them. Labor laws are relaxed so that there is no minimum wage, and slavery has been revived through "company store" corporations. State borders are closed to out-of-state residents, and water costs more than gasoline. A new drug causes people to want to set fires. Its abusers shave their heads and paint their bodies and burn any and everything they can—including each other. Everyone lives in walled neighborhoods, their residents carrying guns and accustomed to the sight of human corpses in their midst. In one small walled community, a fifteen-year-old black girl rejects the teachings of her Baptist minister father. She begins like this to write down in verse things she has discovered about her world:

> All that you touch
> You change.
> All that you Change
> Changes you.
> The only lasting truth
> Is Change.
> God
> Is Change.[1]

It is southern California, July 2024. In Octavia Butler's fictional future world, a young African American woman articulates and spreads the teachings of "Earthseed," the God-is-change philosophy that she has gleaned from her observations of the world. Her thoughts contain many of the same insights of process theology—but they have come in poetic form, out of adversity, and from the mouth and the pen of a black woman. In *Parable of the Sower* and

Parable of the Talents, Octavia Butler deftly weaves together the experience of urban decay, race, gender, science, imagination, the natural world, theology, survival, and hope. She simultaneously captures the sentiments of two groups of theologians—her protagonist seems to be both a process theologian and a womanist theologian. How does Butler accomplish something so elusive, and seemingly unimportant for scholars in process and womanist theologies? Why is there no academic conversation between process and womanist theologies? Do they seem incompatible? Or are they simply not interested in one another?

Discussions between process and black theologies typically employ language of compatibility, consistency, and assessment. Is a process God compatible with the God of black theology who stands unequivocally on the side of the oppressed?[2] Is the "limited power" of a process God consistent with the power God exercises in black theology?[3] Can process theology effectively name and combat the structural social evils, especially racism? Can black theology operate effectively without a metaphysical or "rational" foundation? Gene Reeves identifies points of confluence and tensions between process and black theologies.[4] Both process and black theologies express dissatisfaction with the world as it is, a desire for liberation and freedom, a privileging of empiricism, and a social/relational view of reality and of the importance of God. Yet they diverge on issues of naming the enemy, philosophy and praxis, the metaphysical and the empirical, social location and dualism. Process and black theologians' skeptical mutual assessments have ended in attempts to bring them together[5] or rejection of the entire project.[6]

Butler's lyrical combination of race, gender, science, and process suggests a different direction for conversation between process and womanist theologies. Clear differences exist between them—in origin, content, method, and emphasis. Yet both are evolving theologies with their own set of strengths and weaknesses. I'd like to change the language of compatibility, consistency, and assessment to a metaphor of gift-giving.

Coming together, not as adversaries or evaluators, but as possible friends seeking to transform each other as they grow, process and womanist theologies can offer one another gifts. Various process theologies can provide tools to womanist theologians for directions in which they are already moving. Likewise, resources in womanist theologies can enrich and develop the evolution of process theologies. I propose two touch points between process and womanist theologies that may serve as open hands for this exchange of gifts: (1) a link between the process concept of creative transformation and the womanist expression of "making a way out of no way;" and (2) the privilege of experience and a proposed use of black women's science fiction as a theological source.

The Process Gift to Womanist Theology

In its reduced form, process metaphysics describes how change happens. Everything is constantly in the process of synthesizing a vast diverse past into a subjective, momentary unity. As soon as a new unity is achieved, the new entity contributes itself to the world and becomes one of the many that will be synthesized into a unity in the next moment of experience. This process continues on and on. This process of becoming is influenced by both the past and the future possibilities presented to each entity in the form of the initial aim from God. The process concept of creative transformation elaborates upon this description of the process of becoming.

Cobb's Concept of Creative Transformation

Creative transformation is John Cobb's way of talking about a certain type of change and growth that occurs as a result of God's introduction of novelty. Although Cobb was not the first process thinker to write about creative transformation,[7] I select his articulation of the concept primarily because of the notoriety of his work in the field of process theology. Contrary to classical theism, Cobb asserts that God does *not* sanction the norms and institutions of the past, but calls us beyond the achievements of the past to a new future. Creative transformation is more "a way change occurs rather than the specific content at any given time."[8] Cobb explicitly connects it with a Logos christology. The Logos is the source of novelty in each moment, and when it is incarnate, it is called Christ.[9] Thus he concludes, "where Christ is effectively present, there is creative transformation."[10] I suggest that it is possible to think of creative transformation without the christology that Cobb links to it.

Cobb first articulates a concept of creative transformation as "the call forward." "The call forward" breaks the bonds of determinism and introduces new possibilities into the world.[11] Creative transformation later becomes Cobb's phrase for the process of change itself. But Cobb is clear that not all change is good; creative transformation is positive change for the new. From Cobb's writings, one can identify four characteristics of creative transformation. Creative transformation is (1) contextual and particular; (2) challenging; (3) noncoercive; and (4) universal.

Creative transformation is not a categorical imperative to which one adheres in every situation. Rather, creative transformation is tailor-made for each entity's context,[12] seeking the best possible option in each situation. This option may be the "least of the available evils." In other situations, the divine perspective may lead in a direction that is the best given a wider context that God alone sees. In still other circumstances, the aim pushes us out of our comfort zones. Cobb concludes that creative transformation is not always *felt* as good: "[T]he divine presence is experienced as an other, sometimes recognized as gracious, often felt as judge."[13]

As creative transformation leads us into the future, it necessarily challenges the status quo as we currently experience it:

> Indeed the Logos is threatening to any given world, for it functions to transcend and transform it...In short, the function of the Logos is to introduce tension between what has been and what might be and

continuously to challenge and upset the established order for the sake of the new.[14]

Creative transformation may demand that we give up things to which we are attached. But its challenge moves us beyond the stagnation of the past that would destroy us.[15]

Creative transformation is never forced upon the world. We must make our own decisions about whether or not to embody it. Creative transformation is not a law, but an offering to the world:[16] "We are called to be what in that moment would be fullness. But the calling is not a compulsion. Our actual decision often misses the mark—sometimes rebelliously."[17] Because we have freedom, the efficacy of creative transformation is ultimately our decision.[18]

The universality of creative transformation adds its efficacy to that of our decisions. Creative transformation operates throughout the world.[19] In *The Liberation of Life*, Cobb and coauthor Charles Birch talk about life as working creative transformation in the world.[20] Cobb expands creative transformation from human life to nonhuman life: "Creative transformation...is also the life in all living things...Creative transformation as the immanence of God in the world is not only the way but life itself, the life by which all that is alive lives."[21] Creative transformation is everywhere in everything. It has a universal quality to it.

Creative transformation is, after all, not *all* change. Cobb writes that creative transformation is manifest in the world in a particular manner: " *Christ* must be the life that struggles against the death-dealing powers that threaten us and the way that leads through the chaos of personal and global life to just, participatory, and sustainable society in which personal wholeness is possible."[22] Thus when humans are called to respond to God, creative transformation is that response that liberates humanity and the planet from forces of death.

Cobb draws from the gospel of John to outline creative transformation as a way of articulating his Logos christology. For Cobb, Christ is the power of transformation. Cobb asserts that Christ is most fully effective when recognized by Christians.[23] Cobb's identification of creative transformation as Christ isn't necessary. Because the word *Christ* has assumed a specific connection to Jesus and Christian exclusivism, it allows Christians to identify a Christian reality in non-Christian contexts. The implication of such statements is that Christians must name this normative change as "Christ" for it to be fully effective. This move, intentionally or not, elevates Christianity to a place above other world religious traditions, potentially alienating non-Christians. Yet process theology and a faith conviction insist on connecting the process of change to an entity called God. God has a role in the change that occurs as the world advances, but "Christ" is not necessary for the best that the concept of creative transformation has to offer.

Cobb's concept of creative transformation has invested process theology's process of becoming with a normative valuation. Creative transformation is the change that occurs when God's aims are accepted and incorporated. Creative transformation is contextual and particular, challenging, noncoercive, and found in human and nonhuman life. Creative transformation incorporates the past and moves beyond it in a way that we could not have imagined by ourselves. Cobb tells us that something in this world should and indeed does struggle against the death-dealing powers that threaten us, personally and globally–that there is something moving us toward just, participatory, and sustainable societies in which personal wholeness is possible.

We should retain the nomenclature and concept of "creative transformation." Doing so reminds us that this normative change does not just move us through time, but it transforms us as we become. It transforms the world. The term "creative" affirms the way in which we are created and self-creating in our change. It also reminds us that this change emerges from grasping that which the past alone does not suggest. It surprises us, it amazes us; it is something we might not have seen on our own. If we hold onto *this* "de-Christ-ed" understanding of creative transformation, it can open us up to new possibilities and interaction that heretofore have not been achieved. One of these possibilities is dialogue with womanist theology.

"Making a Way Out of No Way"

Womanist theology has an emphasis on "making a way out of no way"–a way of acknowledging Jesus/God's presence in providing options that do not appear to exist in the experiences of the past. It is a weaving of the past, future, and possibilities offered by God. Such weaving leads to survival, quality of life, and liberating activity on the part of black women. "Making a way out of no way" acknowledges both the role of God and of human agency as new ways break forth into the future. This concept resonates with Cobb's concept of creative transformation, although its connection to christology differs considerably. Womanist theologians do not make the distinctions between God, Christ, and Jesus upon which Cobb insists. Thus it is not clear if it is God, Jesus, or Christ who is part of "making a way out of no way." If, however, we make some of these distinctions and attribute the divine role in "making a way" to God without necessary reference to Jesus or Christ, connections emerge between process and womanist theologians.

Understanding "making a way out of no way" as creative transformation can open womanist theology to several things:

1. a metaphysics/ontology that will necessarily undergird what has previously been asserted by "black women's experience" alone
2. the necessity of addressing ecological justice
3. constructions of womanist theology that are not necessarily Christian

In this sense, womanist theology can benefit and grow from a key concept in process theology.

Linda Thomas defines womanist theology as: "critical reflection upon black women's place in the world that God has created; it takes seriously black women's experience as human beings who are made in the image of God; it affirms and critiques the positive and negative attributes of the church, the African American community, and the larger society."[24] Womanist theology is known for its analysis of religion and society in light of the triple oppression of racism, sexism, and classism that characterizes the experience of many black women.

Womanist theology is a response to sexism in black theology and racism in feminist theology. When black theologians spoke of "the black experience," they only included the experience of black men and boys. They did not address the unique oppression of black women. Feminist theologians, on the other hand, unwittingly spoke only of white women's experience, especially of middle- and upper-class white women. They did not include issues of race and economics in their critiques. Many womanists also feel that feminist theology operates in opposition to men, and as anathema to the church. Womanist theologians want to maintain their connection to black men and remain faithful to the church traditions from which they come. The term *womanist* allows black women to affirm their identity as black while also owning a connection with feminism. Employing Alice Walker's definition of womanist in her 1983 collection of essays *In Search of Our Mother's Gardens*, womanist theology makes significant contributions to the fields of black and liberation theologies.[25]

Womanist theologian Delores Williams states that black people in general, and black women in particular, express their relationship with God as the one who "makes a way out of no way." She writes: "Many times, as a little girl, I sat in the church pew with my mother or grandmother and heard the black believers, mostly women, testify about 'how far they had come by faith.' They expressed their belief that God was involved in their history, that God helped them make a way out of no way."[26] "Making a way out of no way" is more than Williams' own naming of the relationship between black women and God.[27] It is a central theme in black women's experiences of struggle and God's assistance in helping them to overcome struggle.

In *Sisters in the Wilderness*, Delores Williams uses the Genesis stories about Hagar, the slave of Abraham and Sarah, to suggest that the God of womanist theology is not just a God of liberation, but also a God who is interested in the survival and quality of life of black women. From Williams' book, we can identify four characteristics of "making a way out of no way." "Making a way out of no way" involves the following:

1. God's presentation of unforeseen possibilities
2. human agency
3. a telos of justice, survival, and quality of life
4. a challenge to the existing order

Taken literally, "making a way out of no way," suggests that a path forward appears out of nowhere, out of nothing. We cannot understand it this way. Instead, "making a way out of no way" means that the way forward is not contained in the past alone, the only way that is known. A way forward, a way toward life, has come from another source. It comes from unforeseen possibilities. These possibilities come from God. Using the example of Hagar, Williams writes, "God opened Hagar's eyes, and she saw a well of water that she had not seen before. In the context of the survival struggle of poor African American women, this translates into God providing Hagar (read also African American women) with *new vision* to see survival resources where she saw none before."[28] God is the one who presents the way, more properly out of God than out of nowhere. Emilie Townes also acknowledges the grasping of possibilities as a part of womanist spirituality in general:

> Living out womanist spirituality means integrating faith and life…God makes demands on us to live into our faith in radical ways…out of the possibilities we have before us and not out of our well-acknowledged and believed shortcomings.[29]

God's offering of possibilities is felt as a call into the future.

Williams is careful to note that the possibilities God offers are not always *felt* as good. As she struggles with the image of a God who tells Hagar to return to the house of her oppressors, Abraham and Sarah, Williams concludes that God is helping Hagar to survive. God knows that Hagar will not be able to survive childbirth alone in the wilderness and thus encourages Hagar to go home. God is not liberating Hagar, but God is making sure that Hagar survives. God has knowledge of a wider context than Hagar could have and offers this to Hagar. Kelly Brown Douglas refers to this as the way in which womanist theology emphasizes God's role as liberator *and* as judge.[30]

God does not force possibilities onto Hagar, or any human, when "making a way out of no way." Always human agency is involved. "God gave [Hagar] new vision to see survival resources where she had seen none before. Liberation in the Hagar stories is not given by God; it finds its source in human initiative."[31] Williams is so careful to emphasize the role of human freedom that she speaks about "making a way" as something that the human does "with God's help." This is why she has uplifted the stories of Hagar: "The Hagar stories are those which suggest that an *ex-slave* mother could, with God's help, be in complete charge of furnishing her son with survival strategies."[32] "Making a way out of no way" is, therefore, a combination of God's presentation of possibilities and human decision.

"Making a way out of no way" is not a move in just any direction; it has a normative value. "Making a way out of no way" enhances personal and communal life. It promotes liberation, life, and survival. When a way is made, God does more than support basic existence. God encourages quality of life. The ethic of survival/quality-of-life creates freedom, peace, and well-being for the entire African American community.[33] Survival and quality of life is now a guiding ethic for womanist theology. Delores Williams writes, "[A]n ethical principle emerges as a guide in identifying what is to be revalued. The ethical principle yielded is 'survival and a positive quality of life for black women and their families in the presence and care of God.'"[34]

Other womanists refer to the survival and quality of life ethic as a telos of justice. Emilie Townes writes, "God's love moves out to grow in compassion, understanding, and acceptance of one another. It helps begin the formation of a divine-human community based on love that is pointed toward justice."[35] Seeking justice will challenge the societal structures we currently experience. Jacquelyn Grant writes about this in terms of humanity: "In general, womanist principles accent the move toward full humanity for all. To this end, the eradication of all forms of oppression is primary."[36] Karen Baker-Fletcher pushes womanists to extend their understanding of justice in human communities to nonhuman communities as well.[37] Justice for the African American community will necessitate an eradication of the existing structures that oppress people on the basis of racism, sexism, classism, heterosexism, and ecological injustice.

"Making a way out of no way" challenges wider society and our own personal comfort. In the case of Hagar, it moves us into the wilderness. While the wilderness is a difficult place to be, Williams asserts that it is the meeting place for God and humanity. There, God teaches and guides humans into a sense of identity and strength in order to continue the struggle.[38] "Making a way out of no way" is sometimes experienced as release and joy; other times it is experienced as oppression. Either way, it disrupts the past from continuing on as it would without the possibilities God offers.

"Making a way out of no way" is the way of life appearing in situations that threaten death. Williams reminds readers that African American women have not been passive "in the face of the threat of destruction and death."[39] Again, the story of Hagar is illustrative. "One of the constituent ideas in the Hagar-in-the-wilderness symbolism is Hagar's, black women's, and black people's encounter with the threat—and often actuality—of death-dealing circumstances. Alone in the wilderness, pregnant on one occasion and alone with her son in the wilderness on the other occasion, Hagar and child surely would have died had not God intervened."[40] When black women rebel against death-dealing situations and God offers the possibilities that were previously unforeseen, a way is made out of no way.

Womanist Christologies

The model of "making a way out of no way" necessarily involves God. But what about Jesus? Delores Williams acknowledges that her project is specifically Christian.[41] Williams moves easily into christology because of the high christology held by womanist theologians in general. In her survey of womanist christology, A. Elaine Crawford writes that black women, and hence womanists, do not make distinctions between God and Jesus: "God, Jesus, and the Holy Spirit are understood as the three persons of the Trinity and are used interchangeably, especially in the prayers of the African American."[42]

Womanist christologies tend to focus on images of Jesus rather than on distinguishing between Jesus, Christ, and God. In *White Women's Christ, Black Women's Jesus,* Jacquelyn Grant points out that for black women, the historical Jesus is primary.[43] Jesus' lowly birth, ministry to the poor and outcast, wrongful death, and resurrection allow black women to identify with Jesus, and Jesus with black women. This co-suffering and identification is so strong that Jesus can be seen as a black woman. Delores Williams concludes that redemption depends upon black women's participation in the ministerial vision of Jesus. These womanist christologies emphasize Jesus' life, rather than his death or divine-human constitution, as salvific for black women[44] and make no substantive distinctions between Jesus, Christ, and God.

Womanist language about Jesus is broad and conflated with its language about God. Williams writes that it is Jesus who performs the role of "making a way out of no way":

> African American Christians have, for generations, believed in salvation through Jesus Christ. Referring to God and Jesus interchangeably, they have understood the gospel (or good news) to be Jesus' power to deliver the oppressed, Jesus' power to provide healing sustenance and to guide humankind toward a positive quality of life.[45]

Womanist understandings of Jesus are nonspecific and utilitarian:

> Black women's stories…attest to Black women's belief in Jesus/Christ/ God involved in their daily affairs and supporting them. Jesus is their mother, their father, their sister and their brother. Jesus is whoever Jesus has to be to function in a supportive way in the struggle.[46]

Williams does not carefully identify whether or not it is Jesus or God who helps to "make a way out of no way." Nevertheless, a distinction will prove helpful. Identifying the divine agent of "making a way out of no way" as God, rather than Jesus, opens both the concept of "making a way" and womanist theology to important new directions.

Removing the necessary connection between Jesus and God that pervades womanist theology and the concept of "making a way out of no way" allows womanists to receive a meaningful gift from process theologians. Cobb's christology and womanist christologies are largely incompatible.[47] Cobb is concerned to remain faithful to the creedal statements of the church[48] and to distinguish the Jesus of history from the Christ of faith. Womanists, however, do not care about these issues.[49] If we allow Cobb's christology and womanist christologies to have the prevailing voice, womanist and process theologies are understandably incommensurate.

But a "de-Jesus-ed" "making a way out of no way" can be compared with a "de-Christ-ed" creative transformation. Like creative transformation, "making a way out of no way" is a type of change that transforms humanity and the wider world. "Making a way out of no way" comes from the new vision that

God provides to black women, who then have significant agency in moving the future toward a just and participatory society. "Making a way out of no way" challenges the existing status quo. By operating in the situations that black women find life-threatening, it actually does, to use Cobb's language, "struggle against the death-dealing powers that threaten us." Like creative transformation, "making a way out of no way" is contextual, particular, noncoercive, and challenging.

Like "making a way out of no way," creative transformation offers a new vision that does not come completely out of the past. Like "making a way out of no way," creative transformation challenges the oppressive forces of society. Like "making a way out of no way," the aims of creative transformation are particular to each situation and God may not always lead us in ways that feel liberating. Sometimes the God of creative transformation will feel like a judge, but it leads us to a way that will improve the quality of life. Like "making a way out of no way," creative transformation involves God's presentation of unforeseen possibilities, human agency, a telos of justice, survival, and quality of life, and a challenge to the existing order.

Understanding "making a way out of no way" as a type of creative transformation can move womanist theology in three important directions. First, "making a way out of no way" as creative transformation gives womanist theology a metaphysical grounding to what has previously been asserted by examining the experiences of black women. Now we can say with greater strength that "making a way out of no way" is not just particular to the lives of black women or the black community. "Making a way out of no way" gives normative dress to the change that always occurs in a world of change and becoming. "Making a way out of no way" asserts that the aim of God is always toward survival, quality of life, love, and justice. "Making a way out of no way" allows womanist theologians to make a claim for all communities.

Second, "making a way out of no way" as creative transformation necessarily extends to nonhuman communities. Karen Baker-Fletcher's womanist theology incorporates justice for nonhuman environments as well as human communities. "Making a way out of no way" as creative transformation goes several steps further. "Making a way out of no way" as creative transformation states that the aims of God also guide the nonhuman environment. "Making a way out of no way" as creative transformation talks about divine and *creaturely* agency. It will alert African Americans to the ecological crisis and to the fact that the natural world, too, is and must be transformed into a higher quality of its own life.

Third, and perhaps most important, "making a way out of no way" as creative transformation opens womanist theology to non-Christian theological reflection and construction. Womanist theologian Renee Hill criticizes all black theologies for their christocentrism:

> The Christian hegemony that has controlled and defined African American religious discourse is being challenged by African Americans

who practice Islam, African-derived traditional religions (including Santeria, Akan, Yoruba, and Vodun), Buddhism, Judaism, and Humanism among other traditions.[50]

She states that we must remove Christ from the center of African American religious discourse. If Christ is removed from the center of black theologies, new images will emerge. Hill proposes the image of a river:

> It changes and is changed in the process of moving and being...The ability to move with and through difference, the ability to use power to shift, change, and adapt are all characteristics that are well suited to the tasks that black theologies and black power are facing.[51]

This "river" is creative transformation. "Making a way out of no way" as creative transformation gives an indigenous metaphor for both Christian and non-Christian womanist theologies in pluralistic dialogue.

The Womanist Gift to Process Theology

More than church history, doctrine, philosophy, or biblical interpretation, the experiences of black women are the starting point and testing ground for all womanist theologies. Delores Williams insists on the primacy of experience, "[W]e womanists must be guided more by black Christian women's voices, faith and experience than by anything that was decided centuries ago at Chalcedon."[52] Womanist theologians have relied from the beginning upon various forms of literature as sources for providing information about the experiences of black women. Speeches, autobiographies, and slave narratives have provided firsthand records of the experiences of historical figures in black women's history. Yet womanist theologians have also used fictional narratives as lyrical and emblematic representations of the collective experiences of African American women.

It was also Whitehead's vision that the actual experience in the world would be the testing ground and molder of process theology: "The elucidation of immediate experience is the sole justification for any thought; and the starting point for thought is the analytic observation of components of this experience" (PR 4). The majority of process theology documents empirical knowledge of the world through science and philosophy. With such emphasis on science and philosophy, process theology has been able to build a rather solid bridge between science and religion, reason and faith. For that same reason, however, it is often accused of an over-reliance on philosophy and theory, with insufficient grounding in the concrete experiences of people.

Yet process theology contains the requisite elements for using a variety of sources in its commitment to experience. In the oft-quoted analogy of the airplane, Whitehead writes that a true method of discovery will start in one field of observation, make flight into the air of generalization, and land again for observation in another field where the generalization will be tested, adapted, and tried again in yet another field to which the airplane will fly (PR 5). Process theologians have been landing in the fields of physics, biology, philosophy, and psychology for the last several decades, while neglecting the imaginative and creative fields of music and literature.[53]

Womanist theology's use of literature as experience suggests that process theology, also grounded in experience, begin to seriously consider the use of literature, fiction even, as data for its speculative philosophical theology. I suggest a wedding, combining the process emphasis on science and philosophy and the womanist emphasis on history and literature. I go farther and suggest that process theology influenced by womanist concerns will experiment with black women's science fiction. A process theology that uses black women's science fiction

1. expresses a deeper commitment to Whitehead's method of discovery;
2. expands the circle for studies of religious pluralism; and
3. provides a hope that can be missing from many process theologies.

Womanist theologians are recognized for the way in which they have used black women's literature as a source for doing theology. In his 1999 summary of black theology, Dwight Hopkins cites womanist religious scholars as persistently exploring diverse sources of black women's experiences to provide lessons for today—with literature by black women as the most widely drawn upon source.[54] In a foundational essay on womanist theology, Delores Williams summarizes the use of literature in womanist theology: "Female slave narratives, imaginative literature by black women, autobiographies, the work by black women in academic disciplines and the testimonies of black church women will be authoritative sources for womanist theologians."[55] Black women's literature will be, William concludes,

[a] valuable resource for indicating and validating the kind of data upon which womanist theologians can reflect as they bring black women's social, religious, and cultural experience into the discourse of theology, ethics, biblical and religious studies.[56]

Womanist religious scholars use black women's literature as a theological source that describes and elucidates the experiences of black women.

Despite this creative use of black women's literature in the construction of womanist theology, womanist theologians have not drawn upon black women's science fiction as a source for theology, overlooking a critical source in the literary field. Womanist theologians use nineteenth-century slave narratives and autobiographies, as well as twentieth-century authors from the Harlem Renaissance and the 1970s and 1980s. After describing these experiences, which are assumed to be representative, womanist theologians make conclusions about how black women have thought about God, the Bible, or ethics in the past. Yet feminist science fiction writer Joanna Russ offers science fiction as a liberating genre for women because it welcomes the display of alternative attitudes and cultures: "The science fiction arena is particularly appropriate for introducing figures that challenge traditional literary representations of women."[57] Rather than reveal the past experiences of black women and society, black women's science fiction provides visions for the future of society. It offers proposals for what may be.

Science Fiction and Womanist Theology

Black women's science fiction is just beginning to receive the attention it deserves. There are rising numbers of black science fiction writers, many of them female. In addition to the well-known Octavia Butler, Linda Addison, Tananarive Due, Nalo Hopkinson, and Nisi Shawl (to name a few) are constantly adding to the ranks of black female science fiction writers. There are four key aspects of black women's science fiction:

1. It is a critique of current society.
2. It is concerned with issues of social justice.
3. It offers possibilities for the future.
4. It changes its readers.

Black women's science fiction offers a critique of contemporary society. As a utopia, it is constructed, in part, out of dissatisfaction with the world as it is. Utopias do more than reject the author's inherited world. Utopias also offer solutions for ways to make that world better. In rather strong language, literary critic Joseph Wellbank states that justice is a requirement of utopias: "Having an adequate conception of social justice should be of the first importance to every serious utopian thinker and practitioner."[58] Wellbank identifies four criteria of justice that utopic visions must include: a definition of genuine justice, a theoretical frame for the social accomplishment of the demands of justice, a fair schematic for the social structure, and impartiality in these accomplishments.[59] Preston Williams adds that black utopic visions are a combination of freedom, justice, and Christian ethics that entail a reorientation of communal values.[60] A utopia is useless if, in its critique of society, it does not imply or provide a picture of justice. Utopian literature helps its readers to dream and imagine a better life.

Black women's science fiction is also influenced by feminism and feminist science fiction. Rather than positing one idea, feminist science fiction writers write in thought-experiments. Their writing says, "What if…" or "Let's try…" or "what would we get if…" or "I wished I could live like…" Marleen Barr emphasizes this speculative nature of women's science fiction and prefers the term "'feminist speculative fiction' to include feminist utopians, science fiction, fantasy, and sword and sorcery."[61] The female protagonists of feminist speculative fiction destroy patriarchal ideas of femininity: "Women who form communities, become heroes, and take charge of their sexuality behave in a manner which is alien to the established concept of femininity–they show women with mastery and competence."[62] Barr notes that whereas feminist speculative fiction tends to banish men from their ideal communities, "womanist speculative fiction" creates societies in which "women co-exist with men, retain their female characteristics, and function as powerful individuals."[63] In fact, men are crucial to the development of the female hero of womanist speculative fiction. In womanist speculative fiction, "the woman hero dances in the spotlight, eclipsing the male heroine" without causing him to sacrifice his place, purpose, or dignity.[64]

Black women's science fiction changes the world. It offers something that women are often denied in the real world—the possibilities for women to receive support from men.[65] It provides pictures of new relationships between men and women. The protagonist in black women's science fiction changes the imperfect world of the novel and strives to create new societies with new values. Second, these protagonists change their worlds not by sacrificing love for power, but by combining special powers with commitments to others.[66] For Barr, this is a call to the readers of womanist speculative fiction: "[The authors'] visions summon us to rebuild society and make it possible for female heroes to experience both love and public importance."[67]

This quick review of genre influences suggests that there are markers of black women's science fiction. Like the utopia, black women's science fiction offers an ideal society that does not currently exist. It is also a critique of current society—including its patriarchy and limiting roles for men and women. It is interested in freedom, justice, and ethics for the entire community. But it does not just offer one perfect idea; it is speculative. Black women's science fiction offers possibilities and alternatives for the future. In so doing, it changes its readers—encouraging them to rebuild society into the kind of place it can be, or save it from being the kind of place it could be if we are not careful. Because of these functions, critic Dingbo Wu suggests a connection between utopian literature and spirituality: "Utopian literature serves as a spiritual guide demonstrating values and experiences of alternative societies that are in some ways better or worse than the readers' world."[68]

Science fiction has received mixed reviews from American religious scholars. Some critics, such as John V. Lawing, argue that science fiction ignores issues of religion.[69] Others, like Thomas Molnar, critique science fiction for offering salvation without divinity. On the other hand, some religious scholars have embraced science fiction. Stephen May argues that science fiction actually indicates a deep spiritual need within society.[70] Science fiction presents specifically theological concerns.

Like African American religion itself, the religious elements of black women's science fiction encompass a variety of religious sources, including the combination of both Christianity and indigenous religious traditions. Gloria Naylor's *Mama Day* takes place in the Gullah Islands, where wisdom and command of conjure frame the respect for the matriarch, Mama Day.[71] Mama Day's beneficent use of conjure heals her granddaughter from both the ills of the modern world and the evil conjure that have plagued and sickened her.

Octavia Butler's protagonist in the *Parable* series is given a Yoruba middle and surname that relate to traditional Yoruba religion:

> Her second name was 'Oya'...'Oya' is the name of a Nigerian Orisha–goddess–of the Yoruba people. In fact, the original Oya was the goddess of the Niger River, a dynamic, dangerous entity, she was also goddess of the wind, fire, and death, more bringers of great change.[72]

This naming ties Butler's process-womanist religious construction to the religious traditions of West Africa. More directly, Nalo Hopkinson's *Brown Girl in the Ring* explicitly refers to the major *orisha* of traditional Yoruba religion.[73] Although the protagonist initially rejects the "obeah" religion of her grandmother, she comes to embrace her ability to commune with African ancestors. Calling upon their powers is the only way the protagonist can save her community from the dark powers that drain the life from its inhabitants. In these examples, we see that some black women's science fiction refers to traditional African religion as both a source of strength and cure for society's ills. It moves beyond a simple critique or embrace of Christianity and opens the door for the role that African traditional religions play in the lives of black women.

Black women's science fiction ensures that womanist literature is not limited to serving as a source for describing the past experiences of black women. Black women's literature can also have a proscriptive function. Black women's science fiction can tell us what has happened, yes, but it will also provide concrete images, models, and proposals for what *could* happen and/or what *should* happen. A womanist use of science fiction pushes womanist theology to explore lessons from the hard sciences. In so doing, black women's science fiction gives teeth to the eschatological vision. It gives content and possibilities. Some visions provided by black women's science fiction may prove untenable and undesirable. Or we may conclude that they are just what we needed, ideas that have not yet found voice and specificity. By its form and content, black women's science fiction issues womanist theology into the future.

Science Fiction and Process Theology

While process philosophical systems are best known for their rather complex metaphysic of change and evolution, empirical data always has the final word. Process theology leans heavily on the fields of science and philosophy for information about the world, understandably because of Whitehead's background as a physicist and mathematician. Discussing the relation between experience and speculative philosophy, Whitehead highlights the relationship between science and religion: "Philosophy frees itself from the taint of ineffectiveness by its close relations with religion and with science, natural and sociological. It attains its chief importance by fusing the two, namely, religion and science, into one rational scheme of thought" (PR 15–16). Many process theologians have linked process theology with religion and science.[74] Process theologians have not utilized history, literature, or music to the same extent as they have science and philosophy. Notable exceptions are Catherine Keller's *Apocalypse Now and Then* and Ann Pederson's *God, Creation, and All that Jazz*. These feminist process theologians have incorporated the social and aesthetic sciences into their process constructions. But why are they in such a minority? Where is literature? Do process theologians devalue aesthetics in relation to science and philosophy, or have they simply overlooked it because of their own personal and professional interests? By limiting the sources of data for experience, process theologians have failed to conduct Whitehead's metaphorical airplane test of process metaphysics in a variety of fields of practice.

A venture into the use of science fiction as a theological source offers a smooth transition from the focus on the hard sciences to a foray into literature and other aesthetic sciences. Science fiction combines the insights of science, technology, and concrete empiricism with imagination and social critique. Process theology can begin to balance its rational and empirical side with imagination and justice concerns. Science fiction's offer of new possibilities is a potent source of novelty. Science fiction embraces one of the key concepts of process metaphysics—it sifts through the inputs of the past, creates a new thing, and projects this vision into the world.

The use of black women's science fiction as a theological source allows process theologians to receive a meaningful gift from womanists, moving process theology in three important directions. First, it offers process theology a deeper commitment to Whitehead's airplane metaphor for testing truth. Black women's science fiction is yet another field in which the plane of process must land. If a process metaphysic cannot land in the field of literature, it needs to be revised. Yet, the combination of science and fiction may reassure and strengthen the process metaphysic. The experiences and visions of African Americans, black women in particular, may not be so foreign to the speculative philosophy of process theology. A process theology using black women's science fiction will hear voices from the literary community, the scientific community, and African American communities. When process theology explicitly considers the experiences of black Americans, new ground may open for conversation between process and black theologies. Perhaps this time, it will bring new sensitivity and receptivity to change on the part of each dialogue partner.

Second, a process theology that incorporates black women's science fiction expands the circle for conversations in religious pluralism. Griffin, Cobb, Marjorie Suchocki, Gene Reeves, Joseph Bracken, and many other process theologians express strong convictions of religious pluralism and have explored the connections between Christianity and Buddhism through the lens of process thought. They suggest that a process metaphysic may be, at the most, a common thread, and at the least, a starting point, for interreligious discussions. Yet process's religious pluralism suffers from the same myopia as the broader field of religious pluralism; it tends to equate "religions" with Christianity, Judaism, Hinduism, Buddhism, and Islam. Because much of black women's science fiction invokes African traditional religions and their New World variants, a process theology that uses black women's science fiction will enter into conversation with African traditional religions. Bringing African traditional religions into the pluralist discussion can lead to the inclusion of other indigenous religious traditions and will, by necessity, mean extended dialogue with anthropology and art history, as well.

Third, a process theology that incorporates black women's science fiction can provide a hope that can be missing from many process theologies. While process theology does not exclude hope, it provides no guarantee of a happy ending. The future of the world is the result of the cooperative effort between God and the world. Experience has shown us that humanity often chooses options that do not affirm life. If we continue to make these choices, evil may win out over good. This stark realism has resulted in accusations of pessimism and hopelessness against process theology. While process theologians have persistently refuted this critique, a process theology using black women's science fiction will drive their rebuttal home. Black women's science fiction may not save the entire world, but it often reconfigures social and gender relations in ways that re-draw encouraging visions of the future from the point of view of feminist, womanist, and black theologies. It points to another way, requiring change of us as individuals and as society to arrive at a better vision. Womanist theology offers process theology the gift of literature and, in black women's science fiction, the gift of imaginative challenge. Black women's science fiction challenges us, frightens us, and demands of us. Using imagination and just-enough-distance-for-us-to-see-ourselves, black women's science fiction subtly changes its readers to change the world.

In some cultures, to invite someone into your house without offering a gift is impolite. The visitor blesses the host with her presence. The host graces the visitor with an offering from the heart. So I imagine the relationship between process and womanist theologies. They come to the table not to debate, argue, or come to an agreement. They come to visit, learn, and be changed by one another. They are connected by their passions for God, for justice, and for the need to make sense out of experience without giving up on the world. The beliefs in God-initiated change and radical empiricism have provoked the invitation. Octavia Butler is the mediator today. And hands are open–ready for the exchange of gifts that will leave each partner changed.

CHAPTER 14

Feminist Theology in Process Perspective

■ LUCINDA A. HUFFAKER

Feminist theologians have drawn on the resources of process philosophy at least since 1978, when pioneers like Valerie Saiving and Mary Daly participated in the first conference on feminism and process thought.[1] As a theological perspective that gives priority to feminist values and commitments, feminist theology critiques theology that is rooted in and representative of male experience and patriarchal social systems that disadvantage women. Feminist theology advances reinterpretations and/or alternative representations of our systems of ultimate meaning that promote the full humanity of all people, in particular women and others whose voices have not been included in the dominant theological traditions.

Because feminism asserts that theorizing must begin with—and theory is accountable to—the concrete particularities of women's experience, it feels an immediate affinity with process philosophy, which locates its starting point in human experience with a trajectory from concreteness to abstraction rather than vice versa. While both perspectives recognize that what is concrete must have a location (hence experience is subjective and always perspectival), feminists maintain a unique focus on theology from women's experiences.

Process thought also shares with feminism a commitment to the nature of reality as relational. Entities are constituted by their relationships with other entities. Relationships are internal to who we are rather than merely a property or characteristic that we exhibit. The emphasis on the centrality of relationships to all existence is fertile ground for feminist-process dialogue.

Feminist theory emphasizes the significance of relationship and mutuality alongside the values of distinctiveness and personal agency, and process philosophy provides language to explain how it is that the very nature of existence is relational. Moreover, process philosophy offers an analysis of

177

diversity that establishes difference through *contrast* rather than *separation,* providing a crucial epistemological tool for feminists working toward community in a plural world.[2] Process thought provides important philosophical grounding and coherence for feminist theory. Its attunement with contemporary understandings of the nature of existence provides important confirmation for theological construction from women's experience. Given such coincidence of priorities, it is not surprising that the dialogue between feminist and process thought has provided many creative directions for feminist theological critique and constructive work. With no pretense of being comprehensive, this essay provides examples of the contributions of process thought to feminist critiques and reconstructions of some traditional theological doctrines.

Rethinking God

What is God like? Feminist theologians have argued that traditional understandings of God as the Almighty, eternally self-sufficient ruler who demands our obedience and self-denial is oppressive to women and does not connect in helpful ways with our positive experiences of power and goodness. Classical presentations of the divine nature as omnipotent, omniscient, utterly transcendent, and authoritarian are not congruent with feminist values of mutuality, personal dignity, and empathic connection. Alternative threads in the Christian tradition have been lifted up as more helpful to women. Liberation, Trinitarian, and narrative theologies harbor positive images of God that feminist theologians have utilized, and certainly more recent ecological and postcolonial theologies have much in common with feminist theology. However, process philosophy undergirds and expands feminist conceptions of God in particularly helpful ways.

Perhaps the most important place to begin is with God's power. Feminists are committed to the analysis of power for the purpose of replacing oppressive and destructive patterns of *power-over* with more humane arrangements of shared power, that is, *power-with* or *power-alongside.* God as all-powerful has been the template for human power relations, the divine endorsement for hierarchical social structures of power and submission: God over man, man over woman, humans over animals and the rest of creation. Feminists object to the oppressive nature of such unidirectional power and declare the legitimacy of their own experiences of power in collaboration with, in response to, and on behalf of others. Women's experiences of caring for children, creating nurturing environments, and surviving in male-dominated societies necessitate a more nuanced understanding of God's power than mere domination. Feminist attempts to empower women and other marginalized groups rely on the ability to reframe power in ways that do not force us to compete for it. Yet Catherine Keller laments, "in feminist theory and theology the nature of power itself, as distinct from its functions, remains still inadequately illumined."[3]

In their efforts to describe power, feminist theologians have drawn heavily from Bernard Loomer's process conception of power as "the ability both to produce and to undergo an effect."⁴ Whereas unidirectional or linear power has been the dominant understanding that bifurcates the world into winners and losers, relational power recognizes the enduring potency of empowering others. The power both to influence others and to be influenced by others receives profound elaboration in process philosophy's analysis of mutual internal relations. In the creative activity of concrescence and transition, an actual entity draws "the larger whole in which it finds itself" into its own articulation, and in turn it contributes its aspects to this same environment (SMW 96). Relational power is manifested in both giving and receiving and is exercised in collaborative modes of interaction as much or more than through competition.

Process theologians describe God's power as persuasive rather than coercive and dominating, as a lure toward the best possible future rather than a threat of punishment for disobedience. God's lure is the initial aim of every actual entity, but this form of power is persuasive rather than controlling or determinative because of the freedom of the self-authoring entity to incorporate or reject the initial aim in the subjective aim. In addition to persuasion, God's power also has the aspect of receiving the influence of every droplet of experience in its entirety. God feels everything. This describes God's Consequent Nature, and it is our assurance that nothing is lost to God's experience.

God's power to exert and receive influence coexists with our own relational power through the web of interrelations that is our universe. Feminist theologians assert the importance of mutuality in relationships, and this includes the divine-human relationship.⁵ Traditional theism teaches us that God is unchanging and therefore trustworthy, and God's immutability is supposed to give us security. Process and feminist theology describe a God whose receptivity necessitates being influenced or in some manner changed by our feelings, decisions, and actions, thereby demonstrating a responsive and therefore credible love.

Emphasizing the mutuality of the divine-human relationship requires some reframing of the nature of God's transcendence, which has traditionally described God's unknowable, distant Otherness. While feminist theologians have given much attention to God's immanence, or God's presence with us and in the world, they have been criticized for weakening or forfeiting any notion of God's transcendence in their eagerness to make God accessible to those who have had no access to worldly power. God's immanence is well-represented in process philosophy as how God is present in every concrescing occasion. Whitehead associated God's immanence with the Primordial Nature as "being *with* all creation," luring it toward beauty by providing ordered potentials in the form of its initial aim (PR 344). But what about God's transcendence? How does feminist theology account for the mysterious Otherness of God without compromising our essential interconnection?

Feminist theologians have vehemently rejected the image of transcendence that implies "a lack of relatedness in God as the source of divine strength." Such a divine image reinforces the destructive patriarchal model of separate, independent selfhood.[6] Process philosophy provides an alternative picture of transcendence that is aligned more with its root meaning of "crossing over" or "linking" than with its long tradition as a sort of spatial separation. For Whitehead, transcendence bridges the past with the next moment of becoming; it is the freedom to bring new possibilities into existence for "every actual entity, including God" (PR 88, 94). This is an interpretive frame for transcendence that brings an acceptable balance to feminist theology's understanding of immanence, whether divine or human, because it bespeaks nothing less than the fundamental freedom to create or compose self from the parts of our world.

Another aspect of divine perfection, the notion of God's omniscience and omnipresence, presents a particular stumbling block for feminists. An all-seeing, all-knowing God can be painfully associated with the normative and pervasive male gaze, the internalized and media-supported gender police that constrains women's self-image and behavior to prescribed female stereotypes. Consider the pattern of domestic violence enacted by the insanely jealous, possessive partner who insists on watching and controlling every place his victim goes and everything she does.[7] God's abiding presence is a vital and comforting aspect of the divine nature, but omniscience and omnipresence must not violate the private space of self-constitution that in process thought is the concrescing entity. Considerable debate has arisen about the relative presence and absence of God to our experience because of the "moment of sheer individuality...of absolute self-attainment" that Whitehead insists cannot be shared by contemporaries (AI 179). What is at stake is whether God's compassion is real and trustworthy: Is God truly present with us? A feminist theological view, based on women's experience of the omnipresent male gaze, can assert that the moment of private creative self-constitution is essential for the individual dignity and empowerment of humans, and it does not diminish our relation to a loving but limited God.

Often criticized for their image of a "weak" God, process theologians must grapple with the implications of limiting God's control of the world (although reconceiving God's infinite power does provide a more consistent theology of human freedom). If the future is open and creatures make decisions freely, how then can we think of God's unboundedness or ultimacy? For feminists concerned for the just treatment and self-determination of people who have been marginalized and disempowered, God is unlimited in providing for the flourishing of all. God's is the ultimate inclusivity—nothing and no one is wasted or lost or left out. Process thought is well-suited for this conceptual task, for Hartshorne declared that what was worshipful in God are unsurpassability and all-inclusiveness rather than a divine monopoly on power.[8] That God's power is greater than ours and therefore "godly" is due to the inclusivity or "size" of God. That is, God's receptive power includes every entity, excluding no one, and God's persuasive power is that same comprehensive wholeness integrated into the best possible choice for the future as the subjective aim.

God's ultimacy is inclusion rather than domination, hence feminists find in the divine nature a model for collaboration and mutuality with which to resist cultural preoccupation with competition.

Rethinking Creation

Feminists argue that the world is not ordered by opposition and competition, but by relationships of mutuality. Hierarchical patterns that pit humans against each other and make nature subordinate to human desires are dangerously destructive of an interdependent creation. Feminists resist dualisms and dualistic thinking that divide the world into pieces[9] : male/female, thinking/feeling, mind/body, man/nature, white/black, and so on. Such divisions obscure the complexity of these categories and fabricate a basis for stereotypes and exclusion. One pole of the dichotomy usually takes on greater positive value, and that pole is associated with the dominant group, reinforcing the superiority of one side of each dichotomy. So as male is superior to female, thinking should rule feeling, spiritual needs are more important than bodily needs, and so on. The poles of various dichotomies become associated with the corresponding poles of other dichotomies. Attributes of each are generalized accordingly: Women are more attuned to feelings, and men are clear thinkers; women are tempters of the body while men strive to achieve mental excellence; nature is feminine and, like women, should be ruled by men; black people are closer to their animal nature than white people; and so on. Dualism oversimplifies actual existence and becomes a tool to perpetuate false stereotypes and unjust hierarchies.

As feminist theologians seek to dismantle oppressive dualisms, process thought contributes analytical tools that account for distinctions without resorting to oppositional dichotomies. God and world, humans and nature share a continuous organic relation rather than a hierarchy of dominants and subordinates. Classic dualisms like thinking and feeling are subverted by the association of feelings with the fundamental prehensions that are the basis of experience and precursors to all conscious thought. Aesthetics usurps the traditional preeminence of science and technology because, for Whitehead, beauty is the aim of all existence. Concrete particularity is not subordinated to abstract generalizations, and the body is not inferior to mind, soul, or spirit because our body is our concrete location, our avenue of preconscious prehension of experience more fundamental than thought or language. Process thought supports the value that feminists ascribe to *embodied* experience that seeks expression through ritual and sacrament of a *particular* community, as well as deeds of service that attend to the physical needs of people. Finally, nature is not the alien other that must be subdued so that humans can thrive, but humans and nature are interconnected in a complex web that must be nurtured for our mutual sustenance.

These examples illustrate reclamation of what has been denigrated in its stereotypical associations with women and the feminine. Indeed, one method for dismantling traditional dualisms is to enhance the value of the negative pole, as if the two extremes were sides of a scale that needed to be brought into balance. Feminists differ in their assessment of the merit of this approach. Some exalt the heretofore disparaged pole as the feminine essence that will restore our world. At the other extreme are those who avow that any attention to the underside of the dualism will only perpetuate its oppressive power. Another tactic, then, is to counter dualistic interpretations by exposing the complexity of life, to break open the carefully contained categories by exposing their multiple exceptions, to convert the poles to a continuous array.

When dualistic thinking functions to make life simpler, diversity becomes a problem to be solved. Yet process thought demonstrates the benefits of complexity. Even more, process asserts that complexity and order need each other because order supports increasing complexity, which in turn contributes to richer, fuller experience. That places difference in a new light. Difference is not something to solve or avoid because it threatens personal or communal identities. Rather than being adjudicated through separation, difference is incorporated through contrast, thus increasing beauty. Order is not imposed onto difference, forcing it into a preordained structure. Feminist and liberation theologians negatively associate such order with the oppressor's euphemism for quelling resistance. In process thought, order expresses how entities are grouped into greater complexity on the basis of their harmony and intensity.

Naturally, process and feminist emphases on openness and inclusion imply not only complexity but also some chaos; and both perspectives can embrace chaos as an important ingredient for creative advance. Catherine Keller has written eloquently about the Christian tradition's distortion of healthy ambivalence and indeterminateness into the evil to be repressed (like Yahweh's taming of Tehom/Tiamat).[10] Yet only "where there is enough order and enough chaos" in "layering interplay" can new life and possibility emerge.[11] Keller critiques "apocalyptic consciousness" that divides the world into good parts that must battle to subdue or expunge the evil parts. Creativity in process perspective offers something of an antidote to our efforts to control…people, nature, events, the future—something like Keller's "counter-apocalyptic consciousness" that understands and embraces slightly chaotic communities comprised of complexity and difference.[12]

The Problem of Sin

Feminists have argued for the relational nature of the human self, and feminist theologians (among others) extend that relational nature to describe God's character as well. We exist in and through relationships and do not exist apart from them. In process terms, we are constituted by our relationships. As that which prevents us from knowledge of God and from fullness of life, sin describes a lack or loss of relationship, or exclusion or denial of relationship—between humans and God, among humans, from humans toward nature, even an unhealthy relation to one's own body or memories. For feminist theologians, sin comes from a lack of mutuality in any relationship—not a tit-for-tat mutuality of equal exchange, but a rhythmic mutuality of giving and receiving in our co-creation of one another. Certainly we do not expect children to contribute the same amount or type of things to the parent-child relationships as the parent. Nor do we mean "equal" when we describe mutuality in the relations of humans with God or nature. Rather, mutuality suggests receptivity to one another's experience so that we include it in our own self-becoming and consider it in our intentions for the future. These are the dynamics of empathic attunement that feminist psychologists identify as the foundations of psychological development.[13] Sin describes the lack of attunement or empathy or compassion—all words that connote the sharing of some mutual experience.

Sin opposes God's will in that it limits relationship. Process thought states God's will as always directed toward increasing beauty in the world, described as "the evocation of intensities" (PR 111). Intensity and harmony are the complementary components of beauty—greater beauty is the result of as much intensity as can still be synthesized harmoniously in an occasion, and intensity is created by contrast. Receptivity, inclusion, and openness are divine attributes that are central to God's creative activity. God's Consequent Nature describes how God feels the world in its entirety and its particularity—without limitation—and God's Primordial Nature is unbounded in its bringing together or ordering of all our feelings into relevant contrasts. All of this is to say that God's lure is toward taking more into account, expanding our experience to include more of others' experience, increasing contrasts, enlarging our horizons. Our temptation is to protect ourselves or to exert power over others by cutting off our experience of them and limiting their influence on us. God is different from all other actual entities (and without sin) because God's openness to the world's experience is limitless. Nothing is excluded or lost. Bernard Loomer's reference to God's size or stature depicts this ability to perfectly hold the universe of past and present actualities in compatible contrasts, and feeling them as everlastingly present.[14] And Loomer says size can also describe the measure of a person:

> the stature of a person's soul, the range and depth of his [her] love, his [her] capacity for relationships. I mean the volume of life you can take into your being and still maintain your integrity and individuality, the intensity and variety of outlook you can entertain in the unity of your being without feeling defensive or insecure. I mean the strength of your spirit to encourage others to become freer in the development of their diversity and uniqueness. I mean the power to sustain more complex and enriching tensions.[15]

Sin reduces human stature because it cuts off relationship. Our self-protection diminishes us.

Sin as the broken relation between humans and God is well-established in Christian tradition. However, feminists are not satisfied with the traditional explanation that our separation is caused by pride and rebellion against God. It was enormously significant when Valerie Saiving first argued in 1960 that the notion of sin as pride and egotism was predicated on male experience and that women's experience of temptation and sin was different. She described "the feminine situation" of brokenness as "triviality, distractibility, and diffuseness; lack of an organizing center or focus; dependence on others for one's own self-definition; [and] tolerance at the expense of standards of excellence."[16] Her description of feminine sin was groundbreaking as an appeal to women's lived experience as a source for doing theology. While an overactive ego is an understandable temptation for those with social status and power, lack of clarity and frivolity have greater relevance in the experience of their subordinates. Saiving's expansion of the notion of sin laid a path for feminist theologians to explore the nuances of sin as disconnection, denial, or violation of relation.

Process thought recognizes in both egotism and self-negation a common dynamic of failed relation. Relationship can be aborted by one's pride because one has made others the object of his/her inflated subjectivity. In this case, power is exercised unilaterally outward; and rigid personal boundaries limit receptivity and openness to any potential influence from the other. Beauty is diminished because repetition, monotony, and a false sense of security based on predictability are substituted for potential contrast of experience. Alternatively, in sin that feminists describe as hiding or self-negation, relationship is denied because the subject presents no object to enrich others' experience.[17] Power is again unilateral but experienced this time as being influenced or defined by others. A false feeling of safety conceals passivity and fear of risk. Inadequate boundaries allow receptivity to dissolve into loss of integrity, or what Rita Brock has called "loss of heart."[18]

When we act in ways that ignore our connections with other people and parts of our world, sin abounds. Process thought supports feminists' observations that relationship is disabled in two ways: by refusing influence from others or by contributing nothing to others. This helps illumine personal sin. At the same time, feminist theologians are even more concerned to analyze sin and brokenness at social and systemic levels because of the pervasive and interlocking patterns of oppression. Process thought helps explain the weight of limitation on freedom and creativity exercised by one's context and past. Institutions and cultural symbol systems exhibit the same webs of relation and intersubjectivity that describe personal experience. To the extent that they "perpetuate norms of well-being for some at the expense of others," they perpetuate sin through group cohesion and social inheritance.[19] Sin becomes self-generating through systems by habit and lack of critical self-consciousness.

The Problem of Sacrifice

The personal and structural problems of sin, defined as they are by feminist theologians in terms of violated relationships, cannot be resolved (for women) by the Savior's sacrificial death. Feminist objections to soteriology based on the necessity of Christ's suffering and death on the cross are plentiful. Most point to the disproportionate application to women of the model of Jesus' obedience, self-sacrifice, and divine self-giving. Linell Cady has argued, "By making self-sacrifice the primary criterion of the virtuous life, Christianity has given powerful religious validation to the situation of oppression."[20] For those whose temptation is toward hiding rather than self-aggrandizement, Jesus' death as an example of devotion to God's will only reinforces the sin of self-negation. Self-sacrifice on behalf of others, at least as it has been elaborated in Christian tradition, connotes a loss of mutual relation rather than the restoration or empowering of relation. Hence theories of the atonement have presented theological impasses for many feminist theologians. How does Jesus save us?

The problem of sin is addressed by the restoration of right relations, which feminist theology equates with justice.[21] Justice is not order restored by the overwhelming power of the Divine King. Rather, justice is mutual relation and shared power for the well-being of all creation. Jesus demonstrated justice through his life by including the outcasts and marginalized in his circle of human relationships. Process thought shares this profession of justice that insists on inclusion. God's desire is that nothing is lost or wasted (PR 346). God's power is receptive to humans' experience of need. Because we share God's co-creative power to exert and receive influence, both process and feminist theologies emphasize our human responsibility to seek justice through ethical action.

Because right or just relations are at the center of feminist theology, process thought has provided a number of fresh interpretive frames for the person of Jesus, his life, death, and resurrection. Most feminist theologians place significant emphasis on Jesus' life along with or even instead of his death. Process philosophy corroborates that emphasis through its value of concrete, particular experience. As the revelation of God, the Incarnate God, Jesus the Christ is God's openness expressed through self-disclosure. He is also God's completely open receptivity to the world's experience—through the embodied form of a man. Both manifest the divine urge for deeper, fuller, more intense relationship with creation. In our human relationships, we seek to know and be known. Feminists assert that we are ourselves most fully when we share such mutual encounters with others. The Incarnation is God's uniquely receptive and revelatory encounter with humanity.

Authentic relationship always involves risk. In self-disclosure we become vulnerable to rejection. For many feminist theologians, Jesus' death is best understood as evidence of human rejection of relationship with the Divine as well as rejection of life as Jesus lived it in mutual relation with others. Carter Heyward explains, "The rejection and crucifixion of Jesus signaled the extent to which human beings will go to avoid our own relational possibilities."[22] Yet, as we have noted, the point of God's risk in Jesus is not sacrifice, but the profound promise of transformation of destructive powers that require sacrifice. That is why the cross cannot be understood without the resurrection. In process thought, transformative power is grounded in loving openness. Hence, redemption, as Marjorie Suchocki explains it, is God's transformation of our previous decisions against relations with others into new possibilities:

> God's full openness to who we are involves God in the pain of who we are, symbolized most profoundly in the revelation of God in Jesus on a cross. But this unsurpassable truth of God's knowledge is the means whereby God knows precisely what possibilities will be redemptive for us in the next moment of our existence. Through God's crucifixion, God provides us with a resurrection fitted to us.[23]

God's lure in the initial aim is "a resurrection fitted" to each actual entity as it moves from subjective experience to objective satisfaction. On the smallest scale, an entity transcends what was by creating itself anew. On the human scale we transcend what we were by creating something new for ourselves as well as for others in our common future. Just so God's transcendence is expressed in the transformation that is the resurrection. For Christians, the ultimate rejection of relationship that is death turns out not to be ultimate at all. Not only is all experience preserved in unfading importance in God's Consequent Nature, but the resurrection is our assurance that God's Primordial Nature makes the possibility of transformation perpetually present in the world. And this transformation is for the whole world, for, in an interdependent world, both sin and salvation are ecological and communal.

A Few Caveats

Feminist theologians who appropriate process philosophy and theology cite clear benefits that the schema provides, namely a theoretical foundation and conceptual framework for feminist experience, analysis, and practice. It enhances articulation and coherence of certain topics. It points to metaphysical underpinnings for premises such as the centrality of relationships and the focus on experience for analysis and theory. While avoiding claims to comprehensive adequacy, feminists who appeal to process frameworks do affirm its contributions to some preliminary systematizing of feminist models in ways that helpfully respond to critiques of feminist theology as "soft" and lacking in arguable premises and constructive alternatives.

At the same time, feminist theologians have a number of pointed critiques of process thought that qualify their appropriations of it in their work. It is said to be overly abstract, rational, and elitist, and hence not easily accessible to the marginalized communities to which feminists hold themselves accountable. It may be too accommodating and optimistic about evolutionary advancement, and insufficiently attentive to and critical of political dynamics and structures, making it inadequate for supporting feminist commitments to advocacy and praxis. And there is concern that certain strands of process thought perpetuate hidden patriarchal imbalances—for example, overvaluing conscious experience and prioritizing novelty and dynamic process to the disparagement of continuity and rest. These cautions and criticisms indicate that feminist theology contributes to process philosophy by providing arenas for testing the latter's adequacy and extending the fullness of its applications and implications.

Feminist challenges to process thought are significant, and any appropriation should be a critical one. Yet Catherine Keller's optimistic assessment is sound: "The system is therefore capable of self-correction on this score: the theology is no more static than its deity."[24] Their common commitment to mutual openness and influence makes process and feminist theologies' appealing dialogue partners.

Conclusion

That process thought is not widely associated with feminist theology does not mean that it is lacking in influence within the discipline. One can discern its imprint in a host of "relational theologies" that may or may not cite Whitehead or Hartshorne, but which nevertheless employ analogous language to articulate how beings are both connected to one another and distinctly themselves. In addition, a number of female process theologians (and certainly many male feminist sympathizers) do not write from an explicitly feminist perspective but share an appreciation for process/feminist congenialities. The work of these other theologians provides many additional examples of theological reflection that is congruent with process feminist perspectives.

As a brief introduction, this chapter presents a few examples from work that is representative of feminist theology in process perspective. Certainly much more could be mined from process thought to augment feminists' ongoing work to understand and articulate more adequate theological frameworks for just and meaningful life in the twenty-first century. The challenge is for scholars to persist in critical investigation and judicious appropriation of process concepts and categories, and to present fruitful results in publicly accessible and relevant, compelling ways.

CHAPTER 15

A Whiteheadian Perspective on Global Economics

■ CAROL JOHNSTON

Introduction: A Word about History

Current capitalist economic theory (known as neoclassical economics) claims to be "value-free." According to this view, economics operates according to basic "laws," such as that of supply and demand; and these are simply the way the world works. The thesis of this paper is that, contrary to the claim to be "scientific" and "value-free," economic theory is governed by fundamental value-choices and assumptions about human beings and the world that are so deeply embedded in the theory that economists have come to take them for granted. It has been over a hundred years since any mainstream economist seriously examined any of these values and assumptions to see if they are still viable. Instead, they dismiss all attempts to do so, even though in the last hundred years changes in physics and anthropology have changed every other field of inquiry dramatically. At the same time, neoclassical economics, embodied in capitalism, has become the dominant economics of the world; and the capitalist economic model is rapidly changing the whole world to conform to it—regardless of the consequences.

In neoclassical economic theory, human beings are assumed to be individualistic, and so to be essentially self-existent and without necessary relations to each other or the rest of the world. They are also assumed to be "rational actors"—that is, to look at every choice from the point of view of their own individual preferences. In theory, this does not rule out altruism, or concern for others, but it is an altruism chosen by the individual. In practice, the model operates to encourage and reinforce hedonism, or pleasure seeking. Not only human beings are "individualized"—the whole world is assumed to be made up of unrelated parts whose sole value is that imposed by individual human beings. This mechanistic and atomistic world (including all nonhuman creatures) exists solely for human use. Therefore, the only purpose of economics is to exploit the natural world to maximize growth in the production of goods for human use. Since the only way to judge what is "good" for human use is individual choice in the market, we have no way to judge what to produce or how much, beyond letting individuals with access to the market decide as individuals what they want, without regard to any social need. This brings us to the key value choice of capitalism: that the only recognizable good is individual choice.

This state of affairs has a long history of development, with the crucial period spanning from Adam Smith in 1776 to Alfred Marshall around 1900. As the key economists developed their theories, they made value choices and assumptions that were gradually embedded in the theory. However, along the way the economists often had other choices they could have made, and it is very useful to consider these as we search today for ways to deal with the problems capitalism has generated and to try to develop healthier and more sustainable economies. In this consideration, the philosophy of Alfred North Whitehead is most useful. His metaphysics provides a different way of looking at economics, helps to illuminate the embedded assumptions and value choices, and provides a foundation for better ones.

In process philosophy and theology, human beings are not atomistic individuals, but, as Herman Daly and John Cobb put it, "persons-in-community."[1] The world is neither mechanistic nor atomistic, but organic and relational. Every entity has value in its own right, apart from human need or use. A Whiteheadian approach to economics recognizes the impossibility of unlimited growth in the production of things. Instead, it allows for ways to optimize sustainable economic practices for the long-term health of life on earth.

When Adam Smith published his *Inquiry into the Nature and Causes of the Wealth of Nations* in 1776, he was asking if there could be a better way to run economies than the entrenched mercantilism of his day, which operated through state monopolies to benefit an elite. Frustrated with mercantilism, he and many others in his time searched for alternatives. They never imagined that the ideas they wrote about would some day coalesce into what we now call "capitalism," or that they would succeed beyond their wildest dreams. They were just trying to make the system more open to more participation by a wider range of people. I believe that today we are in a similar situation. Capitalism has been wildly successful in its single goal: constant growth in the production of "goods." What things will be produced, and what for, does not matter—as long as someone with money wants them. In addition, capitalism also has serious negative effects on both communities and the natural environment that must be dealt with. It has a built-in tendency to leave many people marginalized—not only unemployed and often unemployable within the capitalist market system, but even worse, stripped of traditional access to subsistence living. Consequently, many of us are searching for solutions—for ways to go beyond cosmetic reforms and really transform capitalism to make it a more equitable and environmentally sustainable system. Surely if Adam Smith and others of his day could think their way through to better ideas about economics than those offered in mercantilism, we can do the same with the economic models available to us today. If they could do it, *we* can do it, too.

Thinking from a Whiteheadian Perspective about Economics and Responsible Action

As a process theologian I already approach economics with a number of assumptions, value choices, and perspectives that come from my tradition. I hope to be clear about what those are and to compare them with those embedded in economics.

First of all, the world (which is both material and spiritual) and every entity in it has intrinsic value. Such value comes just by virtue of the process of concrescence in which the whole universe is embodied in a particular way in that entity, which then embodies concrete values for all subsequent entities to take into account. This is a much different view than that of neoclassical economics, in which human individuals assign all value. Process perspective assumes complex levels of value, which include the recognition that all entities do "assign" value to some extent to other entities–but they also "recognize" intrinsic value, and this must not be ignored. This matters greatly, because it means that unbridled exploitation of human beings and the natural world, justified when value is merely subjective and individual (and therefore not comparable), cannot be supported when value is intrinsic.

Second, insofar as economics has tried to be "scientific," it has also worked within a narrow framework of "facts" that focuses solely on "natural laws" and how things work at a material level. As far as it goes, this is true enough, but it is very inadequate from a process perspective. If economics would carefully stay within its own realm of "fact," economists would have to take into account the (no longer so new) understanding in science that the "material" world is organic, not mechanical, and much more complex than Newtonian physics understood two hundred years ago. However, both capitalism and Soviet-style Marxism have gone far beyond the study of how economies actually work in the world as it actually is and built economic models based on *a priori* deductive premises. These premises are individualistic, materialistic, and place growth in the production of "goods" as the central aim of societies. These have developed into ideologies that are blind to the negative consequences of the models on human and natural communities. One of Whitehead's greatest contributions was his insistence on the importance of testing and re-testing theories and models in actual life, so that when old assumptions are no longer valid, that can be seen and corrected. In *Adventures of Ideas*, Whitehead points out that economics has been particularly guilty of this over-reliance on highly abstracted deduction:

> the doctrines of Commerce have to be founded upon assumptions concerning necessities, habits, technology, and prevalent knowledge. But habits, technology, and knowledge are variable from epoch to

epoch, and even in any one epoch differ in different sections of humanity. Thus any theory of Commerce depends upon presuppositions as to the populations concerned, and cannot be extended beyond these limits apart from a direct investigation of the wider populations (AI 71).

Once we begin to look at actual consequences to the actual world, the problem arises of how the individualism and anthropocentrism of economics has been blind to communities as communities—both human societies and natural ecosystems. In a process perspective, since everything is internally related to everything else, "individuals" are themselves really societies of entities. All individuality takes place in the context of a larger community and is dependent on intrinsic relations with both other human beings and with the rest of the world. Because of this, a process economics will look at the well-being of the community as a community—including the well-being of *all* the individuals within it—rather than measuring only the material wealth of individuals and arbitrarily aggregating the numbers.

At the same time, in a process perspective it is not enough to jump from extreme individualism on the one hand to extreme communalism on the other. Individuality comes to be and is fulfilled in community, but so is community enriched by the unique contributions of individuality. In capitalist economics justice has been defined in two opposing ways: as either social equity for individuals or as freedom for individuals. Either way, communities as such are invisible, and only individuals count. In fact, capitalist economist liberals (whether social equity liberals or laissez-faire liberals) are quite clear that capitalism destroys communities constantly. Most of these economists celebrate this state of affairs as the price to be paid for creativity and material wealth.

When we look to Soviet-style Marxism for an alternative, we find that while the economic model seems very different, the focus is still on *individuals*—only this time on how individuals participate in production. Despite the rhetoric about human solidarity, communities as such are still invisible, still destroyed by the economic model put into practice. So for over 150 years, the terms of the debate about economic justice have been between liberty and equity, but solely for individuals disconnected from their communities and the rest of the natural world.

In a process perspective individuals cannot be divorced from the human and natural communities that sustain them and make their very individuality possible. Individuals are inherently part of communities, and justice is a matter that involves the whole community. In other words, to be healthy persons, individuals need healthy communities in healthy ecosystems. When we think about justice in this broader way, we realize that *both* individual liberty *and* social equity are important, because healthy communities and healthy individuals need both to flourish. For process perspective, then, it is important to look at economic models in terms of what they do for whole *communities*, not just individuals. Process perspective must also view what the economic models do for *all* the individuals in the community.

Critiquing Capitalism from a Whiteheadian Perspective

As has already been noted, the model on which capitalist economies are based is called "neoclassical economic theory." Probably no actual economy embodies neoclassical theory perfectly. Nevertheless, its premises and tools are powerful factors in all capitalist economies (including the state-assisted economies of the East Asian "tigers") and to a certain extent in socialist economies as well. Neoclassical economics is governed completely by one central goal for economics, one fundamental assumption about human nature, and one core value choice embedded in the theory.

The central goal is one of *growth in the production of "goods"–any "goods."* No other goal matters–not economic well-being for all, not health for either individuals or communities, not ecological integrity. Just aggregate economic growth, pure and simple.

The fundamental assumption about human nature is that *human beings are independent individuals who naturally act to maximize their own individual "utility,"* which means whatever an individual chooses to value.[2] Technically, an individual can choose to value community and environment over economic growth, but the economic system never can. In practice the assumption is that each human being is what came to be called, following John Stuart Mill, *homo economicus:* the wealth-maximizing human.[3]

The core value choice embedded in the theory is that *leaving individuals free to choose whatever each wants is good.* This becomes the mechanism whereby the free market operates to achieve economic growth.

How are we to evaluate this goal, assumption, and value? When we look at the results, we have to admit that it works. Capitalism does indeed achieve unbelievable economic growth in the production of "goods" and does it more efficiently than any other system ever tried. If our sole criterion were economic growth and if we understood human beings solely individualistically, neoclassical theory would be judged not only adequate, but highly successful. However, human beings do not live solely on the basis of material goods, and human beings do not live as isolated individuals, making decisions apart from their families and communities. Neoclassical theory tries to wave away this concern by asserting that individuals can choose to "maximize" the good of their families and communities, and an "aggregation" of these choices will sway the outcome at the social level. But notice that any social choice, any community action as such, is ruled out of the picture. And any choices, whether individual or social, in favor of other goals than growth in "goods" are inherently up against the central drive of the economic system for growth in production. This is the reason materialistic consumerism is so powerful: The economy requires it to keep growing, no matter the real needs of the society.

Many other unintended effects of the neoclassical economic model are causing terrible problems throughout the world. The early development of economics isolated three unique but related "factors of production": land, labor, and capital. Over time, capitalism began to treat land and labor more and more as just different forms of capital. This meant that land, and its needs as part of natural systems that must be sustained, became open to abuse and exploitation. So did labor, which caused workers to be treated more and more as interchangeable parts of the production machine. Because labor must follow the most efficient use of capital, laborers (including the managerial class) must constantly move with moving capital. Inevitably communities are disrupted and weakened as companies relocate and workers follow. Families are also weakened because family health ultimately depends on family and neighborhood networks larger than a one- or two-parent family, and extended families and neighborhoods cannot move together. In fact, it is more and more the case that family life, the support of which was once the sole purpose of economic activity, is considered a "voluntary" activity that one may do in one's spare time—as long as it does not interrupt one's work.

The doctrine of free trade exacerbates this problem of community disruption. As long as capital freely crosses national boundaries, firms are free to move their operations to the cheapest sites, and so force nations to bid against each other for the jobs. That pushes wages down worldwide. As the system is more and more globalized, it is driving down manufacturing wages in countries where they once were high, such as the U.S. and Germany. It also makes it very difficult for nations to enforce environmental protections and a social safety net, because companies can simply pick up and move to a less stringent place.

Another problematic effect of the neoclassical model is that its focus on individual choice in the market results in everything else being called "externalities." Air, water, and soil pollution are "external" effects of economic activity, and so is anything else that is not directly done in the market. On one side, this means that the actual social costs of any economic activity are invisible to the market system. This is why the disintegration of communities and families and the destruction of ecosystems are not seen as problems in economic theory. In fact, GNP counts *all* market activity as a plus. This means such costs as environmental clean-up and the burden of paying for larger police forces as societies unravel are actually counted as *positive* contributions! This means that a nation's GNP could be going up while its actual economic well-being, measured in long-term sustainability and social health, is plummeting. It also means that the bottom half or more of the society could be worse off; but as long as GNP is going up, everyone assumes what is happening is good for the country.

This happens especially as people who once fed themselves in subsistence villages lose their land and are pushed into the cities. Since the village economy was not part of the money system, the economic well-being of the people in those economies is not part of GNP. Eventually these subsistence farmers have to leave the land and get work in the cities. Then their families, communities, and culture start to disintegrate, and everyone is both economically and culturally worse off than before. Still, GNP actually counts this situation as good, because the one-time farmers are now earning money wages that add to GNP.

I had a student from Kenya who said, "We used to name our children *Abundance.* Then the 'experts' came and told us we should change from feeding ourselves to growing coffee and tea for export, and we would get rich. So we did, but our coffee and tea don't pay for the expenses of growing them, let alone feed us. Now the trees are gone, the water is bad, the soil is degraded, and our children are hungry." GNP in Kenya has gone up as a result of this change, but my student's people are worse off. So an alternative method of accounting should be devised that actually measures economic welfare, and not just monetary activity. GNP must be abandoned! Luckily, some people are working on this. They call their alternative to GNP the GPI: Genuine Progress Indicator.[4]

One way to cope with "externalities" is to make them "internal"–to put a price on such things as the costs of air pollution and force the players in the market to pay for them. This is often the only effective way to deal with the problem, but it exacerbates the inherent problem of the system–the fact that all the pressure in capitalism is to make "scarce," and so marketable, what once was free and available to all. Worldwide, land, especially arable land, has been almost completely brought into the market system, and the once widespread "commons" whereby anyone could have access to the means to live, is smaller and smaller. Water is next, as oceans are carved up between fishing fleets and fresh water is made more and more scarce by pollution. Will even air some day draw a cost? Certainly clean air already does, as more and more one must be rich to live in less-polluted places.

Critiquing Soviet-style Marxism from a Process Perspective

Historically, Soviet-style Marxian economics has been *the* sole theoretical alternative to capitalism. Karl Marx worked out a truly brilliant analysis of how capitalism works and what both its positive and destructive effects on society are. His analysis holds up to this day, especially his use of historical-critical method and his observations of the effects of the development of factory labor on employment and on traditional agricultural communities. Marx was well aware that industrial development destroys communities, that capital-intensive farming destroys the fertility of the soil, and that the factory system destroys individual initiative and satisfaction with work.[5] He describes in detail the miseries of factory labor at subsistence wages (and less) and the consequences to family and community life.

Marx also had high ideals about the importance of social justice. His economic theory set out to achieve ultimately a kind of utopia of social sharing that sounds (at a material level) remarkably like the kingdom of God as depicted in Christianity. These ideals of equality and justice have given Marxism great power to attract followers. However, Soviet-style Marxism, like capitalist economics, made several crucial choices that have had negative consequences—and, in fact, have proven fatal to Soviet-style Marxism as an economic model.

The first choice was to follow Ricardo, Smith, and Locke in affirming the labor theory of value: the idea that all economic value comes from the labor that goes into producing a commodity. Consequently, while capitalism treats land and labor as forms of capital, Soviet-style Marxism treats land and capital as forms of labor. Unfortunately, this means that the natural world is as much a candidate for misuse in Soviet-style Marxism as in capitalism. In fact, the labor theory of value ended up denying the value caused by absolute scarcity, so that natural limits were ignored. Marxism also denied the inherent value of the natural world—including what might be called the eons of "labor" that it took for life to evolve on earth and the value that it embodies apart from any value to human beings.

Labor itself would seem to fare better, except for the second choice made in Soviet-style Marxism. They chose to affirm economic growth as *the* central goal of the economy, just like in capitalism. And just like in capitalism, they chose to achieve economic growth through indiscriminate industrialization. This choice wiped out much of the benefit labor might have had. So in Soviet-style Marxism, just as in capitalism, labor must move to follow capital, and individuals and communities must be sacrificed for the sake of economic growth. True, individual workers did fare better in Soviet-style Marxian economies than in many capitalist economies in the sense that Marxism kept unemployment low, and created a much better social safety net, and often made better health care and education available to the poorest. However, families, communities, and the environment have more often fared as poorly as in capitalist economies, or worse.

Along with the high ideals of Soviet-style Marxism came some strong prejudices. For instance, the *Communist Manifesto* refers to rescuing people from "the idiocy of rural life" and forging the new "socialist man" in the fires of the factories.[6] It encouraged the destruction of traditional communities and the break-up of extended families and clans because it saw these as impediments to achieving true socialism. When implemented—and it was widely implemented in Soviet-style societies—these ideas caused great destruction and great resistance on the part of traditional communities. In Nicaragua, where Marxism was touted for its "human face," the government nevertheless tried to break up the traditional villages of the Miskito Indians, who resisted fiercely. Similarly, in Rumania, officials decided that the classic rural agricultural villages must actually be bulldozed to end the resistance of the "backward" peasants to "socialism."

A Word about Socialism

Socialism must be discussed differently than capitalism or Soviet-style Marxism, because it has never been developed into a comprehensive theoretical model in the same way. In fact, it is more accurate to discuss "socialisms," because there are so many varieties. Socialisms are really an attempt to find a middle way between capitalism and Marxism, and are usually mixed economies.

Most socialist economies have been much more pragmatic and flexible than Soviet-style Marxism and less individualistic than capitalism. Their strength has been in their recognition that capitalism does not recognize social and community needs and so must be regulated for the sake of the common good and social equity. However, socialisms have tended to make the mistake of allowing for too much central control of the economy by a bureaucracy, similar to Soviet-style Marxism. This ignores the central genius of the free market—that local people can make decisions about their local conditions and needs with far more efficiency than distant bureaucrats can. Consequently, socialist economies that have tried to centralize economic decision making have been notoriously inefficient, while socialist economies that allow for locally free markets have done much better.

Alternative Assumptions and Values for Transforming Economics

Where does our critique of economic models leave us? It seems clear that capitalism is the most successful at producing "goods" for consumption, but that material success comes at a high cost. Soviet-style Marxism is more successful than capitalism at achieving full employment and alleviating the worst forms of poverty, but it also comes at a high cost and in the end has proven a relative failure at improving material standards of living. While production should not be the sole purpose of any economy, it is certainly of basic importance. Certainly capitalism has proven itself to be much more efficient at it. Socialism that uses a free market as the basis of the economy works relatively well, but socialism that relies on a Soviet-style centralized system works poorly.

From a process perspective, we may live in a nation that is capitalist, Marxist, or socialist. Still, we are looking for ways to make the economy more balanced between efficient production, social equity in terms of employment and real participation in economic decision making, and care for the environment that all the rest depends on to be sustained. Ethicists like to call these the "middle axioms" of sufficiency, solidarity, participation, and sustainability. In the face of the massive failures of Soviet-style Marxism, the social trend worldwide is clearly toward capitalism. Attempts to overthrow capitalism through revolutions have proved to be enormously destructive, even where real gains at the most basic levels have been made. Reforms that leave capitalism intact have helped a great deal in the older industrialized nations, but intractable problems of unemployment, social disintegration, and environmental damage remain. The frustration of those who have been most damaged by capitalist development, especially in the Southern Hemisphere, keeps growing.

I suggest that what we need to work on are ways to *transform* capitalism from within. To do that we need alternative goals, assumptions, and values for a transformed economy. That will take a lot of input from a lot of people more expert than I; but I do have some ideas, based on a perspective grounded in process thought, that are meant to be suggestive:

What if, instead of growth in the production of goods, we went back to the suggestion of economist Alfred Marshall that the goal of economies should be *growth in the health and strength of the people?*[7] What if, instead of assuming individuals are isolated entities, as in capitalism, or are only social, as tends to happen in Soviet-style Marxism—what if our assumption were that *human beings are "persons-in-community,"* as Herman Daly and John Cobb have suggested?[8] What if, instead of *homo economicus,* (the wealth-maximizing human of John Stuart Mill) we had *homo salutaris*—the healthy human—as our economic icon? And what if, instead of arbitrarily deciding that the good is what each individual decides it is for themselves alone, we recognized that each entity is inherently good? This would mean that value—even exchange value—must take into account a combination of actual scarcity, usefulness, and basic need, and not be left solely to individual whim.

If *health* instead of wealth were the goal of economics, it would change the way economists measure economic success and the way all of us think about economics. In today's form of capitalism, products—the things made—are getting better and better. We have better cars, better cameras, better computers, better clothes—at least, those of us who have access to these things do. But do we have better people? Do we have a clean environment in which all species can thrive together? If health were the goal, much would stay the same, because with free markets much has improved. But much would also change. Healthy individuals need healthy families, communities, and ecosystems to stay healthy in the long run. They need healthy relationships—including healthy amounts of personal choice—*and* chances to contribute their individual gifts and talents to the larger community.

Health is not an idealistic image. Health is very concrete, which is why it lends itself to economics. It may not be possible to agree on what exactly a single standard of "health" might be, but it is certainly possible to determine if people and their communities are getting healthier or sicker. We also know that no community is healthy that has no conflict, yet too much of the wrong kinds of conflict are unhealthy. Naturally, what is healthy in one culture won't be so healthy in others. Rather than seeing that as a disadvantage, I see it as a strength, because, beyond the basic needs for subsistence, people should be free to determine for themselves what their communities need. As it is, the prescription of capitalism for every community is to rearrange their society and culture to support continuous and insatiable consumption of products, with no debate about what products or for whose benefit.

The main problem I can see in using health as the goal of economics is the inevitable temptation to create a kind of cult of "health" in which healthy people are on top and those judged "unhealthy" are marginalized and denigrated. This could easily develop into a kind of tyranny as bad or worse than the ones that blame desperately poor and starving people for their poverty. We would have to work very hard to avoid this kind of thing and insist that it is indeed a very unhealthy way to deal with illness and handicaps–for individuals and for society. For the truth is, no one is perfectly healthy for long in our mortal lives, and a healthy acceptance of human frailty and limitation is important.

The idea of using health as the goal of economics should be debated. It may be that someone will have a better idea. But even if "health" is not the right goal, that I am convinced we already know of some fundamental changes that must be adopted for a transformed economics.

First of all, economic theories have all relied on Newtonian physics for their basic images of the world. Yet Newtonian physics, which assumes that all entities are individual and unrelated like parts of a machine, has been surpassed for decades by a contemporary physics. This new physics shows how all entities are patterns of energy that are inherently interrelated and interacting–not like a machine at all, but more like a complex living ecosystem. Economics would do much better to return to the early instincts of the French Physiocrats of the eighteenth century such as François Quesnay and look to living natural systems for its patterns instead of abstracted ideals about machinery. Living natural systems have been tested for millions of years and proven effective. As Whitehead comments in *Science and the Modern World*, "a further stage of provisional realism is required in which the scientific scheme is recast, and founded upon the ultimate concept of *organism*" (SMW 64).

Second, economics has relied on purely deductive models for far too long. Early on, when we had few tools for examining actual economies and their effects, it was useful to choose a few crucial *a priori* assumptions and build economic theory on them. But two hundred years later we know much more about human beings and their societies than we did, and we know that the assumptions chosen then are inadequate. Not only should economics revise its assumptions, it should use more inductive and historical-critical research to test the assumptions and adapt the economics to changing situations and different places and times. According to Whitehead, the "men of genius" who created the mechanistic model

> applied the seventeenth century group of scientific abstractions to the analysis of the unbounded universe. Their triumph...was overwhelming. Whatever did not fit into their scheme was ignored, derided, disbelieved...The common sense of the eighteenth century, its grasp of the obvious facts of human suffering, and of the obvious demands of human nature, acted on the world like a bath of moral cleansing... but if men cannot live on bread alone, still less can they do so on

disinfectants...The seventeenth century scheme of concepts was proving a perfect instrument for research...[but] [I]n this century the notion of the mechanical explanation of all the processes of nature finally hardened into a dogma of science. (SMW 59–60)

Third, and following on the second point, we should stop making *ideologies* out of economic models and stop trying to change the world to fit them. This has been enormously destructive on both the left and the right–probably the most destructive thing of all. Global industrialization is being imposed at a terrible cost–a cost made much greater when capitalism is followed as an ideology to be imposed rather than a pragmatic economic tool to be used to improve material life. Capitalist ideology has been used to excuse the destruction of communities and cultures–all in the name of "progress" and never with the consent of those so affected. Ideologies of whatever stripe tend to blind their adherents to what the actual effects on real people are. Such ideologies provide an excuse for doing evil in the name of the hoped-for outcome. Many apologists for capitalism admit that industrial development does indeed destroy traditional communities, and their displaced peoples must suffer terribly both socially and materially. But they justify this with the promise that after the first few generations, the nation will eventually be materially better off, and this makes all the suffering worth it.[9] Yet I have never seen them offer to explain this to the people so affected and let them decide what sacrifices they are willing to make for the sake of their great-grandchildren's future!

Finally, I believe that global capitalism is dualistic and finally exalts the material over the spiritual. Capitalism does make some provision for the spiritual dimension of life, but by treating the spirit, as a practical matter, as separate from matter and unrelated. Capitalism claims to affirm the spirit but privatizes and individualizes it. Spirituality is something you do in your free time and should have no impact on your work, except insofar as such religious doctrines as the Protestant ethic or the Confucian ethic makes you work harder. But the idea that the material should be in service to the spiritual is alien. Even the idea that they should be in balance is effectively denied. Process thought offers a better balance. We must work to transform economics to be less dualistic and more holistic.

A Word of Encouragement

The idea that we can actually make a difference and help to transform global economics for the sake of a healthier and more just world seems impossible. And it is a daunting task that will not be done quickly, easily, or by only a few. But if Adam Smith and his contemporaries could nudge the social/economic trends of their day with their compelling ideas, we can do our best to do the same. Process thought has helped me to understand and value as fact that every entity makes a contribution, however modest, and that that contribution matters–it affects the whole universe.

Sometimes I get discouraged about how hard it is to make a difference. I am depressed about all the hunger and misery in the world. I worry about what environmental degradation is going to do to make things much, much worse in the twenty-first century. At such times I think about those faithful people I know of who faced similarly daunting circumstances and never gave up. Eventually, they made a difference that mattered in the end–that matters to us today. Think of the few Quakers of England and America who began to preach against slavery in the 1700s when no one had thought to question it. They were ridiculed and even actively persecuted, but they persisted, though most of them did not live to see slavery abolished. Yet it was abolished.

In *Adventures of Ideas* Whitehead argues compellingly for the importance of philosophy to the practicalities of economics and explains the role philosophy needs to play:

> I have said enough to show that the modern commercial mentality requires many elements of discipline, scientific and sociological. But the great fact remains that details of relevant knowledge cannot be foreseen. Thus even for mere success, and apart from any question of intrinsic quality of life, an unspecialized aptitude for eliciting generalizations from particulars and for seeing the divergent illustration of generalities in diverse circumstance is required. Such a reflective power is essentially a philosophic habit: it is the survey of society from the standpoint of generality. This habit of general thought, undaunted by novelty, is the gift of philosophy, in the widest sense of that term. (AI 97)

CHAPTER 16

Imagine Peace
Knowing the Real–Imagining the Impossible

■ MARY ELIZABETH MULLINO MOORE

Standing on a busy street corner, I held a sign reading "IMAGINE PEACE." I could have chosen a sign that read "War Is Not the Answer," or "Honk if You Want Peace"; but a simple appeal to imagination seemed the most promising plea for me to make in the midst of our sign-carrying group. How can people engage in peacemaking if they (we) cannot imagine a peaceful world? The purpose of this chapter is to explore the educational challenges of process thought in dialogue with seemingly intractable conflicts in the present world.[1]

For grounding, I will give attention to conflicts in the Middle East and United States involvements in them. I will also explore some of the movements in educational theory of the past thirty years, especially as they bear on social critique and educational reform. These movements are promising, but still lacking. I will thus search for further insight regarding educational practice, focusing particularly on that which has been neglected–the imagination. The role of imagination in process epistemology promises to bear much fruit as a vital, though often missing, element in global peacemaking and in the educational process of most schools and other institutions.

One hallmark of process thought is its attention to the tiniest details of reality and its attempt to grasp the cosmic whole, while envisioning the potential of a world reshaped by immanently transcendent values. For this reason, many religious thinkers, ecologists, and idealists are drawn to process thought. On the other hand, the complexity of process thought explains how it can easily be reduced to one aspect or another. Its uniqueness is in its ability to contemplate life as a whole–the small and the large, the past and the future, the rawness of present reality and the possibilities of a world that could be.

Given possibilities in process-relational theories to engender integrated thinking about complex realities, we turn to process epistemology as a generative source of insight for imagining peace. Five kinds of knowing will be studied in particular: seeking goodness, seeking transcendence, intimate knowing, knowing the stranger and unfamiliar, and imaging and responding to the possible. With such a promise, we turn to the frightening and seemingly intractable realities of violent conflict.

Intractable Violent Conflict

Two women recently talked about the U.S. war in Iraq. Both women had voted for the current U.S. president, but one criticized the war and the other favored it. The first woman said:

> I do not understand why Bush had to wage war on Iraq. I am a student of history, and Bush is asking for trouble if you ask me. The U.S. could lose its position, like the Roman Empire did long ago, or we could abuse our power like Germany did in the last century. Besides, we still have no proof that the war was necessary, even in terms of the hidden weapons that Bush used as his excuse for invading Iraq.

The other woman replied, "But we had to get rid of that evil man!" The first woman replied, somewhat meekly, "Yes, I know."

This conversation reveals a tension that disturbs two ordinary women, both part of the dominant mainstream of U.S. public opinion in 2003, but with different views on war. One was critical of the war against Iraq, but had no alternatives to offer, except to encourage the U.S. not to make war. The second agrees with the war, justified by the evil of Iraq's leader, Saddam Hussein. Both had opinions about war, but nothing to say about peace and peacemaking. Both reveal the intractability of conflict–the historical persistence (first woman) and the necessity for resolving problems (second woman)–but neither offers a constructive alternative. This analysis is not a simple critique of two women; their brief conversation took place in a larger discussion of urgent personal matters. The analysis does, however, point to a common interchange in the U.S., reflecting dominant images of war and minimalist images of peace. Even the signs for recent peace protests (described in the opening paragraph) reveal similar options: "War Is Not the Answer" (a statement of the negative) and "Honk if You Want Peace" (an invitation to express an opinion). Neither gives a constructive alternative.

We see further parallels in the description of H.B. Michel Sabbah, Latin Patriarch of Jerusalem, as he addressed a Christian ecumenical meeting on the present situation of Israel and Palestine.

> Both Israelis and Palestinians want peace and pray for it, despite the fact that the situation on the ground is far from being a situation of peace...Violence reigns everywhere you go in the Holy Land. Violent Israeli military occupation on one hand, and violent Palestinian

resistance on the other hand, leading to terrorism in many cases. Meanwhile Israelis blame it on Palestinians and their terrorist attacks on civilians and non-civilians drawing the conclusion that they do not want peace...Palestinians, in their turn, blame it on Israelis and their protracted non-stop military occupation of the portion of land left for them, in addition to all the practices and collective punishment measures inflicted upon them indiscriminately by the Israeli troops. They too are reaching the conviction that Israel is not willing and does not in fact want to relinquish its military occupation and to give them back their freedom and independence.[2]

We see here the hopelessness of two peoples, stirred by violent skirmishes on both sides. Each side interprets the acts of violence as signs that the other side does not want peace; therefore, peace cannot replace fear in their collective psyches. The cycle continues.

Whenever movement is made toward peace in the Middle East, people are wary of the promises. In a 2003 meeting between Israel's Prime Minister Ariel Sharon and former Palestinian Prime Minister Mahmoud Abbas (Abu Mazen), Abu Mazen explained his success in achieving a cease-fire from Hamas and Islamic Jihad, which added to the military and intelligence cooperation between Israel and Palestine. People continued to be concerned, however, as reported in Israel's newspaper *Ha'aretz*:

> Alongside all this, both the Palestinian and the Israeli leaderships know that declarations that are pleasing to the ear cannot change the reality just like that; they cannot rebuild a trust that has been crushed through three years of harsh violence and cause all the forces on both sides to simply discard the residues of hatred and vengeance. The Palestinians have yet to feel any substantial change in their lives, and they believe the withdrawal from the Gaza Strip and Bethlehem is merely a temporary measure. The Israelis are shrugging off the cease-fire, believing it will not endure and will end in a large terror attack.[3]

This commentary on distrust has been followed, in fact, by more good news *and* bad news; both are likely to continue. Violence poisons the ground upon which people live and the waters from which they drink; violence seeps into every person and every relationship. Peace will require years of dreaming, hoping, and building an alternate world. Yet, efforts leading to the *Ha'aretz* editorial ignite sparks of hope, arising from human decisions and actions and other sources. However threatened these sparks may be, they stir human imagination and point to the possibility of peace beyond violence.

We cannot attend to the intractability of violent conflict without recognizing the complexity and ideological contortions that were used to perpetuate and justify the United States war on Iraq. Months after the initial attacks of the war, President Bush claimed that Saddam Hussein had hidden nuclear weapons and that these would eventually be found. A major piece of evidence used before the war to justify the upcoming conflict was the supposed purchase of uranium from Niger in Africa. The CIA proved this evidence had been based on a forged document signed by a Niger official who had been out of office for many years. The White House argued later that the illegitimacy of the documents had not been passed on to the president, though the CIA claimed to have known of the forgery in early 2002 and to have passed the news to the president long before the State of the Union Address in which he presented this data as fact.[4] Getting the full, true story is difficult, and deception in the interest of promoting an ideological stance and an aggressive action is easy to advance. It shows how easily people can believe, or be led to believe, the justifications for war. Such gullibility reflects a failure of imagination.

The Power of Imagination–A Whiteheadian Cosmology

In a Whiteheadian world view, intractability does not exist as a binding reality, only as a dominant stream of memory. Because all reality is in an ongoing process of emerging, change is always possible, even as the heritage of the past is passed from generation to generation. Even heritage holds within it seeds of novelty and change; the dominant heritage (as the heritage of conflict between Israel and Palestine) is never all there is. Other aspects of heritage also exist, such as instances of peaceful coexistence, successful cooperation, and healthy personal and cultural relationships. These seeds of hope can be uncovered and magnified as sources for recreating relationships in the future. Four aspects of Whiteheadian cosmology are particularly helpful in revealing the power of imagination to evoke a life-filled future–an alternative to violence and destruction that is grounded in the real, but attuned to the possible.

Visions of Peace

For Alfred North Whitehead, "Peace" is an ideal that pulls the individual and the world toward their finest. It is a sense of the whole that transcends the particular, acquisitive desires of an individual. Further, it is a way of knowing; thus, it bears epistemological and educational significance:

[Peace] is a broadening of feeling due to the emergence of some deep metaphysical insight, unverbalized and yet momentous in its coordination of values. Its first effect is the removal of the stress of acquisitive feeling arising from the soul's preoccupation with itself. Thus Peace carries with it a surpassing of personality...It results in a wider sweep of conscious interest. It enlarges the field of attention. Thus Peace is self-control at its widest,–at the width where the "self" has been lost, and interest has been transferred to coordinations wider than personality. (AI 285–86)

This reveals the nature of Peace as an ideal or vision that invokes a sense of wideness or cosmic vision. It enables individuals and communities to transcend themselves. It enables them to transcend values of acquisitiveness and to sense the value of well-being for the entire world. It enables people to let go of fears and other emotions that inhibit, and expand interest in the other, thus intensifying their concerns for the larger world. This vision of peace is far larger than the absence of war; it is an active way of knowing and being in the world–a way that can be cultivated educationally.

Building upon this image, we turn to Whitehead's view of engagement: "The Peace that is here meant is not the negative conception of anaesthesia. It is a positive feeling which crowns the 'life and motion' of the soul" (AI 285). In light of this vision, peace is an active vision, which includes reason and feeling; thus, it can be actively cultivated through active engagement with the world. It is not the absence of war and violence, but the presence of other relationships ("a broadening of feeling") with the wider world.

Whitehead's view of Peace includes special sensitivity to tragedy– encountering the reality of tragedy, and also the unrealized ideal toward which tragedy points:

> [Peace] keeps vivid the sensitiveness to the tragedy; and it sees the tragedy as a living agent persuading the world to aim at fineness beyond the faded level of surrounding fact. Each tragedy is the disclosure of an ideal– What might have been, and was not: What can be. The tragedy was not in vain…The inner feeling belonging to this grasp of the service of tragedy is Peace–the purification of the emotions. (AI 285)

With such a view, Whitehead recognizes that, even the most destructive of situations have within them the possibility of transformation. This will not take place by human effort and reason. "Peace is largely beyond the control of purpose"; thus, peace "comes as a gift" (AI 285). In short, peace is not a thing to be taught, but a gift to be expected and received. Teachers are thus challenged to cultivate expectation and wonder, rather than teaching reliance on human reason and control.

Inheritance and Novelty

The very process of inheritance is promising for transformation. Transformations of the past are evidence that change is possible; indeed faithfulness to the past is *only* possible if emerging occasions are open to the emergence and results of past transformations. In the trajectory of peacemaking, for example, each effort at peace in the history of humankind can potentially contribute to a decision for peace in the present moment. Any regret for violence, or tragic awareness of the devastations of war, can contribute to a decision for peace. At the same time, novelty also enters into the present moment, through the unique integration of past inheritance or through God's initial aim. Novelty might stir a truly new response on behalf of peace. The combination of inheritance and novelty opens endless possibilities for imagining and building peace.

In a process-relational view, the combination of inheritance (continuity) and novelty (change) can be explained metaphysically. Each occasion of experience receives the whole of the past, plus the novelty that emerges from

God's initial aim, and, then, creates itself. In Whitehead's language, "The many become one, and are increased by one."[5] The "manyness" of the past enters into the present moment, but once the new occasion creates itself, it is added to the many. John Cobb and David Griffin explain this in terms of an open window:

> Each of Whitehead's occasions of experience begins…as an open window to the totality of the past, as it prehends all the previous occasions (either immediately or mediately). Once the rush of influences enters in, the window is closed, while the occasion of experience forms itself by response to these influences. But as soon as this process is completed, the windows of the world are again open, as a new occasion of experience takes its rise.[6]

This metaphorical description of inheritance and novelty points to a third aspect of process-relational cosmology, namely that all reality is open to the future.

Open Future

In a way somewhat parallel to Teilhard de Chardin, Whitehead understood the future as "fully and radically open," believing further that progress was possible.[7] This view is easily misunderstood, either by emphasizing the determinism of the past inheritance or by asserting the inevitability of progress. Neither is adequate to capture the cosmology of Whitehead. After many years as an agnostic, Whitehead posited the participation of God in the universe because his metaphysical analyses required some kind of transcending explanation of the world's movements. He came to the view that, through God, people encounter ideals and possibilities. People come to sense a rightness or goodness that is "attained or missed, with more or less completeness of attainment or omission" (RM 60–61). This early insight, developed with more fullness in later writing, reveals Whitehead's hope for progress, devoid of naïve optimism or philosophical necessity. The open future is, thus, open to possibility, but without guarantees of global progress.

Overcoming Dualisms–Converting Opposition into Contrast

Process-relational thought is also highly integrative, resisting dualisms ingrained in Western culture and woven into language as if they were common sense. Whitehead replaced dualistic thought patterns with integrative impulses and with delight in the adventures of ideas. These impulses led him to a philosophy of organism, exploring complex wholes. He sought, in *Science and the Modern World*, to overcome the dualism between the scientific worldview and the values of human experience.[8] In *Process and Reality*, he sought to "accommodate scientific theory and practice, and our social, aesthetic, and religious experience."[9] In both, he drew liberally upon the work of imagination, boldly resisting reductionism and dualistic contradictions as explanations of reality (PR 16–17, 274–75). Such efforts made it possible for Whitehead to make sense of complex realities that people know through radically different experiences of the world; thus, for him, knowing was best approached from many different directions and integrated into wholes.

The dynamic metaphysical process for embracing complexity is converting opposition into contrast—transforming realities assumed to be opposites into wholes that preserve the uniqueness of each, while binding them in relationship (PR 109, 111, 338–41, 348, 350). Contrasts include order and chaos, freedom and necessity, permanence and flux, sadness and joy, even God and the world. Note that Whitehead's view of opposition diverges from human practices of compromise—blending things into a unity that takes a little from each but loses the distinctions. In human terms, the idea of contrast might be depicted as the process of negotiation, or forming unity with diversity. In cosmological terms, the idea of contrasts explains how, in the process of concrescence, realities of difference are brought into a unity that contains each part *and* the distinctions among them.

With such a view, either/or thinking is unthinkable, for one can never fully separate and choose between oppressor and oppressed, comedy and tragedy, right and wrong. In terms of imagining peace, this view suggests that the very act of imagination requires thinking of all parties at once, each with distinctive histories, hurts, and values, and all in relationship with one another. On a global political scale, this view is embodied more by South Africa's Truth and Reconciliation Commission than by the Nuremberg Trials following World War II. The former dealt more fully with the complexities, evils, and tragedies of diverse peoples and political communities; the latter targeted one particular group as war criminals.

This discussion has considerable relevance for education, which even Whitehead acknowledged. He noted that order can function either "as the condition for excellence" or "as stifling the freshness of living" (PR 338). In relation to education, he added:

> The condition for excellence is a thorough training in technique…The paradox which wrecks so many promising theories of education is that the training which produces skill is so very apt to stifle imaginative zest. Skill demands repetition, and imaginative zest is tinged with impulse. Up to a certain point each gain in skill opens new paths for the imagination. But in each individual formal training has its limit of usefulness. (PR 338)

Dangers arise when distinctions are not preserved in contrast—degeneration, triviality, loss of value, and loss of intensity. Educationally, this presents many challenges—maintaining a richness of subject matter and points of view, embracing conflict, and engaging in diverse ways of knowing. Politically, this presents the challenge of upholding the values and powers of diverse peoples, lest one becomes so powerful that it dominates others. According to Whitehead, "The moment of dominance, prayed for, worked for, sacrificed for, by generations of the noblest spirits, marks the turning point where the blessing passes into the curse" (PR 339). In short, no society's order is adequate to preserve and enhance life permanently over time, just as no particular order in school classrooms or family relationships is adequate. Whitehead concludes, "The art of progress is to preserve order amid change, and to preserve change amid order" (PR 339).

These various aspects of Whitehead's cosmology are rich for imagining peace. Visions of peace can become realities through the interplay of inheritance and novelty and the invitation of a radically open future. This view counters the sense of inevitability in the opening case studies, replacing inevitability with possibility. Finally, imagining peace travels a path made possible by converting opposition into contrast, moving away from the sense that one side of a conflict is fully right and the other fully wrong, or that one has been persecuted in a more horrific history than the other. Converting opposition into contrast suggests another way to respond to the "evil man" described by the woman in the first case, and another way for Israel and Palestine to respond to one another, and for the U. S. to respond to Iraq. This way transcends scapegoating and simple answers. It is a way of imagination and negotiation, hard work and bountiful possibility.

Cultivating Imaginative Knowing

People will never be able to make peace until they can imagine it. They can never even long for peace if they cannot imagine it. Imagination, however, has the power to make war as well as peace. Mark Juergensmeyer exemplifies how religious imagination has sometimes contributed to violence by its "propensity to absolutize and to project images of cosmic war."[10] This reality is seen in the conflict between Arabs and Jews, which Juergensmeyer characterizes as "a cosmic struggle of Manichaean proportions."

> Sheik Yassin, for example, described the conflict in virtually eschato-logical terms as "the combat between good and evil." A communiqué issued by Hamas when Americans sent troops to the Saudi Arabian desert following Saddam Hussein's invasion of Kuwait in 1990 declared it to be "another episode in the fight between good and evil" and "a hateful Christian plot against our religion, our civilization and our land."[11]

This analysis suggests that imagination needs to be subjected to critical analysis, as any does other form of thinking. Its power is great, but its power can be used for good or for ill.

At the same time, critical thinking has been given much more extensive attention in modern education than imagination. This has taken several forms—critical thinking in relation to *what* is taught (subject matter), *where* teaching takes place (institutions and other sites), and *how* teaching is done and *by whom* (process and leadership). A few examples will suffice.

- *What?* Paulo Freire critiques the subject matter of education, insisting that educators engage with learners in critical thinking about subject matter from the learners' lives and social worlds.[12] Others argue more specifically that the subject matter for critical reflection should be gender, culture, class, and/or power, with special attention to subject matters related to social oppression and liberation.[13]

- *Where?* As to the sites of educational practice, one of the most profound critiques continues to be that of Ivan Illich, who argued in the early 1970s for disestablishing schools. He explained that "the institutionalization of values leads inevitably to physical pollution, social polarization, and psychological impotence: three dimensions in a process of global degradation and modernized misery."[14] He even linked this critique of institutionalized education with the absence of imagination, quoting a black friend from Chicago as saying "that our imagination was 'all schooled up.'"[15] For Illich, therefore, teaching needs to take place in many sites (family, workplace, and other communities) so that human life, human consciousness, and global well-being will be tended. Illich's agenda has been continued by others, especially in the United States debate regarding educational standards and curriculum.[16] Peace education is another arena that lends itself to widening the venues for teaching, as exemplified by such projects as the "Million Minutes of Peace Appeal," and other initiatives implemented in relation to, and following upon, the United Nations International Year of Peace (1986).[17]

- *How and by whom?* How teaching is done and by whom is a subject for many educational theorists as well, including those already named and others who have focused on educational vision. Consider John Dewey, who fostered a vision of education by and through social experience, and James Botkin, Mahdi Elmandjra, and Mircea Militza, who made one of the early cases for anticipatory and participatory learning.[18] More recently, William Doll has attended to the practices of education, drawing upon process-relational thought and chaos theory, and C.A. Bowers has attended to practices of education that will foster eco-justice and community.[19]

One fruit of all of this work is increased attention to consciousness in education, which has also yielded attention to human agency and cultural action. Some dangers persist, however. Some appeals to envisioning the future focus more on technological readiness or advancement.[20] Other appeals focus on critical thinking with little attention to other ways of knowing. What is most notably missing is attention to imagination, not to replace other forms of thinking, but to enhance and enlarge them with creative possibility. Attending to imagination is particularly important in a process-relational cosmology. According to Whitehead, the influences on an emerging occasion can never be exhausted by the components of a concrescence—"its data, its emotions, its appreciations, its purposes, its phases of subjective aim"; these components will always be transcended by "the final reaction of the self-creative unity of the universe" (PR 47). If self-creativity is thus built into the nature of the universe, then imagination's role in education must be extraordinarily important.

Recognizing imagination as one among many ways of knowing, we move now to consider diverse ways to cultivate imagination for peace. I will name five approaches to education that could bear fruit in the future, as well as the present.

1. Seeking Goodness–The Sustaining Power of Life

I have been touting the promise of imagination for peacemaking, but this requires more than free imagination. It requires *purposive* imagination–a kind of knowing that quests for goodness, seeking to feed the sustaining power of life. I earlier noted that power can be used for purposes that defy goodness, but questing for goodness is searching for the power that exists *within* life and has potential to *tend* life.

This insight is important to education, for power has often been seen as the purpose of education, reflected in the oft-quoted dictum of Francis Bacon, "Knowledge is power."[21] Distorted into human constructions of technological or political power, or distorted into instrumental versions of pragmatism, this emphasis on power can lead to destruction of human culture and the natural world. Bernard Meland appeals to William James' radical empiricism as a wiser and more educationally valuable form of pragmatism. According to him, John Dewey's instrumental version of pragmatism ignored James' emphasis on the human spirit. Meland argues that James' radical empiricism had an implicit educational agenda, namely "a reorientation of the human spirit for a deeper probing of the meaning of existence" and a more specific probing into the meaning of human life; Meland identifies these as educational issues.[22] To encourage such probing is to emphasize both power and goodness and to recognize the relationship between them, rather than assume an independent or antithetical relationship.

This is quite different from a simple and brash quest for power. Bernard Meland argues that the "imbalance of wisdom and the patronage of power has long corrupted our cultural life," even in universities oriented "to advance the arts of the mind."[23] The culture of mind that aims toward power fails to attend to the culture of human spirit. Yet, human spirit is the pathway by which the human mind and imagination can be judged and transformed, thus converting human energy toward good ends. According to Meland, "This implies no simple choice between power and goodness, between knowledge bent on power and knowledge concerned with goodness, but an interrelation of power and goodness."[24] Education that encourages such a relationship will cultivate all forms of thinking. Meland suggests six levels, all of which are important in the educational process: survival thinking; survey of experience; critical appraisal of experience; constructive understanding; imaginative interpretation; and theological and metaphysical thinking, which combines the analytic, constructive, and imaginative.[25] These do not exist in a hierarchy, but in relation to one another.

Please note that many other educational theorists write about educational process in ways similar to Meland; this is not fully new. I hazard a generalization, however: Of all the levels in Meland's list, imagination is the approach to knowing that is most often underplayed by other theorists and educators. This is particularly problematic when we consider that imagination is a critical pathway by which insights and possibilities are evoked and communicated to others. It is also the pathway by which patterns of relationship are established to support the common good.

2. Seeking Transcendence–Touching the Unknown

Closely related to the search for goodness is the search for transcendence–reaching for the beyond and beneath–touching the unknown. Bernard Meland himself posits a connection among goodness, imagination, and transcendence. He encourages educators to seek that which transcends the obvious–not by ignoring facts and figures, but by diving into them more deeply. Educators can thus use facts to transcend facts, or to penetrate "the obvious meaning to its deeper import."[26] This is an aesthetic way of knowing, "for it elicits overtones of feeling and opens vistas in the mind that awaken wonder."[27]

Religious educators have been particularly helpful in reflecting on transcendence as a quality of education and a feature of imagination. Drawing upon the depths of diverse religious traditions in dialogue with contemporary educational literature, they frequently draw connections between transcendence and transformation. Hanan Alexander, for example, says: "Transcendence is the wellspring of hope and creativity because it leaves open the possibility that there is always another, better way to consider any possible situation."[28] When education is attuned to transcendence, however, it requires innovative teaching. Alexander says, "A nondogmatic, transcendent vision of goodness cannot be satisfied with regenerating that which has existed, with mere training and reproduction."[29] Education needs to proceed by inquiry and criticism, seeking better ways for human life. These ways of innovation and creativity are grounded in religious traditions, though not limited to them; certainly, no false dichotomy is assumed between past and future, inheritance and innovation. The rationale for this approach to education is "to strengthen the moral agent within each person," which is the pathway toward goodness, education, moral discourse, and civilized life.[30] Alexander, as Meland earlier, insists on a tight connection among goodness, transcendence, and acts of imagination.

This conversation points to eschatology, a strange topic in an educational discussion. Yet, the future is a recurrent emphasis among process-relational thinkers. The transcendent unknown seeps into the reality of the present world through the initial aim offered to every emerging occasion. This transcendent unknown is variously identified as the kingdom of Heaven, everlasting redemption, reign of God, New Creation, and eschatological future. Many process thinkers emphasize God's role in luring the world toward a better future; others give nontheistic explanations. In either case, the sense of an open future influences the present as well as what is to come. Marjorie Suchocki underscores this: "Clearly, the overcoming of evil which takes place in the everlasting redemption of occasions within God has an effect in the ongoing world...The redemption in heaven demands its likeness on earth."[31] Thus, the interplay of God and the world, and the pull of future possibility, transform the present world.

Similar affirmations can be made without religious language, although contemporary educational theory contains a growing interplay between the disciplines of religion and education, sometimes explicit and sometimes simply drawing upon common concepts and literature. Thirty years ago, for example, the philosopher Philip Phenix addressed transcendence in education.[32] Patrick Slattery continues the emphasis today, turning to eschatology as "a framework for developing and understanding contemporary curriculum," drawing upon philosophical, educational, and theological sources to develop his ideas.[33] Slattery concludes that an eschatological focus is essential for social transformation: "The reconceptualization of eschatology, where the future and transcendence become transformative for the individual and the global community, is an imminent necessity."[34] Surely, if transcendence is of such import for social transformation, the practice of imagining peace is critical to the educational process.

3. Intimate Knowing

The focus on transcendence ironically turns us back to a third way to cultivate imagination for peace—intimate knowing. Elsewhere I have attended to the importance of particularity in educational practice.[35] Here I highlight the need to create spaces for relationships with particular others to deepen, thus nourishing the intimate knowing for which human beings yearn. Intimacy has received little attention by educational theorists. The absence of intimate knowing is implicit in the critiques of schooling offered by such people as Ivan Illich, Pat Farenga, and Linda Dobson; however, what is needed is more than they offer by extension or implication. What is needed is a clear and prominent place for intimate knowing within the educational process, both within and beyond institutions of formal learning.

This concern connects in part with Whitehead's passion for brute facts, and his dream that, in education, abstract generalizations and real facts be interwoven so that the relation between them can be explored and valued (SMW 3, 18, 25, 135, 198–99). Whitehead's elaboration of this is a strong critique of contemporary educational method, though he focused on approaches to education in his day:

> My own criticism of our traditional educational methods is that they
> are far too much occupied with intellectual analysis, and with the

acquirement of formularised information. What I mean is, that we neglect to strengthen habits of concrete appreciation of the individual facts in their full interplay of emergent values. (SMW 198)

Whitehead's attention is on intimacy with particular facts of the world. I suggest that this is a critical aspect, but not a full description, of intimate knowing.

Intimate knowing includes engagement with particular people, beings, observations, and ideas. It includes relating with others from the deep marrow of human experience, what Meland hinted when he pointed toward meaning. It also includes playing with others, and with ideas and combinations of ideas. Such education requires the creation of safe spaces in which people can be honest and open, as they are moved to be, where they can experiment with new ideas and new forms of activity, and where they can be assured of trust and confidentiality insofar as this is possible. Such education is risky, but it responds to a human need and creates a way of being in small communities that will be essential if peace is to be reached in larger social bodies.

4. Knowing the Stranger and the Unfamiliar

Another avenue for stirring imagination is encouraging people to know the stranger and the unfamiliar. This involves crossing cultural, geographic, religious, and age boundaries, what Meland describes as "survey of experience." It also involves crossing disciplinary boundaries, so that scientists and mathematicians engage with the arts and social sciences, and vice versa. Whitehead was persistent in urging educators "to eradicate the fatal disconnection of subjects which kills the vitality of our modern curriculum." He insisted, "There is only one subject-matter for education, and that is Life in all its manifestations" (AE 6–7). If "Life" is the curriculum, then teaching involves meeting the neighbor and stranger, the familiar and unfamiliar. Such meetings stir imagination by opening new windows of experience from which people can draw as they face the particularities of their own lives and their participation in the larger world day by day.

Three issues emerge in any reflection on knowing the stranger and the unfamiliar. One is the danger of collecting otherness as a thing to be accumulated. This danger sometimes involves treating the other as an exotic being to be admired or even laughed at or pitied. It sometimes takes the form of gathering facts about the other as one collects butterflies or bells. Whitehead describes culture in a much more interactive and responsive way: "Culture is activity of thought, and receptiveness to beauty and humane feeling"; to this he adds, "Scraps of information have nothing to do with it" (AE 1). For Whitehead, nothing could be more destructive to good education than "inert ideas," or ideas that are received without being utilized, tested, or "thrown into fresh combinations" (AE 1). We see here a warning about any kind of knowing that is passively received or entertained at a distance. Whitehead, as process-relational philosophers and educators after him, was concerned with genuine, life-changing interactions and the deep knowing that emerges from them.

A second issue in knowing the stranger and the unfamiliar is related to the first—the danger of engaging in boundary-crossing education while ignoring differentials of power. Christine Sleeter has addressed this directly in her work on multicultural education, suggesting that "*empowerment* and *multicultural education* are interwoven, and together suggest powerful and far-reaching school reform."[36] If knowing has to do with relating with the world in a deep and responsive way, then our relationships need to be permeated with awareness and critical response to differentials in power, as well as differentials in language, style, arts, and rituals. Differentials need to be analyzed and critiqued, but more than that. Education needs to cultivate the relative self-sufficiency of each person, each culture, each religious community, contributing to the wholeness of each. Each party needs to be recognized as a whole and not simply in relation to the other. To study African children only as victims of draught, hunger, or AIDS is as demeaning as not studying them at all. To study them as people—with families and communities who love them, with religious and cultural traditions, with lives affected by global political and economic patterns—is to recognize them as real people, and to recognize the multifaceted relationships that affect their lives. Such knowing requires response, which inevitably asks much of the knowers *and* the known, including a redress of inequities and a movement toward equality and interdependence.

A third issue in educating people in difference is the danger that differences will be understood in substantive, nonchanging, and externally related ways; thus, knowing the stranger and unfamiliar is seen as an encounter with a radical other, which may or may not affect learners. The danger here is that people might fall into substantive, disengaged thinking about otherness. This happens often in interreligious education, as when people argue that learners need to know their own tradition well before learning others, lest they become confused. Carl Sterkens argues, however, that religion itself is "not a fixed entity but a dynamic, changeable totality of cognitive processes, associated with affect and behavioural orientations."[37] Further, he argues that all individuals and all religions are polyphonic, embracing a plurality of world views.[38] For these reasons, religious pluralism is not a threat but an unavoidable reality; indeed, the polyphonic self is not a "single, substantive self, existing in its own right and acting in an undivided capacity."[39] It is, rather, a distributed self, located in different situations, times, places, positions, and roles. Sterkens' view is compatible with a process-relational view of human selves and human culture, recognizing that diversity exists both within and beyond individuals' experience.

These dangers are all related, and they all suggest that the learners are nonrelational, static, unitary selves. If, however, the self is relational through and through, and is in a dynamic process of change over time, then the self's unity is not a settled core. It is an emerging integration and reintegration of its stream of inheritance, the influences of the present moment, and the initial aims that enhance novelty and self-transcendence in every new moment. This view of the self suggests that knowing the stranger and unfamiliar has potential to enhance learners' ability to know reality, in all of its manifestations, and to imagine the possible, knowing that the future is radically open.

5. Imaging and Responding to the Possible

One other way to cultivate peace is to envision alternate futures. Such imaginative work has been central for process-relational thinkers, who assume the real possibility for social change. These people exemplify a visionary way of knowing that is significant for education–seeking visions and developing the practical possibilities of those visions. John Cobb, for example, develops an alternative perspective on global politics and economics. He encourages societies to invest maximum power and decision-making in local entities and then to strengthen global entities to address those problems that require global coordination.[40] His proposals are tempered with a realistic assessment that no ideal solution exists, but that some solutions are better than others–avoiding or minimizing catastrophes and building toward a sustainable society. For him, the most hopeful plan is to decentralize the economy and organize the political world into communities of communities.[41] He bases this proposal on building relatively self-sufficient communities so that one community or country is not totally dependent on others for survival.

Cobb's model of imagining and developing an alternate future is a model that can be encouraged in educational institutions. Project learning, simulation gaming, and analyzing social problems to propose alternatives are some ways by which alternate futures can emerge. Further, Cobb's specific idea of relative self-sufficiency is suggestive for the actual shaping of those alternatives. While it discourages dependent and oppressive relationships, it fosters interdependence, both *within* human communities and ecosystems, and *among* them. Such interdependence is important for relationships within the educational process and, also, in the alternate futures that students and teachers envision. Imagining peace is an exercise in imaging relationships that empower each being and community to live as fully as possible *and* to relate with others in ways that nourish life abundant for the entire cosmos.

Conclusion

In conclusion, we return to the three case studies of violent conflict. Without claiming that education has power to change the world in every respect for the better, I do propose that the process-relational epistemology and educational approach sketched here promise to open people to the exercise of imagination. Then, *by way of* imagination, people might also be stirred toward fresh visions of peace, and more just and nourishing ways of engaging with other people and the environment. To practice such education, we need to tap many forms of knowing, which could potentially push the two women of the case study beyond the limits of their present reflection on war, for example. We will also need to engage deeply with difference in both small and large settings and build trust within safe spaces of intimate knowing. Only then might the practice of scapegoating and the active blocking of peace impulses–such as those characterizing Middle East conflicts and U. S. involvements with Iraq–be thwarted and replaced by alternative visions for the future. Is this an exercise in imagination? It certainly is, but I would risk hoping that our imaginative knowing will make all the difference.

CHAPTER 17

Politics in Process Perspective

■ LESLIE A. MURAY

This essay seeks to develop the notion of "an ecological democratic faith" building on the concept of relational power in process thought. Undergirding this effort is a process understanding of the relation between the human and the non-human natural world that is biocentric rather than anthropocentric, affirming the intrinsic value of human and nonhumans alike. As it explores related issues, the essay seeks to broaden the scope of the transformative vision of process thought in relation to politics.[1]

The Concept of Unilateral Power

One of the most important contributions of process thought to a political theology and to political theory is the concept of relational power. Process thinkers develop the concept of relational power in contrast to the notion of unilateral power that has typified most of the Western intellectual tradition and socio-politico-economic-cultural practice. This contrast parallels process thought's rejection of the substantialism of most of the inherited tradition in favor of "event" thinking.

The unilateral conception of power rests on a substantialist view of reality. That is to say, if reality if constituted by discrete, isolated substances that require nothing but themselves (and God) to exist, then the values that become central are self-sufficiency and independence. The consequence of such a view of reality on the conception of power is that power is "a one-way street," the ability to affect, to influence another. Its exercise is the manifestation of unilateral power. Anything that is its opposite—allowing oneself to be influenced by others, as exemplified in receptivity and sensitivity to others and to one's world—is seen as a sign of weakness.

The unilateral conception of power is readily discernible in traditionally stereotyped gender roles. Men are deemed superior because they are active, self-sufficient, independent, unemotional, and unaffected by the vicissitudes of life. Women, on the other hand, are supposed to be dependent, the "weaker sex" in need of both the brains and brawn of men. The most perverted and distorted expressions of the unilateral conception of power are child and spousal abuse, in whatever form.

The ultimate legitimation of unilateral power has been provided by the understanding of divine power as unilateral power. In spite of nuanced philosophical arguments and maneuvers, in effect, God was traditionally conceived as the sole power of the universe, perfect in that power. As part of the very meaning of divine perfection, God was conceived to be supremely unaffected by the world. This was no less true of the deism of the Enlightenment. God created the world by setting the machinery of the universe in motion, perfectly capable of operating according to its own laws. God had very little left to do, although God was perfectly capable of intervening "from the outside" in case the world needed any repairs.

If Jesus Christ is the incarnation of God, then, according to the unilateral conception of power, all of Jesus' power is derived from God. In similar fashion, his own exercise of power is equally one-sided: The people he dealt with were passive recipients of his love, forgiveness, teaching, and healings. In this dimension of the inherited tradition, Jesus' very divinity is contingent on being unaffected by others and by the varied changes of life.

It goes without saying that the political expression of the unilateral conception of power is inclined toward hierarchicalism, authoritarianism, and dictatorship. If being unaffected and influenced by the opinions, thoughts, and feelings of others are seen as signs of weakness, the denigration and suppression of the opinions, thoughts, and feelings of others follow all too easily.

The Concept of Relational Power[2]

To set the stage for a discussion of relational power, let me begin with an allusion to Lord Acton's dictum, "Power corrupts, and absolute power corrupts absolutely." From my understanding of process thought, this statement is true of the unilateral conception of power. However, to claim that Lord Acton's statement holds true about any conception of power is profoundly problematic.

In process thought, anything actual at all, from the tiniest energy event to human beings, has some degree of power. No organism can stay alive without some exercise of some degree of power. A momentary subjective experience, an actual occasion, has *both* a *receptive* side, receiving data from the past, and an *active* side, deciding how it constitutes itself, deciding how it prehends data from the past and actualizes the possibilities of the moment and of future. If then all experience involves both a receptive and an active side, then for process thought power also must have both a receptive and an active side. Power is not only the capacity to affect, to carry out a purpose, but also the capacity to undergo an effect, to be acted upon (PR 351).

Thus, consistent with its vision of a relational and participatory universe, process thought envisions power as relational. One consequence of a relational view of power, consistent with a relational view of the self, is that virtues different from those of independence and self-sufficiency would be cultivated. While in one sense independence and self-sufficiency are to be prized, this is not to be done in an atomistic way that cuts us off from a fundamental sense of relatedness. Rather, we should prize them in a way that fosters *interdependence,* a word that captures both independence and relatedness. Other virtues that at least this process thinker would want to nurture include sensitivity, receptivity, responsiveness, compassion, and creativity. Nurturing these virtues empowers the emergence of a larger, richer self, able to take in greater contrast, greater intensity, leading to greater experiences of beauty.[3]

The relational view of power has important consequences for gender relations. Men's lives can be vastly enriched by nurturing their sense of relatedness without giving up their sense of autonomy. Women's lives can affirm a fundamental sense of autonomy and not be swallowed up in relationships even as they affirm their basic experience of relatedness.

In similar fashion, the exercise of leadership that ensues from a relational understanding of power is significantly different. Instead of a hierarchical, unidirectional, "top down" manner of exercising power, a good leader may be clear about her/his goals yet be sensitive, receptive, and responsive to those whom he/she leads. The leader will affirm them and at the same guide and motivate them, while respecting their freedom. This kind of leadership can steer the team to realize novel possibilities.

If God is the chief exemplification of metaphysical categories, then God is the supreme example of relational power. God is supremely relational on the active side, "the Primordial Nature," as God lures the creatures with ideal possibilities to realize themselves in their fundamental interdependence with one another. God is supremely relational on the receptive side, "the Consequent Nature," as God feels the feelings of the creatures and preserves them everlastingly with no loss of immediacy.

The most adequate understanding of the relationship between the Primordial and Consequent Natures of God is an interactionist one.[4] That is to say, the possibilities God offers every moment arise as divine responses from God's feeling of the feelings of God's creatures. Thus, God, as chief exemplification of the mutuality and reciprocity that characterizes relatedness, is the supreme participant in the lives of God's creatures. If Jesus is the incarnation of God, then the incarnation needs to be understood in relational terms. If Jesus was in any sense human, he was profoundly shaped, as we are, by his human and nonhuman environment, and by the culture and history of his people. Could Jesus have been who he was without the community that gathered around him? As Bernard M. Loomer has written, "Christ owed…his character as a Christological figure…to those people whom he came to serve."[5] "Christ's relations to his fellows and theirs to him were constitutive of his very being."[6] The gospels paint a thoroughly relational picture of Jesus: forgiving, unconditionally accepting and loving, sensitive, receptive, and responsive. This relational Jesus enables others' responses to the possibility of a newness of life that God offers in each moment, and he acts it out through table fellowship with sinners, the oppressed, the marginalized of his day.

We have seen that in Whiteheadian process thought God always acts persuasively rather than coercively. Following Whitehead, process thinkers have rebelled against tyrannical images of God. In keeping with this and in being consistent, coherent, and adequate in upholding the freedom of all actualities, process thinkers have maintained that God does not voluntarily relinquish or limit the divine power. Rather, God is "subject to the rules of the game" much in the manner that constitutional monarchs, presidents, and prime ministers in modern democracies are not above but subject to the laws of their countries.[7] While most process philosophers and theologians prefer to think that they have redefined the attribute of divine omnipotence, that is,, following Anselm in asserting that God's power is that which none greater can be conceived, hence not the only power, I prefer to think of a finite God limited in power.[8] Regardless of which of these directions one follows, the concept of relational divine power in process thought offers an important resource for the development of a "democratic faith" in a "democratic God." This resource is in contact with but also critical and transformative of intellectual currents that foster the exploration of the meanings of democracy and nurture their development.

An Ecological Democratic Faith

In Whiteheadian process thought, the drive toward fulfillment, the experience of beauty, is characteristic of anything actual at all–from the tiniest energy event, to atoms and molecules, to animals with central nervous systems. Consequently, perhaps the most important metaphysical claim a Whiteheadian understanding of nature can make is that experience is the locus of value. In the Whiteheadian scheme, any subjective experiencing, however rudimentary, is of intrinsic value. To be sure, the immediacy and intensity of all subjective experiences "perish," becoming "objective data" in the becoming of other momentary experiencing subjects. Thus, while any experience is of intrinsic value in the immediacy and intensity of the moment, it is also of instrumental value as it contributes to richness of experience of consequent moments of experience. Although all experiences are of intrinsic value, this not to say that all experiences are of equal value. There is an incredible variety in the capacity for "richness of experience," for "intensity of feeling." The capacity for richness of experience depends on the degree of complexity of organization as "actual occasions of experience" come together, extended in space and time.

Positing the locus of value in momentary experiencing is not to be understood in a substantialist, atomistic way, but rather in a relational way. That is to say, as the moment of subjective experiencing prehends data from the past, the past of the entire universe, it arises out of a fundamental web of relationships. This holds true from the tiniest energy event to the complex experiencing of the human self. In the relational universe of Whiteheadian process thought, there is neither *absolute* distinction nor *absolute* identity between the self (or any subjective experience) and "the other," no *absolute* boundary between the self (or any subjective experience) and the world. The web of relationships is the nurturing (or obstructive) matrix for the richness of experience of the becoming moment.

In this manner process thought situates humans in the nonhuman natural world while preserving the distinctiveness of human beings (the difference between the human and nonhuman, human and nonhuman experience being one of degree, not of kind). It also provides a nonanthropocentric grounding for human rights—as well as the rights of nonhuman animals.

Historically in the Western tradition, human rights have been grounded in the unique dignity that humans have simply by virtue of being human, usually connected to a rationality that is a distinctive characteristic of humans alone. In contrast, process thought posits the notion in the capacity to feel, in the capacity for richness of experience that, as we have seen, is of intrinsic value. Moreover, reason is a feature of experience, present in all actualities in however rudimentary a level. Thus, because any experiencing subject is of intrinsic value, in a loose sense we can say that it has rights. However, as we have also seen, not all experiences are equal in richness, hence we may assert that while all creatures have rights, they do not have equal rights. Those rights are contextual and intertwined with the fundamental interdependence of all things.

Deep Ecologists, given their proclivity to defend species equality, will disagree. Moreover, given the long history of the perpetration of horror in the ways humans have treated one another, especially in the twentieth century, as well as in the treatment of the nonhuman natural world, one needs to be very careful in making such a bold claim. The burden of proof is always on the would-be violator. Yet it seems that we cannot help but make ethical judgments, and the category of richness of experience, with its variety of gradations, provides a useful category to make such judgments amidst the ambiguities of actual situations.

The moment of subjective experiencing is the locus of value; yet, it arises out of the web of relationships that includes the past of the entire universe. Thus, the relational metaphysics of process thought can be described as that of the "individual-in-community." As with the notion of interdependence, combining independence and interrelatedness, the concept of the "individual-in-community" suggests an inseparable link rather than inevitable conflict between the individual and the community. To be sure, conflict may occur. However, as I have mentioned, the individual emerges out of a fundamental web of relationships. The communities out of which we emerge as individuals are a part of us and we a part of them. While individuals have the capacity to transcend their communities and realize themselves at times in spite of their communities, those communities can enhance or obstruct individual development.

The notion of the self, human and nonhuman, being an individual-in-community holds true for all actualities, all creatures, human and nonhuman. Indeed, Whitehead considered the question of the "individual-in-community" to be the religious question.[9] In the case of humans, it would be fruitful to build on Bernard E. Meland's concept of "appreciative awareness" and Bernard M. Loomer's idea of "size." These ideas help us cultivate the previously described virtues of sensitivity, receptivity, responsiveness, compassion, and creativity not just in relation to humans but to nonhumans as well. The concept of "appreciative awareness" in Meland and the idea of "size" in Loomer appropriate the Whiteheadian notion of beauty. Our "appreciative awareness" can grow, and we can be persons of greater "size" as we take more and more of the world, greater and greater contrast into ourselves, without violating our integrity. We are called to make the life, the pain, and the joy of the nonhuman "other" part of our own lives, of our own joys and sorrows. This resembles closely what Arne Naess has called the "ecological self," the notion that the community of all living beings is constitutive of our selfhood.[10] If this is the case, then individuals can fulfill themselves only if all living beings realize themselves. And this can occur only if I identify with other living beings, if I can see myself in all living things, or in Meland's words, if I can identify with other living things as instances of "creation in miniature,"[11] with no *absolute* boundary between us.

John Cobb and the economist Herman Daly have called the notion of the "individual-in-community" applied to humans "persons-in-community."[12] This idea provides quite a different grounding for democratic theory than do typical modern democratic theories grounded in an individualistic, atomistic view of the self and in a substantialist view of reality. Process thought emphasizes the dignity of the individual and individual self-realization no less than do individualistic democratic theories. However, unlike atomistic democratic theoreticians, process thinkers emphasize the health of the communities out of which the individual emerges and through which she realizes herself. Process thinkers follow no "party line" and are hardly monolithic. Nevertheless, within their green perspectives those who engage political theory tend to be "communitarian" and "social democratic" in their treatment. This does not mean that process thinkers are collectivists. Process thought, with its emphasis on the "individual-in-community," offers unique resources in affirming both the distinctiveness of the individual and her/his fundamental relatedness. Thus, process thinkers can affirm the concerns of Deep Ecologists and yet resist allowing the "parts" to be swallowed up by the "whole." This is true whether the whole be the ecosystem or the image of some sort of Cosmic Soul/Mind of the Cosmic Social Organism, as in some images of Gaia.[13]

If a community profoundly shapes the development of healthy, creative, free individuals, then the elements that foster that kind of creative development need to be examined. Expressing it in a variety of ways, a number of process thinkers across the generations (from John Dewey, Henry Nelson Wieman, and Daniel Day Williams to John Cobb) emphasize the need for people to participate effectively in the decisions that affect their lives.[14] They emphasize the importance of individual responsibility, of taking responsibility for what we do with the past and for how we respond to the possibilities of the future—that is, for the persons we become.

One implication of efficacious participation in the decisions that shape one's life is the limitation of undue concentrations of power in every overlapping sphere of life, in both institutions and in persons. Politically, this would entail the maximum safeguarding of civil liberties and due process of law. It would include institutional systems of checks and balances. At some levels of community, it could entail representative forms of government; at smaller levels it could and would encourage direct forms of democratic participation.

Undue concentrations of political power are usually inseparably intertwined with undue concentrations of economic power. Transnational corporations have undue influence in the politics within and between nations. The ability to express one's views is all too dependent on the ability to pay for it. The hearing granted to a diverse range on the political spectrum is curtailed by the fact that the media is largely owned by transnational corporations. Most process thinkers want to limit such concentrations of power.

Process thinkers concerned with these issues advocate some form of workers' democracy, workers' ownership and management of their places of employment. In their estimation, political democracy cannot exist without economic democracy. Unlike the neoclassical economists, with individualistic, atomistic presuppositions, process thinkers also advocate subsuming economic life to political life, for the health of the community. That does not necessarily imply state control or ownership; it will involve the use of market mechanisms. However, the use of market is not unhampered; it is for the good of the community.[15]

All of this implies limitations on the undue concentration of power in the state, or in any institution or person. Such limitations become especially needed, as we have seen, with regard to its coercive powers, with regard to civil liberties, due process of law, and the observance of democratic procedures. Nevertheless, the state also has a positive role. The state assures that all parties observe the "rules of the game"—that all elements of society receive fairness, equity, and justice; that all have access to the goods of life. The positive role of the state is to promote the common good, with the maximum participation of all.

Thus, although they show no unanimity on these issues, most process thinkers who deal with them are opposed to globalization, to free trade as practiced today. They take this position because, in their analysis, globalization is destructive of community and the diversity of communities.[16] It imposes an artificial homogeneity destructive of community, of the individual-in-community, human and nonhuman. It keeps wages low. In contrast, process thinkers advocate economic self-sufficiency and the principle of "subsidiarity." This means that "power should be located as close to the people as possible, that is, in the smallest units that are feasible."[17]

While process thinkers encourage the maximization of local participation, they realize that some problems demand solutions on a larger scale, sometimes regional, sometimes national, sometimes international. Thus, their treatment of community envisions an ever-expanding circle of "communities of communities." In all instances, they seek the "common good," the health of the community, of the "individual-in-community."

> In this regard, process thinkers realize that people need to have some minimum standard of living in order to participate effectively in the decisions that shape their lives. Hunger and poverty are not conducive to such participation. The manner in which such a minimum standard of living is guaranteed would encourage both individual responsibility and serving the "common good." It is not atypical to advocate some form of a negative income tax, combined with job training, and gradual reduction in the negative income tax as one's earned salary and or wages grow.[18]

For process thinkers, the "common good"–the health of the community–includes the nonhuman natural world, and not just as something of instrumental value to human beings, but of intrinsic value. Thus, unlike neoclassical economics, most process thinkers concerned with these issues treat the nonhuman natural world not as "externalities" but as integral to economic activity. Consequently, they advocate "sustainable" economies that do not exceed the carrying capacities of the earth's resources; they advocate economies of "scale" that use "appropriate" technologies. Instead of measuring economic welfare by the Gross National Product, they advocate the use of an "Index of Sustainable Welfare," which includes such usually ignored factors as environmental damage, infant mortality, the value of unpaid household work, etc.[19]

The previously described views of process thinkers have much in common with the principles of *The Earth Charter,* which is introduced in Jay McDaniel's essay in this volume. These principles include the following:

1. striving to build free, just, participatory, sustainable, and peaceful societies
2. protecting and restoring the integrity of the Earth's ecosystems, with special concerns for biodiversity
3. treating all living beings with compassion
4. adopting patterns of consumption, production, and reproduction that safeguard the regenerative capacities of the Earth, human rights, and the well-being of the community
5. ensuring that economic activities promote human development in an equitable and sustainable manner
6. the eradication of poverty as a socio-economic-ethical-ecological imperative

7. honoring and defending "the right of all persons, without discrimination, to an environment supportive of their dignity, bodily health, and spiritual well-being"[20]
8. the establishment of access to information, which means inclusive participation, truthfulness, and accountability in governance
9. the affirmation and promotion of gender equality as prerequisite for sustainable development
10. making an integral part of formal education as well as lifelong learning all the knowledge, values, and skills needed to build just and sustainable communities
11. the creation of a culture of peace and cooperation[21]

Both process thought and *The Earth Charter* situate human beings firmly in the nonhuman natural world. Most process thinkers and *The Earth Charter* advocate the quest for a free, democratic, participatory, just, and sustainable community in a nonanthropocentric way, affirming the intrinsic value of the constituent elements of the nonhuman natural world.[22]

I would like to make one last point in keeping with the title of this section, "An Ecological Democratic Faith." In contrast to democratic theories grounded in anthropocentric views of humanity's relationship to the nonhuman natural world, such Deep Ecologists as Joanna Macy have called for "a council of all beings."[23] Thomas Berry has suggested that instead of "democracy" we should start talking of "biocracy."[24] The notion of "biocracy" seeks to convey the idea that we have duties and obligations toward all sentient creatures as well as to the complex, interrelated ecosystems that make life possible.[25] We can strengthen the nonanthropocentric, biocentric, and ecocentric thrust of Berry's notion of "biocracy" by claiming that the nonhuman natural world, speaking metaphorically, has its own system of "checks and balances." Is not the environmental degradation so evident in today's world the result of nonhuman nature's system of checks and balances? This is the vision of an ecological democratic faith, the vision of a participatory universe in which the dignity and creative freedom of all creatures in their fundamental interdependence with one another are affirmed, in which the voices of all creatures are "heard."

Nationalism and Community

In process thought, a sense of community seems to be inseparable from a sense of rootedness, of belonging,[26] what Bernard E. Meland called "at-homeness" in the universe, of being Earth creatures.[27] We experience this sense of rootedness, of belonging, of at-homeness in the universe not in abstract ways but in the concrete experiences of community in a particular place and expressed through shared memories, although those memories may be interpreted in diverse ways. A sense of being at home in the universe, of belonging to the universe, of belonging *everywhere* and *anywhere* is rooted in a sense of belonging *somewhere*.

Following Whitehead, process thinkers maintain that each actual occasion, each momentary subjective experiencing, has its standpoint, its own perspective from which it prehends data from the past and responds to the possibilities of the future. The standpoint includes the physical, geographical location, the community(ies) of which one is a part in space and time.

The need for rootedness, for belonging, as Daniel Day Williams has maintained, is intrinsic to one's identity as a human being.[28] And if this need is inseparable from the particularity of place, then, while repudiating its extreme expressions, we need to recognize that contemporary forms of nationalism, sometimes in twisted, distorted, even demonic ways (i.e. the Balkans), are fundamentally motivated by the search for roots and belonging. The search for roots and belonging that nationalism expresses is, to be sure, complicated by a variety of factors that have unleashed all manner of evil. I shall mention two of those factors here. The first we can see when two or more groups consider the same territory to be "sacred space" with not enough land to go around for everybody. The second we can find in a sanctified exclusivism that sees "the other" as a threat to one's very existence and to that of one's group.

Of course, the expressions of nationalism need not be like that. Traditions within those expressions, such as the "liberal nationalism" of the nineteenth century, are able to affirm the need to belong to a particular group in a particular place while accepting and affirming "the otherness of the other." The challenge for us is to be rooted in our own communities, yet to be so open to other communities that we recognize the bonds of our common humanity—put better and more inclusively, of our common creatureliness—in the search for rootedness and belonging. And this may be the first step in the realization of a "community of communities" in the quest for peace and wholeness.[29]

Conclusion

Building on the concept of relational power in process thought, this essay has attempted to develop the notion of "an ecological democratic faith." In doing so, it seeks to broaden the range of the transformative vision of process thought in relation to political life. Process thought's vision of a free, just, participatory, sustainable, and peaceful society, which parallels that of the *The Earth Charter,* finds especially eloquent expression in the words of William James (who had considerable impact on Whitehead's thought): "Why may not the world be a sort of republican banquet, where all the qualities of being respect one another's personal sacredness, yet sit at the common table of space and time?"[30]

CHAPTER 18

A Process Approach to Ecology

■ JAY MCDANIEL

This essay[1] presents a process approach to ecology. In the first section I offer a general picture of the global challenges to which process theologians respond as they develop theologies of ecology. In so doing I identify six challenges people face in many world religions as they seek to contribute to the common good of the world. A distinctive feature of process theology is that it is not the work of one theologian alone. Rather many theologians, each of whom work on one or another of these challenges, simultaneously realize that they are working in collaboration with others who are addressing other challenges. I hope that this section will give the reader a sense of how process theologians understand the needs of the twenty-first century and how they understand the appropriate agenda of socially engaged theologies, whether Christian or Muslim, Hindu or Buddhist, Jewish or otherwise. As this essay attests in its final section, process theology is already a multireligious theological movement and promises to become even more diverse in the future. The challenges of the twenty-first century will form the agenda for much of its thought.

In the second section I introduce a process understanding of God as it pertains to the larger web of life. Several essays in this volume have focused on God's relations to human life; my aim is to emphasize God's relation to the whole of life. My proposal is that in process theology God is not "One-over-many" but rather "One-embracing-many" and "One-within-many" and "One-between-many." The *many* whom God embraces include other living beings whose ways of living may be strange by human standards yet beautiful by divine standards. An important feature of process theology depicts respect for diversity–human and more-than-human–as a diagnostic feature of authentic trust in God.

In the third section I then outline the general contours of a process approach to environmental concerns, showing how process theology recommends a threefold approach to nature: cosmological, practical, and spiritual. Topics in this section include not only the worldview of process thought as it invites respect and care for the community of life, but also the many forms of feeling through which, according to process theology, humans can enjoy a sense of kinship with, and delight in, other forms of life. My aim in these sections is to introduce the general reader, religiously affiliated and otherwise, to some of the core ideas in process theology as it offers hope for a sustainable future.

The World Situation

Imagine that a terrible catastrophe has occurred–perhaps a nuclear explosion or an ecological collapse–and that a parliament of world religions has been called to assess the situation. Imagine further that you have been asked to give the opening address, offering an assessment of the state of the world and the way forward. You want to be honest about the seriousness of the situation, and yet you also want to offer a word of hope. What would you say?

One possibility would be to read aloud the preamble of the Earth Charter.[2] Originating in discussions among participants in the United Nations, this document was created in the final decade of the twentieth century through a series of consultations held around the world involving people from many walks of life and cultural traditions. Their aim was to assess the state of the world and develop a set of ethical guidelines for just and sustainable living that individuals, families, nations, churches, synagogues, mosques, corporations, and schools might use. Educational circles around the world now use it to apprise citizens of the challenges facing the twenty-first century and to encourage them to help create a *global civil society* conducive to democratic and humane communities. A global civil society is not a government or a church. It is what process thinkers would call a *society* of individuals, coming from many different cultures and religious traditions, who agree in a very general way on a common hope for the future. Consumer culture, for example, now forms a global civil society of sorts, albeit of an unhealthy variety. Its participants do not know each other, yet they share a common set of values and common hope. The values are appearance, affluence, and marketable achievement, understood as a central organizing principle of social life. The hope is for endless material acquisition without ever having to say enough. The Earth Charter envisions another kind of a society, based on a common hope for a sustainable future.

While process theologians alone did not write the Earth Charter, some were involved in the consultation processes that gave rise to it. Its preamble offers a vision of human life and the state of the world that most process thinkers share. The first paragraph sets the general context by pointing out that humans are a part of, not apart from, the larger web of life:

> Humanity is part of a vast evolving universe. Earth, our home, is alive with a unique community of life. The forces of nature make existence a demanding and uncertain adventure, but Earth has provided the

conditions essential to life's evolution. The resilience of the community of life and the well-being of humanity depend upon preserving a healthy biosphere with all its ecological systems, a rich variety of plants and animals, fertile soils, pure waters, and clean air. The global environment with its finite resources is a common concern of all peoples. The protection of Earth's vitality, diversity, and beauty is a sacred trust.[3]

Readers familiar with process theology know that process thinkers share all of these assumptions. They believe that humanity is part of an evolving universe, that the earth is alive with a unique community of life, that living beings depend on one another for their survival and well-being, and that the future of life on earth is uncertain. They also believe that human beings have a responsibility not only to protect the vitality and diversity of the planet, but also its beauty, which takes the form of myriad forms of life both human and more-than-human. In process theology beauty is understood to be the very aim of the universe and the aim of God. To wantonly destroy beauty in the name of progress is itself a form of sin.

The second paragraph presents the bad news, the presence of a great deal of sin on our planet, some of it unintentional but all of it tragic:

The dominant patterns of production and consumption are causing environmental devastation, the depletion of resources, and a massive extinction of species. Communities are being undermined. The benefits of development are not shared equitably and the gap between rich and poor is widening. Injustice, poverty, ignorance, and violent conflict are widespread and the cause of great suffering. An unprecedented rise in human population has overburdened ecological and social systems. The foundations of global security are threatened. These trends are perilous—but not inevitable.[4]

With this paragraph most process thinkers would likewise agree. A healthy approach to life involves an honest appraisal of the myriad ways in which the world is not as it should be. The final two paragraphs provide a word of hope:

The choice is ours: form a global partnership to care for Earth and one another or risk the destruction of ourselves and the diversity of life. Fundamental changes are needed in our values, institutions, and ways of living. We must realize that when basic needs have been met, human development is primarily about being more, not having more. We have the knowledge and technology to provide for all and to reduce our impacts on the environment. The emergence of a global civil society is creating new opportunities to build a democratic and humane world. Our environmental, economic, political, social, and spiritual challenges are interconnected, and together we can forge inclusive solutions.

To realize these aspirations, we must decide to live with a sense of universal responsibility, identifying ourselves with the whole Earth community as well as our local communities. We are at once citizens of different nations and of one world in which the local and global are linked. Everyone shares responsibility for the present and future well-being of the human family and the larger living world. The spirit of human solidarity and kinship with all life is strengthened when we live with reverence for the mystery of being, gratitude for the gift of life, and humility regarding the human place in nature.[5]

The previous two paragraphs, then, present what most process thinkers would take to be the best hope of our planet: that a global civil society emerge that emphasizes respect and care for the community of life. Are the world's religions up to the task of helping create such a society? Can the people of the different religions truly forge inclusive solutions to problems of injustice, poverty, ignorance, violent conflict, environmental devastation, resource depletion, and an extinction of species?

The Six Challenges

From a process perspective the answer is, "Maybe." The capacity of the world's religions to help create a global civil society depends on the degree to which people from different religions can respond to six challenges, all of which pertain to the well-being of the planet. From the vantage point of the earth's future it may not matter whether we understand ourselves as Christian or Buddhist, Jewish or Hindu, Muslim or Bahai. What matters is that we respond to the following challenges:

- *The Compassion Challenge:* that is, the challenge to identify resources within our traditions that are conducive to compassion—understood as respect and care for the community of life—and to live from these traditions in daily and community life.

- *The Repentance Challenge:* that is, the challenge to acknowledge teachings and practices within our traditions that lend themselves to arrogance and violence, prejudice and ignorance, and to repent from them, thus adding new chapters to their ongoing histories in a spirit of religious and cultural reconstruction. In Christianity, for example, the process of reconstruction involves coming to grips with patriarchy, racism, anti-Semitism, classism, and a host of other "isms" that have shaped Christian life and thought.

- *The Simplicity Challenge:* that is, the challenge to provide a meaningful alternative to what is arguably the dominant religion of our planet, namely consumerism. We must do more than lament the social and environmental costs of excessive consumption. We must show that life can be lived frugally and joyfully without the tragedy of poverty and the trappings of affluence.

- *The Diversity Challenge:* that is, to appreciate religious and cultural diversity by respecting people of different religions and cultures, trustful that there are many valuable forms of religious and cultural expression and that all make the whole of life richer.

- *The Science Challenge:* that is, to enter into meaningful dialogue with the natural sciences, acknowledging the epistemological power of their understandings of the universe and life on earth, while at the same time developing religious ways of looking at the world that lift up a sacred dimension to life.

- *The Environmental Challenge:* that is, to adopt an ecological outlook on life that acknowledges our biological and spiritual kinship with other creatures. Such an outlook will encourage the building of communities that are ecologically sustainable, compassionate toward other living beings, and protective of the earth's beauty for future generations, human and nonhuman alike.

Of course, these challenges will be more challenging to some people than to others. It may be easier for indigenous peoples to recognize kinship with other creatures than for some Muslims, Jews, and Christians. Equally important, not all of the challenges are relevant to all people. For example, the challenge to live frugally is most relevant to the one-fifth of the world's population who consume more than half the world's resources, thus depleting the world's nonrenewable resources and living in a way the world could not possibly emulate. The affluent are called to live more simply so the poor can simply live. In short, when considered in relation to concrete circumstances, the six challenges are on a sliding scale of objective urgency and perceived need.

Nevertheless, for many readers of this anthology—as for me—the six challenges are all relevant and *challenging.*[6] We are called

- to live compassionately even if compassion makes us feel vulnerable
- to live self-critically even if we are afraid of change and find it easier to criticize others than ourselves
- to reject a lifestyle based on appearance, affluence, and marketable achievement even if we are deeply absorbed in it and gain from it
- to welcome religious diversity even if we are initially fearful of strangers and what they might teach us
- to learn from science even if we might fear the consequences
- to recognize that we are kin to other creatures even if we prefer to think of ourselves as set apart and special

But here another question emerges: Can process theology help? Here again the answer is, "Maybe." A distinct feature of process theology is that its various writings address each of the challenges individually. In a more general way, it offers an outlook on life that enables a person to address all of them simultaneously, chiefly through its offering an ecological outlook on life. My focus in the remainder of this essay, then, is on the sixth challenge—the environmental challenge–as it so often provides a window into the other challenges.

In process theology "the environment" is not simply an issue among issues but rather a context for all issues. It is the web of life on earth and more generally the vast, evolving universe. This web includes not only what surrounds human beings but also our own free response to these surroundings. Moreover, our freedom is itself an expression of, not an exception to, a capacity for spontaneous self-structuring that is found throughout the whole of nature. This means that the ultimate reality of the universe is not God but rather "Creativity," which is manifest in everything that happens, whatever happens. It is to the process understanding of God, then, and God's relation to Creativity, that I turn.

God's Fondness for Beetles

When asked what he had learned about God after a lifetime of studying nature, the British biologist J.B.S. Haldane is alleged to have said: "I have learned that God has an inordinate fondness for beetles."[7]

It is not clear that Haldane ever really said this–the source has not been found–but if he did, he had a good point. Beetles have inhabited our planet for some 250 million years, compared to modern humans who have been on earth for only a few hundred thousand years. At least 500,000 species of beetles crawl the earth. This amounts to a quarter of all known animal species. This suggests that God may have not just a fondness for beetles, but–how to say this?–a rather magnificent obsession.

Of course, if Haldane did make the remark, he would have been speaking facetiously. He was a skeptic, and his remark would have been designed to poke fun at theists who unwittingly assume that God is a humanlike deity residing three miles off the planet, whose entire purpose in creation is to create humans. This would mean that fifteen billion years of galactic history and five billion years of earth history were designed for the primary purpose of producing human beings. The question naturally emerges: If humans were the sole purpose of galactic and biological evolution, why did God wait so long? Why not simply begin with humans and simultaneously create the rest for their enjoyment? For process thinkers, the answer is fairly straightforward. Each entity in our universe is an end in itself and not simply a means to other ends. Thus these means have been countless ends to creative evolution–as many as there are beings. This understanding also points to the fact that humans have not been the sole aim of creation and that, in the billions of years of evolution that preceded human life on earth, God was not waiting for humans. As evolution was unfolding, God saw something good in the planets and stars, the hills and the rivers, birds and the insects. Our task as humans is to add to the beauty, partly by recognizing the many other forms of beauty that already exist. This, then, is how a process theologian would offer a creative interpretation of the first creation story in Genesis. The point of the story is not to say that humans alone are good, but rather that the diverse whole is very good, humans included.

Haldane is known for another quote as well, the source for which is also difficult to find, but which also bears upon an understanding of God. It is that the universe is not only stranger than we imagine, but stranger than we *can* imagine.[8] Here, too, process theologians can agree. A healthy religious life must include what one science writer, Ursula Goodenough, calls a *covenant with mystery*, if it is to avoid the idolatry of making a god of its own beliefs and pretending a certainty it lacks.[9] Indeed, following Haldane, we might even speak of a covenant with strangeness.

By strangeness I mean the sheer mystery of being itself–the mystery that anything at all exists when there would, instead, be nothing at all. Whitehead alludes to this mystery in the first part of *Process and Reality* when he writes:

> There remains the final reflection, how shallow, puny, and imperfect are attempts to sound *the depths in the nature of things.* In philosophical discussion the merest hint of dogmatic certainty as to finality of statement is an exhibition of folly. (PR xiv)

A covenant with strangeness will include a humble recognition that theologies and philosophies of human design–including process theologies–can never fully plumb the depths in the nature of things. Reality is always more than our conception of it.

By strangeness I also mean something a little closer to home. I mean the subjective worlds of other living beings, whose ways of feeling the world may be very different from our own, but may nevertheless be beautiful in their own right. Here I use the word *beauty* in a Whiteheadian sense. I mean harmony and intensity of subjective feeling.

Beetles, then, would be a good example of this second kind of strangeness. From a process perspective they are, indeed, subjects of their own lives and not simply objects of human observation because they feel the presence of the world around them and respond in their own unique ways. In the language of process theology they have "intrinsic value" and not simply "instrumental value." And yet their subjective worlds must be very different from what we humans know.

What does it mean, though, to say that beetles are subjects? It does not mean that they exist in isolation from their environments or apart from their relations with the surrounding world, but rather that they feel the presence of their worlds from subjective points of view. When a living being experiences the surrounding world, the subject of the experience is not different from the act of experiencing itself. Moreover, the act of experience can be conscious or unconscious.

By "consciousness," process thinkers mean a particular kind of experience, or, more accurately, a certain way of experiencing the world, characterized by clarity and a sense that things could be otherwise. Consider the act of seeing and recognizing another human face. In this activity the face is in the foreground of our awareness; and we are "conscious" of it, while there remains something in the background of which we are "less conscious" because we are focusing on the face. In recognizing the face we have a dim intuition that things could be different: Our friend could not be "here" at all, and yet "here she is." We take note. This taking note is what process thinkers mean by consciousness. It is a highly developed form of experience that is characteristic of certain kinds of sense perception and certain kinds of reflection. Most of our experience in sleep and at the edges of ordinary waking consciousness is not like this at all. We take things into account and are affected by them and yet they are not objects of clear focus. By implication most beetle experience may likewise lack this kind of clarity. Beetle experience may well be vague, dim, and subconscious–and by human standards very strange.

But strangeness lies in the eye of the beholder. If beetles are somehow aware of humans in a conscious way, we can only imagine that from their point of view we humans would be the strange ones. Moreover, if we abandon all caution and playfully imagine that beetles have something like theistic religion, we can only trust that for them God will be an omnipresent "Beetle" in whose image all beetles are made. Beetles could legitimately argue that they, not we, have dominion over the earth; that they, not we, have been most faithful to God's commandment to be fruitful and multiply.

Of course, imagining the world from a beetle's point of view is fanciful, and some might ridicule it as irrelevant to any real concerns. But from a process perspective such an imaginative exercise is, in its own way, a kind of prayer, because it is a way of sharing in the divine life. In process theology God is immanent within all living beings as a lure to live with satisfaction. God knows not only humans but nonhumans with an intimacy beyond compare. God does indeed know what it is like to be a beetle, even if we can only have a dim intuition. Accordingly, a playful meditation on "what it might be like to be a beetle" can be a spiritual practice in its own right, a finite and human sharing in divine empathy for each and every creature.

Equally important, such imagining can be a healthy antidote to a kind of anthropocentrism that too often and unnecessarily creeps into monotheistic consciousness. Too often we monotheists imagine the earth as a castle of divine making, designed for human use and pleasure, with the rest of creation as mere backdrop. Process theology recommends a more ecological perspective, in which God is pictured as including, not excluding, the whole of creation.

What, then, is God in process theology? The first thing to make clear is that, in process theology, God is *not* the ultimate reality. This requires explanation.

Creativity and God

The well-known interpreter of world religions, Huston Smith, suggests that the history of human thought evidences at least four approaches to God: atheism, polytheism, monotheism, and monism. Atheism says there is no god; polytheism says there are many gods; monotheism says there is one God; and monism says there is only God.[10]

Monotheism is the prevailing option among members of the Abrahamic traditions. When process theologians use the word *God,* they typically mean the one God of monotheism. They recognize, though, that this one God can have many names and faces and that the deities of polytheistic religions can reveal certain dimensions of the one God. Thus, at least for process thinkers, a polytheistic consciousness has value because it reminds monotheists of these many faces and names and thus helps them overcome the idolatry of confusing the one God with a single image. Atheism's value comes as it helps theists remember that so many images of divine reality are the product, not of divine revelation, but of human projection.

Among some more mystically minded people, though, the word *God* is properly used, not to name the one God of monotheism, but rather to name an ultimate reality of which all things are manifestations. This reality is sometimes called the "Godhead." From a process perspective this intuition of an ultimate reality carries wisdom, and an awakening to its nature can be of religious significance. But they do not use the word *God* to name this reality. Instead they use the word *Creativity.* The proposal, then, is that Creativity is the ultimate reality and that God is the ultimate actuality.

These ultimates are not necessarily competitive but can instead be complementary, because each is ultimate in a different way. God answers the questions: "Are we loved?" and, "Is there hope for life on earth?" Creativity answers the question: "Of what is everything a manifestation, God or no God?"

A further word is in order about Creativity, because without it the process understanding of God does not make sense. For purposes of explanation I ask you, my reader, to imagine that all entities in the universe are indeed expressions of a common something. Let us speak of this common something as pure energy or pure becoming or pure activity or, as one Chinese philosopher speaks of it, *continuous creativity.*[11] The fact that all entities are expressions of this continuous creativity does not mean that the many entities are reducible to one another. Cats will be cats, and beetles will be beetles. They will feel the world in different ways. Still they are varied expressions of a pure activity that is manifest in various shapes and tonalities. This is part of what process thinkers mean by Creativity. They mean *that pure activity or continuous creativity of which all things are expressions.*

Now imagine further that the living beings on our planet are subjects of their own lives and not simply objects for others. Their subjectivity consists, not only of their feelings or prehensions of what surrounds them, but also of the spontaneous decisions they make, moment by moment, in responding to their environmental influences. By "decision," I do not mean conscious decision. I do not mean an act of reflecting upon alternative courses of action and choosing one. Most human decisions do not even involve this kind of conscious and deliberative reflection. Rather I mean the internal act of responding to stimuli in one way or another, thereby excluding possibilities for responding in another way. This is another part of what process thinkers mean by Creativity. They speak of this act of responding as *self-creativity*, because in the act itself the self of that moment–the center of feeling–emerges. The self does not precede the decision; it is the decision and its result.

Now consider the fact that, at least in human life, this capacity for spontaneous response can unfold in ways–both constructive and destructive, both violent and tender. We see spontaneous response in acts of human kindness but also in acts of human cruelty. This points to still a third aspect of what Whiteheadians mean by Creativity. They mean the pure activity of which all existing things are expressions, which, considered in itself, is devoid of particular purpose, because it is found in all purposes.

If we pull these various ideas together, we have a general idea of what is meant by Creativity in process theology. Creativity is the ultimate reality: a pure activity, beyond good and evil, which is manifest in all individual beings, including those who have capacities for creative response, in which case Creativity is their own self-creativity.

And what, then, is God? In process theology God is the primordial but not exclusive manifestation of this Creativity, whose decisions to love the world and lure it toward various forms of goodness, truth, and beauty form the encompassing background for the unfolding of continuous creativity. Creativity is the ultimate reality; God is the ultimate actuality.

This emphasis on Creativity as the ultimate reality is important both religiously and scientifically. Scientifically it means that evolution itself is a creative process, both in its galactic dimensions and in its biological and cultural dimensions, and that this creativity is not reducible to the choices of a single, divine creator. The results of evolution may be tragic or happy, beautiful or horrible–either way they are creative. Religiously an emphasis on Creativity means that forms of religious experience can be centered in Creativity rather than God, and that they have wisdom in their own right, God or no God. Many process thinkers believe that Buddhist awakenings to Emptiness and Hindu awakenings to Nirguna Brahman are of this kind. In these awakenings something ultimate is seen that is not God. Equally important, the emphasis on Creativity helps process thinkers deal with the question of God and tragedy. There is tragedy in the world which God neither does prevent nor can prevent and which is tragic even to God. Here, then, a further word about God is in order.

One-embracing-many

With most monotheists, process theologians believe that God is One. However, in the spirit of J.B.S. Haldane, process thinkers recommend that we begin our thinking about God's oneness with strangeness. We should not begin with images of a male deity residing off the planet who favors a single way of life. Rather, we should begin with intuitions of a large and strange universe, filled with billions upon billions of galaxies, in which we humans are small but included.

Of course, some who begin with this intuition might then imagine God as an entity spatially separated from the universe by an invisible boundary, whose oneness excludes diversity. In effect they will be imagining God as One-over-many or perhaps–if they are more mystical–as One-absorbing-many. A process approach differs from these two approaches. It invites us to imagine God as One-embracing-many. In this view God is a universal consciousness–everywhere at once–who is equally present to each and every creature: to the smallest of sparrows on earth, and also to the most distant of black holes. Indeed God encircles the universe, which means that the universe is inside God, not unlike the way in which fish are inside an ocean, or embryos are inside a womb, or clouds are inside the sky. This does not mean that God wills everything that happens in the universe. Just as embryos within a womb have creativity that is not reducible to the mother and as fish in the sea have creativity not reducible to the ocean, so things happen in the universe that are not reducible to God or God's will. Horrible things happen that God cannot prevent. Such things are tragic even to God. Children are murdered; women are raped; animals are abused; forests are needlessly destroyed. Still, the universe is inside God, and it affects God at all times.

The implications of this perspective are significant. If we believe that the universe is inside God, this means that when we witness terrible tragedies that inflict horrible suffering on living beings, the tragedies happen to God even as they happen to the living beings who suffer. It means that when we look lovingly at another human being or we gaze in awe at the multicolored textures of beetles, we are seeing part of what makes God "God." The universe is God's body. Not a sparrow falls without God being moved. God is the unity of the universe: the larger whole in which the universe unfolds.

This larger whole can be felt but not grasped, because we are always inside it. It is not "this object" or "that object" or even "all of them added together." Rather it is the receptacle in which all living beings live and breathe and have their being. Many of us sense this larger whole–this One-embracing-many– when we gaze into the sky on a dark and starlit night. Just as the dark sky is not a star among stars but rather encompasses all the stars and the earth as well, so we sense an encompassing wisdom that is not an entity among entities within the universe, but rather a womblike mystery that embraces the heavens and the earth. This reality is what process thinkers have in mind when they say "God." They mean One-embracing-many.

One-within-many

They also mean One-*within*-many. In process thought the spirit of God is also within each creature as its innermost lure to live with satisfaction relative to the situation at hand: its very breath of life. In a general way the spirit is also a counter-entropic lure. Despite the tendencies of energy toward chaos, the universe has been drawn by the spirit to create new wholes from pre-existent parts: atoms from subatomic events, molecules from atoms, stars from molecules, galaxies from stars and, at least in life on earth, living cells from molecules, tissues from living cells, bodies from cells, and so on. This does not mean that galactic or biological evolution is the result of a preexistent design on God's part, but rather that God lures the universe into the self-creation of new forms of order relative to what is possible in the situation at hand. Evolution is an ongoing process, not yet finished, that is prompted but not coerced by the indwelling spirit of God into newness.

The idea that God is within living beings can help us understand how religion emerges in human life. In human life this divine breathing takes many forms. Certainly it is within each of us as our own innermost lure to live with satisfaction, as expressed among other ways in our simple will to live. When we see people struggling to survive against difficult odds, as in situations of poverty or warfare or abuse, we see the presence of God in them. The divine spirit animates their own spirits; and they are responding in the most natural of ways, by creatively adapting to the situation at hand. Biologists tell us that this creative adaptation serves an evolutionary purpose, increasing the chances that their genes will survive into new generations. Process thinkers will add that, even if their genes do not survive, the creative adaptation has value in its own right, moment by moment. God is in creative adaptivity itself.

In process thought, though, the lure of God within each human life is not only a lure to live. It is also a lure to live well; that is, to live with beauty—with harmony and intensity—relative to the situation at hand.[12] In other words, the indwelling lure of God within each human life is more than an inner impulse to creatively adapt to new situations. It is also an impulse to seek the good, to be open to what is true, and to celebrate what is beautiful. The good, the true, and the beautiful are themselves forms of creative adaptation. Some outward expressions include the creation of music, enjoyment of friendships, cooking of food, pursuit of knowledge, telling of stories, pursuit of justice, building of community, dancing in the moonlight, courage in suffering, and befriending of strangers. The lure of God within human life takes many forms, all of which make the whole richer.

At their best, then, the world's religions are responses to this indwelling lure to live well. On the one hand, they are embodiments of a human struggle to survive with satisfaction. Some of their strategies may involve *useful fictions* that facilitate that survival. For example, if a world religion teaches that "we have the only truth," this teaching may serve as a means by which people in the religion promote their own survival and help assure the prospects of future generations of believers, even as the teaching contradicts the divine lure toward goodness. Just because an idea is conducive to survival doesn't mean that the idea is right. The idea may be wrong but useful.

In this essay, of course, I am assuming that the world's religions involve more than useful fictions. Over time, and through trial and error in response to the divine lure toward truth, they have uncovered wisdom worthy of universal appreciation. In this sense all religions are partly inspired by God, just as all science and all art are partly inspired by God. Not only the lure to survive, but also the lure toward wisdom, is a deep and ineradicable dimension of the human heart; and religion contains part of this wisdom.

It is important to emphasize, though, that to be wise and important, divinely inspired wisdom in religion does not need to be about God. Buddhists, for example, are especially wise about the impermanence of all things, which is itself "ultimate" in its own way. Without awareness of impermanence, we humans cannot be saved from our excessive clinging to finite things—sometimes quite beautiful—that inevitably pass away in time. Buddhists rightly tell us that our clinging usually leads to great suffering and sadness, not only in ourselves, but also in others upon whom we foist our projections of permanence. The wisdom of Buddhism is saving then, not because it points to God who saves us, but because it helps us make peace with impermanence. It can help us live more lightly on the earth and gently with each other.

To offer another example, many indigenous religions traditions in Africa, Asia, and the Americas are remarkably wise about our kinship with other creatures. More than most of the classical and text-based traditions, the indigenous traditions often emphasize that we humans are part of a wider community of life that includes other creatures. This does not mean that indigenous traditions always treat other creatures in a friendly way. No human traditions have a monopoly on ecological wisdom, even as all have something to offer. But it does mean that the indigenous traditions typically recognize more than others the importance of establishing reciprocal relations with the more-than-human world. In this sense they help us realize with Thomas Berry, that the universe itself is a communion of subjects and not simply a collection of objects.[13] Thus the wisdom of indigenous traditions is saving, too, not because it points to a saving God of the kind emphasized in Abrahamic religions, but because it points to an attitude that can save us from ecological collapse. In process theology the guiding axiom is not that the Truth is One while the Paths are Many, but rather that the Truths are Many and all Make the Whole Richer. These truths are part of the many that are embraced by God, even if not about God.

One-between-many

So far I have said that, from a process point of view, God is One-embracing-many and One-within-many. It is important to add that God is also One-between-many. By this I mean that God is not only inside each living being and beyond each living being, but also between all living beings, inasmuch as living beings dwell in mutually enhancing relations.

This emphasis on mutually enhancing relationships raises a profound question for all theists, process theists included, as they attend to certain aspects of biological life, specifically predator-prey relations. The question is fairly simple: If God is a lure toward wholeness within each living being, whose side is God on as the fox chases the rabbit? Does God want the fox to win, or the rabbit?

The process view is that God is on the side of each: luring the fox to find the rabbit, since it is the only way that the fox can survive given his or her genetic dispositions, and luring the rabbit to escape the fox, given that it is the only way for the rabbit to survive, too. This can mean either that God is deeply pained by the relationship, precisely because it is not mutually enhancing since one individual must be frustrated; or it can mean, as many environmentally minded thinkers might prefer, that God is in the relationship itself, as a necessary way that life has to unfold on earth.

The first response is one way that process thinkers would make sense of the idea, found in the Christian tradition and also other traditions such as Jainism, that nature itself has a tragic and fallen dimension that falls short of pure harmony. The "fall" is not the result of human sin, but rather the result of necessary ways in which life must unfold, given the evolution of life on earth. The second response is a way that process thinkers make sense of the idea, found in many traditions, that there is somehow something beautiful in nature, including predatory-prey relations, because it exemplifies a deep and necessary interdependence, by which one living being feeds another. For my part, I see wisdom in both points of view, yet neither is entirely satisfactory. With other theists I remain mystified as to why so much killing has to occur on earth, quite apart from human killing, which is equally mystifying.

In any case, many of the world religions find something sacred in mutually enhancing relations. In indigenous traditions, as noted above, human-earth relations can be mutually enhancing. And in many of the text-based religions, something very special and even sacred can found in human-human relations. We see this in Jewish emphases on collective fidelity to the bonds of covenant, in Confucian emphases on the primary value of family life, in Buddhists' emphases on *sangha* or living in community, in Christian and Muslim emphases on developing trans-cultural and trans-ethnic communities of believers. In many traditions the key to this solidarity lies in empathy, which is a feeling of the feelings of others and in acts of loving kindness. The prophetic traditions then add that this solidarity also includes justice, understood as fidelity to the bonds of relationship. On a more personal and intimate vein, Christianity adds further that one of the most sacred of relationships, which is itself a lesson in love, is marriage.

A process approach to God is sympathetic to all of these emphases, because it finds God in relationship itself, particularly when relationship involves empathy and loving kindness. It then adds, as do several religious traditions, that God calls humans into expanding circles of empathy, beginning with family but reaching out to include many others, human and nonhuman, in horizons of care. As humans respond to this call by dwelling responsibly and lovingly in community, they make the sacred reality still more visible on earth. In Christian terms the word or spirit of God becomes flesh, not simply within individual hearts and lives, but also in community. This is one reason that peace on earth is so important. It enables God to become more fully incarnate in the world.

Cosmology, Practice, Spirituality

How, then, might we help God become more incarnate? The answer, so we learn from the Earth Charter, is not to accrue more and more material goods in an endless quest for appearance, affluence, and achievement. Once our basic needs are met, says the Charter, our vocation in life is not to *have* more, but rather to *be* more. Moreover, it is to be more in community with others, human and more-than-human, because our relations with others constitute part of who we are. We help God become more incarnate in the world by helping to create communities that are just, compassionate, nonviolent, participatory, and ecologically wise.

In our time many speak of these communities as "sustainable communities." The Earth Charter adds that a building of these communities requires *respect and care for the community of life*. This means that the builders themselves need to have certain qualities of consciousness—certain virtues—that are conducive to flourishing community. These virtues include forgiveness and patience, creativity and courage, tenderness and empathy, and also a capacity to act without attachment to the fruits of fame, fortune, and power.

Most advocates of sustainable community hope that religion can help in a building of these communities, and they also trust that science can help. They do not turn to science for the development of virtues, but rather for information and wider cosmological perspective. At the level of information, they assume that the building of sustainable communities can be guided by scientific knowledge. Such knowledge concerns the limits of the earth to absorb pollution, its capacities to supply nonrenewable resources (oil and minerals) that lie within the carrying capacity of the planet, and its capacities to supply renewable resources (water and timber) that do not exceed nature's capacities for renewal. The argument is that, guided by this information, humans can then build buildings and design cities, till soils and extract resources, in ways that recognize limits to growth.

For many advocates of sustainability, though, the hope is that science can also contribute to sustainable community in a more philosophical way. In particular they hope that insights from evolutionary biology and astrophysics might elicit a healthy recognition that we humans are part of a much larger story in which we are small but included. This story is that of the evolving universe, some fifteen billion years in the making, whose future is not yet decided. The idea is that our acquaintance with the *epic of evolution* can help us understand that we are not the center of things or the whole of things. Rather, we are creative expressions of a deeper and continuous Creativity (see above) that is also manifest in the stars and planets, the hills and rivers, the trees and plants. We then realize that our vocation as humans is not to escape the responsibilities of creativity, as if the future were already determined by God or fate, but to add our voice to a more universal adventure. This is to understand human creativity on the analogy of worship: a collaborative process in which many voices come together to produce something that is more than the sum of its parts. Inspired by this sense of collaboration, we can then try to design communities in which fertile soils, clean waters, and healthy atmospheres are preserved for future generations of living beings. If, as Muslims say, the universe itself is a mosque, then the epic of evolution tells us that the universe is a mosque-in-the-making. Our calling as humans is to help create and protect one small corner of it.

Thus the hope is that science in its way, and religion in its way, might help human beings participate in the great work of helping build sustainable communities. Are these hopes justified? Can science and religion help us understand that the universe is—once again with Thomas Berry—a communion of subjects, not a collection of objects? This is where some advocates of sustainable community turn to process theology. Process thought offers at least three planks for a bridge to sustainable community:

1. a cosmology that supports the "epic of evolution" approach named above
2. an image of sustainable community that includes practical guidelines for the treatment of other forms of life
3. a recognition that sustainable community requires, not only philosophy and ethics, but also heightened capacities for discernment and spiritual awareness

Cosmology

At the level of cosmology, process thinkers advocate many ideas concerning religion and nature that, taken together, form what might called a "philosophy of nature" or "theology of nature" that is conducive to sustainable living. A distinctive feature of the process cosmology is that its various ideas can be, and have been, appropriated by people from different religious traditions to articulate their religious points of view. Accordingly, process theology can provide a neutral conceptual vocabulary for friendship between people of different religions, even as it also serves as a bridge to sustainability. This is important, because sustainable community itself requires respect for religious and religious diversity as well as biological diversity. Here, then, are twelve ideas at the heart of a process approach to nature.

1. Nature as Creative. The first and most basic idea, already introduced above, is that nature is a continuously creative process, with galactic as well as terrestrial dimensions, of which humans are an integral part. Creativity is the ultimate reality.

2. Nature as Visible and Invisible. The second is that nature includes invisible as well as visible dimensions, as exemplified in feelings and other conscious states of mammals (invisible) and the human brain (visible), and that both of these dimensions are expressions of the same kind of creative energy and in this sense "natural."

3. Intrinsic Value and Pan-Experientialism. The third idea is that each living being on earth (and anywhere else) is a subject for itself not just an object for others. Every living being has intrinsic value and some capacity for experiencing its environment (consciously or unconsciously) from its own unique point of view. Here the word *living* includes God (see below) *and* carbon-based forms of life such as single-celled organisms and animals. *Living* more generally means any being of any sort that has subjectivity of any kind, on the basis of which it can take into account its surrounding environment in a conscious or nonconscious way, creatively responding in novel ways. We can combine this idea with Whitehead's view that nature includes many planes of existence, not just the three-dimensional plane of space as evident to the vision. This understanding of "living" opens up the possibility, characteristic of many indigenous societies, that forms of actuality (spirits, living ancestors) are part of the larger ecology of a community. It also opens up the possibility, emphasized by empirical studies in parapsychology, that the human self (and perhaps other forms of life) undertake a continuing journey after death, which likewise widens a sense of "ecology" in a way that resembles Chinese emphases on an ecological trinity of heaven-earth-human relations.

4. Two Kinds of Wholes. The fourth idea is the view that inorganic materials–mountains, for example–are aggregate expressions of subatomic forms of energy that are, if not living in a biological sense, then at least possessive of some capacity for nonconscious prehending of their immediate environments. The idea that all actual entities have capacities for taking into account their environments, either consciously or nonconsciously, is called pan-experientialism or pan-psychism. To avoid the idea that this implies that macroscopic entities (rocks, for example) are experiencing subjects in their own right, process theologians draw a distinction between two kinds of natural wholes:

- wholes that have unified subjectivity on the basis of which they have reality for themselves (living cells, animals)
- wholes that are aggregate-expressions of energetic phenomena with nonconscious prehending capacities, but that lack unified subjectivity (rocks)

5. Inter-Being[14] *or Mutual Presence.* The fifth idea is that all living beings have their existence and identities in relation to, not apart from, all other living beings. This means that the very identity of a living being, including each plant and animal, is partly determined by the material and cultural environment in which it is situated. Process theology goes further, in a sense reminiscent of Buddhism, to say that each entity is "present in" every other entity, such that interconnectedness implies inter-being or inter-containment. This means that all entities are thoroughly ecological in nature and that human beings are themselves ecological in being persons-in-community, not persons-in-isolation. In a process context, "community" includes the entire web of life in which a human (or other living being) is nested. This means that respect for the intrinsic value of individual living beings cannot be separated from considerations of the instrumental value, positive or negative, that these beings have for others in their biotic communities.

6. Teleology. The sixth idea is that the universe as a whole, over vast periods of time, has evolved toward heightened degrees of intrinsic value. These are equated with heightened capacities for richness of experience, as evident in the capacities of animals (humans included) to respond to new situations in unpredictable and creative ways, experiencing both the joys and sorrows of mortal existence.

7. God in Nature. The seventh idea is that the whole of nature is embraced by a divine reality–the One-embracing-many. This divine reality is influential throughout nature in a continuous way as an indwelling lure toward satisfactory survival within individual living beings and as a more generalized lure toward new forms of order and novelty within evolution as a whole.

8. Non-Supernaturalism. The eighth idea is that this divine lure does not interrupt the causal operations of nature as understood in physics and chemistry. Among other things, this means that the divine lure is best understood as ultra-natural rather than super-natural. This leads some process theologians to speak of process theology as a form of naturalistic theism.

9. Divine Empathy. The ninth idea is that the One-embracing-many is not only influential throughout nature in a noncoercive way, but also acted upon by nature in a continuous way, such that it empathically shares in the experiences of all forms of existence and in the joys and sufferings of all living beings.

10. Diversity in God. The tenth idea is that, by virtue of this empathy, the One-embracing-many is enriched both by the experiences of individual living beings and by the diverse kinds of lives that inhabit the planet. An unnecessary depletion of biological diversity, then, is a tragedy not only for the earth, but also for the divine life itself.

11. Sin as Unnecessary Violence against Creation.[15] The eleventh idea is that, because nature is itself creative at all levels, things happen in evolution itself and in human interactions with other living beings and forms of existence that are tragic, even for God. This leads process theologians such as Marjorie Suchocki to define sin as unnecessary violence against creation, from which even God suffers.

12. Co-creativity. The twelfth idea is that human beings, as creatures among creatures, can help prevent these tragedies by cooperating with the divine lure toward the fullness of life, and that this kind of response is their true vocation in life. In process theology the whole of nature is historical or evolutionary, and the future is not preordained, not even by God. What happens in the future depends on decisions made in the present by human beings and other living beings, moment by moment.

Social Ethics

All twelve ideas have implications for social ethics. The idea that all living beings have intrinsic value entails the view that humans have moral obligations to other creatures–animals, for example–under human domestication and in the wild. It simultaneously means that economic institutions and policies ought to aim at the promotion of human well-being in an ecologically responsible context. This aim would replace aiming at economic growth for its own sake. Human communities reach fruition when they live in fruitful cooperation with other forms of life and natural systems and when they are limited in scope, making space for the habitats of other living beings. This does not imply that any living being, including even human beings, have absolute rights to life. It does imply that respect and care for the community of life is the defining characteristic of healthy human community. The idea of degrees of intrinsic value entails the view that it is more morally problematic to inflict violence on a gazelle than to take the life of a bacterium, even though both the gazelle and the bacterium possess subjectivity. The idea that God is enriched by biological diversity and harmed by violence against creation means that ethical relations with nonhuman forms of life cannot be separated from faithful relations to God. And the idea that humans are co-creative with God means that the very will of God, that nature itself flourish in its fullness, depends for its realization on human responsiveness.

If we seek a simple way of understanding a process approach to ethics, we might say that, in process theology, a building of sustainable communities requires a capacity for *mutually enhancing relations* at three levels: human-human relations, human-earth relations, and human-animal relations. Mutually enhancing relations between humans include forms of governance that are democratic. In these democratic forms humans participate in the decisions that affect their lives. Such relations also demand forms of social organization that are just, availing humans of the essentials of life, such as food, clothing, shelter, health care, education, and opportunities for meaningful employment. Law and politics can and must assure many of these relations. But these relations also depend on what process thinkers would label a culture of peace; that is, a culture in which people listen to one another, care for each other, and have a sense that they share a common destiny.

For some people, of course, the word *peace* has somewhat boring connotations. It suggests a state of affairs that is nonviolent and harmonious, but not necessarily intense or surprising. Process theologians typically define peace more creatively, proposing that peace at its deepest level has a musical quality, like an improvisational jazz concert. Such a concert will consist of a creative and evolving harmony of sound, created by different musicians with different instruments, who have the material wherewithal to purchase their instruments, and who are cooperatively responding to one another in an ongoing live performance, often in surprising and joyful ways. If the concert is to continue, the musicians must be willing to keep on playing even when things threaten to fall apart. They must be willing to forgive one another of the mistakes they might make. Process theologians say that peace is like this. It can be unpredictable, filled with creative tensions; and it can have its sad and mournful moments. But it is cooperative and creative, surprising and sometimes joyful, and its competitive dimensions do not issue into violence.

Equally important, peace requires listening to the silences between the sounds, because it is the silences that give the sounds their meaning. In communities that embody peace, these silences are the things people cannot say or have not yet said, but that are part of their deeper intentions and hopes. In peace at its deepest and best level, then, the participants who create peace listen for these silences and handle them with respect. The spiritual foundation of peace does not simply lie in a capacity to make peace and build communities that are just and sustainable. It lies also in listening sympathetically and deeply to the subjective aims of others, responding with sounds that are new, surprising, and beautiful. A unique feature of process thought is that it begins with listening to others, on their own terms and for their own sakes, and allowing oneself to be shaped by what one hears. Ethics begins not just with principles, but with empathy.

Of course, in a process context listening to humans is by no means enough. Process thought suggests that we can also listen to other living beings and to the earth, because all are expressions of a common Creativity and all are expressions of various forms of feeling, conscious or nonconscious. Thus process thought recommends both a land ethic and an animal welfare ethic. A land ethic typically emphasizes the responsibility of humans to respect and protect the integrity, stability, and beauty of biotic communities and habitats. An animal welfare ethic emphasizes human responsibility to protect individual animals from unnecessary suffering. A process approach emphasizes both. It seeks what might be called *humane, sustainable communities.*

In process theology the word *sustainability* can be used in a very general way to name a quality of community that includes peace, democracy, participation, justice, and ecological wisdom; or it can be used more specifically to name that aspect of the community that is ecologically wise. When sustainability is used in the second sense, it refers to communities that embody what I called "land ethic."

In process theology such an ethic rests on a recognition that human beings are not only *em-*bodied and *en-*cultured, but also, as it were, *en-*landed. To be en-landed is to know that you are dependent on a wider community of life for your existence, that the members of that wider community (the flora and fauna, the earth and air and water) are part of who you are even as they are more than what you are, and that you have ethical responsibilities to care for them not only for the sake of present generations but also for future generations of human and nonhuman beings.

Spirituality

Process theology recognizes that religious life is more than theology and ethics, understanding and moral behavior. It includes prayerful states of awareness that are sensitive to the intrinsic value of each living being. It practices forms of ritual that help awaken people to the mystery and grandeur of landscapes, waterways, and galactic vistas. It undertakes inner journeys toward integration between consciousness and the energies and archetypes that well up within the unconscious, some of which are encoded within human genes. It makes humble acknowledgment that humans are small but included in larger wholes that far transcend their finite concerns. In process theology, all of these forms of spirituality are natural and part of nature understood in general terms.

Moreover, the philosophy of Whitehead is open to the possibility of forms of empathic connection. The connection is not only between humans and other humans, but also between humans and nonhuman forms of life. The very journey toward peaceable selfhood, toward which all living beings strive in their own unique ways, may well continue after death until wholeness is realized. Should such connections and continuation prove to be true, they, too, would be part of nature broadly understood.

Finally and importantly, from a process perspective it is wrong to think that spirituality as such begins with human beings. Each living being has its own unique relationship to God. All living beings, indeed the whole of the cosmos, are embraced within the larger and divine whole. How other living beings experience this embrace is a mystery to humans. But that they are part of this embrace is central to process theology. Spirituality begins, not with formal belief or even with social ethics, but with nonverbal attunements to the divine embrace. This embrace takes the form of an indwelling call to survive with satisfaction relative to the situation at hand. For many creatures in nature, humans much included, the simple desire to survive with satisfaction, even amid sometimes insurmountable odds, is a form of spirituality.

Criticisms and Responses

Process theology is not without its critics, all of whom raise important questions for the process perspective. Three kinds of criticism are illustrative.

First, inasmuch as process theology speaks of degrees of intrinsic value in accordance with degrees of sentience, some environmental thinkers argue that this approach privileges sentient beings, perhaps especially those with highly developed nervous systems over ostensibly insentient beings, such as mountains and water. Indeed, process theology offers what might best be called a biocentric approach over a geocentric approach, proposing that while ostensibly inorganic realities do indeed contain intrinsic value, their value is best understood in terms of their instrumental value to living beings.

Second, process theology is open to the possibility of continued existence for humans and other animals after death. It thus opens up, but fails to answer, the difficult question of whether, in a journey toward peaceable selfhood, impulses toward predation—which seem natural and necessary in life on earth— would be transcended. This seemingly speculative question bears upon the deeper question of whether predator-prey relations on earth are unambiguously good, as some Deep Ecologists might suggest. Or do they contain an element of tragedy as well, as process theologians aver. In the latter respect process theology has sympathy with classical traditions, ranging from Jainism to Judaism, that see something tragic in the more violent dimensions of nature. Whereas some environmentally oriented traditions see the evolutionary unfolding of creation as divine will, process theology views this unfolding as partly the result of divine influence and partly the result of nature's own creativity, which itself can unfold in ways both beautiful and tragic.

Third, and finally, classical theists in the Abrahamic traditions, while appreciating the process image of God as one who shares in the joys and sufferings of all living beings, nevertheless prefer to think of this sharing as something that God chooses to do, as if God would choose otherwise. Process theology proposes, by contrast, that even God is an exemplification of metaphysical principles. One of these is the ecological principle that, to be actual at all, one must be affected by other realities and partly composed of other realities. Thus process theology speaks of the universe as the very body of God. This means, not only that to be fully divine God must dwell in relation to a universe, but also that divine power is limited by the power of the universe itself, such that it cannot be unilateral or one-sided. Classical theists often criticize process theology for offering a view of God that denies omnipotence in the classical sense. Process theologians respond that only through such a denial can theists make sense of the unnecessary violence in creation, as well as the goodness and beauty of creation that largely results from the creativity of the universe itself, as inspired but not manipulated by the divine lure. Among Christian and Jewish process theologians, it is as important to recognize that the intrinsic value of all living beings, while appreciated by God, is not reducible to God. This respect for otherness—even on God's part—is a key feature of process theology. As this essay has emphasized, God has an inordinate fondness for beetles and all forms of life, humans much included. The call of God to humans is for humans to share in this divine delight by protecting a habitat for other creatures, by treating individual animals with kindness, and by creating communities that are socially just, ecologically sustainable, and spiritually satisfying.

SECTION IV

Emerging Process Traditions

Although the theological use of process thought began within the Christian tradition (reflecting Whitehead's own Christian orientation), and although it has been identified in its short history primarily with liberal Protestant Christianity, recent experience and current work powerfully demonstrate that process theology is not limited to one tradition. Indeed, it may prove to be equally or even more at home in other Christian streams or in other religions. Some of the most vital and active scholarship in process theology is currently taking place outside of the liberal Christianity most closely associated with it. There seems to be every reason to believe that these growing movements will continue to be fruitful and that their contributions will continue to enrich the process tradition.

The three essays in this section are a small sample of the many and diverse avenues of thought and practice now being opened up within the process community. Thomas Jay Oord surveys the rapidly growing field of process thought informed by evangelical concerns and concepts. He identifies the core affirmations of evangelical piety, notes how dialogue with process thinkers on these issues proceeds, and connects the discussion with recent work in the "open theism" movement. Jeffery Long demonstrates how Whiteheadian concepts can be used in Hindu theology, with special attention to the tension in both Hindu and Whiteheadian thought between theistic and nontheistic ultimates. Sandra Lubarsky concludes with an explication of Jewish process theology centered on the notion of covenant as it has been reimagined after the rending experience of the Holocaust.

CHAPTER 19

Evangelical Theologies

■ THOMAS JAY OORD

I seek to identify how process theology approaches the diverse traditions and theologies are typically identified as evangelical.[1] I have in mind what are labeled evangelical theologies in the American context. Most of my comments will hold true of the thought and practices of evangelicals worldwide. Evangelicalism is a broad socio-theological movement, and the dogmatic claims its members make are quite diverse. Considering this, evangelicalism is an essentially contested tradition. Within it an intense debate occurs about how best to develop and explain its essential ingredients.[2] Because who should be identified as evangelical and what counts as evangelical theology are hotly contested issues, I begin by noting how process theology might consider five affirmations that many would consider the core of evangelicalism.[3] These five characteristics of evangelical thought provide orienting concerns from which one might gauge various affinities and disparities that evangelical theology might have with process theology. I look at the fifth affirmation, having to do with the doctrine of God, in greater detail than the others. In that discussion, I address the dialogue that has emerged between process theology and a way of evangelical thinking called "Openness Theology."

The *first affirmation* at the core of evangelical piety and theology is this: The Bible is principally authoritative for matters pertaining to salvation. At first glance, this affirmation may appear to be a major point of contention between evangelicals and process thinkers. Although those whom process thought has influenced make important contributions to biblical studies,[4] one rarely if ever hears process theists characterized as "back to the Bible" advocates or proponents of *sola scriptura*. In fact, many biblical scholars with ties to process theism have been at the forefront of identifying ways in which some biblical passages have actually undermined the well-being of women, nonhumans, and minorities.

More than a few evangelicals have suggested that process theology subverts the biblical witness. Some have suggested that process theology considers philosophy–rather than the Bible–its most authoritative source. Ronald Nash, in a book he edited that was written primarily by evangelicals who oppose process theology, argues that "most process theologians appear to have a highly selective biblical hermeneutic. Scripture is welcomed as authoritative when it agrees with [process] panentheist opinions. But when Scripture conflicts with panentheist beliefs, it is conveniently ignored or casually discarded."[5] Generally speaking, evangelicals have suggested that process scholars place more emphasis upon reason and contemporary experience as sources for constructive theology than the biblical witness.

When considering a process approach to evangelicalism's core belief about biblical authority, a more interesting question might be asked: "*Must* the principal authority of the Bible be a source of contention between evangelical and process theists?" Although process theists may or may not look to the Bible as authoritative for matters of salvation, process thought as such does not require one to reject the Bible as supremely authoritative for such matters. Nothing at the core of process thought prevents a process theist from claiming that one document or individual is more effective in revealing who God is and what salvation entails.[6]

Even if a process theist were to take the Bible as supremely authoritative for matters pertaining to salvation, the questions of interpretation would still need to be addressed. Within evangelicalism a wide range of interpretive techniques, practices, traditions, and rules are adopted. Anabaptists typically interpret scripture differently from Wesleyans, and both groups interpret scripture differently from those in Calvinist traditions. Just as there is no uniform hermeneutic within evangelicalism, biblical scholars with a process orientation differ among themselves on interpretive concerns.[7]

A *second core affirmation* of evangelicalism is that a conversion from sin, made possible by Jesus Christ, is necessary for full salvation. The issues of salvation typically lead one to ask whether Christianity is the only religion offering salvation. Process thought is at odds with evangelical theologies that are exclusivistic. Inherent in the basic process understandings of God and God's relation to the world is the claim that God self-reveals to *all* peoples. While evangelicals have not typically embraced a thoroughgoing pluralism that says that any religion is as good as Christianity, some traditions within evangelicalism have adopted an inclusivist position. In fact, evangelicals in the Wesleyan theological tradition have typically affirmed that God's prevenient grace provides a measure of light for salvation to all peoples.[8] While process thought affirms the evangelical tenet that salvation can be found in Jesus Christ, it only sharply disagrees with particular traditions within evangelicalism claiming that *only* Christianity contains salvific truth.[9]

Also at stake in the question of full salvation is the issue of life after death. Evangelicals typically claim that life after death is an important aspect of salvific hope. While early process figures such as Alfred North Whitehead and Charles Hartshorne were at best ambivalent to the idea of an afterlife and at worst hostile, many contemporary process theologians affirm life after death as an important doctrine supporting Christian hope. Such process thinkers contend that human souls have the capacity to survive bodily death. And such souls continue to exist indefinitely in new modes of existence.[10]

A *third affirmation* that lies at the core of evangelicalism claims Christians should be active in the midst of a decadent culture, attempting to evangelize and transform it. One of the characteristics of evangelicals is their evangelistic fervor to spread the good news of Jesus. And evangelicals believe that the spreading of this gospel is necessary because so many live in sin. It is not uncommon for evangelicals to talk of overcoming the world. Evangelicals intend to be in the world but not of it.

Process theology affirms this evangelical tenet. Like Evangelical theologies and practices, process traditions typically emphasize the importance of transformation, both individual and corporate. But process theologians themselves typically differ from evangelicals about what needs to be done to transform a decadent culture. And they typically differ on what particular features of culture *cause* decadence. Evangelicals typically align themselves with the conservative, socio-political side of various cultural-ethical issues. Process theists typically align themselves with the progressive/liberal side. For instance, process theists have generally been supportive of the push to recognize Christian ordination status for homosexuals. Evangelicals have generally thought that such ordination would not be a step forward in the transformation of culture.

When it comes to evangelizing and transforming culture, one might summarize the substantive disparity in this way: both process and evangelical theists want to increase the common good, but theists in these traditions generally have differing ideas about what needs to be done to increase overall flourishing. In theory, however, an evangelical might embrace process theology while also affirming conservative socio-political positions. "Process theology" and "liberal Christianity" are not synonyms, although most process thinkers to date have sympathies with liberal Christianity. Some evangelicals may have distanced themselves from process thought due chiefly to the social and political views of particular process thinkers rather than due to core notions of process theology itself. Core notions of process theology itself, however, transcend the conservative-liberal split.

The *fourth affirmation* I find at the core of evangelicalism is that Christian formation (labeled variously as "Christian spirituality," "holiness," "discipleship," "Christian morality," "growth in Christ," etc.) is indispensable to the Christian life. Those engaged in the process-evangelical dialogue have probably explored this affirmation least. At its best, process theology joins evangelical theology in offering conceptual resources for accessing and embodying habits of holiness. While process theologians may disagree with evangelicals about which specific disciplines and behaviors are most conducive to the promotion of abundant life, both traditions recognize the importance of developing various virtues in response to God's call to creative transformation.

One branch of evangelicalism—the pentecostal-charismatic—may be a key conversation partner with regard to the issue of Christian formation in an evangelical-process dialogue. While the majority of Christian process theists have been more comfortable adopting forms of worship and religious expression typical of mainline denominations, process theism offers conceptual tools to pentecostals and charismatics who wish to speak of direct encounters with God. Most process theologians affirm that all individuals directly perceive God through nonsensory perception. According to process theism, all Christians intuit, albeit variably, God's call and power. Because pentecostals and charismatics claim to be in direct communication with God, they should find a sophisticated philosophical basis in process philosophy for their claim. In fact, such genuine experiences of God might be expected from individuals who are intensely attuned to God's moment-by-moment calls to action.[11]

Process thought can do more than provide a basis for conceptualizing the divine origin of ecstatic religious experience—as intellectually important as that is. It can also provide pentecostals and charismatics with tools for qualifying their claims about what God has revealed to those with ears to hear. Because process thought includes the speculation—for a variety of reasons, not least being the problem of evil—that God cannot unilaterally determine any creaturely state of affairs, it also provides a basis for being cautious about claims that God desires particular actions. Rather than absolute certainty with regard to knowing God's call for how to act in one situation or another, process thought suggests that the convictions of individuals should lay along a range of degrees of confidence. One may be extremely, somewhat, or hardly confident that God desires a particular action. This tool of qualification prevents one from equating God's Word absolutely with one's own words, without denying that one can possess a degree of confidence that God desires some particular course of action instead of another. It is this confidence of God's direct leading that, from a process perspective, pentecostals and charismatics rightly champion.

I turn to the *fifth evangelical affirmation:* that concerning how one conceives of God. Most evangelicals would affirm the following: God is perfect in love, almighty, without beginning or end, One (although Trinitarian), personal, free, omniscient, the Creator and Sustainer, both transcendent and immanent in relation to the world, the ground of hope for the final victory of good over evil, and the proper object of worship.

The conversation—perhaps mostly mutual criticism—has been most intense here.[12] Process theology's conceptions of God are often at odds with evangelical-ism's reformed theological traditions (especially Calvinism). In particular, the notions of divine omnipotence, omniscience, and temporality that process theists proffer oppose what the reformed tradition regards as orthodox. Process theists deny that God can unilaterally determine any creaturely state of affairs. Reformed theologies stress such theological determinism, at least as a possibility.

Process theists deny that God knows actual future events, because the future is not yet knowable. Reformed evangelicals typically believe that God knows actual future events, because God is a nontemporal being who sees all of time in an eternal now. While process theists can agree with reformed evangelicals with regard to the formal aspects of affirmation five listed above, reformed evangelicals and process theists strongly disagree with how each of these formal terms are best understood.

Evangelicalism, however, is comprised of many groups and individuals who embrace theological underpinnings other than those whose source is the reformed tradition. In particular, Arminian, Wesleyan, and pentecostal traditions share many general theological affinities with process thought.[13] The most fruitful theological interaction between process theists and evangelicals comes from evangelicals who describe their theological position as the "Open View."[14] In their 1994 landmark book, *The Openness of God*, Clark H. Pinnock and coauthors laid out an evangelical position that shares several affinities with process theology.[15] These authors argue that their position is more theologically faithful to the broad biblical witness than other theological options in the evangelical tradition.[16] If "Open" evangelicals are correct about their faithfulness to scripture and if the affinities that their view shares with process theism are grounded in this theologically faithful interpretation, perhaps, as I suggested earlier, the principal authority of scripture for matters pertaining to salvation need not be a stumbling block in the evangelical-process dialogue.[17]

Clark Pinnock's words of justification for offering the Open view of God might just as easily have been spoken by a process theist. Pinnock argues that, "theological integrity and the credibility of the concept of God in our time are both at stake. It is difficult to believe the conventional model of God because of its intellectual contradictions and lack of existential appeal."[18] Pinnock continues by noting that, "apologetically, the open view of God embraces a modern understanding of reality as dynamic not static."[19] Open theists join with process theists in identifying the metaphysics at the heart of classical theism as inadequate. Pinnock speaks of "excessive Hellenization" that has caused numerous conceptual distortions in formal Christian theologies.[20] Rather than eschew constructive philosophy altogether as many in recent years have (unsuccessfully) attempted to do, Open theists look to relational categories for philosophical support.

Process theists share the Open intention to talk about God's actual existence and how that existence affects all reality. It also speculates and offers provisional statements about who God is and what this divine being is doing. The process and Open approaches to theology differ from those that merely discuss community beliefs, linguistic referents, or parts of symbol-systems. As John B. Cobb Jr. puts it, "Evangelicals and process theologians are both concerned about the way things are…Because process theology is proposing ideas about questions that are real questions for evangelicals and claiming continuity between its answers and biblical ones, a good many evangelicals take it seriously."[21]

Atop the list of theological affinities that Open and process theists share is the conviction that love should be the principal theme in Christian theology.[22] Richard Rice, who offers a segment on the biblical grounding of *The Openness of God*, claims that the Open view expresses well the basic convictions of scripture pertaining to love. From a Christian perspective, says Rice, love is the first and last word in the biblical portrait of God.[23] When one enumerates God's qualities, one must not only *include* love on the list, but, to be faithful to the Bible, one must put love at the *head* of that list. Love is the most important quality that humans attribute to God. And love is more than care and commitment; it also involves sensitivity and responsiveness.[24] A doctrine of God faithful to the Bible must show that all God's characteristics derive from love.[25] "Love, therefore, is the very essence of the divine nature," argues Rice.[26] He notes elsewhere that "Process thought is often described as a metaphysics of love, an attempt to develop a full-fledged metaphysical system from the fundamental insight that God is love. The open view of God shares this emphasis upon the priority of love."[27]

Openness theists follow process theists in rejecting some traditional doctrines of God. They believe that some classic theologies have characterized God as an aloof Monarch removed from the world's contingencies. "The Christian life involves a genuine interaction between God and human beings," says Pinnock. "We respond to God's gracious initiatives and God responds to our responses…and on it goes."[28] Open theists embrace the notion that God is like a loving parent who, as Pinnock puts it, possesses "qualities of love and responsiveness, generosity and sensitivity, openness and vulnerability."[29] God is a person who experiences the world, responds to what happens, relates to humans, and interacts dynamically with creatures. God's experience changes in the divine give-and-take of interactive relationship.

What gets Pinnock and his Open cohorts tangled in the roughest of intra-evangelical tussles is their denial that God exhaustively foreknows free creaturely actions.[30] Like process theists, Open theologians like Pinnock argue that "God knows everything it is possible to know, but this cannot include future free decisions because they cannot in principle be known by simple definition. If they could be known, they would not be free."[31] This uncertainty upon God's part establishes that the future remains open, not completely determined. Their belief that the future is in some sense genuinely open is one reason these evangelicals label their position the "Open" view of God.[32]

Hand-in-hand with the Open denial that God knows exhaustively the actual future is the denial that God is nontemporal. Open theists join process theists in claiming that we best conceive of God as temporally everlasting rather than timelessly eternal. Conventional theism's notion that God is nontemporal implies that deity is totally actualized, immutable, impassible, and outside of time and sequence. The idea of God as temporally everlasting, by contrast, means, says Pinnock, that "the everlasting One is active and dynamic through all of this flow" and that "the past, present, and future are real to God."[33]

In his monograph, *Most Moved Mover: A Theology of God's Openness*, Pinnock provides a list of convictions that process and Open theists hold in common. "We:

- make the love of God a priority;
- hold to libertarian human freedom;
- are both critical of conventional theism;
- seek a more dynamic model of God;
- contend that God has real, not merely rational, relationships with the world;
- believe that God is affected by what happens in the world;
- say that God knows what can be known, which does not amount to exhaustive foreknowledge;
- appreciate the value of philosophy in helping to shape theological convictions;
- connect positively to Wesleyan/Arminian traditions."[34]

Given these affinities, Pinnock acknowledges that "conventional theists often characterize the open view as a form of process thought." His additional remark indicates the political ramifications of this characterization: "[I]n an evangelical context, [that] is tantamount to proving it heretical without any further ado."[35]

Open evangelical theists are to be commended for understanding process thought–both aspects that they appreciate and aspects that they reject much better than most contemporary evangelicals.[36] Some criticisms of process thought that Open theists render, however, might be shown to be less consequential than Open theists believe. For instance, one important difference between Open theism and Process theism is the God-world relationship each supposes. Process theists suppose that God necessarily relates to some realm of nondivine individuals or another. Open theists suppose that God's relations with the world are essentially accidental, such that at one time God existed apart from any world whatsoever. Pinnock implies that, to exist, the God of process theism requires some world or another: "The openness view...denies the process conviction that God is ontologically dependent on the world and that God always has and must have a world to experience. [God] does not need a world in order to be God."[37] Richard Rice describes the process doctrine of the God-world relation in this way: "Without a creaturely world, God would have no actuality and hence no existence."[38]

While Rice and Pinnock are correct that classic process texts, such as Alfred North Whitehead's *Process and Reality*, can be interpreted as stating that God could not exist without some world or another, this claim opposes the core process notion that God exists necessarily. After all, a being that exists necessarily requires nothing else to exist. The point of the more robust form of process theism is not that God cannot exist unless some world or another exists. Rather, the point is that a metaphysical scheme supposing that God necessarily (involuntarily) and everlastingly relates to some world is preferable to a scheme that claims that God's relations to the world are accidental (wholly voluntary) and provisional. If process theists were to attack the Open conception of the social Trinity by claiming that, to exist, this social Trinitarian God requires intra-Trinitarian relations, process theists would commit this same conceptual error. After all, Open theists believe that God exists necessarily. In short, both Open and process theists affirm that God necessarily exists such that nothing could end God's existence. At issue is the comparative strength of the two different metaphysical visions concerning *with whom* and *by what mode* God relates.

The classical Christian doctrine of *creatio ex nihilo* often arises in the Open-process dialogue about God's mode of relation to the world.[39] Process theists reject this doctrine on a variety of grounds, not the least of which is its implications for the problem of evil.[40] If God at one time possessed the power to create unilaterally from absolutely nothing, God would always retain essentially the ability to determine unilaterally. The God capable of exercising total control through unilateral determination is culpable for failing to prevent the genuine evils that occur in life. As David Griffin puts it, "The doctrine of *creatio ex nihilo*...[implies] (1) that the creatures have no inherent power with which to offer any resistance to the divine will, and (2) that there are no metaphysical principles, inherent in the nature of things, descriptive of the kinds of relations that necessarily obtain either between God and the creatures or among the creatures themselves."[41] Given these implications, the problem of evil remains insoluble.[42] For God to be exonerated for failing to prevent genuine evils from occurring, God must not possess the ability to withdraw or override the power for freedom that creatures inherently possess.

The concept of divine unilateral power implied in *creatio ex nihilo* also has implications for how one understands God's activity in biblical inspiration, evolution, the oppression of women and minorities, and the sanctioning of political authorities. Process theists wonder why the Bible is not crystal-clear, unambiguous, and inerrant if God can totally control any event and if crystal-clear unambiguous revelation would assist humans in securing salvation. And if God can unilaterally determine events, why did God allow a multibillion year evolution, complete with immense nonhuman suffering? Or, if God can totally control events, why has God permitted the oppression and domination of women (especially by Westerners) and minorities? Or, finally, if God can unilaterally determine any course of events, does this mean that present and past political regimes are divinely sanctioned?

Some Open theists are cognizant of the difficulties that arise from the problem of evil and other matters when they affirm *creatio ex nihilo* and the doctrine of divine power that it implies.[43] They continue to affirm this church doctrine, however, for a variety of reasons. For instance, Open theists believe that accounting for various miracles recorded in scripture requires this traditional creation doctrine. As David Basinger puts it, "God not only created this world *ex nihilo* but can, and at times does, intervene unilaterally in earthly affairs."[44]

Pinnock argues that "certain events in world history can be the special effects of divine activity."[45] The miracle of Jesus' resurrection "goes beyond persuasion." Pinnock continues, "God brought it into effect unilaterally without consultation."[46] Open theists also contend that the type of power necessary for *creatio ex nihilo* supports an eschatology that guarantees God's eventual victory over evil.

Process theists might respond, however, that divine unilateral determination (i.e., metaphysical coercion) is not required for the creation of the world, the triumph of good over evil, or the occurrence of miracles. David Ray Griffin presents this line of argumentation. Griffin argues that the idea that God only creates persuasively is more plausible given the age and pain-ridden evolution of the world. He suggests that the "Big Bang" beginning of our universe through the divine persuasion of chaotic elements, however, "could produce quasi-coercive effects."[47] After this initial activity bringing order out of chaos, God would not be capable of quasi-coercion due to the evolution of increasingly complex power and freedom in those with whom God subsequently relates. Griffin also defends his belief that (1) God will ultimately be victorious over evil and (2) salvation can be experienced in a life beyond bodily death.[48] It is important to note, however, that his vision is not based upon his belief that God can unilaterally guarantee this victory. Rather, victory can be gained only through divine persuasive love along with appropriate creaturely responses. Finally, Griffin turns to evidence from parapsychology to argue that events traditionally considered miracles caused by divine unilateral determination could rather be understood as events in which God's persuasive call, alongside the extraordinary powers of certain humans, instigates astonishing occurrences.[49]

A glance at core notions of Open theism when compared with core notions of process theology suggests that affinities are many and the prospect for mutual transformation promising. Perhaps a way forward in this interaction is to address the metaphysics and logic of a claim that each prizes highly: "God is love." Both theologies consider God in relational love categories. Both theological trajectories wish to affirm that God's nature or essence is love.

Process theists wonder whether the Open claim that God's essence is love is valid given the Open claim that God does not essentially or necessarily love the world. "If divine compassion for creatures is purely voluntary, not inherent in the very nature of who God is," argues Griffin in criticism of the Open view, "we cannot say that God simply *is* love."[50] John B. Cobb Jr. suggests that this emphasis upon God's voluntary love leads to unwarranted anthropomorphism, because it implies that God's will precedes or controls the divine nature.[51] For love to be God's essence, God's actions must arise involuntarily from the divine nature. The abstract features of God's nature were not chosen, according to Cobb's formulation, but these features are true of God by definition.

Open theists, however, endorse the widely assumed notion that love requires freedom. We don't typically think someone loving if that one is required to give a gift rather than freely doing so. Besides, it seems odd to express praise and gratitude to someone who acts by necessity rather than freely. Pinnock describes the position this way:

> Imagine a happily married couple. Having a baby is something they could freely choose to do and they would certainly love it. But one must say that, while their love for the child expresses their love for one another, they are not required to have a child in order to love. God's love for the world expresses his loving essence too, but it is not a necessary expression of his essence...Putting it bluntly, God's nature would be complete and his love fulfilled even without a world to love.[52]

To the process criticism that God's social attributes, e.g., love, require a world to which God must relate, Open theists reply that the God they envision should be considered socially loving, because deity expresses love in the everlasting relations of intra-Trinitarian life.[53] Pinnock explains the Open position in this way: "[W]e hold that God is ontologically other than the world and in a certain sense 'requires' no world. God does not have to relate to some other reality because he is internally social, loving and self-sufficient."[54]

A partial resolution to the debate may emerge in the process notion of divine dipolarity that Open theists such as Richard Rice accept. Rice argues that because "God's love *never* changes, God's experience *must* change."[55] In light of dipolarity, it might be said that the fact *that* God expresses love is a necessary and involuntary aspect of the divine nature. God did not choose this abstract characteristic; it comprises one element of who God is by definition. However, *how* God expresses love is free choice on God's part. God decides how to express love when considering and feeling how the world has responded to God in the past.[56] A worshiper need have no qualms about expressing praise and gratitude to the God who freely chooses the manner in which divine love is revealed.

This resolution helps with one aspect of the Open-process dialogue, but it does not solve the issue that most divides Open evangelicals and process theologians: divine power. After all the qualifications are made, neither process nor Open theists currently appear willing to budge on this issue.[57] While, on one hand, process theists consider ways in which the theory of divine power they espouse might portray divine activity as more effective or faithful to the biblical witness, they apparently will not eschew the claim that God cannot unilaterally determine any state of affairs. This claim resides at the heart of their answer to the problem of evil, the theory of evolution, their interaction with relational feminist theologians, and other concerns. On the other hand, while Open theists are eager to consider ways in which the theory of divine power that they espouse can cohere with a coherent doctrine of divine love, they apparently will not eschew the claim that God *can* unilaterally determine some states of affairs. They believe that evangelical doctrines of eschatology, christology, and miracles are undermined if God is conceived as unable to exercise coercive power on occasion. At present, the issue of divine power seems to have created an impasse.

In this essay, I have briefly identified how process theology approaches evangelical theology. I've noted some affinities and disparities that the two theological traditions share. Perhaps a passage of scripture serves as an appropriate conclusion to this enterprise. As process and evangelical theologians wrestle with how Christians ought to think and live, these words from the great love chapter might be appropriate:

> For now we see in a mirror, dimly, but then we will see face to face. Now I know only in part; then I will know fully, even as I have been fully known. And now faith, hope, and love abide, these three; and the greatest of these is love. (1 Cor. 13:12–13)

CHAPTER 20

A Whiteheadian Vedanta

Outline of a Hindu Process Theology

■JEFFERY D. LONG

Clarifying Our Terms: Hinduism, Vedanta, and Process Theology

One of the most notoriously difficult terms to define in religious studies, perhaps as difficult as the very term "religion," is the term "Hinduism." Why is Hinduism so difficult to define? First of all, the term "Hinduism" does not point to any one specific institution that can be traced to a historical founding figure. Unlike Buddhism, which looks to the Buddha, or Christianity, which looks to Christ, or Islam, which looks to Muhammad, Hinduism has no one founder. In fact, no one is really even sure when Hinduism began. There is a widespread disagreement among scholars as to the dating of the earliest known Hindu texts, the *Vedas*. Western scholars tend to place the composition of these texts between 1500 and 1000 B.C.E., but Hindu scholars generally regard them as products of a period at least a thousand years prior to this. Archaeological evidence suggests a considerable continuity of culture in India–and, one may presume, of religion–going back almost to the end of the last ice age. So "Hinduism," if one takes all of this information into account, would seem to refer to the collective religious beliefs and practices of the people of India dating back to the dawn of civilization.

But this does not give us many specifics, because, at least during the period about which we have more certain knowledge–roughly the last 2500 to 3000 years–the religious beliefs and practices of India have displayed a mind-boggling internal diversity. Belief systems recognized as Hindu include everything from monotheism to polytheism to pantheism to atheism. Practices vary from sect to sect, from region to region, and even from family to family. Some have said there is as much religious variety within Hinduism as among the rest of the world's religions combined! So just as the term "Hinduism" does not point to any one historical institution; it does not point to any one belief either.

This does not mean, however, that one can say nothing about Hinduism, that one cannot generalize about Hindu beliefs and practices. One can make generalizations about Hinduism, as long as one recognizes that a generalization is just that—a generalization, to which exceptions will be inevitable. In the course of this essay, therefore, whenever any claims are made about Hinduism, or about what Hindus do or believe, the reader should understand that there will inevitably be Hindus—maybe quite a few—who would not accept what is being said as an accurate description of their religion. But there are many more that would, and the reader will simply have to take it on faith that the author knows what he is talking about! This, indeed, is part of the beauty of Hinduism—the great freedom of belief that is possible within it, and the variety that the exercise of this freedom inevitably creates. In fact, this is the first generalization we can make about Hinduism—that it takes as a matter of course that there are many perspectives and approaches to truth, and that all are to some degree valid and to be respected. Hinduism is a radically pluralistic religion.

A second generalization that can be made about Hinduism is that the vast majority of Hindus regard a body of literature called the *Vedas*—mentioned earlier—as sacred. This does not mean that most Hindus have read this Vedic literature. It is written in Sanskrit, an ancient language generally accessible only to scholars, even since ancient times, and has become available in translation only since the nineteenth century. Most Hindus are more familiar with later texts that base their authority on the Vedas than they are with the Vedas themselves. These are texts like the *Ramayana*, the *Mahabharata* (of which the famous *Bhagavad-Gita* is a portion), the *Puranas*, the *Dharma Shastras*, or Law Books, and the texts of the various systems of Indian philosophy, or *Darshanas*. But most Hindu schools of thought define themselves as, broadly speaking, Vedic. This means they look to the Vedas as their original source of inspiration, even if the texts they more commonly employ are drawn from later Hindu literature. This later literature is called *smriti*, "that which is remembered"—the sacred tradition. This is in contrast with the Vedas, which go by the term *shruti*, or "that which was heard"—the primordial divine revelation.

Among the many Hindu schools of thought, the one that has become predominant to the point where it is simply identified by many authors as *the* Hindu philosophy is that which is called *Vedanta*. *Vedanta* literally means the "end of the Veda"—*Veda anta*—that is, the goal or the purpose of the Veda, the essential inner meaning or core of the Vedic literature. This term originally referred to a specific portion of the Vedic literature—a set of texts known as the *Upanishads*, meaning "secret doctrine."[1] But it has come to refer collectively to all schools of thought that take the *Upanishads* to represent the apotheosis of the Vedas, the highest truths of the Vedic revelation.

The *Upanishads*, however, read in isolation, do not present the reader with a clear or consistent philosophical vision. They require interpretation, and ideally, the guidance of a living teacher, or guru, to make their meaning clear.

They are therefore traditionally read not in isolation, but in the context of a particular interpretive framework provided by the teaching of a particular school of Vedanta; and, Hinduism being a pluralistic tradition, there are many schools of Vedanta. Each tends to emphasize a particular set of claims set forth in the *Upanishads* as the literal, metaphysical truth, and to interpret the remainder of the texts in the light of these great proclamations, or *mahavakyas*.

These schools of thought are distinguished from one another chiefly with regard to their stance on whether unity or diversity is the defining characteristic of existence. Some portions of the *Upanishads* proclaim, quite clearly, that reality is one–an ultimate unity. The form of Vedanta that emphasizes unity as the main characteristic of existence, to the point where it actually regards diversity as a result of cosmic illusion, or *Maya*, is Advaita, or Nondualist, Vedanta. Other portions of the *Upanishads* proclaim, however, equally clearly, the ultimate reality of diversity, particularly the all-important distinction, for theistic belief systems, between God and the world. The form of Vedanta that gives the most emphasis to this distinction is Dvaita, or Dualist, Vedanta. The other schools of Vedanta fall somewhere between these two on this spectrum of unity and diversity, such as Vishishtadvaita, which affirms an *organic* unity, a unity-in-diversity.

Process theology is, of course, not a traditional form of Vedanta. It is a modern, or postmodern, approach to theology that takes its inspiration from the thought of Alfred North Whitehead and such subsequent thinkers as Charles Hartshorne, John Cobb, and David Ray Griffin, among others. Process thought, however, has considerable affinities with Vedanta, especially Vishishtadvaita– more, in my opinion, than with Christianity, the religious tradition in which the vast majority of process theology has been undertaken.

A major concern of Hindu intellectuals since the nineteenth century has been the development of Hinduism as a tradition with universal relevance. "Hinduism," as we have already seen, is the collective designation of the ancient religious beliefs and practices of the people of India. Indeed, the word *Hindu* refers to a geographical feature–the Sindhu or Indus River from which India gets its name. But in the minds of Hindus, Hinduism is the *Sanatana Dharma*, the eternal or universal religion or way of life, a tradition having important themes, like respect for diversity and the divinity of all beings, from which all of humanity could benefit. Hinduism has never been a proselytizing religion. Believing that all paths can eventually lead to salvation and enlightenment, the Hindu tradition has been largely content to remain a phenomenon local to the Indian subcontinent. However, especially since the colonization of India, first by the forces of Islam and then by those of the West (the British Empire and the more recent globalization of Western capitalism), Hindus have increasingly felt obliged to engage with the outside world. The recognition has dawned that Hinduism is a tradition with an important message for the world.

Process thought, therefore, is an approach to the deep questions of existence that is rooted in the philosophical and theological conventions and concerns of the West. It also has striking affinities to and overlaps with the mainstream of Hindu—and more specifically, of Vedantic—thought. Process theology is thus in an excellent position to provide an idiom through which Hinduism can express itself in Western terms, thus making its universal message available and known to the world. Process thought, in other words, can serve as a kind of bridge between Hinduism and Western thought, a theology for the new global Hinduism.

Translating Vedanta: The First Task of a Hindu Process Theology

The first task, then, of the Hindu process theologian is to translate the concepts of Vedanta—the dominant form of Hindu theology—into the terms of process thought. The goal is both to communicate the concepts of Vedanta to a Western audience and to rethink Vedanta in process terms. Translation, even between languages, is never merely a matter of making one-to-one correspondences between the terms of two systems, for a perfect correspondence never exists. Translation thus always involves a reconstruction and—to borrow a term from process thought—*creative transformation* of the original in the idiom of the new language—or, in this case, the new conceptual system. A Hindu process theology is therefore not simply a restatement of the themes of Vedanta in the terms of process thought, but something new—an addition to the already diverse Hindu tradition, a distinctively new Vedanta for a new age. The consciousness of the Hindu process theologian is the locus of the convergence of these two cultures and systems of thought, and a Hindu process theology is a hybrid of the same. A Hindu process theology is, again, a conceptual statement and a reflection of the new global Hinduism that seeks to have relevance broader than the local concerns of the Indian subcontinent. It does not supersede or try to replace these local concerns, or the more ancient formulations that have traditionally reflected them. Indeed, it draws upon the more traditional formulations as vital resources and as guides for its own reflections. But it also tries to go beyond them, to speak to the new international and multicultural situation of the Hindu tradition.

What are the fundamental concepts of Vedanta, the concepts that a Hindu process theology seeks to translate and understand using the terms of process thought? A close examination of the Vedanta tradition reveals several fundamental concepts with which a Hindu process theology needs to concern itself. These are:

Brahman, in both its Nirguna and Saguna aspects;
Ishvara, or God, and the relationship of God to the entities making up the universe;
Maya, meaning illusion, but also creativity;
Karma, Samsara, the cycle of rebirth; and
Moksha, liberation from this cycle.

But the most fundamental is *Brahman.*

"All This Is Indeed Brahman"

What is reality? What is the character of existence? *Brahman*, the foundational concept of Vedanta, is the most common Hindu answer to these two questions. In most Hindu systems of thought, at least the majority of the Vedanta schools, the totality of all that exists, the whole of reality, encompassing all actuality and possibility, is designated by this term "Brahman." Brahman—which is also known as "the Real" (*sat*)—is coextensive with reality as such. It is that which is real preeminently, and of which the existence of all other entities is derivative and in which it participates. It is that, by knowing which, all things are known.[2] It is also the ultimate object of religious aspiration, of the ancient Upanishadic prayer, "Lead me from the unreal to the Real, from darkness to light, from death to immortality."[3] It is eternal. "It is the immortal; it is Brahman; it is the Whole."[4] To understand Hindu metaphysics is to come to grips with the idea of Brahman.

So what exactly is Brahman? Brahman is a Sanskrit term that can be translated as "that which is expansive"—literally "that which makes things great." It is described in the Upanishads—the philosophical portion of the sacred Vedic literature of Hinduism—as the sweet essence of all that is, the "honey of all beings."[5] It is Brahman that has become all things, that in which they live, move, and have their being. It is from Brahman that all things have emerged and to which all shall inevitably return. And it is Brahman that all things really *are*, in their essence, throughout the course of their existence—including our very selves. *Tat tvam asi*, goes one of the most famous formulations, or *mahavakyas*, of the *Chandogya Upanishad*: "You are That." There is nothing that is not Brahman. As the Upanishads say, *Sarvam khalvidam Brahman*: "All this is indeed Brahman."

Brahman is a universal, all-pervading substance that has become all things. Contemporary Vedanta uses an image of a vibrating energy field to explain Brahman. The vibrations of Brahman correspond to the entire range of existing entities—from solid to liquid to gas to energy to consciousness—conceived as quantum realities vibrating at different frequencies, modifications of the same fundamental "stuff" of reality.

Brahman: One Infinite Being, Consciousness, and Bliss

The essential characteristics of Brahman, according to Vedanta, include, first of all, unity. Brahman is "one alone, without a second,"[6] and is consistently referred to in the singular as "that" (*tat*) or "that one" (*tadekam*). But Brahman also possesses the three characteristics of infinite being, consciousness, and bliss (*anantaram sat-chit-anandam*).[7]

This set of characteristics immediately raises a philosophical issue. If Brahman is the totality of all that exists—or, to put it as we did a moment ago, if there is nothing that is *not* Brahman—then how is it that consciousness and bliss can characterize Brahman? This is a question because consciousness and bliss, at least as these are commonly understood, are forms of *experience*. As forms of experience, they necessarily involve a subject and an object, an experiencer and that which is experienced. Consciousness, or awareness, must involve a knower and a thing known, and bliss an enjoyer and a thing enjoyed.

Brahman, however, is "one alone, without a second." What is there outside itself for Brahman to know or to enjoy? If Brahman is also all that exists, the answer must be "Nothing." But then how can Brahman be characterized by consciousness and bliss?

Because there is nothing else for Brahman to know or to enjoy, the necessary conclusion is that Brahman must know and enjoy itself. This is the Hindu answer to the question of creation: Why does the universe exist? This is not the metaphysical question, "Why is there anything at all?" The answer to this is that it is in the very character of reality to exist; for existence, as well as consciousness and bliss, is one of the essential characteristics of Brahman. But why *this* universe? Why a universe of infinite variety, of manifold entities, of human beings and plants and animals, of stars and planets and galaxies, of atoms and quarks? The very nature of Brahman is being, consciousness, and bliss. For Brahman, therefore, to be fully what it is—for it to *be* being, consciousness, and bliss—it must become many. That One, by its very nature, by its own internal necessity, must manifest as a plurality—indeed an infinity—of conscious, enjoying, existing beings—or, to use the terminology of process thought, *actual entities.* The One *is* the Many.

Nirguna and Saguna Brahman: Formless Creativity and Informed Theocosm

From the perspective of eternity, seeing Brahman as it is within itself, from the perspective of its own nature, one could say Brahman is a unitary state of infinite being, consciousness, and bliss. But the very nature of its basic characteristics necessitates the manifestation of Brahman in—or rather, *as*—time and space and the infinite beings therein. From the perspective of time and space, then, from our perspective, Brahman can be seen as a kind of inner necessity or dynamism in all things that sustains them in their existence and gives them a kind of trajectory, propelling them in the direction of the realization of infinite bliss and infinite consciousness—a dynamism the Hindu tradition also calls *Maya.*

This inner dynamism and trajectory toward the intensification of experience that characterizes all things, a trajectory that involves the evolution of increasingly complex forms of experience (such as consciousness) and a drive toward beauty (the experience of which could be called bliss) is called, in process thought, the principle of *creativity*—another meaning, again, of the Hindu term *Maya.* It is the principle that, according to process thought, underlies all existence, potential and actual. The first contribution of a Hindu process theology to the Hindu tradition is this insight: Brahman is creativity.

Creativity, however, in process thought, is not, as Brahman is, the sum total of all existence. Creativity is, rather, an abstract, eternal principle that *informs* all things. It is the fundamental principle of existence that underlies all forms; but it is, itself, formless. In contrast with the entities that make up the universe of time and space, creativity, "can be called the *formless ultimate*," the "ultimate behind all forms."[8]

A process theologian, then, would not say that creativity *is*, like Brahman, all things. Brahman *is* creativity, but is not exhausted by it. A process Hindu theologian, it seems, would need to say that the sum total of reality–Brahman–contains within itself a formless aspect, corresponding to the process concept of creativity, but that Brahman also possesses an aspect *with* form, corresponding to the universe of actual entities. But is such a postulation of a dual nature of Brahman warranted within the Hindu tradition?

In fact, Brahman, according to Vedanta, *does* have a dual nature–a *Nirguna* aspect and a *Saguna* aspect. The literal meaning of *Nirguna* is "without qualities"–Brahman as unqualified and unconditioned by form. *Saguna*, in contrast, means "with qualities"–Brahman as qualified by the limitations of time and space, as the sum total of all actual entities. So Nirguna Brahman corresponds to Whitehead's understanding of creativity as nonactual and formless. Saguna Brahman corresponds to the two realities that Whitehead calls "the contrasted opposites in terms of which Creativity achieves its supreme task of transforming disjoined multiplicity, with its diversities in opposition, into concrescent unity, with its diversities in contrast"–namely, God and the world.[9] God and the world are conceived, both in Vedanta and in process thought, as realities that necessitate one another, realities that, in Whitehead's terms, "stand to each other in mutual requirement." This leads me to suggest as a term for referring to the joint entity that they together constitute the word *theocosm*–the God-world complex. This Western, Greek term would correspond to the Vedantic concept of Saguna Brahman.

Ishvara/Paramatman: God as the Soul of All Beings

Arguably the most central doctrine of process thought is its doctrine of God. God is also central to Hinduism–though the reader may have begun wondering, by this point, when God was going to make an appearance! God, or Ishvara, and Brahman, at least on the understanding of most schools of Vedanta, are not identical. Like creativity, God is a subset of Brahman, the sum total of reality, the Whole. Brahman is generally conceived as ultimately impersonal–or, more accurately, beyond or encompassing both personal and impersonal qualities. Brahman is Being Itself. Ishvara, on the other hand, although the Supreme Being, is nevertheless *a* being, an inhabitant of the spatio-temporal realm, albeit the most important being. Ishvara is the only metaphysically *necessary* one, without whom no possible world could exist. God, or Ishvara, is therefore dependent, ultimately, upon Brahman, and is a derivative reality therefrom–this despite the absolutely central role that God plays in Hindu piety.

The same is true of God in process thought. God is the preeminent exemplar of the principle of creativity underlying all beings, the one who makes creativity available to the other beings that make up the universe–the reality that mediates between the realms of form and formlessness.

But God did not create creativity. God, in both Hinduism and process thought, is not a creator *ex nihilo*. The inner logic of creativity, rather, necessitated (as it continues to necessitate, at each moment of the universal creative advance) God. From the perspective of classical Christian theology, this appears to reduce God's role. It makes God subject to a logical necessity beyond the control of the divine will. This apparent reductionism is one of the chief reasons Christian theologians have given for rejecting process theology as incompatible with the Christian tradition. But this same formulation places process thought squarely within the mainstream of the Hindu tradition and gives Hindu thinkers all the more reason to be comfortable with a Hindu process theology.

But why is God necessary either to process thought or to Vedanta? As Whitehead explains, the universe is conceived in process thought, and also in Vedantic thought, as a closed system, a self-contained whole, without a creator or an imposition of order from outside. This necessitates some *internal* principle of order that guarantees the universe will not slide into chaos and creates the conditions for the very possibility of a universe:

> In fact, the Universe, as understood in accordance with the doctrine of Immanence, should exhibit itself as including a stable actuality whose mutual implication with the remainder of things secures an inevitable trend towards order.[10]

This "stable actuality" is what process theology means by *God*.

It is important to point out that God, in both process thought and in Hinduism, is a being that is *internal* to all things, and is yet, at the same time, distinct from them.[11] Both systems could be called *panentheistic*.[12] Panentheism is, of course, the belief, not that God *is* all beings (which is called pantheism), but that God is *in* all beings, and all beings, at the same time, are *in* God.

This view is expressed by Hindu thinkers such as Swami Muktananda, known for his expression, "God dwells in you as you." Swami Vivekananda refers to God as "the soul of our souls."[13] Another Vedantic term for God is paramatman, or the Supreme Self, the Self, or atman, of all beings. "He who sees Me everywhere and sees all in Me, to him I am not lost, nor is he lost to Me."[14] The Hindu tradition frequently uses language that sounds more literally pantheistic than panentheistic. Nevertheless, the distinction between deity and worshiper is absolutely vital to popular Hindu practice, such as the practice of *puja*, or devotional worship addressed to a personal manifestation of God in a particular form, or *murti*–a practice mistakenly decried for centuries by many Muslims and Christians as idolatry. The God-world distinction is especially central to the Vaishnava faith. It might be accurate to say that Hinduism sees God and the world as neither wholly distinct nor wholly identical, but as existing in symbiotic continuity.

The concept of the relationship between the individual self and God in Hinduism, dating back at least to the *Upanishads*, is neither one of simplistic identification nor of absolute separation. Living beings are depicted in such texts as the *Taittiriya Upanishad* as being made up of multiple layers or levels, with the outermost, physical layer being the most changeable, the most superficial, and the inner layers being successively more and more permanent, more and more real.[15] Deeper than the physical self, for example, is the personality we have developed over the course of our experiences in this life—our habits, memories, predispositions, etc., called in Sanskrit *samskaras.* But even deeper than this personality would be the traces of personality and memory that we carry in our subconscious minds—in our souls—from our previous lives. Going beyond even this deep level, and others, still more profound, God exists within and experiences through us from our fundamental core or center. A well-known metaphor for this divine indwelling is given in the *Bhagavad-Gita*: the metaphor of a string of pearls, with God dwelling within and connecting all beings just as the string connects the pearls that rest upon it. "On Me all that is here is strung like pearls upon a thread."[16]

Maya/Karma/Samsara: Infinite Beings Seeking Infinite Consciousness and Bliss

Turning now, though, from the vast scale of God and Being to the scale of human existence, what is the meaning and purpose of life in the universe as conceived by Hindu process theology? To summarize briefly what we have seen thus far, the sum total of all of reality is conceived in Hinduism as Brahman. Creativity corresponds to the concept of Nirguna, or formless, Brahman. But the manifestation of this creativity as the propelling force underlying all things corresponds to the concept of Maya, and the totality of actual entities, including God—the *theocosm*—to Saguna Brahman. In both Hindu and process thought, as we have seen, God is postulated as a necessary element of Saguna Brahman, as a kind of bridge between the Nirguna and the Saguna realms—the realms of form and formlessness. God makes available to all beings the creative potentials that they have the ability to embody. According to process thought, an actual entity can only be related to another actual entity. For a universe to exist for more than a mere instant, for it to have stability and continuity, an actual entity is necessary. This entity must be able to embody and present to the rest of the actual entities making up the universe the sum total of future possibilities they are capable of actualizing. This necessary being is a necessary condition for the possibility of any possible future. This necessary being is God.

But what is our role—we, the actual beings who make up the universe? Our role is to make Brahman, in actuality, what it is capable of becoming as a pure potentiality. Our role is to manifest infinite being, infinite consciousness, and infinite bliss. In the terms of process thought, our role is to evolve forms of experience capable of the potentially limitless enjoyment of potentially limitless beauty. God's role is to act as a center of universal consciousness, to coordinate the experiences of the many beings making up the universe such that they constitute a unity, a universe, in the first place. God is to bring unity and order out of the chaos of the multitude of individual decisions being made by the actual entities at each new moment of the creative advance. God already embodies this infinite being, consciousness, and bliss, and by so doing lures us to do the same.

The situation from which we begin, however, as human beings, makes our role in the actualization, the ongoing creation and self-expression, of the universe far from self-evident. We do not always *feel* that the fundamental basis of our existence is a potential for infinite being, consciousness, and bliss. We do not always *feel* like beings in whom God perpetually dwells, and whom God is perpetually calling from the depths of our preconscious experience to higher and higher levels of awareness and enjoyment. We feel, to use a term from the philosopher Martin Heidegger (whose philosophy has many affinities with process thought), "thrown" into this world, with little or no sense of our purpose or of our connectedness, through God, with all other beings. We arrive into this world in a state of *avidya*, or ignorance of our true potential. From this ignorance arises suffering—the fear of death, of losing oneself, which gives rise to the fear of losing one's property, and so to fear, and eventually hatred, of the other, whom one views as a threat. We remain unaware that God dwells within all beings, including ourselves. But what is the cause of this ignorance? What is Hindu process theology's response to the problem of evil?

The fact of primordial spiritual ignorance, of *avidya*, is a necessary side effect of the process by which Brahman is actualized, by which creative potential is transformed, through us and through God, through the beings making up the universe, into a spatio-temporal reality. Recall the earlier discussion of the problem raised by the nature of Brahman as both one and as infinite being, consciousness, and bliss. For the One to become fully (actually) what it already really is in eternity (potentially), for it to manifest its nature in time, it is necessary for the One to become the Many. The One must take on the limitation of being a finite subject experiencing the finite objects of the spatio-temporal world.[17] Put another way, one cannot experience consciousness or bliss, much less infinite consciousness and bliss, without the experience of finitude. The purpose of our existence is to move from our current state of *avidya*, or ignorance, to *vidya*, or wisdom—from the finite to the infinite. To again invoke the ancient prayer of the Vedic sages, we must move from the unreal to the real, from darkness to light, from death to immortality.

The fact that the very nature of the creative process necessitates the state of "original ignorance" in which we find ourselves is expressed by the Hindu tradition with the concept of Maya. Maya, significantly, is translatable as both "illusion" and "creative power." The basic concept of Maya is that the very creative process by which Ishvara coordinates the experiences of the entities making up the world and guides them toward the realization of their full potential—the realization of Brahman—is also the process by which ignorance and darkness arise; for this process necessarily veils from us the true nature of reality. It is precisely by overcoming and learning to see through and beyond this veil that our true potential can be realized. Imagine God is an invisible man. Only by wearing a mask and clothes can God be seen. The mask and the clothes are not God. They hide his true nature. But without them, he would remain a mystery. This mask and clothes are what are meant by Maya.

But Maya, as creative power, has a purpose: the coordination of the experiences of the entities making up the world such that they can eventually realize their true nature and experience the infinite consciousness and bliss that is their destiny. Maya manifests a world of regularities, of universal laws, like the laws of physics, or the laws of morality. The fundamental principle on which Maya operates is the principle of action, or *Karma*. Karma can be understood as the sum total of the effects of all the previous actions undertaken by the entities constituting the universe, including our own past selves, and the future effects that we are currently creating with our present choices, our present actions. Karma, one could say, is another form of creativity.

By engaging in activity, by making choices, by exercising our freedom, we gradually learn, through trial and error, the deep truths of existence. According to Hindu thought, this can take an entity many lifetimes. The compatibility of this doctrine of rebirth, or *punarjanma*, with process thought is something that David Ray Griffin, among others, has affirmed.[18] The process of rebirth, literally "wandering about," through which the soul gradually realizes its true nature and purpose is called *Samsara*.

Moksha: Liberation

The ultimate goal of most Hindu religious practice, and certainly within Vedanta, is *Moksha*, or liberation from Samsara, from the process of wandering from rebirth to rebirth in search of one's true self.

This, of course, naturally raises the question, "What happens next?" What is the fate of an entity who has escaped the process of rebirth? The answer to this question varies a great deal within the Hindu tradition, depending upon which system of belief and practice one consults. In Advaita Vedanta, which emphasizes the "illusion" part of the concept of Maya and claims that Nirguna Brahman is ultimately all that exists, liberation from rebirth involves a loss of personal identity, or rather, a realization that one never had a separate identity to begin with. From the perspective of time and space—which is, from the point of view of this school, a deluded perspective—the liberated soul, in effect, ceases to exist. The more dualistic, theistic, and devotional schools, however, such as those that are part of the Vaishnava tradition, envision liberation as a loving union with divinity. They even speak of a heavenly afterworld—called Vaikuntha, in which the liberated soul lives forever enjoying the infinite beauty of God, not unlike the heaven of Christianity or the paradise of Islam.

From a process perspective, I would postulate that liberation would mean taking part with God, as a fully conscious participant, in the never-ending creative process of the actualization of infinite being, consciousness, and bliss in the universe. Much as in some forms of Mahayana Buddhism, the difference between Samsara and Liberation, on this understanding, is not so much an ontological difference between two different realms of existence, but a revolution in the consciousness of the liberated being. A being in Samsara is subject to Karma–that is, on a process understanding, it is minimally free with regard to the collective influence of the past. Such a being, ignorant or dimly aware of its interconnections with all other beings, is a perpetual victim, an object of experience. Life happens *to* such a being.

But a liberated being, having attained a higher degree of cognizance of the causal relations between the past and the present–and the potentials for the future existing in the present–becomes a master of Karma. Rather than drowning again and again in the ocean of Samsara, such a being learns to surf the waves of cosmic consciousness. In tune with God, perhaps through meditation or some other yogic or devotional practice, and with its fellow beings, the liberated master becomes a conscious coparticipant with God in the unfolding of the divine vision of creative potential, an instrument of God in the world. For such a liberated being, God becomes, as the *Gita* says, the true doer of action, and the ultimate enjoyer of its results.

Conclusion

In this essay, I have at least begun to outline a Hindu process theology. In this theology, Nirguna Brahman is conceived as creativity. Saguna Brahman is conceived as both God and the entities making up the world–what I have called the *theocosm.* Ishvara, or God, is conceived essentially as God is conceived in process thought–as the necessary bridge between creativity and the world. Maya is conceived as creativity in its role as a limiting factor, giving rise to limited, finite beings precisely so the infinite can thereby be realized. Karma, in this view, is the regularity, the "inevitable trend toward order," that the divinely coordinated universe exhibits. Samsara is the process of rebirth, of wandering through the karmically ordered world and learning from one's experiences until one reaches Moksha. Moksha is a state characterized by a true understanding of the interdependence of all beings, including their mutual implication with divine existence, a conscious participation in the divine creative process.

Through such an experiment, and further, future elaborations thereon, it is hoped that the Hindu tradition can begin to articulate its vision of reality with a greater clarity to the wider world. Then the Hindu tradition can draw out its implications of respect for the diversity, the interdependence, and the potential divinity–meaning the divine consciousness, or cosmic consciousness, the *theocosmic* consciousness–of all beings.

CHAPTER 21

Covenant and Responsible Creativity

Toward a Jewish Process Theology

▪ SANDRA B. LUBARSKY

So central is covenant (*brit*) to the whole structure of Judaism that it is fair to name it the controlling metaphor of Judaism. Not only does it describe the way Jews have understood both their personal and their corporate relationship with God, it also implies the Jewish view of an ideal God-world relation.[1] "Follow me!" and "Listen, Sh'ma!" are the core exhortations to which Israel voluntarily consents; what it means "to follow" and "to listen" is spelled out and interpreted over the course of millennia. Within the covenantal structure, prophets called for ethical commitment, rabbis delineated acceptable personal behavior and public action, hasids promoted the celebration of the created order, and mystics practiced ways to attain direct experience of God. All sought to be open to the presence of a living God, to connect with that presence, to respond to it by "holy" living, seeking to improve an imperfect world and living in hope that perfection was not eternally elusive. Covenant has been the orienting structure for Jewish life, a way to understand the meaning, purpose, and goal of life lived in relationship with God, the community, the non-Jewish world, and nature.

A process-relational Judaism will begin with the idea of covenant, wrestle with its meaning in the modern world, and explore the ways in which process philosophy helps to clarify the internal process and external expectations of the covenantal relationship.

Covenantal Partnership

Early on in the biblical narrative, it becomes clear that the covenantal relationship is much more than a legal structure, for the defining feature of the Jewish notion of covenant is the relationship of partnership between God and human beings. Though God is greater in all ways, human beings are called to be partners with God in creating, sustaining, and perfecting the world. Next to the basic belief in divinity, the idea of a divine-human partnership is the fundamental "leap of faith" essential to Judaism. This idea asserts that the Creator of the universe desires, for unknown reasons, to have a partnership with creatures who are both created in God's image and "but dust and ashes."

Because of partnership, the encounter with God may not simply elicit obedience or awe; it may call forth that quintessential Jewish interaction with God: "Godwrestling." To be in a covenantal relationship of partnership is to encounter God dialogically, to be in conversation with God not only about what God wishes and expects, but also what you expect and desire. In rabbinic tradition, Abraham is considered to be superior to Noah, even though Noah was completely obedient to God. When Noah was informed that the world would be destroyed and that he should build an ark, he did just that. Abraham, on the other hand, once the impending destruction of Sodom was revealed to him, asked God to reconsider. "Will you indeed sweep away the righteous with the wicked? Suppose there are fifty righteous within the city; will you then sweep away the place and not forgive it for the fifty righteous who are in it?" (Gen. 18:23–24). Because Abraham engaged God as a responsible partner rather than simply accepting God's dictum, he is judged to be more admirable than Noah. God's response is not always what the human partner hopes to hear. Sometimes, as in the story of Job, God will argue back: "Shall a faultfinder contend with the Almighty?" (Job 40:2). But it is this give-and-take that exemplifies the intimate, relational structure of covenant in which "wrestling" is a legitimate form of coming to terms with the duties and responsibilities of partnership.

The Covenant Reconceived

The covenant has been the subject of revision, necessitated by the to-and-fro of historical events and the position that Jews found themselves in within the larger cultures around them. Particularly in the period following the destruction of the second temple, Rabbinic Judaism reestablished the terms of the covenant—and thus saved the covenantal relationship. They did this by declaring that though the temple was destroyed, the priesthood thus undermined, and national sovereignty lost, God was yet present in the life of the Jewish people, even to the point of being in exile with them. Under these dramatically changed circumstances, the rabbis declared that the covenant no longer mandated rituals that were connected with temple and land except in a transmuted form that became embedded in the worship of God through prayer, study, and good deeds.

In the modern period of Jewish life the covenant has been redefined, primarily in reaction to Immanuel Kant's judgment of Judaism and in response to Kant's greater philosophical vision. Kant did not speak positively about Judaism. He designated Judaism as the archetypical heteronomous religion and set it against Christianity and, more importantly, against Enlightenment thinking as a whole. According to Kant, Judaism was based on submission to external authority and bound to archaic, irrational rituals. Leading Jewish thinkers of the eighteenth and nineteenth centuries spent their creative energies responding to this disparaging depiction of Judaism. Hoping to secure the external benefits of political emancipation as well as to reconcile Jewish tradition with modernity, they set out to contradict Kant by embracing Kantian rationalism. Judaism was reformulated into a system of ethics based on universal, rational truths and disconnected from the ritual and legal structures that had shaped community life.

The God who was imaged as a Lawgiver who demanded obedience to laws without regard to reason was rejected by liberal Jewish thinkers. They, instead, granted priority to individual autonomy. Under the guidance of the Kantian philosopher, Hermann Cohen, Judaism was reconstructed as a religion of "ethical monotheism." Leo Baeck, a student of Cohen's, went so far as to designate the "essence" of Judaism to be ethical monotheism. Even Martin Buber, who decried the Kantian reduction of God to an idea and spoke instead of the I-Thou relationship, maintained a modernist allegiance to the authority of the individual. The whole of Reform Judaism, founded in Germany during the height of Kant's prestige, was shaped by the desire to show European society that Judaism was *the* religion of reason, that its commandments were universalizable, and that its salvific goal was the establishment of a perfectly moral world.

Liberal Judaism became an attractive alternative to orthodoxy because it appealed to the intellectual needs and desires of many Jews, as well as accommodating the demands of the non-Jewish world. As Mordecai Kaplan felicitously stated, the past would have a vote, not a veto, and thus individual Jews would have greater power to determine belief and practice in ways that complemented their new social and culture conditions. Judaism thus reformulated had tremendous liberalizing consequences within the Jewish community at the same time that it eased the way toward civil emancipation.

But the attendant costs of this restructuring were and continue to be significant. In making modern Judaism the most Kantian of traditions, Jewish thinkers succeeded in gaining the admission of individual Jews into the wider culture. Over the course of a century and a half, under the spell of Kantian thought and the enticements of political and social emancipation, the legal, ceremonial, communal, and mystical traditions of Judaism were delegitimized. Constrained by the requirement that authority lies within the individual and cannot be imposed without forfeiting the ethical basis of decision, liberal thinkers turned to the notion of "contentless revelation." God's presence was asserted, but what God stood for, other than an assurance that the ethical impulse within us had universal warrant, was unclear. For many liberal Jews, the most that could be salvaged of the traditional divine-human relationship was the "still, small voice" of the human conscience. Any recognition of divine or communal restraints on individual decision-making were recognized to be sociological, not theological.

In the twentieth century, the Holocaust compounded the challenges to the idea of covenant. God's presence came under question as well as God's redemptive capacity. Had God gone into "hiding" during the Hitler years? Was it now possible only to speak of a "voluntary covenant" to which Jews no longer owe obedience?[2] Between the nineteenth-century philosophical denunciation of Judaism and the twentieth-century physical annihilation of the Jewish people, what had been central to Jewish self-understanding—the idea of the covenant—came to be described as a "broken myth" whose "traditional force has been neutralized."[3]

The contemporary Jewish thinker, Arnold Eisen, has correctly linked covenantal renewal with "the larger healing awaited by Jewish faith and the Jewish people"[4] in the post-Holocaust period. But it is hard to imagine how covenantal healing can happen within a Kantian framework.[5] What Whitehead said about Kant in regard to philosophy in general seems also to hold true for postmodern Jewish covenantal theology: We must go around rather than through him. The Kantian challenge to Jewish covenantal thinking assumed both that covenant could be reduced to divine legislation and that divine contact with the human world necessarily violates human freedom. The covenant thus loses its relationship of mutuality and becomes inadequate. Healing the covenant will depend first on extracting it from this world view and second on placing it within a process-relational paradigm in which the notion of covenant can be broadened, a metaphysics of internal relations embraced, and the core insights of covenantal theology—the affirmation of creativity and relationality—affirmed.

A growing number of Jewish thinkers support the move away from a modernist, Kantian world view. Among them is Arthur Waskow, who considers the contemporary struggle to find a new way of apprehending God to be a continuation of the tradition of Godwrestling. He is one of the leaders of an emerging movement in American liberal Judaism—"Jewish Renewal"—that is intentionally seeking a new philosophical paradigm, one that distinguishes between the "creative and destructive" features of modernity and that recognizes the interrelatedness of spirituality and community life. Such aspects as gender equality, participatory democracy, and religious pluralism are affirmed; restricting religious expression, destroying communities, and seeking to rule the world are among the rejected aspects. This "paradigm shift" has much in common with the description of "constructive postmodernism" spelled out by process philosopher David Griffin. Indeed, process theology has been named as one of the sources for the positive transformation of Jewish thought.[6]

The remainder of this essay is devoted to exploring the idea of covenant from within a process-relational paradigm. This is an initial exercise in covenantal revisioning, undertaken within a very different historical climate than either the rabbinic or the Kantian revisions. Jews today face neither the exigencies of exile nor the oppressions of preemancipation life. But modernity has more than threatened all forms of spirituality, and Judaism has been particularly vulnerable to its pressures. Can a revised notion of covenant help us to dislodge the individualism, materialism, and militarism that dominated the modernist paradigm and thereby infiltrated our own religious self-understandings? Can it be the source of envisioning healthy God-world and human-human relationships in this postmodern world? Can it again offer guidance for life-affirmation, for living abundantly but not destructively?

A Covenant of Responsible Creativity: Reenvisioning the Covenant

The mythic narrative of the Jewish covenant begins in the shadow of Mount Sinai as a singular experience. Jewish ritual, however, not only keeps the event alive as a "living past," but makes it function as a way "back to the future." The contemporary Jewish experience is vastly different from that of ancient Judaism; nonetheless, the modern Jew is shaped by a liturgy that insists on a personal memory of having been a slave in Egypt and covenanted at Mount Sinai. The covenantal story told each spring at the Passover *seder* reinforces the relationship that is recorded in the Hebrew Bible and is felt to be ongoing despite dramatically different circumstances.

Even where theological commitment is absent or nearly so, observances that secure a sense of covenantal continuity and reinforce particular patterns of sensitivity continue to be practiced.[7] Indeed, as Arnold Eisen has pointed out in a recent study on the rise of ritual observance in American Jewish communities, many contemporary Jews have settled for ritual that functions apart from belief in the presence of an authoritative God.[8] For these Jews, ritual serves as a sort of theological compromise with modernity, particularly with modernity's attack on God's power and authority and its concomitant veneration of human freedom. But one wonders how long such ritual and the orienting structure of which it is an expression can retain their vitality apart from a viable way of speaking about the divine-human partnership.

A process-relational approach to Judaism offers a way of recovering the emotional, moral, personal, and interpersonal relationship of covenant for our post-Holocaust, postmodern age. Rather than reducing covenant to a legalistic formula and then having to either defend it in the face of the Kantian challenge or reject it as an archaic model that violates human freedom, covenant can instead be seen as *the site for responsible creativity*. To describe the covenant as fundamentally a relationship of responsible creativity, reciprocity, and life-affirmation is very different from describing it as a contract or a system of divine legislation. It is to assert that behind the ritual and ethical codes that developed as part of Jewish tradition is an experience of personal connection with and gratefulness toward a being who calls for intentional, full-hearted participation in life.

This point is illustrated in a famous midrash on the Sinai event, which tells the story of God's desire for "guarantors" of the gift of the Torah. At first the people offered the patriarchs as guardians. But they were deemed unacceptable. The prophets, too, were turned down. It is only upon the offering of their children that God said, "They are certainly good guarantors. For their sake I give the Torah to you."[9] In a covenant in which the divine imperative is to "choose life," God accepts the people's children and the generations to come as their gift of reciprocity. Future life is the promise given to the God who is the source of life. The connection of covenant with children is made repeatedly throughout the Torah. The drama of the binding of Isaac revolves around whether Abraham will indeed "follow" God and whether God will indeed bless Abraham with the generation of life. At a crucial point, it becomes clear that covenantal faithfulness does not entail child sacrifice; to the contrary, covenant is first and foremost a relationship of life-affirming activity.

The halakha or religious guidelines developed in response to the covenantal affirmation of life provided Jews a way to "walk" with God; Torah, as divine legislation, is an expression of this relationship. But the covenantal relationship is greater than Torah, understood in this circumscribed way. It is a way of living a life in coordination with other lives—divine, human, and nonhuman—and in gratitude for them.[10]

This interpretation emphasizes certain aspects of covenant as it has been traditionally understood and deemphasizes others. Divine-human partnership and the freedom and responsibility that it entails are unquestionably central characteristics of the traditional Jewish notion of covenant. But rarely has covenant been spoken of as a relationship in which creativity is explicitly valued and encouraged. The reasons for this are numerous, complicated, and contradictory. To consider them briefly is hardly to explain them. Suffice it to say that on the one hand, creativity is implied in the transformative work of redeeming the world—covenant thus induces creative effort without naming it as a separate activity. On the other hand, creativity as an attribute of human power can be seen as in tension with divine omnipotence and the idea that God is the sole cause of all things—thus creativity is not always directly attributed to human beings. A further reason, and likely the most significant, is that much of Jewish thought was developed under the influence of a substance metaphysics and the ideal of an eternal, unchanging order. Thus although Jews understood themselves to be in a relationship of co-creativity with God, the tradition became disposed toward securing creative insight within a legal frame that would promote and maintain righteous action. Creativity was embedded in the legal tradition and thus both routinized and restrained. Thus it is fair to say that to think of covenant as a relationship of responsible creativity is both to affirm and recast tradition. It is to accept John Cobb's description of God's influence on human beings as a valuable midrash on the covenantal idea.

> Creative freedom and personal responsibility have been accented where belief in the biblical God has been alive…[W]here the biblical God was understood to hold before human beings new possibilities

for their lives—indeed a new historical order, and finally a new world—there human beings have experienced themselves as free to transcend the bounds of the past and to live from the not yet realized possibilities.[11]

In this rendering, not only are creative freedom and personal responsibility valued, but the covenant itself is understood as a potentially transformative process.

A theology of covenant will have much in common with what process theologians have named a "spirituality of creativity" and the process of "creative transformation."[12] In this way of seeing things, creativity is the defining feature of life and the basic force of the world. Freedom and power are the means by which all beings participate in the creative process. God is understood as "the supreme, all-inclusive embodiment of creative power" and all other beings are understood as "embodiments of creativity."[13] God alone offers every creature a set of possibilities on which to act—the "initial aims"—and in this way, God's creativity differs from that of other creatures. But all living beings are involved in the creative process, making decisions about how they will respond to the past and what they will contribute to the future. Rather than Lawgiver or Sovereign or Judge, God's foremost role in the world is Creator-Sustainer and Creator-Redeemer. As Creator-Sustainer, God "implants" possibility into the world and works to sustain life-affirming, creative response to those possibilities. As Creator-Redeemer, God transforms the creative efforts of all beings and recasts them in relation to new possibilities.

This sense of a world of creative effort is captured by the Chassidic rabbi Simchah Bunam of Przysucha (1765–1827) in the following gloss on Genesis 1:

The Lord created the world in a state of beginning. The universe is always in an uncompleted state, in the form of its beginning. It is not like a vessel at which the master works to finish it; it requires continuous labor and renewal by creative forces. Should these cease for only a second, the universe would return to primeval chaos.[14]

Bunam's commentary complements a process-relational world view in which creativity is ongoing and is undertaken by "creative forces" working in partnership with God and in which creating the world is a way of saving the world.

To live in a covenantal relationship in a world infused with creativity is very different from living in a world legislated by a divine authority. Rather than obedience to specific directives, we are called to use our freedom in ways that are life affirming and to be open to new possibilities as they arise, recreating ourselves in responsiveness to God. Though the power differential between human beings and God remains, the partnership between God and human individuals is heightened within a theology of creativity. "Serving" God means something different in a paradigm marked by creativity rather than obedience.

Free choice and responsibility are played out in relation to creativity and interconnectedness and to a God whose goal is to enrich the world. To be responsive to God is to consciously participate in the creative process so that life is affirmed. In this scenario, God does not want obedience but attentiveness, sensitivity, and responsible action that will help to further life itself. The exodus story thus links liberation with reorientation. The Hebrews are emancipated from slavery, not to become slaves to God, but to enjoy a relationship in which their self-determination is coupled with God's vision of a redeemed world. "You shall be holy," God says, not "you shall be subservient or obedient or submissive." As David Griffin writes,

> To "obey" the will of God in our lives is to become more rather than less creative. True obedience is therefore manifested in a life of maximal creativity...The divine call is to exert our creative energies to the fullest in a wide variety of dimensions. The divine "no" is directed only against those expressions that are really destructive rather than creative, in that they cripple or destroy the creative capacities of others, including one's own future experiences.[15]

Covenantal partnership is a particularly Jewish way of expressing engagement with creative transformation. Within this relationship, Jews will wrestle with God and with others, akin to Jacob's nighttime match, struggling with the entanglements of partnership and the responsible creative action that it requires.

In this framework, covenant itself becomes subject to the creative activity that is at work in the universe. Although covenant is an enduring relationship, it may not be an unalterable one. This is something the rabbis already acknowledged as they undertook their interpretive work in the face of changed historical conditions. Legal and social structures will be developed to hold on to the beauty and holiness that has been achieved. But these behavioral obligations may become irrelevant or even detrimental in the face of change. Although as participants in a covenantal relationship we live in hopes of a redeemed world, even our assumptions about such a world are subject to radical change. There is simply no way to secure the creative advance. Our only choice is to be open to it and seek to meet creativity with creativity.

Internal Relatedness and Divine-Human Interaction

Once creativity is emphasized as the defining feature of covenant, modernist assumptions about how God interacts with the world must be rethought. A process-relational paradigm offers two significant strategies for building an alternative understanding of revelation: the notion of divine power as noncoercive influence and the idea of internal relations.

Since Kant's accusation that God's revelation was heteronomous, nonorthodox Jewish thinkers have sought a theory of divine-human interaction that is noncoercive either in form or in content. The alternatives mostly resulted in substituting divine "presence" for divine "word." Both Martin Buber and

Franz Rosenzweig, for example, concurred that what happens in the revelatory moment is an encounter with the presence of God. It is the experience of being in relationship that constitutes revelation; no objective content—neither legislation nor propositional truths—is relayed. For Rosenzweig, Torah is a response to revelation, but not itself part of the revelatory experience. For Buber, not even this much significance is given to Torah. Even Abraham Heschel, who maintained a more traditional approach in which Torah is valued as divine word, nonetheless claimed that any revelatory content can only be known midrashically, that is, in a nonliteral way. Thus interpretive authority lies with humans. In short, then, for nontraditional thinkers, content has been sacrificed to preserve human freedom and authority.

A process-relational metaphysics offers a way to think of revelation as an event in which human freedom is respected and yet content imparted. Because God is not conceived of either as all-powerful or totally transcendent, God acts in the world without overpowering it. Such an understanding of God is consistent with the traditional understanding of covenant. Though the idea of divine omnipotence was almost never rejected outright, it was constrained by the belief that God self-limits divine power to establish covenantal relationships—and in that relationship, God's self-restraint is unassailable. In actuality, the central Jewish narrative has imaged God as involved in the world and the world as the location of free beings in relation to God. The intellectual inconsistency in holding that God is both omnipotent and relational has been mostly disregarded in the face of the covenantal intuition of partnership.

Nonetheless, no modern Jewish thinker has laid out a systematic approach to how God's power and human power intermingle. And because the idea of omnipotence, though overshadowed by the idea of covenant, still lingered, so too did the hope that in times of great travail God would exercise God's ability to end evil. Despite the affirmation of human freedom and responsibility, it was nonetheless expected that the very affection and obligation that arise from within the covenantal relationship would mandate God's exercise of power. In a partnership of care and responsibility, how could one partner suffer so much pain when the other had the capacity to alleviate it?

The analysis of power offered by process philosophy is of much use here, both in clarifying the extent and kind of power that God yields and in reminding Jews of the logic that is implicit in the covenant itself. A process conception of divine power offers the only way to maintain the divine-human covenant and untangle the theological jumble that results when two conflicting ideas—freedom and omnipotence—are simultaneously affirmed. The process notion that omnipotence is a theological mistake ought to be obvious from within a covenantal structure. Human freedom presupposes a limitation of divine power. God cannot be both omnipotent and in relation with free and responsible beings. On the one hand, God's power is curtailed by the very fact that there is power throughout the created world. On the other hand, God's power is only meaningful in relation to the power of others, for a being who embodies all the power in the cosmos must thereby exist in a place that is devoid of any other living beings. A process metaphysics holds that God's power, like all power, is relational power. This means that God does not choose to give up omnipotence to be in relationship with other beings, but that divine power is relational by necessity. Thus, divine supervention is not an option, no matter how terrible the evil that may arise.

Perhaps even more important than the critique of omnipotence is the clarification that process thinkers have made regarding the kind of power that God holds. It is not enough to deny omnipotence, for that does not in itself overcome the possibility that God, as most-but-not-all powerful, might still act in ways that would compromise human freedom. The much more vital shift involves the distinction between brute power and persuasive power—and the recognition that the former is flawed both because it can be used to increase suffering and because it operates by violating the very freedom that is life-preserving. Moreover, in the long run, brute power seems to be less influential than persuasive power.

The idea of revelation changes rather sharply when God's power is conceived of as persuasive influence. It is no longer one in which a divine commander addresses a subservient crowd who thus feels compelled to obedience. A picture of revelation in which God calls to the people, "Come, join me in a relationship of mutual commitment," in which "I will be your God and you will be my people," aligns the covenantal recognition of human dignity with modern respect for human freedom. Godwrestling has only ever been a possibility because humans are free to struggle with God's will and their personal desires, to seek meaning and connection, to "listen" and "follow." A process-relational understanding of divine power as influence and persuasion, operating in confluence with the freedom of other lives, articulates what has been profoundly assumed but not clearly expressed by covenantal logic. Covenant has always attributed a great deal of dignity to humans and presumed a great deal of human influence on the world—in process-relational language, humans have been understood to have the two-fold powers of self-determination and of influence on others, including God's life and the life of the world. For example, though they differed on details, Jewish mystics agreed that human beings are "the perfecting agent in the structure of the cosmos."[16] All traditional Jews have held that the practice of halakhah was the way to perfect the world and usher in the messiah. When divine power is conceived as the power of persuasive influence, operative within a relationship of partnership, heteronomy and autonomy are no longer relevant categories. In a process-relational framework, divine revelation assumes relationality that cannot be violated either by God's presence or God's word.

Moreover, noncoercive power in a world of relations must be understood as acting *in* and *with* the world, rather than *on* the world. Divine persuasive power is the inverse of brute force that bears down on its target like a thunderbolt strike. In a process-relational metaphysics, revelation works in tandem with creativity and the self-determination of an individual. God influences all beings as they are in the process of shaping themselves, offering initial aims or possibilities so that new life arises in relation both to past actuality and ideal potentiality. At each moment, God's will is revealed, not as an outside imposition, but as a part of the context within which every subject arises. Real content is thus imparted to the individual. God's revelation is felt by the becoming individual as a lure that is life-affirmative. But it is also a communication that is both very personal–the gradation of possibilities offered to each individual, reflecting the details of that individual's becoming–and very communal–offered to the individual in relation to the history in which it arises. Thus a process-relational model enables divine revelation that includes both the felt presence of God and propositions aimed at unifying creativity with God's hope for the world. The becoming subject chooses how God's influence will be actualized, responding to divine revelation that is direct and intimate even as it yields to the self-determination of the individual.

Conclusion

A covenantal life, traditionally understood as being "commanded," entails living life in ways that are life-affirming. Even among nonorthodox Jews who have rejected the idea of an omnipotent God who hands down divine legislation, there remains the belief that certain behaviors are incumbent upon those who understand themselves as consecrated to a covenantal relationship. Partnership involves obligation and commitment that are emotionally felt as being commanded, even as the idea of divine legislation is rejected and human freedom is affirmed. "Follow me." "Choose life." "Love your neighbor." "Care for the widow, the poor, and the hungry." No longer considered to be "legislation," these instructions are so profoundly a part of covenantal expectations that they are felt as divine imperatives. "Must and ought–the two are one," states Arthur Waskow, in nearly the same breath as he speaks of "God-wrestling."[17] What words can express these feelings of obligation that arise in relationship with a God whose power is persuasive? Franz Rosenzweig, responding to the Kantian critique, distinguished between "law" and "command," arguing that law is impersonal and hence to be disassociated from religion, but command is addressed to the individual within a personal relationship and is thus to be honored. "The commandments, just as a lover's expressions of affection, are governed by the presence and implicit wishes of the beloved."[18] Emmanual Levinas, too, speaks convincingly of the encounter with the Other, which issues in "a command that commands commanding."[19] Here the imperative–to unite love and justice–comes from the face of the Other, but it is expressive of the ethical passion that characterizes the covenantal relationship itself. Christian theologian, John Cobb, advises that, from a process-relational understanding of the persuasive God, we should:

> Cease to think of God as the one cause of all things or the sole cause of any event or entity and think of God instead as the giver of life and

freedom, the source of creative novelty, and the one who in love creates the possibility of our love.[20]

What is the response to such a God? Within a covenantal relationship where trust and affection are exchanged, obligations of intimacy—answering love with love—are inevitable. Though not imposed, they may nonetheless be experienced as commanded, necessary, and appropriate. Thus it might be said that there is a commanding quality to the covenantal relationship—as with every relationship of love—only perhaps more so in relationship with a God who lovingly responds to each life and all of life.

The Jewish understanding of covenant has always entailed a divine-human partnership based on freedom, reciprocity, trust, and love—all for the purpose of enhancing both the source of life and the bearers of life. The legislative aspects of covenant are secondary to this insight of relationality. As with a *ketubah* that traditionally sets forth the obligations of marriage, there is an assumption that behind the contract lies a greater promise: the promise of affection reciprocated. Covenant understood as a relationship of responsible creativity in which life is to be affirmed is well served by a process-relational metaphysics. Such a metaphysics helps to articulate the traditional insight of covenant as an alternative to either blind subservience or random, unchecked acts of freedom. Covenant is that structure that affords creative response to God's will, occurring within the bounds of a relationship of listening, following, and loving. To live covenantally is to live in conscious relationship with the creativity that inspires life.

Notes

Chapter 1: God For Us

[1]David Hume, *Natural History* (New York: Oxford University Press, 1993 [1757]), 155.
[2]Ibid.
[3]Cf. Robert C. Neville, *Creativity and God: A Challenge to Process Theology* (New York: Seabury Press, 1980).
[4]By "perfect being" theism, I mean the classical monotheistic formulation influenced by the Greek notion of perfection in the Platonic, Aristotelian, and Neo-Platonic traditions. This notion of perfection includes the assumption that any change in the perfect being or object is precluded, because a change could only be away from the perfect state, which is unitary and singular.
[5]The dogma of radical grace, while a valuable corrective to any tendency to domesticate God, can be expressed in such a way that it becomes a Protestant overreaction to supposed (Catholic or even Jewish) "works-righteousness." This position turns out to be largely a polemic against a straw man. Liberal theologians tried to reclaim human power, not in the Pelagian sense of manufacturing our own salvation, as Protestant polemic would have it, but with the nuance that what human power exists is limited and even frustrated by the conditions under which humans exist, requiring redemption and salvation that humans cannot themselves provide. Process thought shares with the liberal theology of the nineteenth century and its twentieth-century inheritors, such as Tillich and Niebuhr, the conviction that it is the existential situation of the human being that makes her evaluation of her own power incongruent with her actual ability to influence the forces at work in the world. In other words, what separates the human being from her ideal self is woven into the very fabric of existence: the inability to escape being affected and defined by outside forces, although tragically we seek to fully define ourselves. This view stands in opposition to the persistent conservative strain, strongly identified with Protestantism, that we are separated from God and rendered impotent by our objective "sinfulness," "fallenness," or similar description, a state for which a primordial human event is responsible.

Chapter 2: Jesus and Christ in Process Perspective

[1]See Karl Barth, *The Word of God and the Word of Man* (New York: Harper, 1957).
[2]See Wolfhart Pannenberg et al., *Revelation as History* (New York: Macmillan, 1968).
[3]See Wolfhart Pannenberg, *Jesus–God and Man* (Philadelphia: Westminster Press, 1968).

Chapter 3: Coming to Salvation

[1]*Process and Reality* provided the primary statements of this metaphysical understanding of the God that "...dwells upon the tender elements in the world, which slowly and in quietness operate by love; and it finds purpose in the present immediacy of a kingdom not of this world" (343). See 350 where Whitehead describes succession without loss of immediate unison. See 15–16 where Whitehead talks about the relationships of philosophy, religion, and science. On 244, Whitehead describes God as the source of valuation and order.
[2]Individuals such as Lionel Thornton (John Culp, "Modern Thought Challenges Christian Theology: Process Philosophy and Anglican Theologian Lionel Thornton," *Anglican Theological Review* 76, no. 3 [Summer 1994]: 329–51) made early theological appropriations of these metaphysical statements. Fully developed theological statements about salvation appear later with theologians such as John B. Cobb Jr. (see note 16) and Schubert Ogden (e.g., "'For Freedom Christ Has Set Us Free': The Christian Understanding of Ultimate Transformation," in *The Whirlwind in Culture*, ed. Donald W. Musser and Joseph L. Price [Bloomington, Indiana: Meyer Stone Books, 1988], 200–213).
[3]See David L. Wheeler, "Toward a Process-Relational Christian Soteriology," *Process Studies* 18, no. 2 (Summer 1989). See also Wheeler, *A Relational View of the Atonement: Prolegomenon to a Reconstruction of the Doctrine* (New York: Peter Lang, 1989).
[4]See PR 4, 36, and 157–67. For an analysis of Whitehead's understanding of experience, see Olav Bryant Smith and David Ray Griffin, "The Mystery of the Subjectivist Principle," *Process Studies* 32, no. 1 (Spring-Summer 2003): 3–36.

[5]Wheeler, "Soteriology," 106, and *Atonement*, 4.

[6]2 Corinthians 13:4; Philippians 2:6–8; 1 Corinthians 13:4.

[7]The biblical account of Hosea's patient work to recover his wife illustrates the defeat of evil without the destruction of evil. This symbolizes God's patient loving of the nation of Israel.

[8]See Wheeler, *Atonement*, 53, 103, 199, 220, 226; "Soteriology," 111; and David L. Wheeler, "Toward a Process-Relational Christian Eschatology," *Process Studies* 22, no. 4 (Winter 1993): 228, for discussions of God as the source and end of the world and thus salvation. Also see Donna Bowman, *The Divine Decision: A Process Doctrine of Election* (Louisville: Westminster John Knox Press, 2002), for another way of emphasizing God's initiative in salvation.

[9]See Bowman, *Divine Decision*, 21, 72, and 163. See also Roland Faber, "Apocalypse in God: On the Power of God in Process Eschatology," *Process Studies* 31, no. 2 (Fall-Winter 2002): 64–96.

[10]John B. Cobb Jr. (see note 16), Delwin Brown (e.g., "Notes on the Nature and Destiny of Sin, or How a Niebuhrian Process Theology of Liberation Is Possible," in *Theology, Politics, and Peace*, ed. Theodore Runyon [Maryknoll, N.Y.: Orbis Books, 1989], 159–66), and Marjorie Hewitt Suchocki (e.g., *The Fall to Violence: Original Sin in Relational Theology* [New York: Continuum Publishing Company, 1994]) provide representative process descriptions of salvation, although Daniel Day Williams (e.g., "Therapy and Salvation: The Dimension of Human Need," *Union Seminary Quarterly Review* 15:4 [May 1960], 303–17), Schubert Ogden (see note 2), and other thinkers have also made valuable contributions to the process theological development of these themes.

[11]Acts 17:22–34.

[12]This analysis of sin depends heavily on Delwin Brown, *To Set at Liberty: Christian Faith and Human Freedom* (Maryknoll, N.Y.: Orbis Books, 1981).

[13]Ibid., 66, citing Reinhold Niebuhr, *The Nature and Destiny of Man*, vol. 1, (New York: Scribner's, 1955), ch. 6–9.

[14]Brown's discussion of the kingdom of God in *To Set At Liberty: Christian Faith and Human Freedom* provides the basis for much of this development.

[15]John B. Cobb Jr. and David Ray Griffin, *Process Theology: An Introductory Exposition* (Philadelphia: Westminster, 1976), 124.

[16]Helpful works on salvation in process thought include John B. Cobb Jr., "The Meaning of Salvation," *Mid-stream* 9 (Spring 1970) ; John B. Cobb Jr. and David Ray Griffin, *Process Theology: An Introductory Exposition* (Philadelphia: WestminsterPress, 1976); John B. Cobb Jr., *God and the World* (Philadelphia: The Westminster Press, 1969); John B. Cobb Jr., *The Structure of Christian Existence* (Philadelphia: The Westminster Press, l967); John B. Cobb Jr., *A Christian Natural Theology: Based on the Thought of Alfred North Whitehead* (Philadelphia: The Westminster Press, 1965); John B. Cobb Jr., *Grace and Responsibility: A Wesleyan Theology for Today* (Nashville: Abingdon Press, 1995); and John B. Cobb Jr., "Justification by Faith," *Master Sermon Series* (August 1970).

[17]John B. Cobb Jr., "The Resurrection of the Soul: Ingersoll Lecture on Immortality delivered at the Divinity School, Harvard University, 2 March 1987," *Harvard Theological Review* 80, no. 2 (1987): 216.

[18]Cobb, "Resurrection," 226. Marjorie Suchocki argues that a concept of subjective immortality consistent with Whitehead's and Hartshorne's understanding of existence in God after death describes a new type of existence. See Marjorie Hewitt Suchocki, "Charles Hartshorne and Subjective Immorality," *Process Studies* 21, no. 2 (Summer 1992): 118–22.

[19]Cobb, "Meaning of Salvation," 152–54. For similar understanding, see Schubert M. Ogden, *The Reality of God and Other Essays* (San Francisco: Harper & Row, 1977), 224–26.

[20]RM 83. See also AI 18, 25.

[21]For Whitehead's careful reflection on this question, see "Immortality," in Alfred North Whitehead, *His Reflections on Man and Nature*, selected by Ruth Nanda Anshen (New York: Harper and Brothers Publishers, 1961), 164.

Chapter 4: Religious Pluralism

[1]For examples of Jewish, Muslim, and Buddhist process pluralism, respectively, see Sandra B. Lubarsky, *Tolerance and Transformation: Jewish Approaches to Religious Pluralism*

(Cincinnati: Hebrew Union College Press, 1990); Sir Mohammad Iqbal, *The Reconstruction of Religious Thought in Islam* (London: Oxford University Press, 1934); and Ryusei Takeda, "Mutual Transformation of Pure Land Buddhism and Christianity: Methodology and Possibilities in the Light of Shinran's Doctrine," *Bulletin of the Nanzan Institute for Religion and Culture* 22 (Spring 1998), 6–40.

²John Hick, *A Christian Theology of Religions: The Rainbow of Faiths* (Louisville: Westminster John Knox Press, 1995), 24.

³Ibid., 125.

⁴Alan Race introduced this typology of exclusivism, inclusivism, and pluralism in *Christians and Religious Pluralism: Patterns in Christian Theology of Religions* (Maryknoll, N.Y.: Orbis, 1983).

⁵John Hick, *Philosophy of Religion*, 3d ed. (Englewood Cliffs, N. J.: Prentice-Hall, 1983), 117–18.

⁶Paul F. Knitter, *No Other Name? A Critical Survey of Christian Attitudes Toward the World Religions* (Maryknoll, N.Y.: Orbis, 1985), 121, 125, 116–17, 140.

⁷Mark S. Heim, *Salvations: Truth and Difference in Religion* (Maryknoll, N.Y.: Orbis, 1995), 72.

⁸John Hick, "The Non-Absoluteness of Christianity," in *The Myth of Christian Uniqueness: Toward a Pluralistic Theology of Religions*, ed. John Hick and Paul F. Knitter (Maryknoll, N.Y.: Orbis, 1987), 16–36, at 18.

⁹Hick, *Christian Theology*, 123.

¹⁰Ibid., 13.

¹¹I develop this point in David Ray Griffin, *Religion and Scientific Naturalism: Overcoming the Conflicts* (Albany: State University of New York Press, 2000).

¹²Hick, *Christian Theology*, 53.

¹³Knitter, *No Other Name*, 25.

¹⁴Smith, "Idolatry in Comparative Perspective," in *Myth of Christian Uniqueness*, ed. Hick and Knitter, 59.

¹⁵Hick, *Christian Theology*, 15.

¹⁶John B. Cobb Jr., *Christ in a Pluralistic Age* (Philadelphia: Westminster, 1975), 27, 163.

¹⁷Hick, *Christian Theology*, 16–18.

¹⁸John B. Cobb Jr., in Leonard Swidler, John B. Cobb Jr., Paul F. Knitter, and Monica K. Hellwig, *Death or Dialogue? From the Age of Monologue to the Age of Dialogue* (Philadelphia: Trinity Press; London: SCM Press, 1990), 1–18, at 13.

¹⁹David Lochhead, *The Dialogical Imperative: A Christian Reflection on Interfaith Encounter* (Maryknoll, N.Y.: Orbis, 1988).

²⁰Paul F. Knitter, "Interreligious Dialogue: What? Why? How?" in *Death or Dialogue*, ed. Swidler et al., 27.

²¹Knitter, *No Other Name*, 36; Knitter, *Jesus and the Other Names: Christian Mission and Global Responsibility* (Maryknoll, N.Y.: Orbis, 1996), 29, 31.

²²Race, *Christians and Religious Pluralism*, 90, 78.

²³Langdon Gilkey, "Plurality and Its Theological Implications," in *Myth of Christian Uniqueness*, ed. Hick and Knitter, 44–46.

²⁴John B. Cobb Jr., *Beyond Dialogue: Toward a Mutual Transformation of Buddhism and Christianity* (Philadelphia: Fortress Press, 1982), 13 .

²⁵When Hick's *Christian Theology* was published in 1995, a bibliography of critiques of his position filled almost five pages.

²⁶Kevin Meeker and Philip L. Quinn, "Introduction: The Philosophical Challenge of Religious Diversity," in *The Philosophical Challenge of Religious Diversity*, ed. Quinn and Meeker (New York: Oxford University Press, 2000), , 3.

²⁷Heim, *Salvations*, 8, 42.

²⁸Caroline Franks Davis, *The Evidential Force of Religious Experience* (Oxford: Clarendon Press, 1989), 167.

²⁹Cobb, *Beyond Dialogue*, 96.

³⁰John Hick, *An Interpretation of Religion* (New Haven: Yale University Press, 1989), 249.

³¹Davis, *Evidential Force*, 172–73.

³²Hick, *Interpretation of Religion*, 245.

³³Ibid., 239.
³⁴Ibid., 300; emphasis added.
³⁵Ibid., 301.
³⁶For negative critiques of Hick's position, see Heim, *Salvations*; Quinn and Meeker, eds., *The Philosophical Challenge of Religious Diversity*; and Gavin D'Costa, ed., *Christian Uniqueness Reconsidered: The Myth of a Pluralistic Theology of Religions* (Maryknoll, N.Y.: Orbis, 1990).
³⁷Hick, *Interpretation of Religion*, 300.
³⁸Heim, *Salvations*, 125. The criticism that Hick's position is "not really pluralistic" is somewhat misleading, because Hick does affirm pluralism as defined in the first section. But Hick's position, by virtue of affirming that all religions are oriented to an identical ultimate and aim at an identical salvation, can be called "identist pluralism."
³⁹Ibid., 23.
⁴⁰Ibid., 129–30.
⁴¹Ibid., 16, 87, 88, 89, 90, 101, 103, 109, 125, 129, 130, 228.
⁴²Ibid., 226.
⁴³This is suggested by the fact that Paul J. Griffiths' (rave) review of the book is titled "Beyond Pluralism" (*First Things*, [January 1996]: 50–52).
⁴⁴Gavin D'Costa, having criticized the pluralist project as defined in Hick and Knitter's *Myth of Christian Uniqueness,* questions "whether 'pluralistic theology' is an appropriate or even adequate interpretation of religious plurality" (*Christian Uniqueness Reconsidered*, x–xi). See also Paul Griffiths' review in the previous note.
⁴⁵Although it has widely been assumed that the Bible teaches creation out of nothing, this doctrine did not arise until near the end of the second century of Christian thought. See David Ray Griffin, "Creation Out of Nothing, Creation Out of Chaos, and the Problem of Evil," in *Encountering Evil: Live Options in Theodicy*, ed. Stephen T. Davis, new ed. (Louisville: Westminster John Knox Press, 2001), 108–25.
⁴⁶See, besides the essay mentioned in the previous note, David Ray Griffin, *God, Power, and Evil: A Process Theodicy* (Philadelphia: Westminster Press, 1976 [reprinted with a new preface, Lanham, Md.: University Press of America, 1991]), and Griffin, *Evil Revisited: Responses and Reconsiderations* (Albany: State University of New York Press, 1991).
⁴⁷Marjorie Hewitt Suchocki, *Divinity and Diversity: A Christian Affirmation of Religious Pluralism* (Nashville: Abingdon Press, 2003), 29–35.
⁴⁸Ibid., 86.
⁴⁹See note 38 above.
⁵⁰Cobb, *Death or Dialogue*, 116; *Beyond Dialogue*, 124–28; *Transforming Christianity and the World: A Way beyond Absolutism and Relativism*, ed. Paul F. Knitter (Maryknoll: Orbis, 1999), 184–85 .
⁵¹Cobb, *Beyond Dialogue*, 43.
⁵²Cobb, *Transforming Christianity*, 79.
⁵³Cobb, *Death or Dialogue*, DOD 6.
⁵⁴Cobb, *Transforming Christianity*, 186.
⁵⁵Ibid., 74; Cobb, *Death or Dialogue*, 120.
⁵⁶Cobb, *Death or Dialogue*, 14.
⁵⁷Cobb, *Transforming Christianity*, 140.
⁵⁸Ibid., 86–87.
⁵⁹Race, *Christians and Religious Pluralism*, 98.
⁶⁰Cobb, *Transforming Christianity*, 137.

Chapter 5: The Dialogue between Jews and Christians

¹*Nostra Aetate* can be found in *The Documents of Vatican II*, ed. Walter M. Abbott, S. J. (New York: Guild Press, 1966), 660–68. A group of Jewish scholars produced *Christianity in Jewish Terms*, ed. Tikva Frymer-Kensky, David Novak, Peter Ochs, David Fox Sandmel, and Michael A. Signer (Boulder: Westview Press, 2000), in which both Jewish and Christian scholars discuss a wide range of theological topics.
²Among the many writers in this group, students of process theology would be particularly interested in: Michael E. Lodahl, *Shekhinah/Spirit: Divine Spirit in Jewish and Christian Religion* (New York: Paulist Press, 1992); Bernard J. Lee, S.M., *The Galilean Jewishness of Jesus* (New York: Paulist Press, 1988); Sandra B. Lubarksy and David Ray Griffin, eds., *Jewish Theology and Process Thought* (Albany: SUNY Press, 1996); and Clark M. Williamson, *A Guest*

in the House of Israel (Louisville: Westminster/John Knox Press, 1993) and Williamson, *Way of Blessing, Way of Life: A Christian Theology* (St. Louis: Chalice Press, 1999).

[3]Mordecai Kaplan, *Communings of the Spirit: The Journals of Mordecai M. Kaplan,* Vol. I 1913–1934, ed. Mel Scult (Detroit: Wayne State University Press and The Reconstructionist Press, 2001), 376.

[4]Ibid., 377.

[5]Ibid., 459.

[6]Ibid., 462.

[7]Ibid., 500.

[8]Robert M. Seltzer, "Kaplan and Jewish Modernity," in *The American Judaism of Mordecai M. Kaplan,* ed. Emanuel S. Goldsmith, Mel Scult, and Robert M. Seltzer (New York and London: New York University Press, 1990), 11.

[9]Max Kadushin, *Organic Thinking: A Study in Rabbinic Thought* (New York: Bloch, 1938).

[10]Milton Steinberg, "The Theological Issue of the Hour," *Proceedings of Rabbinical Assembly,* 1949.

[11]William Kaufman, *The Evolving God in Jewish Process Theology* (Lampeter, Wales: Edwin Mellen Press, 1997) and *The Case for God* (St. Louis: Chalice Press, 1991).

[12]Emanuel S. Goldsmith, "Kaplan and Henry Nelson Wieman," in *The American Judaism of Mordecai Kaplan,* 197–220.

[13]Lori Krafte-Jacobs, "The 'Essence' of Judaism: A Process-Relational Critique," in *Jewish Theology and Process Thought,* 75–88.

[14]Quoted in Simon Noveck, "Kaplan and Milton Steinberg," in *The American Judaism of Mordecai M. Kaplan,* 145.

[15]Ibid., 165.

[16]Sandra B. Lubarsky, "Judaism and Process Thought," in *Jewish Theology and Process Thought,* 55.

[17]See particularly Cobb's *Christ in a Pluralistic Age* (Philadelphia: Westminster Press, 1975) for a treatment of Christ as the incarnation of the creative, transformative Logos.

[18]Henry N. Wieman, *The Source of Human Good* (Carbondale, Ill.: Southern Illinois University Press, 1946).

[19]Kaplan, quoted in Emanuel S. Goldsmith, "Kaplan and Henry Nelson Wieman," in *The American Judaism of Mordecai M. Kaplan,* 208–9.

[20]Goldsmith, "Kaplan and Wieman," 215.

[21]Ibid.

[22]Nahum Ward, "Living Torah," in *Jewish Theology and Process Thought,* 250.

[23]Ibid., 251.

[24]See, e.g., Lawrence A. Englander, "Revelation from a Limited God: A Re-evaluation of Torah as Blueprint," *Journal of Reform Judaism* (Spring 1988): 65–75.

[25]Edward Farley, *Deep Symbols* (Valley Forge: Trinity Press International, 1996), 82.

[26]Abraham Joshua Heschel, quoted in Edward K. Kaplan and Samuel H. Dresner, *Abraham Joshua Heschel: Prophetic Witness* (New Haven: Yale University Press, 1998), 167. Heschel's dissertation, *Das Prophetische Bewusstsein,* was published by the University of Berlin in 1935, which by then was, ironically, under Nazi control.

[27]Ibid., 168.

[28]Ibid.

[39]Ibid., 261.

[30]Ibid., 262.

[31]Parmenides founded the Eleactic school of philosophy in the sixth century B.C.E. that taught the unity of all things and the impossibility of change.

[32]See S. Daniel Breslauer's "Modernizing Biblical Religion: Abraham Heschel and Charles Hartshorne," *Encounter* 38, no. 4 (Autumn 1997): 337–46.

[33]Kaufman, *The Evolving God,* 72.

[34]Harold Schulweis, "Charles Hartshorne and the Defenders of Heschel," *Judaism* 24 (Jan. 1975): 59.

[35]Ibid., 61. Schulweis' primary opposition here is to Hartshorne.

[36]Ibid. Schulweis here quotes AI 345.

[37]Ibid., 62. Jacob J. Staub concurs with Schulweis in his otherwise sympathetic treatment of process theology; see Staub, "Kaplan and Process Theology," in *The American Judaism of Mordecai M. Kaplan,* 291.

[38]See, e.g., discussions of intrinsic value in John B. Cobb Jr. and Charles Birch, *The Liberation of Life* (Cambridge: Cambridge University Press, 1981), 152–68, 216–17; and in Jay B. McDaniel, *Earth, Sky, Gods & Mortals* (Mystic, Conn.: Twenty-Third Publications, 1990), 66–67, 91–92, 160.

[39]See Martin Buber, *On Zion: The History of an Idea*, trans. Stanley Godman (New York: Schocken Books, 1973), xix; Carol Johnston, *And the Leaves of the Tree Are for the Healing of the Nations* (Louisville: Presbyterian Church, USA: Office of Environmental Justice, 1997); and Clark Williamson, *Way of Blessing*, 142–48.

[40]From the Avoth of Rabbi Natan, text B, as quoted in Jacob Neusner, *A Life of Rabban Yohanan ben Zakkai* (Leiden: E. J. Brill, 1962), 134.

[41]John Merkle, ed., *Faith Transformed: Christian Encounters with Jews and Judaism* (Collegeville: The Liturgical Press, 2003).

[42]For an analysis of this structural supersessionism, see R. Kendall Soulen, *The God of Israel and Christian Theology* (Minneapolis: Fortress Press, 1996).

[43]Jules Isaac coined the term "teaching of contempt" in his *The Teaching of Contempt* (New York: Holt, Rinehart & Winston, 1964).

[44]Schubert M. Ogden, *Christ Without Myth* (New York: Harper & Brothers, 1961), 156.

[45]Lee, *The Galilean Jewishness of Jesus*.

[46]Lodahl, *Shekhinah/Spirit*.

[47]Pamela Payne, *A Christic World's Unfolding: A Feminist Post-Shoah Christological Vision*. Ph.D. Dissertation, Vanderbilt University, 2003.

[48]Clark M. Williamson, *A Guest in the House of Israel: Post-Holocaust Church Theology* (Louisville: Westminster/John Knox Press, 1993; *Way of Blessing, Way of Life: A Christian Theology* (St. Louis: Chalice Press, 1999); *Has God Rejected His People? Anti-Judaism in the Christian Church* (Nashville: Abingdon Press, 1982); *When Jews and Christians Meet* (St. Louis: CBP Press, 1989); *Interpreting Difficult Texts: Anti-Judaism and Christian Preaching*, with Ronald J. Allen (Philadelphia: Trinity Press International, 1989); and Clark M. Williamson, ed., *A Mutual Witness: Toward Critical Solidarity between Jews and Christians* (St. Louis: Chalice Press, 1992).

Chapter 6: Scripture and Revelation

[1]H. Richard Niebuhr, *The Meaning of Revelation* (New York: Macmillian, 1941), 93; quotation from RM 32.

[2]Marjorie Hewitt Suchocki, *God-Christ-Church: A Practical Guide to Process Theology* (New York: Crossroad, 1982), 49–52.

[3]Ibid., 51–52.

[4]Ibid., 54.

[5]Schubert M. Ogden, *The Reality of God and Other Essays* (New York: Harper and Row, 1963), 180.

[6]Ibid., 181–83.

[7]Ibid., 184.

[8]David Ray Griffin, *A Process Christology* (Philadelphia: Westminster, 1973), 219–20, citing Schubert M. Ogden, "Bultmann's Project of Demythologizing and the Problem of Theology and Philosophy," *Journal of Religion* 37 (1957): 169.

[9]Ibid., 219.

[10]Ibid., 220–21; italics original.

[11]Ogden, *The Reality of God*, 185.

[12]See, e.g., Schubert M. Ogden, *On Theology* (San Francisco: Harper and Row, 1986), 22ff.

[13]John B. Cobb Jr., "Trajectories and Historic Routes," *Semeia* 24 (1982), 89–98, and *Beyond Dialogue: Toward a Mutual Transformation of Christianity and Buddhism* (Philadelphia: Fortress Press, 1982); Benjamin A. Reist, *Processive Revelation* (Louisville: Westminster/John Knox Press, 1992), 24; Delwin Brown, "Struggle Toward Daybreak: On the Nature of Authority in Theology," *The Journal of Religion* 65 (January 1985).

[14]See David H. Kelsey, "The Theological Use of Scripture in Process Hermeneutics," *Process Studies* 13 (1983): 184, and the reply by David J. Lull, "What Is 'Process Hermeneutics'?" *Process Studies* 13 (1983): 190.

[15]Russell Pregeant, *Christology Beyond Dogma: Matthew's Christ in Process Hermeneutic* (Philadelphia: Fortress Press, 1978), 33–34.

[16]Lyman Lundeen, *Risk and Rhetoric in Religion: Whitehead's Theory of Language and the Discourse of Faith* (Philadelphia: Fortress Press, 1972), 39.

[17]Griffin, *A Process Christology*, 151–67.

[18]Schubert M. Ogden, *The Point of Christology* (Dallas: Southern Methodist University Press, 1992), 51–63.

[19]Schubert M. Ogden, *Christ without Myth* (New York: Harper and Brothers, 1961), 146–64; Ogden, *The Point of Christology*, 94f.

[20]See Kelsey, "Theological Use of Scripture," 182–83.

[21]Robert K. Gnuse, *The Old Testament and Process Theology* (St. Louis: Chalice Press, 2000).

[22]J. Gerald Janzen, "Metaphor and Reality in Hosea 11," *Semeia* 24 (1982): 7–44.

[23]Terence Fretheim, *The Suffering God* (Philadelphia: Fortress Press, 1984).

[24]Gnuse, *Old Testament and Process*, 111–123.

[25]Ronald Farmer, *Beyond the Impasse: The Promise of a Process Hermeneutic* (Macon, Georgia: Mercer University Press, 1997). An earlier full-length treatment of process hermeneutic was Barry Woodbridge's Claremont dissertation, "The Role of the Text and Emergent Possibilities in the Interpretation of Christian Tradition: A Process Hermeneutic in Response to the German Hermeneutical Discussion." Briefer treatments are found in William A. Beardslee, "Whitehead and Hermeneutic," *Journal of the American Academy of Religion* 47, no. 1 (March 1979): 31–37 and Pregeant, *Christology Beyond Dogma.*

[26]William A. Beardslee, "Whitehead and Hermeneutic," *Journal of the American Academy of Religion* 47, no. 1 (March 1979): 32.

[27]Ibid., 34.

[28]PR 16; see Pregeant, *Christology Beyond Dogma*, and Farmer, *Beyond the Impasse*, 105f.; see also Pregeant, "Where Is the Meaning? Metaphysical Criticism and the Problem of Indeterminacy," *The Journal of Religion* 63, no. 2 (1983): 107–24.

[29]Farmer, *Beyond the Impasse*, 161.

[30]Pregeant, *Christology Beyond Dogma*, 126.

[31]David J. Lull, "The Spirit and the Creative Transformation of Human Existence," *Journal of the American Academy of Religion* 47, No. 1 (March, 1979): 46; see also Lull, *The Spirit in Galatia: Paul's Interpretation of Pneuma as Divine Power* (Chico, California: Scholars Press, 1980).

[32]Catherine Keller, *Apocalypse Now and Then: A Feminist Guide to the End of the World* (Boston: Beacon, 1996), esp. 274.

[33]Gnuse, *Old Testament and Process*, 58–63, 141–70.

[34]Lewis S. Ford, *The Lure of God: A Biblical Background for Process Theism* (Philadelphia: Fortress Press, 1978), 127–35.

[35]Cobb, "Trajectories and Historic Routes."

[36]Gnuse, *Old Testament and Process*, 58–59.

[37]This spirit of inclusive progressivism pervades much of the work of process-oriented biblical scholars. William A. Beardslee particularly exemplified this spirit. Beardslee should be credited with providing the most important early impetus to relate process thought to biblical studies, as well as acknowledged for guiding the process hermeneutic movement to maturity. Early on, in 1972, in *A House for Hope: A Study in Process and Biblical Thought*, he brought biblical apocalypticism into creative conversation with Whitehead to address important questions in contemporary theological discourse. And all of his work has been characterized by fair-mindedness and a generous attempt to locate what is valuable in a variety of competing perspectives. It is therefore entirely fitting that the present essay should be dedicated to his memory.

Chapter 7: Preaching as Conversation among Proposals

[1]For surveys of the relationships of theological viewpoints and sermons, see Donald K. McKim, *The Bible in Theology and Preaching* (Eugene: Wipf and Stock Publishers, 1999 [1994]); Ronald J. Allen, *Preaching as Believing: The Sermon as Theological Reflection* (Louisville: Westminster John Knox Press, 2002), 129–41.

[2]Whitehead referred to "proposals" as "propositions" (see n. 4 below). I join William A. Beardslee et al., *Biblical Preaching on the Death of Jesus* (Nashville: Abingdon Press, 1989), 60–64, in using the language of "proposal" for "propositions." Elsewhere, I have spoken of proposals as "invitations": Clark M. Williamson and Ronald J. Allen, *Adventures of the Spirit: A*

Guide to Worship from the Perspective of Process Theology (Lanham, Md.: University Press of America, 1997), 137–58.
[3]The most comprehensive account of all phases of the sermon from a process-relational perspective is Marjorie Suchocki, *The Whispered Word* (St. Louis: Chalice Press, 1999).
[4]Clark M. Williamson, "Preaching the Easter Faith," *Encounter* 37 (1976): 43–44. For a lyrical commentary on God offering invitations (propositions, lures) to the world, see Suchocki, *The Whispered Word,* 1–12.
[5]Susanne K. Langer, *Problems in Art* (New York: Charles Scribner's Sons, 1957), 15.
[6]Susanne K. Langer, *Philosophical Sketches* (Baltimore: Johns Hopkins University Press, 1962), 89.
[7]Cited in Bernard Meland, *Fallible Forms and Symbols* (Philadelphia: Fortress Press, 1976), 60.
[8]Ibid., 28.
[9]Ibid., 187.
[10]Beardslee et al., *Biblical Teaching,* 61.
[11]Ibid., 24.
[12]Ibid., 38–49.
[13]PR 193. "A judgment is the critique of a lure for feeling."
[14]Though Suchocki does not dwell on the notion of conversation to describe preaching, the conversational spirit pervades her *The Whispered Word,* esp. 39–53.
[15]The preacher does not primarily aim to initiate the congregation into the technical vocabulary of process-relational conceptuality (although that may be helpful from time to time). The preacher primarily wants to help the community deepen its awareness of (and response to) God's presence and movement.
[16]On honoring otherness in all phases of preaching, see John S. McClure, *Otherwise Preaching: A Postmodern Ethic for Homiletics* (St. Louis: Chalice Press, 2002). Cf. Ronald J. Allen, "Preaching and the Other," *Worship* 76 (2002): 211–24; id., "Preaching and Postmodernism," *Interpretation* 55 (2001): 34–48.
[17]The idea of preaching having conversational qualities is as old as the Bible. The term "homily" translates the Greek *homileo*–"conversation." The early church used *homileo* (and cognates) for "the sermon." The root of *homileo* is associated with companionship. See W. Bauer, W.F. Arndt, F.W. Gingrich, and F.W. Danker, *A Greek English Lexicon of the New Testament and Other Early Christian Literature* (Chicago: University of Chicago Press, 1961), 565; cf. G.W.H. Lampe, editor, *A Patristic Greek Lexicon* (Oxford: The Clarendon Press, 1961), 951–52. The homilist is a companion with the congregation in identifying divine lures. For the sermon as conversation as a motif in contemporary preaching, see the bibliography in Ronald J. Allen, *Interpreting the Gospel: An Introduction to Preaching* (St. Louis: Chalice Press, 1998), 299, n. 2.
[18]David Tracy, *Plurality and Ambiguity* (San Francisco: Harper and Row Publishers, 1987), 20, emphasis added. Cf. Robert M. Grant and David Tracy, *A Short History of the Interpretation of the Bible,* 2nd edition (Philadelphia: Fortress Press, 1996), 153–87, esp. 169–74.
[19]Tracy, *Plurality and Ambiguity,* 18. Cf. Hans-Georg Gadamer, *Truth and Method,* trans. Garret Barden and John Cumming (New York: Crossroad, 1982), 325–41, 347–51; and Clark M. Williamson, "Process Hermeneutics and Christianity's Post-Holocaust Interpretation of Itself," *Process Studies* 12 (1982): 80.
[20]Tracy, *Plurality and Ambiguity,* 19.
[21]Ibid., 20.
[22]Ibid., 19.
[23]For an exquisite discussion of the relationship of the various voices, see Suchocki, *The Whispered Word,* 24–25.
[24]Cf. Lyman Lundeen, *Risk and Rhetoric in Religion* (Philadelphia: Fortress Press, 1972), 226ff.
[25]Beardslee et al., *Biblical Preaching,* 30ff.
[26]For a process-relational approach to the Bible, see Ronald L. Farmer, *Beyond the Impasse: The Promise of Process Hermeneutic* (Macon, Ga.: Mercer University Press, 1997). Cf. Robert K. Gnuse, *The Old Testament and Process Theology* (St. Louis: Chalice Press, 2001); Williamson and Allen, *Adventures of the Spirit,* 113–35; cf. Clark M. Williamson, "The Authority of Scripture after the Shoah" in *Faith and Creativity,* ed. George Nordgulen and George Shields (St. Louis: CBP Press, 1987), 135–38; John B. Cobb Jr., "The Authority of the Bible" in *Hermeneutics and*

the Worldliness of Faith, ed. Charles Courtney, Olin Ivey, and Gordon Michaelson, *The Drew Gateway* 45 (1974–75): 200.

[27]A sermon usually develops around one biblical passage or two. Preachers can also prepare sermons that focus on biblical themes, that is, ideas that develop across several passages or books. See Ronald J. Allen, *Wholly Scripture: Preaching Themes from the Bible* (St. Louis: Chalice Press, 2004).

[28]Delwin Brown, *Boundaries of Our Habitations: Tradition and Theological Construction* (Albany: State University of New York Press, 1994). Indeed, only a small part of the past is known to us in clear and articulate documents or concise events with singular meanings. Much of Christian tradition is available to us as a vague, inarticulate, but powerful fabric of feeling.

[29]For a practical pattern for such reflection, see Suchocki, *The Whispered Word,* 39–53.

[30]Reliable reference works (e.g., dictionaries of the Bible, church history, theology, worship, and ethics) often assist the preacher in locating conversation partners on particular issues. Suchocki offers a practical guide in her *The Whispered Word,* 45–46.

[31]Clark M. Williamson, *Way of Blessing, Way of Life: A Christian Theology* (St. Louis: Chalice Press, 1999), 32–38; cf. Suchocki, *The Whispered Word,* 41ff.

[32]For guides to helping describe the culture of a congregation, see Nora Tubbs Tisdale, *Preaching as Local Theology and Folk Art,* Fortress Guides to Preaching (Minneapolis: Fortress Press, 1997), and Stephen Farris, *Preaching that Matters: The Bible and Our Lives* (Louisville: Westminster John Knox Press, 1998), 25–38.

[33]For the relationship between the one and the many in the congregation, see Suchocki, *The Whispered Word,* 28–37. In a sense, each listener hears a different sermon. God works with each congregant to optimize the value of the sermon that she or he hears. God also works with the community as community to intensify their sense of relatedness with one another. Cf. Beardslee et al., 64–72.

[34]For different expressions of diversity in a local congregation, see James R. Neiman and Thomas G. Rogers, *Preaching to Every Pew* (Minneapolis: Fortress Press, 2001), as well as Joseph R. Jeter Jr. and Ronald J. Allen, *One Gospel, Many Ears: Preaching and Different Listeners in the Congregation* (St. Louis: Chalice Press, 2002).

[35]John S. McClure proposes a feed-forward process in which the preacher meets weekly with members of the community to discuss the biblical text and other resources for the upcoming sermon in his *The Round Table Pulpit: Where Leadership and Preaching Meet* (Nashville: Abingdon Press, 1995).

[36]On the importance of explicitly naming one's theological perspective, see Suchocki, *The Whispered Word,* 51–52.

[37]Beardslee et al. use the language of the "Spirit" to speak of the aims preaching serves (preaching serves the Spirit) and its animation (by the Spirit) (24ff).

[38]Meland, *Fallible Forms and Symbols,* 43; cf. xiii, 48, 174–75.

[39]Ibid., xiv and 150ff. Cf. Bernard Meland, *Faith and Culture* (New York: Oxford University Press, 1962), 212ff. See further, Stephen T. Franklin's comments on religious language in his *Speaking from the Depths* (Grand Rapids: Wm. B. Eerdmans, 1990), 358.

[40]On the importance of naming the presence of the Divine, see Mary Catherine Hilkert, *Naming Grace: Preaching and the Sacramental Imagination* (New York: Continuum, 1997).

[41]On judgment, see PR 192ff.

[42]Meland, *Fallible Forms and Symbols,* 32–33. Reason is not a single faculty among many but is the activity involving the total organism (128ff).

[43]Bernard Lee proposes conversation as a way to describe preaching. However, Father Lee calls for preacher and congregation to create the sermon together on the spot, in the sanctuary, during the moment of preaching: Bernard Lee, "Shared Homily: Conversation that Puts Communities at Risk," in *Alternative Futures for Worship: The Eucharist,* ed. Bernard Lee (Collegeville: The Liturgical Press, 1987), vol. 3, 157ff.

[44]Reuel Howe, *Partners in Preaching* (New York: Seabury Press, 1967), 47.

[45]Ibid., 53.

[46]For practical suggestions along this line, see ibid., 57–83.

[47]Beardslee et al. note that making the community aware of conflicts among various proposals (or propositions) increases the sense of the listener's freedom (38–49).

[48]Fred B. Craddock, *As One Without Authority: Revised and with New Sermons* (St. Louis: Chalice Press, 2001 [1971]), 114, Craddock's emphasis.

[49]Meland, *Fallible Forms and Symbols,* 57. For imagination in preaching, see especially Paul Scott Wilson, *The Imagination of the Heart* (Nashville: Abingdon Press, 1988), and Thomas H. Troeger, *Imagining a Sermon* (Nashville; Abingdon Press, 1990).

[50]David G. Buttrick, *Homiletic* (Philadelphia: Fortress Press, 1987), 310ff.

[51]Nathaniel Lawrence, *Whitehead's Philosophical Development* (Berkeley: University of California Press, 1956), xx, cited in Lundeen, *Risk and Rhetoric in Religion,* 24.

[52]E.g., Thomas G. Long, *Preaching and the Literary Forms of the Bible* (Philadelphia: Fortress Press, 1989). Cf. Buttrick, *Homiletic,* 333ff.

[53]Craddock, *As One Without Authority,* 99–100.

[54]Ibid., 98–99.

[55]For an analogy from the world of teaching, see Mary Elizabeth Moore, "Narrative Teaching: An Organic Methodology," *Process Studies* 17 (1988): 253ff.; id., *Teaching from the Heart* (Minneapolis: Fortress Press, 1991), 131–62

[56]For a catalogue of approaches to the movement of sermons, see Ronald J. Allen, ed., *Patterns of Preaching: A Sermon Sampler* (St. Louis: Chalice Press, 1998).

[57]On "letting the sermon go" into the congregation, and, indeed, into the world, see Suchocki, *The Whispered Word,* 55ff.

[58]MT 45. Cf. PR 403 and Lundeen, *Risk and Rhetoric in Religion,* 49–51. For fuller discussion of orality and aurality see Walter J. Ong, *The Presence of the Word* (New Haven: Yale University Press, 1967); id., *Orality and Literacy* (New York: Methuen Press, 1982).

[59]Franklin, *Speaking from the Depths,* 237, 234–41, 379.

[60]Meland, *Fallible Forms and Symbols,* 30. Meland's emphasis.

[61]Ibid.

[62]Preachers are frequently uneasy with silence. They are accustomed to our noisy culture. Preachers are often afraid of loss of control that threatens during silence. Preachers are anxious that the community's attention may wander. To alleviate anxieties, preachers often bypass silence. Preachers who seek to incorporate silence into preaching may need to school themselves and the community on the revelatory power of silence.

[63]Suchocki gives the most eloquent statement I have seen regarding the divine presence in the sermon in *The Whispered Word,* 1–12, 27–35, 67–68. For a significant discussion of a similar point from the standpoint of another discipline, see Jay McDaniel, "The Role of God in Religious Education," *Religious Education* 29 (1984): 414ff.

[64]Suchocki, *The Whispered Word,* 59–60.

Chapter 8: Process Theology and the Healing Adventure

[1]For discussions of the current research, see Jeff Levin, *God, Faith, and Health* (New York: John Wiley and Sons, 2001); Harold Koenig, *Is Religion Good for Your Health?* (New York: Haworth Pastoral Press, 1997); Harold Koenig, *The Healing Power of Faith* (New York: Simon and Schuster, 1999).

[2]I purposely use the term "associated" in referring to the relationship between spiritual practices, religious commitment, and physical well-being. Health and illness result from many factors rather than one factor. From a scientific as well as metaphysical viewpoint, we can affirm the positive benefits of religious practices, while also affirming that other factors condition health and illness.

[3]Koenig, *The Healing Power of Faith,* 34–40, 105–12.

[4]For a comprehensive discussion of the research on intercessory prayer as well as the metaphysics of prayer, see Larry Dossey, *Healing Words* (San Francisco: HarperSanFrancisco, 1993).

[5]Herbert Benson, *Timeless Healing* (New York: Scribners, 1996).

[6]For an extended discussion on the healing ministry of Jesus from a process-relational perspective, see Bruce Epperly, *God's Touch: Faith, Wholeness, and the Healing Miracles of Jesus* (Louisville: Westminster John Knox Press, 2001).

[7]George Engel, "The Need for a New Medical Model: A Challenge for Biomedicine," *Science* 196, no. 4286 (April 8, 1977): 129.

[8]Ibid., 130.

[9]For a more comprehensive discussion of the role of process-relational thought in the transformation of medicine, see Bruce Epperly, *At the Edges of Life* (St. Louis: Chalice Press, 1992), 67–136.

[10]Quoted in M. Todd, "The Challenge of Medicine: Prevention of Illness," in *Inner Balance: The Power of Holistic Healing*, ed. E.M. Goldway (Englewood Cliffs, N.J., 1979), 2.

[11]Ibid., 3.

[12]Gary Gunderson, *Deeply Woven Roots* (Minneapolis: Fortress Press, 1997).

Chapter 9: The Creative Adventure of Pastoral Counseling

[1]While I will be referring to pastoral counseling in this essay, all the points have implicit relevance for the broader field of pastoral care.

[2]Cf. David E. Roy, *Toward a Process Psychotherapy: A Model of Integration* (Fresno, Calif.: Adobe Creations Press, 2000), 93, and PR 7.

[3]In this essay, the terms *psychotherapy* and *therapy* are used interchangeably with *pastoral counseling*. Psychotherapy literally means "psyche healing." *Psyche*, of course, is the Greek word we translate as soul.

[4]The *subjective form* of a given moment includes *how* the person is experiencing the content of that moment. Often, this is an emotion.

[5]For more information, see Roy, *Toward a Process Psychology*, 97.

[6]Roy, "The Clinical Use of Whitehead's Anthropology," *Process Studies* 29, no.1 (2000): 124–150.

[7]See source in previous note for further clarification at this point.

[8]See Roy, *Toward a Process Psychology*, chapter 3 for a summary of Whitehead's theory of perception.

[9]This is supported by watching how infants learn to perceive, struggling to put together patches of color into meaningful wholes. Learning to perceive even what adults consider to be simple objects takes a great deal of time, effort, and learning.

[10]Roy, *Toward a Process Psychology*, 160–66.

[11]Roy, "The Clinical Use of Whitehead's Anthropology," 142–46.

[12]The name of this phase was inspired by the work of John B. Cobb Jr., in particular his book, *The Structure of Christian Existence* (Philadelphia: Westminster Press, 1967).

[13]"Discern: *v.t.* 1. to perceive by the sight or some other sense or by the intellect; see, recognize, or apprehend clearly. 2. to distinguish mentally; recognize as distinct or different; discriminate. *v.i.* 3. to distinguish or discriminate. L *discernere* to separate" (*Webster's Encyclopedic Unabridged Dictionary of the English Language* [New York: Gramercy Books, 1989]).

[14]Alfred North Whitehead, *Symbolism, Its Meaning and Effect* (New York: Macmillan, 1927), 23.

[15]In addition to PR, see also discussion in Whitehead's *Symbolism*.

[16]This is virtually the same dynamic as occurs in the initial mode of perception, causal efficacy.

[17]David Ray Griffin, private communication.

[18]Roy, "The Clinical Use of Whitehead's Anthropology," 128–30.

[19]Ibid., 137–38.

[20]Ibid., 134–35.

[21]Ibid., 135–37.

[22]More than 300 practitioners from these and related fields attended the six-day "Silver Anniversary International Whitehead Conference: Process Thought and the Common Good" in Claremont, Calif., from Aug. 4–9, 1998. There were more than 40 different sections with more than 250 presentations.

Chapter 10: Process Perspectives on Sexuality, Love, and Marriage

[1]Due to the limitations of length for this essay, I will only consider process theologians published in the U.S. and Great Britain.

[2]For a critique of the association of *Eros* with sexuality, see Rita Nakashima Brock, *Journeys by Heart: A Christology of Erotic Power* (New York: Crossroad, 1991).

[3]Henry Nelson Wieman, *The Source of Human Good* (Carbondale and Edwardsville: Southern Illinois University Press, 1946), 17, 19.

[4]Throughout this paper I will change "man" to "human" in quotations from early process thinkers because I believe they would have used inclusive language had they been aware of this issue.

[5]Wieman, *Source of Human Good*, 236.
[6]Ibid., 236
[7]Ibid.
[8]Ibid., 237.
[9]Ibid., 238.
[10]Ibid., 237.
[11]Ibid.
[12]Ibid., 242.
[13]Ibid., 239.
[14]See the discussion of this debate in James C. Livingston, *Modern Christian Thought: From the Enlightenment to Vatican II* (New York: Macmillan Publishing Co., Inc., 1971), 429.
[15]John B. Cobb Jr. (Unpublished paper, Claremont, California: Center for Process Studies, 1960), 8.
[16]John B. Cobb. Jr., *A Christian Natural Theology* (Philadelphia: Westminster Press, 1965), 126.
[17]Ibid., 126–27.
[18]Daniel Day Williams, *The Spirit and the Forms of Love* (Lanham, Md.: University Press of America, 1981), 8–9, 13, 219.
[19]Ibid., 235.
[20]Ibid.
[21]Ibid.
[22]Ibid.
[23]Ibid., 236.
[24]Ibid., 232.
[25]Ibid.
[26]W. Norman Pittenger, *The Only Meaning* (Oxford, England: A. R. Mowbray and Co., 1969), 126.
[27]Ibid, 112, 120–21.
[28]Ibid., 113.
[29]W. Norman Pittenger, *Making Sexuality Human* (New York: Pilgrim Press, 1979), 5.
[30]Ibid., 14.
[31]Ibid., 15–16.
[32]Ibid., 83–85.
[33]Ibid., 88, 51, 33.
[34]Ibid., 88.
[35]W. Norman Pittenger, *Love and Control in Sexuality* (Philadelphia: United Church Press, 1974), 37.
[36]Ibid., 45.
[37]Ibid., 45–46.
[38]Ibid., 42–43.
[39]W. Norman Pittenger, *Time for Consent: A Christian's Approach to Homosexuality* (London: SCM Press Ltd., 1976), 45, 103.
[40]W. Norman Pittenger, *Gay Lifestyles: A Christian Interpretation of Homosexuality and the Homosexual* (Los Angeles: Universal Fellowship Press, 1977), 105.
[41]Pittenger, *Gay Lifestyles*, 109–14. Here Pittenger is drawing on the work of George O'Neill and Nena O'Neill in their book *Open Marriage* (London: Peter Owen, Ltd., 1973).
[42]W. Norman Pittenger, *The Lure of Divine Love: Human Experience and Christian Faith in a Process Perspective* (New York: Pilgrim Press, 1979), 66–67.
[43]W. Norman Pittenger, *The Meaning of Being Human* (New York: Pilgrim Press, 1982), 68, 77–78.
[44]Ibid., 72.
[45]John B. Cobb. Jr., "Is the Church Ready to Legislate on Sex?" *Occasional Papers* 55 (Nashville: The United Methodist Board of Higher Education and Ministry, 25 January, 1984), 10.
[46]Ibid., 6.
[47]John B. Cobb Jr., "Being Christian about Homosexuality" in *Homosexuality and Christian Faith: Questions of Conscience for the Churches*, ed. Walter Wink (Minneapolis: Fortress Press, 1999), 89–90.

[48]John B. Cobb Jr., *Matters of Life and Death* (Louisville: Westminster/John Knox Press, 1991), 119.

[49]Ibid., 96.

[50]Ibid., 118.

[51]Ibid., 120.

[52]John B. Cobb Jr., "The Mission of the Church, Part II," *Creative Transformation* 1, no. 3 (Spring 1992): 1, 8.

[53]Ibid., 1.

[54]Ibid., 8.

[55]Ibid.

[56]Ibid.

[57]Mary Ellen Kilsby, John B. Cobb Jr., and William A. Beardslee, "What Shall the Church Say about Homosexuality?" In *Now What's a Christian to Do?* ed. David P. Polk (St. Louis: Chalice Press, 1994), 93–94.

[58]Ibid., 94–95.

[59]Ibid., 95.

[60]Ibid., 60.

[61]Ibid., 96.

[62]Ibid., 97.

[63]Cobb, "Being Christian about Homosexuality," 89–93.

[64]Ibid., 93.

[65]Ibid.

[66]John B. Cobb Jr., *Postmodernism and Public Policy: Reframing Religion, Culture, Education, Sexuality, Class, Race, Politics, and the Economy* (Albany: State University of New York Press, 2002).

[67]Ibid., 99.

[68]Ibid.

[69]Ibid., 100.

[70]Portions of this section have been previously published as Kathlyn A. Breazeale, "Marriage after Patriarchy," *Creative Transformation* 8:3 (spring 1999) and as Kathlyn A. Breazeale, "Marriage after Patriarchy?: Partner Relationships and Public Religion," in *Religion in a Pluralistic Age: Proceedings of the Third International Conference on Philosophical Theology,* ed. Donald A. Crosby and Charley D. Hardwick (New York: Peter Lang Press, 2001).

[71]See Dalma Heyn, *Marriage Shock: The Transformation of Women into Wives* (New York: Villard Books, 1997), 18.

[72]Alfred North Whitehead, "Mathematics and the Good," in *The Philosophy of Alfred North Whitehead,* ed. Paul Arthur Schilpp (Lasalle: Open Court, 1941), 670.

[73]Marjorie Hewitt Suchocki, *God Christ Church: A Practical Guide to Process Theology* (New York: Crossroad, 1988), 22.

[74]Suchocki explains how the Whiteheadian concept of relationality is the structure that allows both evil and redemption to occur with her development of "freedom in community." See chapter IV in Suchocki, *God Christ Church,* 61–80.

[75]For a discussion of *pater familias,* see Sarah B. Pomeroy, *Goddesses, Whores, Wives, and Slaves: Women in Classical Antiquity* (New York: Schocken Books, 1975), 150–51. Only those few women who became Vestal Virgins were automatically exempt from the power of the *pater familias.*

[76]For a discussion of the practice of the "Rule of Thumb," see Lawrence Stone, *The Family, Sex and Marriage in England 1500-1899* (New York: Harper & Row, 1977), 326.

[77]The relationship between the Christian tradition and violence against wives is cogently described by Rosemary Radford Ruether in her article, "The Western Religious Tradition and Violence Against Women in the Home," in *Christianity, Patriarchy, and Abuse: A Feminist Critique,* ed. Joanne Carlson Brown and Carole R. Bohn (Cleveland: Pilgrim Press, 1989), 31–41.

[78]In the nineteenth century, Western married women's civil status was nonexistent in English common law, and they were treated as minors according to the Napoleonic Code. See Barbara Corrado Pope, "Angels in the Devil's Workshop: Leisured and Charitable Women in Nineteenth-Century England and France," in *Becoming Visible: Women in European History,* ed. Renate Bridenthal and Claudia Koonz (Boston: Houghton Mifflin, 1977), 309.

[79]From "Battering Statistics" compiled in October 1996 by the Los Angeles Commission on Assaults Against Women, 605 West Olympic Boulevard, Suite 400, Los Angeles, Calif., 90015.

[80]Bernard Loomer, "Two Conceptions of Power," *Process Studies* 6, no.1 (spring 1976): 19.

[81]Brock, *Journeys by Heart,* 32.

[82]Loomer, "Two Conceptions," 19.

[83]Brock, *Journeys by Heart,* 34.

[84]Loomer, "Two Conceptions," 19.

[85]Ibid., 20–21.

[86]Kenneth Woodward, "Using the Bully Pulpit?" *Newsweek* (22 June, 1988): 69.

[87]I am indebted to Barbara Keiller for stimulating my imagination and thinking about intimacy and the Whiteheadian notion of God.

[88]For John Cobb's discussion of Whitehead's philosophy of the relationship between body and soul, see Cobb, *Postmodernism,* 86–89.

[89]For a extended discussion of this devaluation of women, the body, and sexuality, see Rosemary Radford Ruether, "Misogynism and Virginal Feminism in the Fathers of the Church," in *Religion and Sexism: Images of Woman in the Jewish and Christian Traditions,* ed. Rosemary Radford Ruether (New York: Simon and Schuster, 1974), 150–83.

[90]Marjorie Hewitt Suchocki, *The End of Evil: Process Eschatology in Historical Context* (Albany: State University of New York Press, 1988), 75.

[91]Loomer, "Two Conceptions," 26.

Chapter 11: Reflections on Cinema, Spirituality, and Process

[1]Whitehead's term is the "ontological principle": "Actual occasions form the ground from which all other types of existence are derived and abstracted" (PR 75); "'Actual entities'– also termed 'actual occasions'–are the final real things of which the world is made up. There is no going behind actual entities to find anything more real" (PR 18); "The ontological principle can be summarized as: no actual entity, then no reason [i.e., cause pursuant to some effect]" (PR 19).

[2]Critic and filmmaker Paul Schrader identified an entire school of filmmaking with these characteristics, calling it "transcendental cinema." By this phrase he distinguished a type of filmmaking that highlighted philosophical concerns and conflicts through a deliberate, aestheticized style. Ozu Yasujiro (1903–1963), Robert Bresson (1901–1999), and Carl Dreyer (1889–1968) are considered the paradigmatic transcendental directors. See Schrader's *Transcendental Style in Film: Ozu, Bresson, Dreyer* (Berkeley: University of California Press, 1972).

[3]Stop-motion animation is a term that encompasses processes like claymation (Gumby cartoons, Wallace and Gromit, *Chicken Run*) and three-dimensional model work (Willis O'Brien's work on the ape in *King Kong,* Ray Harryhausen's skeleton army in *Jason and the Argonauts,* ED-209 in *Robocop*).

[4]E.g., Tom Twyker's *Lola rennt (Run Lola Run),* Michael Haneke's *Code inconnu (Code Unknown),* Michel Gondry's *Eternal Sunshine of the Spotless Mind.*

[5]E.g., Christopher Nolan's *Memento,* Gaspar Noë's *Irreversible.*

Chapter 12: Process Theological Ethics

[1]Henry Nelson Wieman, *The Source of Human Good* (Chicago: University of Chicago Press, 1947).

[2]Schubert Ogden, *Faith and Freedom: Toward a Theology of Liberation* (Nashville: Abingdon Press, 1979).

[3]Franklin Gamwell, *The Divine Good: Modern Moral Theory and the Necessity of God* (Dallas: Southern Methodist University Press, 1996).

[4]Marjorie Suchocki, *God, Christ, Church: A Practical Guide to Process Theology* (New York: Crossroad, 1982).

[5]Katherine Keller, *From a Broken Web: Separation, Sexism and Self* (Boston: Beacon Press, 1986).

[6]Cf. AI 252ff., and Charles Hartshorne, *Creative Synthesis and Philosophic Method* (New York: University Press of America, 1983 [1970]), 303ff.

[7]See Hartshorne, *Creative Synthesis,* 303, and AI 252–253.

[8]John B. Cobb Jr., *A Christian Natural Theology Based on the Thought of Alfred North Whitehead* (Philadelphia: Westminster Press, 1965).

[9]Charles Birch and John B. Cobb Jr., *The Liberation of Life: From the Cell to the Community* (Cambridge, England: Cambridge University Press, 1981).

[10]Hartshorne, *Creative Synthesis,* 303.

[11]Ibid.

[12]Charles Hartshorne, *Born to Sing: An Interpretation and World Survey of Bird Song* (Bloomington, Ind.: Indiana University Press, 1973).

[13]AI chapter XVII.

[14]T.S. Eliot, "The Hollow Men," in *Collected Poems 1909–1935,* by T.S. Eliot (Faber & Faber, 1936), 82.

[15]Hartshorne, *Creative Synthesis,* 304.

[16]Cobb, *Christian Natural Theology,* 114 ff.

[17]Hartshorne, *Creative Synthesis,* 304.

[18]AI chapter XX.

[19]Cobb, *Christian Natural Theology,* 96.

[20]H. Richard Niebuhr, *The Responsible Self: An Essay in Christian Moral Philosophy* (New York: Harper & Row, 1963), 55–57.

[21]Birch and Cobb, *Liberation of Life,* 79 ff.

[22]David Landis Barnhill and Roger S. Gottlieb, "Introduction" in *Deep Ecology and World Religions: New Essays on Sacred Ground,* ed. Barnhill and Gottlieb (Albany, N.Y.: State University of New York Press, 2001), 6.

[23]John B. Cobb Jr., "Protestant Theology and Deep Ecology," in *Deep Ecology,* ed. Barnhill and Gottlieb, 216–19.

[24]Birch and Cobb, *Liberation of Life,* 158–59.

[25]James M. Gustafson, *A Sense of the Divine: The Natural Environment from a Theocentric Perspective* (Cleveland, Ohio: The Pilgrim Press, 1994) 66, 73.

[26]Hartshorne, *Creative Synthesis,* 305.

[27]See Birch and Cobb, *Liberation of Life,* 158–59, where they justify the killing of chicken for food so long as suffering is minimized.

[28]John B. Cobb Jr., *Christ in a Pluralistic Age* (Philadelphia: Westminster Press, 1975); Schubert H. Ogden, *The Point of Christology* (San Francisco: Harper and Row, 1982).

[29]See John B. Cobb Jr., "Christ Beyond Creative Transformation," in *Encountering Jesus,* ed. Stephen T. Davis (Atlanta: John Knox Press, 1988).

[30]Birch and Cobb, *Liberation of Life,* 236.

[31]See Lois Livezey, "Women, Power, and Politics: Feminist Theology in Process Perspective," *Process Studies* 17, no. 2 (1988): 70.

[32]Douglas Sturm, "Religion as Critique and the Critique of Religion: The Problem of the Self in the Modern World" (paper delivered at the University of Kansas, October 14, 1989), 19–20, quoting Hanna Pitkin and Sara Shumer in Richard Bernstein, *Beyond Objectivism and Relativism: Science, Hermeneutics, and Praxis* (Oxford: B. Blackwell, 1983), 223–24.

[33]Ibid., 21.

[34]Reinhold Niebuhr, *Moral Man and Immoral Society* (New York: Charles Scribner's Sons, 1932), 57.

[35]Douglas Sturm, *Community and Alienation: Essays on Process Thought and Public Life* (Notre Dame, Ind.: University of Notre Dame Press, 1988), 185.

[36]Ibid., 66–69.

[37]Herman E. Daly and John B. Cobb Jr., *For the Common Good: Redirecting the Economy Toward Community, the Environment, and a Sustainable Future* (Boston: Beacon Press, 1989).

[38]Ibid., chapter 9.

Chapter 13: An Exchange of Gifts

[1]Octavia Butler, *Parable of the Sower* (New York: Warner, 1993), 3.

[2]See Theodore Walker Jr., "Hartshorne's Neoclassical Theism and Black Theology," *Process Studies* 18, no. 4 (Winter 1989): 240–58; and Henry Young, "Process Theology and Black Liberation: Testing the Metaphysical Foundations," *Process Studies* 18, no. 4 (Winter 1989): 259–67.

³Ronald C. Potter, "A Comparison of the Conceptions of God in Process and Black Theologies," *The Journal of the Interdenominational Center* 12, no.1–2 (Fall 1984–Spring 1985): 50–61.

⁴Gene Reeves, "Liberation: Process Theology and Black Experience," *Process Studies* 18, no. 4 (Winter 1989): 225–39.

⁵See the works of black process theologians Henry Young, Edward Smith, and Theodore Walker Jr.

⁶Thandeka, "I've Known Rivers: Black Theology's Response to Process Theology," *Process Studies* 18, no. 4 (Winter 1989): 282–93.

⁷Independent of Whitehead, Pierre Teilhard de Chardin describes a process of creative transformation that occurs in the world. See Pierre Teilhard de Chardin, *Christianity and Evolution* (London: Collins, 1971), 21–24. Relying on Whitehead's thought, Henry Nelson Wieman also discusses creative transformation. See Henry N. Wieman, *The Source of Human Good* (Chicago: University of Chicago Press, 1946). Cobb acknowledges his indebtedness and departure from Teilhard and Wieman—see John B. Cobb Jr., *God and the World* (Eugene, Oreg.: Wipf and Stock Publishers, 1998 [1965]), 51–57.

⁸John B. Cobb Jr., "Can Christ Become Good News Again?" (originally presented in 1989), in *Can Christ Become Good News Again?* (St. Louis: Chalice Press, 1991), 97.

⁹Cobb's goal in *Christ in a Pluralistic Age* (Philadelphia: Westminster Press, 1975) is to articulate a christology that will open Christians to religious pluralism: "Christ, as the image of creative transformation, can provide a unity within which the many centers of meaning and existence can be appreciated and encouraged and through which openness to the other great Ways of mankind can lead to a deepening of Christian existence," *Christ in a Pluralistic Age*, 21.

¹⁰John B. Cobb Jr. and David Ray Griffin, *Process Theology: An Introductory Exposition* (Philadelphia: The Westminster Press, 1976), 100.

¹¹Cobb, *God and the World*, 49–50.

¹²John B. Cobb Jr., "Christ Beyond Creative Transformation," in *Encountering Jesus: A Debate on Christology,* ed. Stephen T. Davis (Atlanta: John Knox Press, 1988), 72.

¹³Cobb and Griffin, *Process Theology*, 105.

¹⁴Ibid., 84.

¹⁵Ibid., 85.

¹⁶John B. Cobb Jr., "Kingdom Come and the Present Church" (originally presented in 1975), in *Can Christ Become Good News Again?,* 116.

¹⁷John B. Cobb Jr., "Christology in Process-Relational Perspective," *Word and Spirit: A Monastic Review* 8 (1986): 86.

¹⁸Cobb, "Christ Beyond Creative Transformation," 144.

¹⁹John B. Cobb Jr., "Christian Universality Revisited" (originally presented in 1989), in *Can Christ Become Good News Again?,* 85.

²⁰Charles Birch and John B. Cobb Jr., *The Liberation of Life: From the Cell to the Community* (Denton, Tex.: Environmental Ethics Books, 1990), 188.

²¹Cobb, "Christ Beyond Creative Transformation," 144. By this point, Cobb's understanding of creative transformation has been influenced by his work with biology, evolution, and ecological justice. He admits that what he has called "life" in the book *Liberation of Life* is also Christ and creative transformation. In his early work, Cobb identified creative transformation as "the way." In this late work, creative transformation becomes the life and the truth, following the christological statement in the gospel of John.

²²Ibid., 143.

²³Griffin and Cobb, *Process Theology*, 101.

²⁴Linda E. Thomas, "Womanist Theology, Epistemology, and a New Anthropological Paradigm," *Cross Currents* 48 (1998–1999): 489.

²⁵Alice Walker, *In Search of Our Mothers' Gardens: Womanist Prose* (San Diego: Harcourt Brace Jovanovich, 1983).

²⁶Delores S. Williams, *Sisters in the Wilderness: The Challenge of Womanist God-Talk.* (Maryknoll, N.Y.: Orbis, 1993), ix.

²⁷Williams notes that Alice Walker dedicates one of her books to her mother, who "makes a way out of no way," and the 1982 conference of The National Black Sisters, Clergy and Seminarians Conference was entitled "Making a Way Out of No Way" (ibid., 241 n. 2).

²⁸Ibid., 198.
²⁹Emilie Townes, *In a Blaze of Glory: Womanist Spirituality as Social Witness* (Nashville: Abingdon Press, 1995), 140.
³⁰Kelly Brown Douglas, "Womanist Theology: What Is Its Relationship to Black Theology?" in *Black Theology: A Documentary History, vol. 2.,* ed. James Cone and Gayraud S. Wilmore (Maryknoll, N.Y.: Orbis, 1993), 296.
³¹Williams, *Sisters,* 5.
³²Ibid., 129.
³³Ibid., 177.
³⁴Ibid., 175.
³⁵Townes, *Blaze of Glory,* 140.
³⁶Jacquelyn Grant, "Servanthood Revisited: Womanist Explorations of Servanthood Theology," in *Black Faith and Public Talk,* ed. Dwight N. Hopkins (Maryknoll, N.Y.: Orbis, 1999), 134.
³⁷Karen Baker-Fletcher, *Sisters of Dust, Sisters of Spirit: Womanist Wordings of God and Creation* (Minneapolis: Fortress Press, 1995).
³⁸Williams, *Sisters,* 113–20.
³⁹Ibid., 136.
⁴⁰Ibid., 130.
⁴¹Ibid., 202.
⁴²A. Elaine Crawford, "Womanist Christology: Where Have We Come from and Where Are We Going?" *Review and Expositor* 95 (1998): 376.
⁴³Jacquelyn Grant, *White Women's Christ and Black Women's Jesus: Feminist Christology and Womanist Response* (Atlanta: Scholars Press, 1989).
⁴⁴Only recently has the constitution of Jesus become important for womanist christologies. In *Sisters of Dust, Sisters of Spirit,* Baker-Fletcher describes Jesus' constitution as dust and spirit, earthly and heavenly, divine and human. In her lecture "Jesus as Dust and Spirit: An Incarnational Theology" at the 2001 Annual Meeting of the American Academy of Religion, Baker-Fletcher admits that she is looking toward a process metaphysic to support this assertion.
⁴⁵Delores S. Williams, "Straight Talk, Plain Talk: Womanist Words about Salvation in a Social Context," in *Embracing the Spirit: Womanist Perspectives on Hope, Salvation, and Transformation,* ed. Emilie M. Townes (Maryknoll, NY: Orbis, 1997), 118.
⁴⁶Williams, *Sisters,* 203.
⁴⁷Womanist christologies and Cobb also have different starting points and different interests. Cobb uses the prologue to John in his development of his Logos, and later Sophia, christology. Womanists, on the other hand, explicitly reject the biblical witness of John and Paul and focus on the synoptic gospels, Luke in particular. See JoAnne Marie Terrell, *Power in the Blood?: The Cross in the African American Experience* (Maryknoll, N.Y.: Orbis, 1998), 111.
⁴⁸Cobb, *Christ in a Pluralistic Age,* 147–73.
⁴⁹Williams, *Sisters,* 203.
⁵⁰Renee Leslie Hill, "Disrupted/Disruptive Movements: Black Theology and Black Power 1969/1999," in *Black Theology,* ed. Cone and Wilmore, 147.
⁵¹Ibid., 148.
⁵²Williams, *Sisters,* 203.
⁵³One indication of this is the process-affiliated organizations listed on the Web site for the Center for Process Studies (http://www.ctr4process.org/Links/CPSLinks.htm). There are organizations that focus on process and philosophy, science, psychology, education, and environment; yet there are none expressly looking at process and aesthetic fields.
⁵⁴Dwight Hopkins, *Introducing Black Theology of Liberation* (Maryknoll, N.Y.: Orbis, 1999), 156.
⁵⁵Delores Williams, "Womanist Theology: Black Women's Voices," in *Black Theology,* ed. Cone and Wilmore, 266.
⁵⁶Ibid.
⁵⁷Joanna Russ, "What Can a Heroine Do? Or Why Women Can't Write," in *Images of Women in Fiction,* ed. Susan Comillon (Bowling Green, Ohio: Bowling Green University Popular Press, 1972), 18.
⁵⁸Joseph H. Wellbank, "Utopia and the Constraints of Justice," in *Utopia/ Dystopia?* Ed. Peyton E. Richter (Cambridge, Mass.: Schenkman Publishing Co., 1975), 33.

[59]Ibid. 33–34

[60]Preston Williams, "Black Perspectives on Utopia," in *Utopia/ Dystopia?* ed. Richter, 49–51.

[61]Marleen Barr, *Alien to Femininity: Speculative Fiction and Feminist Theory* (New York: Greenwood Press, 1987), xxii, n. 1.

[62]Ibid., xvii–xviii.

[63]Ibid., 61.

[64]Ibid., 72; Barr asserts that, in womanist speculative fiction, the male and female reverse roles of hero and heroine. The female is now the hero with vision and power who inspires and requires followers; the male is the traditional "heroine" who obeys and falls into line.

[65]Ibid., 73.

[66]Ibid., 80.

[67]Ibid., 81.

[68]Dingbo Wu, "Understanding Utopian Literature," *Extrapolation* 34 no. 3 (Fall 1993): 243.

[69]John V. Lawing, "Sniffing Out Science Fiction," *Christianity Today* 20 (Feb. 27, 1976): 19.

[70]Stephen May, "Salvation, culture and science fiction," in *Christ in Our Place* (Allison Park, Pa.: Pickwick Publications, 1989), 343.

[71]Gloria Naylor, *Mama Day* (New York: Vintage Books, 1993).

[72]Butler, *Parable,* 48.

[73]Nalo Hopkinson, *Brown Girl in the Ring* (New York: Warner Books, 1998).

[74]John B. Cobb Jr. and biologist Charles Birch came together to write *The Liberation of Life,* a liberative theology for the natural world based on the insights of evolution. Likewise, David Griffin has written and edited numerous works dealing with science, philosophy, and process theology including *The Reenchantment of Science: Postmodern Proposals; Religion and Scientific Naturalism: Overcoming the Conflicts,* (Albany: State University of New York Press, 1988) and "Science and Religion: A Postmodern Perspective" in *Beyond Conflict and Reduction: Between Philosophy, Science and Religion,* ed. William Desmond, John Steffen, Koen (Decoster. Leuven, Belgium : Leuven University Press, 2001).. Numerous process and process-relational theologians ground their theologies in a study of the hard sciences, such as Jay McDaniel, Sallie McFague, Anne Primavesi…and the list continues.

Chapter 14: Feminist Theology in Process Perspective

[1]The conference took place at Harvard University in autumn 1978, and most of the papers were subsequently published in Sheila Greeve Davaney, ed., *Feminism and Process Thought* (New York: Edwin Mellen Press, 1981).

[2]Process philosophy suggests that identity coalesces through multiple connections and contrasts rather than contracting through successive separations from the potential pollution of the "other." Hence one's identity thrives in diverse communities, made more interesting and beautiful by the rich plurality of encounters with others. See Lucinda A. Huffaker, *Creative Dwelling: Empathy and Clarity in God and Self* (Atlanta: Scholars Press, 1998).

[3]Catherine Keller, "Power Lines," in *Power, Powerlessness, and the Divine: New Inquiries in Bible and Theology,* ed. Cynthia L. Rigby (Atlanta: Scholars Press, 1997), 57–77.

[4]Bernard M. Loomer, "Two Conceptions of Power," *Process Studies* 6, no. 1 (spring 1976): 17

[5]Carter Heyward, *The Redemption of God: A Theology of Mutual Relation* (Washington, D.C.: University Press of America, 1982).

[6]Beverly Wildung Harrison, "The Power of Anger in the Work of Love," in Weaving the Visions: New Patterns in Feminist Spirituality, ed. Judith Plaskow and Carol P. Christ (San Francisco: Harper & Row, 1989), 221.

[7]Anne Marie Hunter, "Numbering the Hairs of Our Heads: Male Social Control and the All-Seeing Male God," Journal of Feminist Studies in Religion 8, no. 2 (1992): 7–26.

[8]Anna Case-Winters, "The Question of God in an Age of Science: Constructions of Reality and Ultimate Reality in Theology and Science," Zygon 32, no. 3 (September 1997): 369.

[9]Rosemary Radford Ruether, "Motherearth and the Megamachine: A Theology of Liberation in a Feminine, Somatic, and Ecological Perspective," in Womanspirit Rising, ed. Carol P. Christ and Judith Plaskow (San Francisco: Harper & Row, 1979 [1960]), 43–52.

[10] *Tehom* is the Hebrew word for the chaos of the ocean depths in Genesis 1, while *Tiamat* is the name of the a primordial goddess in the Babylonian *Enuma Elish*, in which the younger god Marduk slays Tiamat, the mother of the divine world, and uses her body to create the dome or firmament for the sky.

[11] Catherine Keller, "No More Sea: The Lost Chaos of the Eschaton," in *Christianity and Ecology: Seeking the Well-Being of Earth and Humans*, ed. Dieter T. Hessel and Rosemary Radford Ruether (Cambridge: Harvard University Press, 2000), 194.

[12] Catherine Keller, *Apocalypse Now and Then: A Feminist Guide to the End of the World* (Boston: Beacon Press, 1996).

[13] See Huffaker, *Creative Dwelling.*

[14] Bernard M. Loomer, "S-I-Z-E Is the Measure," in *Religious Experience and Process Theology: The Pastoral Implications of a Major Modern Movement*, ed. Harry James Cargas and Bernard Lee (New York: Paulist Press, 1976), 51.

[15] Ibid., 70.

[16] Valerie Saiving, "The Human Situation: A Feminine View," in *Womanspirit Rising*, ed. Christ and Plaskow, 37.

[17] Marjorie Hewitt Suchocki, *The Fall to Violence: Original Sin in Relational Theology* (New York: Continuum Publishing, 1995), 40.

[18] Rita Nakashima Brock, *Journeys by Heart: A Christology of Erotic Power* (New York: Crossroad, 1988), 10.

[19] Suchocki, *The Fall to Violence*, 164.

[20] Linell E. Cady, "Relational Love: A Feminist Christian Vision," in *Embodied Love: Sensuality and Relationship as Feminist Values*, ed. Paula M. Cooey, Sharon A. Farmer, and Mary Ellen Ross (San Francisco: Harper & Row, 1987), 140.

[21] Carter Heyward, *Touching Our Strength: The Erotic as Power and the Love of God* (San Francisco: Harper & Row, 1989).

[22] Carter Heyward, *The Redemption of God*, 48.

[23] Marjorie Hewitt Suchocki, *God, Christ, Church: A Practical Guide to Process Theology* (New York: Crossroad, 1982), 110.

[24] Keller, "Power Lines," 70.

Chapter 15: A Whiteheadian Perspective on Global Economics

[1] Herman E. Daly and John B. Cobb Jr., *For the Common Good: Redirecting the Economy Toward Community, the Environment, and a Sustainable Future* (Boston: Beacon Press, 1989), 159ff.

[2] Lionel Robbins, *An Essay on the Nature and Significance of Economic Science*, 2nd ed. (London: Macmillan, 1935), excerpted in *The Philosophy of Economics*, ed. Daniel Hausman (Cambridge: Cambridge University Press, 1984), 123, and Kenneth Arrow, *Collected Papers, vol. 1: Social Choice and Justice* (Cambridge: Harvard University Press, 1983), 11–12.

[3] John Stuart Mill, "On the Definition and Method of Political Economy," in Hausman, *Philosophy of Economics*, 52–53.

[4] See Clifford Cobb, Ted Halstead, and Jonathan Rowe, "If the GDP Is Up Why Is America Down?" *The Atlantic Monthly* (October 1995): 59–78.

[5] Karl Marx, *Capital*, ed. Friedrich Engels, trans. of 3d German ed. by Samuel Moore and Edward Aveling (New York.: Modern Library, 1906), 554.

[6] Karl Marx and Friedrich Engels, *Manifesto of the Communist Party* (1848), ed. Friedrich Engels and trans. Samuel Moore (New York: International Publishers, 1932), reprinted in *Marx on Economics*, ed. Robert Freedman (New York: Harcourt, Brace & World, 1961), 17.R

[7] Alfred Marshall, *Principles of Economics*, 8th ed. (London: MacMillan, 1925), 139.

[8] Daly and Cobb, *For the Common Good*, 159–75.

[9] See Peter L. Berger, *The Capitalist Revolution: Fifty Propositions About Prosperity, Equality, and Liberty* (New York.: Basic Books, 1986).

Chapter 16: Imagine Peace

[1] I am grateful to two communities who engaged with me in reflecting on oral versions of this essay: Association of Process Philosophy of Education, St. Paul, Minnesota, 11–14 July

2003, and Center for Process Studies Seminar, Claremont, California, 5 November 2003. This chapter is also published in *Process Papers*, vol. 8, 2004.

[2]H.B. Michel Sabbah, Latin Patriarch of Jerusalem, delivered in Oekumenische Kirchentag, Berlin, 30 May 2003.

[3]The Move to a Political Conflict," Editorial, *Ha'aretz*, 4 July 2003, published online 6 July 2003 (http://www.haaretz.com/hasen/pages/ShArt.jhtml?).

[4]See discussions in public media: "CIA Questioned Documents Linking Iraq, Uranium Ore," *Washington Post* (22 March 2003); "Italy May Have been Misled by Fake Iraq Arms Papers, U.S. Says," *Los Angeles Times* (15 March 2003); "(Over)selling the World on War," *Newsweek* (9 June 2003): 24; "CIA Did Not Share Doubt on Iraq Data: Bush Used Report of Uranium Bid," *Washington Post* (12 June 2003); Representative Henry Waxman, "New Questions on President's Use of Forged Nuclear Evidence," House Committee on Government Reform, 12 June 2003 (http://www.house.gov/reform/min/inves_admin/admin_nuclear_evidence.htm).

[5]PR 21; cf. 21–22, 40, 56–57.

[6]John B. Cobb Jr. and David Ray Griffin, *Process Theology: An Introductory Exposition* (Philadelphia: Westminster Press, 1976), 20.

[7]Ibid., 112.

[8]Whitehead concludes that neither pure objectivism nor pure subjectivism is adequate to explain the world. Reality is best described in terms of dynamic relationships.

[9]Victor Lowe, *Alfred North Whitehead: The Man and His Work, Vol. I–1861–1910* (Baltimore: John Hopkins University Press, 1985), 5; cf. PR 3–17, 266–81, 342–51.

[10]Mark Juergensmeyer, *Terror in the Mind of God: The Global Rise of Religious Violence* (Berkeley: University of California Press, 2000), 242.

[11]Ibid., 153. Quoting Hamas communiqué no. 64, 26 September 1990, quoted in Jean-Francois Legrain, "A Defining Moment: Palestinian Islamic Fundamentalism," in *Islamic Fundamentalisms and the Gulf Crisis*, ed. James Piscatori (Chicago: Fundamentalism Project, American Academy of Arts and Sciences, 1991), 75–76.

[12]Paulo Freire, *Pedagogy of the Oppressed* (New York: Harper and Row, 1971); id., *Pedagogy in Process: The Letters from Guinea-Bissau* (New York: Seabury Press, 1978); id., *The Politics of Education* (South Hadley, Mass.: Bergin and Garvey, 1985).

[13]Kathleen Weiler, *Women Teaching for Change: Gender, Class and Power* (South Hadley, Mass.: Bergin and Garvey, 1988); Weiler, "The Lives of Teachers: Feminism and Life History Narratives," *Educational Researcher* 23, no. 4 (May 1994): 30–33; William F. Pinar, ed., *Curriculum Theorizing: The Reconceptualists* (Berkeley: McCutchan, 1975); Pinar, "Understanding Curriculum as Gender Text: Notes on Reproduction, Resistance, and Male-Male Relations," in Stephen Appel, ed., *Psychoanalysis and Pedagogy* (Westport, Conn.: Bergin & Garvey, 1999), 103–24; Pinar, William M. Reynolds, Patrick Slattery, and Peter M. Taubman, *Understanding Curriculum* (New York: Peter Lang, 1995); Pinar, ed., *Contemporary Curriculum Discourses: Twenty Years of JCT* (New York: Peter Lang, 1999); Petra Munro, "Resisting 'Resistance': Stories Women Teachers Tell," *Journal of Curriculum Theorizing* 12, no. 1: 16–28; Christine E. Sleeter, ed., *Empowerment through Multicultural Education* (New York: State University of New York, 1991); Sleeter, *Multicultural Education as Social Activism* (Albany: State University of New York, 1996).

[14]Ivan Illich, *Deschooling Society* (New York: Harper and Row, 1971 [1970]), 1. Illich explains that the school is not the only modern institution with the primary purpose of shaping human visions of reality; however, the school "enslaves more profoundly and more systematically, since only school is credited with the principal function of forming critical judgment, and, paradoxically, tries to do so by making learning about oneself, about others, and about nature depend on a prepackaged process" (47).

[15]Ibid., 23; cf: 40.

[16]Ron Miller, ed., *Educational Freedom for a Democratic Society: A Critique of National Goals, Standards, and Curriculum* (Brandon, Vt.: Resource Center for Redesigning Education, 1995). See particularly Pat Farenga, "Unschooling 2000," on 208–25 and Linda Dobson, "Thoughts from a Free Mom," on 226–40.

[17]Jagdish Chander Hassija and Mohini Panjabi, eds., *Visions of a Better World* (London: Brahma Kumaris World Spiritual University, 1994 [1992]).

[18]John Dewey, *Democracy and Education* (New York: Macmillan, The Free Press, 1997); Dewey, *Experience and Education* (New York: Macmillan, 1997); James W. Botkin, Mahdi Elmandjra, and Mircea Malitza, *No Limits to Learning: Bridging the Human Gap: A Report to the Club of Rome* (New York: Pergamon, 1979), esp. 24–33.

[19]William E. Doll Jr., *A Post-Modern Perspective on Curriculum* (New York: Teachers College, 1993); William E. Doll Jr. and Noel Gough, eds., *Curriculum Visions* (New York: Peter Lang, 2002); C.A. Bowers and David Flinders, *Responsive Teaching: An Ecological Approach to Classroom Patterns of Language, Culture, and Thought* (New York: Teachers College, 1990); C.A. Bowers, *The Culture of Denial: Why the Environmental Movement Needs a Strategy for Reforming Universities and Public Schools* (Albany: State University of New York Press, 1997); Bowers, *Educating for Eco-Justice and Community* (Athens, Ga.: University of Georgia Press, 2001).

[20]James W. Botkin, Mahdi Elmandjra, Mircea Malitza, James Botkin, Dan Dimancescu, Ray Stata, with John McClellan, eds., *Global Stakes: The Future of High Technology in America* (Harmondsworth, England: Penguin, 1984 [1982]).

[21]Bernard E. Meland, *Higher Education and the Human Spirit* (Chicago: University of Chicago Press, 1953), 33, cf. 33-47.

[22]Ibid., 45.

[23]Ibid., 47.

[24]Ibid.

[25]Ibid., 26-30.

[26]Ibid., 28.

[27]Ibid.; see also Bernard E. Meland, "Some Philosophical Aspects of Poetic Perception," *The Personalist* 22, no. 4 (1941): 384-92.

[28]Hanan A. Alexander, *Reclaiming Goodness: Education and the Spiritual Quest* (Notre Dame: University of Notre Dame Press, 2001), 146.

[29]Ibid., 186.

[30]Ibid., 187-88.

[31]Marjorie Hewitt Suchocki, *The End of Evil: Process Eschatology in Historical Context* (New York: State University of New York Press, 1988), 116. Suchocki develops these ideas with a more explicit connection with Christian tradition in: *God, Christ, Church: A Practical Guide to Process Theology* (New York: Crossroad, 1989 [1982]), 183-224.

[32]See, for example: Philip Phenix, "Transcendence and the Curriculum," in Pinar, *Curriculum Theorizing*, 323-40.

[33]Patrick Slattery, "Toward an Eschatological Curriculum Theory," in Pinar, *Contemporary Curriculum Discourses*, 281, cf. 278-88; originally published in *Journal of Curriculum Theorizing* 9, no. 3 (1992): 7-22.

[34]Ibid., 283, cf. 284, 286.

[35]Mary Elizabeth Mullino Moore, "Ethnic Diversity and Biodiversity: Richness at the Center of Education," *Interchange* 31, nos. 2 & 3 (2000): 259-78.

[36]Christine E. Sleeter, ed., *Empowerment through Multicultural Education*, 2. See also: Christine E. Sleeter and Peter L. McLaren, eds., *Multicultural Education, Critical Pedagogy, and the Politics of Difference* (Albany: State University of New York Press, 1995); Sleeter, *Multicultural Education as Social Activism*.

[37]Carl Jozef Alfons Sterkens, *Interreligious Learning: The Problem of Interreligious Dialogue in Primary Education* (Proefschrift, Katholieke Universiteit Nijmegen, Nijmegen, 2001), 81.

[38]Ibid., 76-85.

[39]Ibid., 85.

[40]John B. Cobb Jr., *Sustaining the Common Good: A Christian Perspective on the Global Economy* (Cleveland: Pilgrim Press, 1994), 111-31. See also id., *Postmodernism and Public Policy: Reframing Religion, Culture, Education, Sexuality, Class, Race, Politics, and the Economy* (Albany: State University of New York Press, 2002); id., *The Earthist Challenge to Economism: A Theological Critique of the World Bank* (New York: St. Martin's, 1999); Herman E. Daly and John B. Cobb Jr., *For the Common Good: Redirecting the Economy toward Community, the Environment, and a Sustainable Future* (Boston: Beacon, 1994); David Ray Griffin and Richard Falk, eds., *Postmodern Politics for a Planet in Crisis: Policy, Process, and Presidential Vision* (Albany: State University of New York Press, 1993).

[41]Cobb, *Sustaining the Common Good*, 130-31. See also Daly and Cobb, *For the Common Good*.

Chapter 17: Politics in Process Perspective

[1]My treatment of politics attempts to include the concerns of liberation theology. The literature dealing with process theology, political theology, and liberation theology is abundant. For representative treatments of process theology, political theology, and liberation theology,

see Delwin Brown, *To Set at Liberty: Christian Faith and Human Freedom* (Maryknoll, N.Y.: Orbis Books, 1981); John B. Cobb Jr., *Process Theology as Political Theology* (Philadelphia: The Westminster Press, 1982); John B. Cobb Jr. and W. Widick Schroeder, eds., *Process Philosophy and Social Thought* (Chicago: Center for the Scientific Study of Religion, 1981); Charles Birch and John B. Cobb Jr., *The Liberation of Life: From the Cell to the Human Community* (New York: Cambridge University Press, 1981); Herman E. Daly and John B Cobb Jr., *For the Common Good: Redirecting the Economy toward Community, the Environment, and a Sustainable Future,* 2d ed. (Boston: Beacon Press, 1994); John B. Cobb Jr., *Sustainability: Economics, Ecology, and Justice* (Maryknoll, N.Y.: Orbis Books, 1992); John B. Cobb Jr., *Sustaining the Common Good: A Christian Perspective on the Global Economy* (Cleveland: The Pilgrim Press, 1994); Schubert M. Ogden, *Faith and Freedom: Toward a Theology of Liberation,* rev. ed. (Nashville: Abingdon Press, 1989); essays on the theme of faith and justice, an interface between process and liberation theologies in *Process Studies* 14, no. 2 (Summer 1985); Dermot A. Lane, *Foundations for a Social Theology: Praxis, Process, and Salvation* (New York: Paulist Press, 1984); Jay McDaniel, "The God of the Oppressed and the God Who Is Empty," in *God and Global Justice: Religion and Poverty in an Unequal World,* ed. Frederick Ferre and Rita Matragnon (New York: Paragon House, 1985). See also the special issue of *Process Studies* devoted to process theology and the Black Experience: *Process Studies* 18, no. 4 (Winter 1989). The works of the members of the Social Ethics Seminar, a group of social ethicists informed by process thought, situated for the most part in the Midwest, tend to be more positive in their estimate of modernity than such "constructive postmodernists" as John B. Cobb Jr. and David Ray Griffin, with some favoring economic growth.

[2]I am indebted for the distinction between unilateral and relational power to Bernard M. Loomer's classic essay, "Two Conceptions of Power," *Process Studies* 6, no. 1 (Summer 1976): 5–32. See also Rita Nakashima Brock, *Journeys by Heart: A Christology of Erotic Power* (New York: Crossroad Publishing Co., 1988); Leslie A. Muray, "A Democratic Faith in a Democratic God" (unpublished paper); Muray, " Democratic Vistas on Faith and God" (Part I), *Creative Transformation* 6, no. 4 (Summer 1997): 22–23; and Muray "Democratic Vistas on Faith and God" (Part II and III), *Creative Transformation* 7, no. 1 (Fall 1997): 14–16. See also James Newton Poling, *The Abuse of Power: A Theological Problem* (Nashville: Abingdon Press, 1991).

[3]For lengthier treatments of these themes, see Leslie A. Muray, *An Introduction to the Process Understanding of Science, Society and the Self: A Philosophy for Modern Humanity* (Lewiston, N.Y.: E. Mellen Press, 1988), 17–29; and Muray, "Confessional Postmodernism and the Process-Relational Vision," *Process Studies* 18, no. 2 (Summer 1989): 83–94. My development of an ethics of character and virtue from a process perspective is influenced by Bernard Loomer's notion of "size" and Bernard Meland's concept of "appreciative awareness." See Bernard M. Loomer, "S-I-Z-E Is the Measure," in *Religious Experience and Process Theology: The Pastoral Implications of a Major Modern Movement,* ed. Harry James Cargas and Bernard Lee (New York: Paulist Press, 1976), 69–76; and Loomer, "The Size of God," in *The Size of God: The Theology of Bernard Loomer in Context* ed. William Dean and Larry E. Axel (Macon, Ga.: Mercer University Press, 1987), 20–51; see Bernard E. Meland, *Faith and Culture* (Carbondale, Ill.: Southern Illinois University, 1953), 119–22, 174–75; and especially Meland, *Higher Education and the Human Spirit* (Chicago: the University of Chicago Press, 1953), 48–78.

[4]Leslie A. Muray, "The Doctrine of Grace in Whiteheadian Categories," *Encounter* 45, no. 4 (Autumn 1984): 359–71.

[5]Bernard M. Loomer, "Empirical Theology within Process Thought," in *The Future of Empirical Theology,* ed., Bernard E. Meland (Chicago: University of Chicago, 1969), 162.

[6]Ibid., 163.

[7]See Muray, "A Democratic Faith in a Democratic God" and "Democratic Vistas on Faith and God" (Parts I, II and III) for lengthier treatments of these ideas. For parallels between concepts and images of deity and of political power, I am indebted to the insights of David Nicholls. See especially his *Deity and Domination: Images of God and the State in the Nineteenth and Twentieth Centuries* (London and New York: Routledge, 1994 [1989]).

[8]See Muray, "A Democratic Faith in a Democratic God" and Leslie A. Muray, "Democracy and God in Gerald Birney Smith," *Encounter* 62, no. 1 (Winter 2001): 67–88.

[9]RM 86. In Leslie A. Muray, "Meland's Mystical Naturalism and Ecological Responsibility," in *Religious Experience and Ecological Responsibility,* ed., Donald A. Crosby and Charley D. Hardwick (New York: Peter Lang Publishing, Inc., 1996): 257–75, I appropriate

Meland's use of the notion of the "individual-in-community" to argue that to foster the ecological ethos requisite for dealing adequately with ecological crisis, we need extend the doctrine of the "imago dei" to the nonhuman natural world. Langdon Gilkey makes a similar argument in *Nature, Reality, and the Sacred: The Nexus of Science and Religion* (Minneapolis: Augsburg Fortress, 1993) and Gilkey, "Nature as the Image of God: Signs of the Sacred," *Theology Today* 51, no.1 (April 1994): 127–41.

¹⁰Arne Naess, "*Self-*Realization: An Ecological Approach to Being in the World," in *Thinking Like a Mountain: Towards a Council of All Beings*, ed. John Seed, Joanna Macy, Pat Fleming, Arne Naess (Philadelphia, Pa.: New Society Publishers, 1988), 20.

¹¹Meland, *Faith and Culture*, 140.

¹²Daly and Cobb, *For the Common Good*, 159–75.

¹³See the works of Frederick Ferré that deal with "personalistic organicism," his concept for situating humans in the nonhuman natural world while simultaneously defending the distinctiveness of humans: Ferré, "The Integrity of Creation," in *Empirical Theology: A Handbook*, ed. Randolph Crump Miller (Birmingham, Ala.: Religious Education Press, 1992), 222–43; Ferré, "Personalistic Organicism: Paradox or Paradigm?" in *Philosophy and the Natural Environment*, ed. Robin Attfield and Andrew Belsey (New York: Cambridge University Press, 1994), 59–73; Ferré, *Being and Value: Toward a Constructive Postmodern Metaphysics* (Albany, N.Y.: State University of New York Press, 1996); and Ferré, *Living and Value: Toward a Constructive Postmodern Ethics Metaphysics* (Albany, N.Y.: State University of New York Press, 2001). See also Leslie A. Muray, "The Transformation of Ethics: A Response to Frederick Ferré," *American Journal of Theology and Philosophy* 23, no. 1 (January 2002): 3–12. For another treatment of these issues, see my joint review of *Gaia & God* by Rosemary Radford Ruether (San Francisco: HarperSanFrancisco, 1992) and *Sustainability* by John B. Cobb Jr. (Maryknoll, N.Y.: Orbis, 1992) in *Process Studies* 22, no. 3 (Fall 1993): 149–62. Ferré and I both defend the notion of "personalistic organicism." We see as profoundly problematic the attribution of subjective agency to aggregates, societies, and systems, with the historic usage of organic metaphors, particularly ones that use some sort of a "soul" that dominates the body and in which the "whole" in effect overwhelms "the parts." Such metaphors have tended to legitimize domination and exploitation. Obviously evident in feudalism, it is even more blatant in the rhetoric of fascism (and in a different way, Stalinism), in which the value of individuals resides solely in the degree to which they are of use to the state. The state embodies "the whole" that is society. The "Party," whether fascist, national socialist, or communist, embodies the vanguard that should lead the state. In effect the Party is the state, as party and state overlap and are collapsed in one another to a considerable extent. Society, "the people," "the working" class, the state, the party are all then embodied in the omniscient leader–"Il Duce," "Der Fuehrer," "the Master" (Stalin). In effect, in various ways, the state, the party, "the Leader" all embody the "Soul" that dominates the inferior "Body" that is human society.

¹⁴Daly and Cobb, *For the Common Good*, 298–304.

¹⁵Ibid., 14–15, 138–58, 298–304.

¹⁶Ibid., 209–35.

¹⁷Ibid., 174.

¹⁸Ibid., 315–18. See also Warren Copeland, *And the Poor Get Welfare* (Nashville: Abingdon Press, in cooperation with the Churches' Center for Theology and Public Policy, Washington, D.C., 1994), 163–92.

¹⁹Daly and Cobb, *For the Common Good*, 443–507.

²⁰Earth Charter Initiative, *The Earth Charter*, Benchmark Draft 2, April 1999, Principle 11, p. 4.

²¹*The Earth Charter.*

²²"The 1994 Declaration of Principles on Human Rights and the Environment" also attempts to affirm the right of humans and nonhumans. It stresses human responsibility to such an extent that the document winds up underemphasizing the intrinsic value of nonhumans, raising the question of whether, in spite of its intentions, the document succeeds in avoiding anthropocentrism. See the document at http://tufts.edu/departments/fletcher/multi/www/1994-decl.html.

²³Pat Fleming and Joanna Macy, "The Council of All Beings," in *Thinking Like a Mountain*, ed. Seed et al., 79–90.

²⁴Thomas Berry, "Teilhard in the Age of Ecology," Video Interview (Mystic, Conn.: Twenty-Third Publications, 1988).

[25]Ibid.

[26]Daniel Day Williams, *The Spirit and the Forms of Love* (New York and Evanston: Harper and Row Publishers, 1968) 146.

[27]Bernard E. Meland, *Modern Man's Worship: A Search for Reality in Religion* (New York: Harper and Brothers Publishers, 1934) 143.

[28]Williams, *Spirit*, 146.

[29]For an autobiographical treatment of this topic, see Leslie A. Muray, "Rootedness and Openness," in *Culture and History*, ed. Boris Gubman (Tver, Russia: Tver State University, 2000), 148–49 (in Russian, trans. Boris Gubman).

[30]William James, *The Will to Believe* (1897; reprint, New York: Dover Publications, 1956), 270

Chapter 18: A Process Approach to Ecology

[1]Versions of this chapter appeared in my book, Jay McDaniel, *Gandhi's Hope: Learning from Other Religions as a Path to Peace* (Maryknoll, N.Y.: Orbis Press, 2005).

[2]The Earth Charter: Values and Principles for a Sustainable Future, www.earthcharter.org (15 June 2004).

[3]Ibid.

[4]Ibid.

[5]Ibid.

[6]Of course, many process thinkers focus primarily on one or two of the challenges. Often, for example, process theologians in the Christian tradition focus primarily on the first two challenges. Their writings are aimed at fellow Christians, and they attempt to mine the Christian tradition for various teachings and practices that, as reinterpreted in a process vein, might enable Christians to live compassionately and with a spirit of openness to change. These theologians assume that Christianity itself is a tradition-in-process capable of growth and change. They are seeking to add their voice to its development. On the other hand, some process philosophers have been primarily interested in the dialogue between process philosophy and science and have not been as concerned with intra-Christian discussions. Their aim has been to show how process thought provides a unique and plausible way of interpreting evolutionary biology, animal behavior, relativity theory, and quantum theory. But all things considered, most process thinkers operate in a spirit of collegiality with other process thinkers, feeling that they are part of a large collaborative process that addresses all six issues named above. They hope that process thought might contribute to that global civil society in which Whiteheadian and neo-Whiteheadian ways of thinking contribute to the common good of the world.

[7]J.B.S. Haldane, quoted in G.E. Hutchison, "Homage to Santa Rosalia, or Why Are There So Many Kinds of Animals?" *The American Naturalist* 93 (1959): 145–59.

[8]From J.B.S. Haldane, "On Being the Right Size," *Possible Worlds and Other Essays* (London: Chatto and Windus, 1927). Quoted in http://www.vanderbilt.edu/~parker/quotes.html (June 15, 2004).

[9]Ursula Goodenough, *The Sacred Depths of Nature* (New York: Oxford University Press, 1998), 12.

[10]Huston Smith, *Why Religion Matters: The Fate of the Human Spirit in an Age of Disbelief* (San Francisco: HarperSanFrancisco, 2001), chapter 15.

[11]Tu Weiming, "The Continuity of Being: Chinese Visions of Nature," in *Worldviews, Religion, and the Environment: A Global Anthology* ed. Richard C. Foltz (Belmont, Calif.: Wadsworth, 2003), 210.

[12]Alfred North Whitehead, *The Function of Reason* (Princeton, N.J.: Princeton University Press, 1929), 8. See also the discussion of these three aims of life in Charles Birch and John B. Cobb Jr., *The Liberation of Life: From Cell to Community* (Cambridge: Cambridge University Press, 1981), 106.

[13]Thomas Berry and Brianne Swimme, *The Universe Story: From the Primal Flaring Forth to the Ecozoic Era: A Celebration of the Unfolding of the Cosmos* (San Francisco: HarperCollins, 1992), 243.

[14]I borrow the phrase "inter-being" from Thich Nhat Hanh, "The Sun My Heart," in *Dharma Rain: Sources of Buddhist Environmentalism*, ed. Stephanie Kaza and Kenneth Kraft

(Boston: Shambhala, 2000). Hanh's felicitous phrase captures Whitehead's sense that all entities are present in all other entities.
    [15]This understanding of sin is richly developed by Marjorie Hewitt Suchocki in *The Fall to Violence: Original Sin in Relational Theology* (New York: Continuum, 1995), 16. .

Chapter 19: Evangelical Theologies

[1]Timothy P. Weber considers the definition of evangelicalism "one of the biggest problems in American religious historiography" ("Premillennialism and the Branches of Evangelicalism," in *The Variety of American Evangelicalism*, ed. Donald W. Dayton and Robert K. Johnston [Knoxville: University of Tennessee Press, 1991], 12).
    [2]For more on this, see William J. Abraham, *The Coming Great Revival: Recovering the Full Evangelical Tradition* (San Francisco: Harper & Row, 1984), 9. Some dispense with the task of identifying essential ingredients of evangelicalism and speak instead of "family resemblances." Unfortunately, however, this practice typically fails to identify what commonality members of this family share.
    [3]I offer examples here of those whose list of basic evangelical affirmations is the same or similar to mine. Affirmation five is excepted from the comparisons I make here, because those who offer their lists of evangelical core convictions rarely, if ever, include an explicit affirmation pertaining to the doctrine of God. My list of core characteristics is the same as the list given by Martin E. Marty in "The Revival of Evangelicalism and Southern Religion," in *The Varieties of Southern Evangelicalism*, ed. David Edwin Harrell Jr. (Macon, Ga.: Mercer University Press, 1981), 9–10. The list Thomas A. Askew offers is the same as well ("A Response to David F. Wells," in *A Time to Speak: The Evangelical-Jewish Encounter*, ed. A. James Rudin and Marvin R. Wilson [Grand Rapids, Mich.: Eerdmans, 1987], 41–42). George Marsden, in a volume of essays he edited entitled *Evangelicalism and Modern America*, offers core aspects nearly identical to my own except that he stresses that God's saving work is recorded in scripture (Grand Rapids, Mich.: Eerdmans, 1984), ix–x. James Davison Hunter, in *American Evangelicalism: Conservative Religion and the Quandry of Modernity* (New Brunswick, N.J.: Rutgers University Press, 1983), stresses the inerrancy of the Bible as important for evangelicals while adding the second coming of Christ and the "individuated conception of personal, social, and institutional problems" as characteristic of evangelicals (47). However, in his later book *Evangelicalism: The Coming Generation*, these additional stresses are downplayed (Chicago: University of Chicago Press, 1987), ch. 2. Richard Quebedeaux, in *The Young Evangelicals* (New York: Harper & Row, 1974) includes the four convictions I suggest except the emphasis on spiritual growth (3–4). Donald Bloesch, in *The Future of Evangelical Christianity: A Call for Unity and Diversity* (Garden City, N.Y.: Doubleday, 1983), 5–6, 17–18, follows the same form as Quebedeaux. Jon Johnston also does not include the spiritual growth aspect, although he implies it throughout his work (*Will Evangelicalism Survive Its Own Popularity?* [Grand Rapids, Mich.: Zondervan, 1980], 20–25). Mark Ellingsen includes as an additional characteristic the notion that evangelicals are those who explicitly identify themselves as such (*The Evangelical Movement* [Minneapolis: Augsburg, 1988], 47–48). Alister McGrath's list is the same as mine except that he adds the Lordship of the Holy Spirit (*Evangelicalism and the Future of Christianity* (Downers Grove, Ill.: InterVarsity, 1995), 56.
    [4]Published biblical scholars with a process orientation include William Beardslee, Ronald Farmer, Terrence Fretheim, Robert Gnuse, David Lull, and Russell Pregeant. See also Lewis Ford, *The Lure of God: A Biblical Background for Process Theism* (Philadelphia: Fortress, 1978).
    [5]Ronald Nash, "Process Theology and Classical Theism," in *Process Theology*, ed. Ronald Nash (Grand Rapids, Mich.: Baker, 1987), 3–29. "Panentheism" is a conception of the God-world relationship adopted by many process theologians in which God has always and necessarily been related to some world or another.
    [6]Of course, this raises the question, "What are the core notions of process theology?" If David Ray Griffin's list of ten core notions of process philosophy were presupposed, however, one would find no essential disagreement between evangelicals and process theology on this point. Furthermore, one could claim that Christian Scripture is a source that emerged thanks to what Griffin calls a high degree of "variable divine influence" (*Reenchantment Without Supernaturalism: A Process Philosophy of Religion* [Ithaca, N.Y.: Cornell University Press, 2001], 5–7. See especially core notion seven.)

[7]For guides to ways in which biblical scholars with a process orientation address issues of hermeneutics, see Ronald L. Farmer, *Beyond the Impasse: The Promise of a Process Hermeneutic*, Studies in American Biblical Hermeneutics, no. 13 (Macon, Ga: Mercer University Press, 1997) and Terrence Fretheim's half of the book he cowrote with Karlfried Froehlich, *The Bible as Word of God in a Postmodern Age* (Minneapolis: Fortress, 1998).

[8]Among evangelical works that might be labeled "inclusivist" because they affirm the possibility of salvation for the unevangelized, see Clark H. Pinnock, "An Inclusivist View" in *More Than One Way?* ed. Dennis Okholm and Timothy Phillips (Grand Rapids, Mich.: Zondervan, 1995), 112–23, and Pinnock, *A Wideness in God's Mercy: The Finality of Jesus Christ in a World of Religions* (Grand Rapids, Mich.: Zondervan, 1992); Randy L. Maddox, "Wesley and the Question of Truth or Salvation Through Other Religions," *Wesleyan Theological Journal* (Spring/Fall 1992): 7–29; John Sanders, *No Other Name: An Investigation into the Destiny of the Unevangelized* (Grand Rapids, Mich.: Eerdmans, 1992); Amos Yong, "Whither Theological Inclusivism? The Development and Critique of an Evangelical Theology of Religions," *The Evangelical Quarterly* 71:4 (October 1999): 327–48.

[9]For a discussion of exclusivism, inclusivism, and pluralism, see Mark Grear Mann, "Religious Pluralism," in *Philosophy of Religion: Introductory Essays*, ed. Thomas Jay Oord (Kansas City: Beacon Hill, 2003), 259–74.

[10]David Ray Griffin argues this way in his work *Reenchantment Without Supernaturalism*, 246.

[11]For a discussion of how a process conception of nonsensory perception might be helpful for the evangelical Wesleyan doctrine of prevenient grace, see Thomas Jay Oord, "A Postmodern Wesleyan Philosophy and David Ray Griffin's Postmodern Vision," *Wesleyan Theological Journal* 35:1 (April/May, 2000), and Oord, "Prevenient Grace and Nonsensory Perception of God in a Postmodern Wesleyan Philosophy," in *Between Nature and Grace: Mapping the Interface of Wesleyan Theology and Psychology* (San Diego, Calif.: Point Loma Press, 2000).

[12]For evangelical criticisms of process thought, see Ronald Nash's edited volume, *Process Theology*. For a criticism of evangelicalism by one sympathetic to process thought, see Nicholas F. Gier, *God, Reason, and the Evangelicals* (Lantham: University Press of America, 1987).

[13]See, for instance, Bryan P. Stone and Thomas Jay Oord, eds., *Thy Nature and Thy Name Is Love: Wesleyan and Process Theologies in Dialogue* (Nashville, Tenn.: Kingswood, 2001). John Culp was one of the first evangelicals to consider positively how process resources may be helpful to evangelicals ("A Dialogue with the Process Theology of John B. Cobb Jr.," *Wesleyan Theological Journal* 17 [Fall 1980]: 33–44).

[14]The label, "openness of God," was first presented in the title of Richard Rice's Open theism book: *The Openness of God* (Nashville, Tenn.: Review and Herald, 1980). Donald Wayne Viney has noted that Charles Hartshorne wrote of God's openness in several publications, but Hartshorne apparently never used the phrase "openness of God."

[15]The book is divided into five sections, each written by separate authors. Richard Rice provides the "Biblical Support for a New Perspective"; John Sanders addresses Christian tradition in "Historical Considerations"; Clark H. Pinnock addresses the view as "Systematic Theology"; William Hasker provides "A Philosophical Perspective"; and David Basinger suggests some "Practical Implications" in *The Openness of God: A Biblical Challenge to the Traditional Understanding of God*, ed. Clark H. Pinnock et al. (Downers Grove, Ill.: InterVarsity, 1994).

[16]Among Openness books that are particularly noteworthy are the following: Gregory A. Boyd, *God of the Possible: A Biblical Introduction to the Open View of God* (Grand Rapids, Mich.: Baker, 2001); Clark H. Pinnock, *Most Moved Mover: A Theology of God's Openness* (Grand Rapids, Mich.: Baker Academic, 2001); Richard Rice, *God's Foreknowledge and Man's Free Will* (Minneapolis: Bethany House, 1984), and John Sanders, *The God Who Risks: A Theology of Providence* (Downers Grove, Ill.: InterVarsity, 1998).

[17]Two especially important conferences involved Open and process theists in face-to-face dialogue. The first, "The Enlightenment in Evangelical and Process Perspectives," was held in 1997, and the second, an evangelical subsection of the International Whitehead Conference of 1998, produced a variety of fruit, not the least of which is a collection of five essays titled, *Searching for an Adequate God: A Dialogue Between Process and Free Will Theists*, ed. John B. Cobb Jr. and Clark H. Pinnock (Grand Rapids, Mich.: Eerdmans, 2000).

[18]Pinnock, *Most Moved Mover*, 118.

[19]Ibid.

[20]Ibid., 101.

[21]John B. Cobb Jr., "Evangelical Theology in Process Perspective," unpublished manuscript presented at *The Enlightenment in Evangelical and Process Perspectives* conference, Claremont, California, 20–22 March, 1997. Manuscript available at the *Center for Process Studies,* Claremont, California.

[22]This emphasis upon divine love is the overriding theme in a book by Wesleyans in dialogue with process thought titled, *Thy Nature and Thy Name Is Love,* ed. Stone and Oord. It also is the central theme in my forthcoming book, Thomas Jay Oord, *An Essentially Loving God: An Open and Relational Theology of Love.*

[23]Richard Rice, "Biblical Support for a New Perspective," in *Openness of God,* 18.

[24]Ibid., 15.

[25]Ibid., 21.

[26]Ibid., 19.

[27]Richard Rice, "Process Theism and the Open View of God: The Crucial Difference," in *Searching for an Adequate God,* 183–84.

[28]Pinnock et al., "Preface," *The Openness of God,* 7.

[29]Pinnock, "Systematic Theology," in *The Openness of God,* 103.

[30]Pinnock briefly documents this turmoil in the introductory chapter of *Most Moved Mover.* For a monograph-length explication of Pinnock's theological journey, including summaries of some theological tussles, see Barry L. Callen, *Clark H. Pinnock: Journey Toward Renewal, An Intellectual Biography* (Nappanee, Ind.: Evangel, 2000).

[31]Clark H. Pinnock, "Between Classical and Process Theism," in *Process Theology,* ed. Ronald Nash (Grand Rapids, Mich.: Baker, 1987), 325.

[32]Gregory A. Boyd presents a very accessible book-length defense of Open theism's denial of exhaustive divine foreknowledge in *God of the Possible: A Biblical Introduction to the Open View of God* (Grand Rapids, Mich.: Baker, 2001). Christopher Hall and John Sanders debate the issue in *Christianity Today,* "Does God Know Your Next Move?" 45:7 (2001): 39–45; 45:8 (2001): 50–56.

[33]Pinnock, "Systematic Theology," in *Openness of God,* 120.

[34]Pinnock, *Most Moved Mover,* 142–43. For an illuminating discussion of Open and process theism, see Donald Wayne Viney, "The Varieties of Theism and the Openness of God: Charles Hartshorne and Free-Will Theism," in *The Personalist Forum* 14/2 (Fall 1998): 199–238.

[35]Pinnock, *Most Moved Mover,* 141.

[36]Stephen T. Franklin is an evangelical who knows process thought very well and works toward the mutual transformation of process and evangelical theisms. Franklin's major work to date is *Speaking from the Depths: Alfred North Whitehead's Hermeneutical Metaphysics of Propositions, Experience, Symbolism, Language, and Religion* (Grand Rapids, Mich.: Eerdmans, 1990).

[37]Pinnock, *Most Moved Mover,* 145.

[38]Rice, "Process Theism," in *Searching for an Adequate God,* 185.

[39]Michael E. Lodahl provides a chapter-length discussion of what is at stake in *creatio ex nihilo* in his essay, "Creation Out of Nothing? Or Is *Next* to Nothing Good Enough?" in *Thy Nature and Thy Name Is Love,* chapter nine. Amos Yong is a pentecostal theologian whose work addresses the value of process theology for pentecostal thought. See his exploration of doctrines of creation, "Possibility and Actuality: The Doctrine of Creation and Its Implications for Divine Omniscience," *The Wesleyan Philosophical Society Online Journal* [http://david.snu.edu/~brint.fs/wpsjnl/v1n1.htm] 1:1 (2001).

[40]Lewis S. Ford has written numerous reviews and articles on the evangelical-process dialogue in a variety of journals. One of his best essays is his review of *The Openness of God:* "Evangelical Appraisals of Process Theism," *Christian Scholars Review* 20:2 (December 1990): 149–63.

[41]David Ray Griffin, "Creation and the Problem of Evil," in *Encountering Evil: Live Options in Theodicy: A New Edition,* ed. Stephen T. Davis (Louisville: Westminster John Knox Press, 2001), 115. Griffin offers a sustained discussion of *creatio ex nihilo* in this chapter. See also Catherine Keller's book-length rejection of *creatio ex nihilo:* Keller, *Face of the Deep: A Theology of Becoming* (London: Routledge, 2003).

[42]I also make this point in my essay, Thomas Jay Oord, "A Process Wesleyan Theodicy: Freedom, Embodiment, and the Almighty God," in *Thy Nature and Thy Name Is Love,* chapter

8, and in Oord, "Divine Power and Love: An Evangelical Process Proposal," *Koinonia: The Princeton Theological Seminary Graduate Forum* X.1 (Spring 1998): 1–18.

[43]Pinnock acknowledges "that Genesis 1 does not itself teach *ex nihilo* creation but presents God as imposing order on chaos..." (*Most Moved Mover*, 146). Rather than follow process thought by speculating that God created from chaotic nondivine entities, however, Pinnock speculates that the chaos of Genesis refers to God's warfare with "rebellious angels" (ibid.). Although Pinnock likely does not intend this, one might interpret this second speculative move to support the argument that God always faces forces over which God cannot exert total control. For an Open argument concerning the possibility of demonic warfare, see Gregory Boyd, *God at War: The Bible and Spiritual Conflict* (Downers Grove, Ill.: InterVarsity, 1997).

[44]Basinger, "Practical Implications," in *The Openness of God*, 156. See also Basinger's influential work, *Divine Power in Process Theism: A Philosophical Critique* (Albany, N.Y.: State University of New York Press, 1988).

[45]Pinnock, *Most Moved Mover*, 147.

[46]Ibid., 148.

[47]David Ray Griffin, "Process Theology and the Christian Good News: A Response to Classical Free Will Theism," in *Searching for an Adequate God*, 30. This divine activity would be quasi-coercive, because God would have no competition from the habits and histories of enduring things. Enduring things would not exist in the chaotic state prior to the Big Bang. A divine decision in relation to such whiffs of existence would only be subject to the metaphysical principles that reside as aspects of God's own essence.

[48]Ibid., 36–38.

[49]Ibid., 23.

[50]Ibid., 17.

[51]John B. Cobb Jr., "Introduction," *Searching for an Adequate God*, xiii.

[52]Pinnock, *Most Moved Mover*, 145. Gregory Boyd provides a lengthy argument for why the Trinity provides a better relational metaphysics than a process hypothesis in *Trinity and Process: A Critical Evaluation and Reconstruction of Hartshorne's Di-Polar Theism Towards a Trinitarian Metaphysics* (New York: Peter Lang, 1992).

[53]I discuss these issues in detail in my manuscript, Oord, *An Essentially Loving God* (forthcoming).

[54]Pinnock, *Most Moved Mover*, 145.

[55]Rice, "Biblical Support," in *The Openness of God*, 48.

[56]I develop this issue in my manuscript, Oord, *An Essentially Loving God* (forthcoming).

[57]For a relational theodicy attuned to both process and openness concerns about divine love and power, see Thomas Jay Oord, "Evil, Providence, and a Relational God," *Quarterly Review* 23:3 (Fall 2003): 238–50.

Chapter 20: A Whiteheadian Vedanta

[1]The Vedas are divided into four portions, each of which serves as a philosophical commentary or elaboration upon the one that precedes it–the Samhitas, the Brahmanas, the Aranyakas, and the Upanishads. The first and oldest of these portions, the Samhitas, consists of the four collections of Sanskrit poems that, at first glance, appear to be hymns to natural forces personified as gods or *devas* (literally "shining ones"). These poems are regarded by the tradition, however, as having profound philosophical meanings that are gradually unpacked over the course of the later portions of the Vedic literature. The culmination of this process takes place in the philosophical dialogues of the Upanishads, which are regarded, at least by the adherents of the Vedanta schools, as expressing the most profound truths of Vedic thought.

[2]Chandogya Upanishad 6:1.

[3]Translated. In original, "Asato ma sad gamaya, tamaso ma jyotir gamaya, mrityor ma amritam gamaya."

[4]Brihadaranyaka Upanishad 2:5.

[5]Brihadaranyaka Upanishad 2:5.

[6]Chandogya Upanishad 6:2.

[7]Pravrajika Vrajaprana, *Vedanta: A Simple Introduction* (Hollywood, Calif.: Vedanta Press, 1991), 2.

[8]David Ray Griffin, *Reenchantment without Supernaturalism* (Ithaca, N. Y.: Cornell University Press, 2001), 261; and PR 20.

[9]PR 348. Note that Whitehead conceives of creativity in terms of the resolution of multiplicity into unity, within the being of a single actual entity, whereas the Hindu tradition tends to come from the opposite direction–beginning with an original metaphysical unity and moving to the universe of perceived multiplicity. A widespread conception explains the fundamental difference in philosophical styles between the West and India. This conception says the East begins from within, with the essence of a thing, and moves to the empirical reality, from the abstract to the particular. On the other hand, the West begins with the perceived reality and moves to a generalized ultimate unity, from the particular to the abstract. All such generalizations, of course, have exceptions and run the risk of becoming stereotypical. To the degree that this is a valid observation I think the correspondences between Hindu and process thought that I am outlining in this paper support a case for the Hindu idea that many paths can lead to truth. The path one takes, the path that is most appropriate for one, depends upon one's starting point. Regardless of one's starting point, we can still end up reaching the same conclusion.

[10]AI 115. The importance of what Whitehead calls the "doctrine of Immanence," in contrast with classical Christian notions of the universe as wholly dependent upon an external reality for its existence, is that only such a doctrine of immanence can yield logical coherence. According to Whitehead, "God is not to be treated as an exception to all metaphysical principles, invoked to save their collapse. He is their chief exemplification" (PR 343).

[11]It is perhaps significant in this regard that the name of one of the most important of the forms of divinity in Hinduism, Vishnu, means, literally, "the pervader," "the one who pervades all things."

[12]Satguru Sivaya Subramuniyaswami, using language strikingly reminiscent of process thought, refers to the theology of his particular Hindu school of thought, Advaita Ishvaravada, as "dipolar panentheism" (*Merging with Shiva: Hinduism's Contemporary Metaphysics* [Himalayan Academy, 1999], 1186).

[13]Swami Vivekananda coined this phrase, which he uses throughout his works, from *Kena Upanishad* v. 4.

[14]*Bhagavad-Gita* 6:30, translation of Sri Aurobindo.

[15]Taittiriya Upanishad 2:1–5.

[16]*Bhagavad-Gita* 7:7, translation of Sri Aurobindo.

[17]This language of "becoming" and "taking on" finitude should not be taken to suggest that this is a temporal process–that there was a "beginning" when there was only the One and then the One "acted" in order to become the many. Though the Hindu tradition sometimes uses anthropomorphic–and therefore necessarily temporal–language and imagery to describe it, the process in question is happening at each and every moment.

[18]See David Ray Griffin, *Parapsychology, Philosophy, and Spirituality: A Postmodern Exploration* (Albany, N.Y.: State University of New York Press, 1997).

Chapter 21: Covenant and Responsible Creativity

[1]Neil Gillman summarizes this assertion well when he writes: "There is no more central theme in Jewish self-perception than that of covenant. It is the single indispensable key to understanding the way Jewish religion evolved from its earliest beginnings…[I]t is the linchpin of the Jewish myth, that structure that Jews use to lend meaning to their experience in the world and to locate their place in the flow of nature and history" (*Sacred Fragments: Recovering Theology for the Modern Jew* [Philadelphia: The Jewish Publication Society, 1990], 41).

[2]See Irving Greenberg, "Voluntary Covenant," *Perspectives* no. 3 (New York: National Jewish Resource Center).

[3]Arnold Eisen, "Covenant," in *Contemporary Jewish Religious Thought: Original Essays on Critical Concepts, Movements, and Beliefs*, ed. Arthur A. Cohen and Paul Mendes-Flohr (New York: Charles Scribner's Sons, 1987), 111.

[4]Ibid.

[5]The best that might be achieved is something akin to what Eugene Borowitz has proposed as a "postliberal/post-orthodox" position, in which "I live from a Jewish faith that

my personhood derives from God who commands me yet also dignifies me with independent personal responsibility." Such a position is clearly "post-orthodox," but much less clearly post-liberal, for it maintains the position that individual autonomy is in conflict with God and community (Eugene B. Borowitz, *Renewing the Covenant: A Theology for the Postmodern Jew* [Philadelphia: Jewish Publication Society, 1991], 31).

⁶ALEPH, a major renewal organization, offers the following additional detail on spiritual sources: "Among our guides to interpretation of Torah are the Prophetic, Kabbalistic, and Hassidic traditions as they are now being transformed in the light of contemporary feminist spirituality, process theology, and our own direct experience of the Divine" (www.aleph.org/html/principles.html).

⁷As Arnold Eisen notes, "Observance at century's end seems to have moved even farther out in front of belief than was the case previously in twentieth-century Judaism and seems not terribly concerned about whether belief will struggle...to catch up" (*Rethinking Modern Judaism: Ritual, Commandment, Community* [Chicago: University of Chicago Press, 1998], 257).

⁸"Commandment continues to evince a robust independence of divine revelation, a diversity of sources, an array of enactments" (ibid., 263).

⁹Cant. Rabba I, 24, cited in Nahum N. Glatzer, ed., *The Judaic Tradition* (Boston: Beacon Press, 1969), 220–21.

¹⁰Thus the covenant is not simply shorthand for a legal or ethical system. It is primarily a structure in which the connection between God and human beings is declared to be inescapable, enduring, and intimate. This is not to say that the biblical narrative provides ample support for a covenant of parity that includes mutual obligations. "If you follow my statutes and keep my commandments and observe them faithfully, I will give you your rains in their season, and the land shall yield its produce..." (Lev. 26:3–4a). But once this pattern of expectations was not fulfilled, religious leaders faced the interpretive challenge of securing the covenant despite the seeming abrogation of responsibilities. Well before modernity and the Holocaust, the contractual elements of covenant had given way to a broader reading in response to the myriad historical catastrophes that threatened the covenantal meaning-structure. So, for example, in response to the massacres of Rhineland Jewry during the Crusades, Ashkenazi rabbis conceived of the idea of "afflictions from love" to replace the idea of "punishment for sin." Suffering became a sign of righteousness, not a consequence of sin. And thus a "covenantal explanation" that could withstand the great suffering of the period was created and covenant as a meaning-securing, world-orienting structure maintained its plausibility.

¹¹John B. Cobb Jr. and David Tracy, *Talking about God: Doing Theology in the Context of Modern Pluralism* (Seabury Press, 1984), 54

¹²See for example, David Griffin, *God and Religion in the Postmodern World* (Albany: State University of New York Press, 1989); and John B. Cobb Jr., *Christ in a Pluralistic Age* (Philadelphia: The Westminster Press, 1975).

¹³Griffin, *God and Religion*, 63, 37.

¹⁴Rabbi Simchah Bunam, cited in W. Gunther Plaut, ed., *The Torah, A Modern Commentary* (New York: Union of American Hebrew Congregations, 1981), 25.

¹⁵Griffin, *God and Religion*, 45.

¹⁶Gershom Scholem, *Kabbalah* (New York: New American Library, 1974), 152.

¹⁷Arthur Waskow, *Godwrestling Round 2: Ancient Wisdom, Future Paths* (Woodstock, Vt.: Jewish Lights Pub., 1996), 28–29.

¹⁸Gillman explicating Franz Rosenzweig, *Sacred Fragments*, 23, 24.

¹⁹Emmanuel Levinas, *Totality and Infinity* (The Hague; Boston: M. Nijhoff Publishers, 1979), 212.

²⁰Cobb and Tracy, *Talking about God*, 75.

Index

transmutation, 109; *see also:*
perception
Trinity, 51, 167, 178, 254, 260; social:
258; *see also:* Christ, God, Holy
Spirit
triumphalism, 24
triviality, 46–47, 184; *see also:* evil
Troeltsch, Ernst, 51, 53
truth, 6, 10, 24, 49, 52, 54–55, 57,
69–70, 74, 80, 103, 109, 136, 139,
144–45, 175, 186, 238, 263–64,
272, 276; complementary: 55, 57–
58; propositional: 68–70, 282; *see
also:* epistemology, knowledge
Tsai Ming–liang, 141

U

ultimate, 6, 57, 249; nontheistic:
249; theistic: 249
uncertainty, 24
United States, 137
unity, 6–7, 45, 75, 161–62, 183, 264,
266, 268, 270; *see also:* diversity,
many
universals, 139–41, 144, 162
universe, 5, 6, 23, 39, 43, 46, 60, 68,
72, 75, 87, 145, 179, 183, 190,
198–99, 242, 265, 267–71, 273,
275, 280–81; as God's body: 6,
74; order in: 7, 269; *see also:*
cosmos
University of Chicago, 4
Upanishads, 263–64, 266; *Chandogya*:
266; *Taittiriya*: 270; *also:*
Hinduism
utility, 192
utopia, 172–73, 195

V

Vaikuntha, 272; *see also:* Hinduism
Vaishnava, 269, 272; *see also:*
Hinduism
valuation, 7, 17, 71, 76
value, 6–8, 17, 19, 24, 26, 37, 39–41,

46–47, 52, 63, 71, 86, 117, 136–37,
139, 141, 144–47, 150, 166, 173,
177–78, 181–82, 185, 188–90, 192,
197, 199, 207, 279; aesthetic: 7;
economic: 195; instrumental:
233; intrinsic: 63, 190, 220, 233;
transmission: 12, 47; *see also:*
beauty, God, experience,
subjective aim
Vedanta, 262–73; Advaita: 54, 57,
264, 272; concepts: 265; Dvaita:
264; schools: 263–64;
Vishishtadvaita: 264; *see also:*
Hinduism
Vedas, 262–63, 266, 271; *see also:*
Hinduism
victory, 24, 65, 254, 259
vidya, 271; *see also:* Hinduism,
wisdom
violence, 36, 180, 202–8, 218
virtue, 156, 185, 219, 222, 231, 254;
see also: sin
Vodun, 170; *see also:* religions

W

Walker, Alice, 165
Ward, Nahum, 61–62
Waskow, Arthu, 277, 284
Wavelength, 141
wealth, 191
well–being, 38, 61, 63, 64, 92, 94,
96–97, 99–101, 124, 155, 157, 166,
184–85, 191, 193–94, 251; *see also:*
flourishing, health
Wellbank, Joseph, 172
Wesley, John, 81
Wesleyanism, 252, 255, 257
whales, 155; *see also:* animals
*White Woman's Christ, Black Woman's
Jesus,* 168
Whitehead, Alfred North, , 3, 5, 12,
15, 18, 29–30, 34–36, 38, 46, 55–
57, 60, 63–65, 68, 70, 72–79, 96,
105–19, 132–33, 147, 149, 153,